The Nature of Classical Collecting

The Nature of Classical Collecting
Collectors and Collections, 100 BCE–100 CE

ALEXANDRA BOUNIA
University of the Aegean, Greece

ASHGATE

Published by
Ashgate Publishing Limited
Gower House
Croft Road
Aldershot
Hampshire GU11 3HR
England

Ashgate Publishing Company
Suite 420
101 Cherry Street
Burlington, VT 05401-4405
USA

Ashgate website: http://www.ashgate.com

British Library Cataloguing in Publication Data
Bounia, Alexandra
   The nature of classical collecting : collectors and
   collections, 100 BCE–100 CE. – (Perspectives on collecting)
   1. Collectors and collecting – History 2. Collectors and
   collecting – Philosophy 3. Antiquities – Collection and
   preservation – History
   I. Title
   069.5'09014

Library of Congress Cataloging-in-Publication Data
Bounia, Alexandra.
   The nature of classical collecting : collectors and collections, 100
BCE–100 CE / Alexandra Bounia.
      p. cm. – (Perspectives on collecting)
Includes bibliographical references and index.
   ISBN 0-7546-0012-2 (alk. paper)
   1. Classical antiquities–Collectors and collecting. 2. Civilization,
Classical–Collectors and collecting. 3. Collectors and
collecting–Philosophy. 4. Collectors and collecting–History. I.
Title. II. Series.

DE60.B68 2003
069'.5'0938–dc 21

2003052110

ISBN 0 7546 0012 2

Printed and bound in Great Britain by MPG Books Ltd, Bodmin, Cornwall

Contents

Acknowledgements

Acknowledgment is made for permission to use the following figures and plates:

Figure 0.1 reproduced from Pearce, S.M., *On Collecting: an Investigation into Collecting in the European Tradition*, Routledge, (1995), with the permission of the author and Routledge;

Figure 1.1 reproduced from Barthes, R., *The Fashion System*, fig. 3.9, p. 37, with the permission of Farrar, Strauss and Giroux;

Figures 3.5 and 3.7 reprinted from C. Morgan, *Athletes and Oracles, The Transformation of Olympia and Delphi in the Eighth Century BC*, pages 27 and 128 respectively, with the permission of Cambridge University Press;

Figure 9.4 reprinted from *Cicero's Verrine Oration II.4: with notes and vocabulary* by Shelia K. Dickison (1992), with the permission of Wayne State University Press;

Plates 3.1, 3.2, 3.3 and 3.4 reprinted with the permission of the École Nationale Supérieure des Beaux-Arts.

List of Figures

List of Plates

Abbreviations

AAHG	*Anzeiger für Altertumswissenshaft, hrsg. von der Österreichischen Humanistischen Gesellschaft*, Innsbruck, Wagner.
ad Attic.	Marcus Tullius Cicero, *Ad Atticum.*
ad Fam.	Marcus Tullius Cicero, *Ad Familiares.*
ad Lucil.	Lucius Annaeus Seneca, *Epistulae morales ad Lucilium.*
AJA	*American Journal of Archaeology*, New York, Archaeological Institute of America.
AJPh	*American Journal of Philology* (Baltimore).
ANRW	*Aufstieg und Niedergang der Römischen Welt*, Berlin.
AP	*Anthologia Graeca (=Palatina)*, edited by Beckby, 4Bde, Munich, 2nd edn, 1965-1968.
Appian *BellCiv*	Appian, *Bella Civilia.*
Arist., *Cael.*	Aristotle, *De caelo.*
Arist., *De part. an,.*	Aristotle, *De partibus animalium.*
Arist., *Inc.*	Aristotle, *De incessu animalium.*
Augustine, Cat.	Augustine, *De Catechizandis Rudibus* (399 CE).
BCH	*Bulletin de Correspondence Hellénique*, Paris, de Boccard.
BICS	*Bulletin of the Institute of Classical Studies.*
BSA	*Annual of the British School at Athens.*
Budé	Collection des Universités de France, publiée sous le patronage de l'Association Guillaume Budé (Paris).
CIL	*Corpus Inscriptionum Latinarum* (Berlin, 1863).
CRAI	*Comptes rendus de l'Académie des Inscriptions et Belles-Lettres*, Paris, Klincksieck.
De brev. vit.	Lucius Annaeus Seneca, *De brevitate vitae (Dial. 10).*
De invent.	M. T. Cicero, *De inventione.*
De Leg.	M. T. Cicero, *De Legibus.*
De Off.	M. T. Cicero, *De Officiis.*
Demetrius, *Eloc.*	Demetrius [Phalereus], De Elocutione = Περί Ἑρμηνείας.
Dessau *ILS*	H. Dessau, *Inscriptiones Latinae Selectae*, Berlin, 1892-1916.
Div.	M. T. Cicero, *De divinatione.*
EAD	*Éxplorations Arhaeologiques de Delos.*
Ep.	*Epistles* (of Horace, Pliny the Younger, or other authors).
Eu.	Aeschylus, *Eumenides.*

FdD	*Fouilles de Delphes.*
FGrH	Jacoby, F. *et al.* (eds), *Die Fragmente der griechischen Historiker*, in progress, Leiden, 1923.
Fin.	M. T. Cicero, *de Finibus.*
frg.	fragment(s).
Fronto, Nab.	Marcus Cornelius Fronto, edn S. A. Naber (Leipzig, 1867).
FS	R. Barthes, *The Fashion System*, translated by M. Ward and R. Howard, Berkeley: University of California Press, 1990.
Geo.	Vergilius Maro, Publius, *Georgics.*
GRBS	*Greek, Roman and Byzantine Studies*, Durham, North Carolina.
IDélos	*Inscriptions de Délos* (1926, Paris: Champion); (1929, edited by Durrbach, F., Paris: Champion); (1950, edited by Plassart, A., Paris: Champion); (1972, edited by Courpy, J., Paris: Depositaire Éditions E. de Boccard).
Il.	Homer, *Iliad.*
Inst. Orat.	Quintilianus, Marcus Fabius, *Institutio Oratoria.*
JDAI	*Jahrbuch des Deutschen Archäologischen Instituts*, Berlin, de Gruyter.
JHS	*Journal of Hellenic Studies*, London.
Josephus, *BellJud*	Josephus, *Bellum Judaicum.*
JRA	*Journal of Roman Archaeology.*
JRS	*Journal of Roman Studies*, London.
L.L.	Marcus Terentius Varro, De *lingua Latina.*
Loeb CL	*The Loeb Classical Library* (co-published by William Heinemann, London, and the Harvard University Press in Cambridge Mass.).
LS	Long, A.A. and Sedley, D.N., 1987, *The Hellenistic Philosophers*, 2 vols, Cambridge: Cambridge University Press.
MDAI (R.)	*Mitteilungen des Deutschen Archäologischen Instituts (Röm. Abt.)*, Berlin, Mann.
MEFR	*Melanges d'Archéologie et d'Histoire de l'École Française de Rome*, Paris, de Boccard.
MEFRA	*Melanges d'Archéologie et d'Histoire de l'École Française de Rome, Antiquité*, Paris, de Boccard.
Mem.	Xenophon, *Memorabilia Socratis.*
Met.	Ovidius Naso, Publius, *Metamorphoses.*
Od.	Homer, *Odyssey.*
OLD	*Oxford Latin Dictionary*, edited by P. G. W. Glare, Oxford: Clarendon Press, 1976-1982.
PCPhS	*Proceedings of the Cambridge Philological Society.*
Phys.	Aristotle, *Physics.*

Pindar, *Pyth.*   Pindar, *Pythian Odes.*
Plut., *De Pyth. Orac.* Plutarch, *De Pythiae oraculis.*
Plut., *Lys.*   Plutarch, *Vitae Parallelae, Lysander.*
Plut., *Quaest. conv.*   Plutarch, *Quaestionum convivialum.*
Plut., *Quaest. Graec.* Plutarch, *Quaestiones Graecae.*
Plut., *Sept. Sap. Conv.*Plutarch, *Convivium septem sapientium.*
Plut., *Thes.*   Plutarch, *Vitae Parallelae, Theseus.*
Pro Arch.   M. T. Cicero, *Pro Archia.*
RE   *Paulys Real-Encyclopädie der classischen Altertumswissenschaft*, edited by G. Wissowa, *et al.*, Stuttgart, 1893.
REL   *Revue des Études Latines.*
RhM   *Rheinisches Museum für Philologie.*
Rose   Rose, V., *Texts and Testimonia of fragments of Aristotle's works*, Leipzig, 1866.
R. R.   Marcus Terentius Varro, *De re rustica.*
S-B   Loeb translations of Martial's Epigrams, by D. R. Shackleton Bailey, 1993.
SVF   H. von Arnim, *Stoicorum Veterum Fragmenta*, Leipzig, 1903.
TAPA   *Transactions and Proceedings of the American Philological Association*, Chico, Cal., Scholars Press.
TAPhS   *Transactions of the American Philosophical Society*, Philadelphia, Indepedence Square.
Tertullian, *Apol.*   Tertullian, *Apologeticus.*
Tranq. An.   Lucius Annaeus Seneca, *De Tranquillitate animi.*
Tusc. Disp.   M. T. Cicero, *Tusculan Disputations.*
Wehrli   Wehrli, F. E. (ed.), *Die Schule des Aristoteles* (frgs. of the Peripatetic philosophers), 10 volumes, Basel, 1944-1959.

General Preface to the Series

The study of collecting is a crucial facet in the contemporary turn towards the understanding of social practice, seen as the medium through which individuals and communities create self-identity. Social construction of the meanings of material culture is at the heart of this project, and the collecting process, through which objects are put into meaningful relationships seen as producing knowledge, value, aesthetic and prestige, is central to it. *Perspectives on Collecting* is intended to bring together detailed studies and broader over-views, drawn from the analysis of a wide range of collecting practices, which together will develop a sustained exploration of the field.

Susan Pearce, General Editor

Preface

This book developed as the result of the wish to combine my interest in the classical past, and my belief that it is only through thorough examination of the origins of museums and collections that we will be able to reach the dismantling of the modern museum and its reassemblage in an abstruse metamorphosis; this requires extensive research in the ancestry of the cultural institution of the museum and collecting, a field which has much to offer. The subject of this book is the nature of classical collecting as illustrated by four Latin writers, Marcus Tullius Cicero, Gaius Plinius Secundus, Marcus Valerius Martialis and Titus Petronius Arbiter, who lived and wrote during the first century BCE and the first century CE. The book originated from my Ph.D. thesis that I submitted at the University of Leicester in 1998. In the book it has not been possible, as it was in the thesis, to include the text and translation of all the relevant paragraphs of the four authors mentioned above in an appendix. Nevertheless, some of the most important paragraphs have been added in the text, and the references will guide those who might want to pursue the issue further to the relevant sources.

The transliteration of Greek words follows accepted usage with, as I fear, the usual inconsistencies. The language used in this book is non-inclusive, not as a result of a sexist intention, but just in order to avoid the inelegant double types.

It is my great pleasure to acknowledge here the support I have received at different stages of the development of the ideas presented in this book. Warm thanks are due to my supervisor, Professor Susan Pearce, for all her help, encouragement, and advice. I would also like to acknowledge the financial support received from the State Scholarship Foundation of Greece. The Public Benefit Foundation Maria Kassimati also financed part of my studies, and I am deeply grateful for that.

I am also indebted to Dr Ian Jenkins, Michael Vickers, and Dr Graham Shipley, for providing much needed encouragement, bibliography, and advice at different stages of this work. My thesis' examiners, Dr Mary Beard and Janet Owen, are also to be sincerely thanked. Naturally, the final outcome is my own responsibility.

Over the years I have had the privilege to enjoy the friendship of many people: Martha Karagilanis and Tassos Kokkinis, Dr Maria Mouliou, Dr Diogo Fernandez-Thomaz and Maria-Christina, Dr Özlem Görey, Eirene Marathaki, Elizabeth Myrogiani, Elli Kollia, Dr Paul Martin, Dr Pedro Lorente, Dr Pedro Casaleiro and Xana Faria de Almeida, Dr Theano Moussouri and Alice Semedo have been always available for my personal and academic problems alike.

Special thanks are due to Mike Bieber, who besides being a good friend, found the time and the patience to read and improve the English of my thesis. I am also grateful to Jim Roberts who produced some of the figures.

I would not have started a Ph.D. thesis without the trust of my family, and their unfailing support of every kind. My sincere and warmest thanks must go to my aunts, Ms Apostolia Karabetsou and Ms Demetra Patellis, my uncle Mr Leonidas Anastassopoulos, and my sister, Dina, who have been always there for me. My first debt of gratitude, though, is to my mother. I owe to her more than words can express.

Finally, sincere thanks go to Argiris Mamais, for his unfailing support through all the stages of the thesis and the book preparation.

Introduction

Like Noah's Ark, those great civic collections, the library and the museum, seek to represent experience within a mode of control and confinement. One cannot know everything about the world, but one can at least approach closed knowledge through the collection. Although transcendent and comprehensive in regard to its own context, such knowledge is both eclectic and eccentric. Thus the ahistoricism of such knowledge makes it particularistic and consequently random. In writing of collecting one constantly finds discussion of the collection as a mode of knowledge.

(Stewart, 1993: 161)

Collecting is the desire of the Museum.

(Elsner, 1994a: 155)

The phenomenon of collecting as a systematic activity that refers to the satisfaction of symbolic rather than actual needs, is traditionally taken to originate in the middle of the fifteenth century, when the collections of the Medicis and the first cabinets of curiosities were formulated as a result of the Renaissance Humanism, and 'the fundamental Humanist concept that Man could be understood through his creations and Nature through the systematic study of Her manifestations' (Cannon-Brookes, 1992: 500).

Nevertheless, the practice of collecting had started long before that; its genesis can be located in the European prehistoric communities of around 3,000 BCE. Since then and up to the present day, it has been through different phases, each characterised by a set of notions, whose deployment will contribute invaluably to the discussion concerning collecting and museums. Pearce (1992: 90; 1995: 55) discusses the history of collecting in the long term (*longue durée*) of European tradition, and discerns four phases of development: the 'archaic prologue', the 'early modern', the 'classic modern' and the 'post-modern'. Out of these four, the first, i.e. the 'archaic', which includes the early hoards and grave goods, the accumulations of Greek temples and open-air shrines, the royal collections of Hellenistic kings, the art and curiosity collections held by the Romans, and the relics treasured by the medieval princes and churches, has attracted the least attention. Its presence in the 'pre-history' of collecting is acknowledged unanimously by historians of museums and/or collecting, but there has been no attempt at a closer examination of that phase, which was both very long-lasting and as critical as are all early phases for the crystallisation of a phenomenon.

This book aims to address this gap, and to offer a contribution to the history of collecting that will go beyond historical knowledge, an analysis of the origins of the phenomenon that has defined Western tradition, and continues to do so.

The introduction will be structured in the following manner: first, we will discuss briefly the relation between collecting and museums, in order to put the subject of collecting in the wider context of the museological discourse. Then, we will present a literature review: the historiography of collecting, approaches to collecting theory, and background literature on classical collecting (the focus of this book) will be discussed. Then the aims of the book and its justification will be presented, along with a few methodological concerns regarding the discussion of the nature of collecting and the use of the data assembled. Finally, the book outline will be provided.

Museums and Collections

The role and importance of the museum as an inseparable part of the cultural identity of modern societies has been acknowledged for a long time, and in various ways. The museum's importance lies in the fact that it holds the

> true data ... upon which in the last analysis the materialistic meta-narratives depended for their verification. With this is linked the other side of the unique museum mode, the ability to display, to demonstrate, to show the nature of the world and of man within it by arranging the collected material in particular patterns which reflect, confirm and project the contemporary world view. (Pearce, 1992: 4).

Museums, in other words, occupy the unique role of being 'the defining source of the phenomenon of the *original*, while simultaneously generating its circulation in reproduced form as a part of a commodity culture' (Sherman and Rogoff, 1994: xvii, emphasis in the original). During the last decades of the twentieth century, and due to rapid changes in fields like cultural theory, anthropology and philosophy, and of theoretical apparatuses like those devised by post-structuralism, post-modernism and feminism (Porter, 1991; 1994), museologists became aware of the multiple possibilities which exist within museums to 'create', codify and often manipulate cultural and historical knowledge, in their attempt to 'naturalise the concreteness of the social and historical processes in which they participate' (Sherman and Rogoff, 1994: x). As a result, the need for a closer critical inspection and intervention of museums' development and history seems mandatory for contemporary cultural historians, in order to acquire a clear picture of the development of our society and its interrelation with museums (Duclos, 1994: 6; Pearce, 1992: 115-116).

However, until recently, and despite the need for a more analytical approach to the history of museums, this has been limited to historical narratives concerning individual institutions. One way to replace this mode of thought would stem from examining in detail the traditional definition of the museum: an institution to collect, document, preserve, exhibit and interpret material culture and related information for the public benefit (e.g. Museums Association, 1994/5: 445; ICOM, Art. 3, Statutes). The history of the museum emerges from the public histories of collecting, documenting, preserving, exhibiting and educating, or, in the words of Sherman and Rogoff (1994: x), 'between the social histories of collecting, classifying, displaying, entertaining, and legitimating'.

In all this, major importance accrues to collecting, which is the dynamic process that lies behind the genesis of the museum and, consequently, of the other activities and histories. In Elsner's words: 'While the museum is a kind of entombment, a display of once lived activity (the activity whereby real people collected objects associated with other real people or living beings), collecting is the process of the museum's creation, the living act that the museum embalms' (1994a: 155). Although the former part of this assertion can be contested as adherent to a static and monolithic approach toward museums, which denies interaction between past and present collecting activities, the latter part encapsulates the relation between museums and collections.

This relation has been the theme of many debates. The museum usually is connected primarily to the Public and the State, while collecting is considered as a private pursuit. Furthermore, museums are supposed to be in a condition of permanence, while the collector is always suspected of dispersing his collection. The museum, additionally, is supposed to be the holder of all the scholarship concerning its field of collecting. The collector, on the other hand, is thought to have a personal preoccupation, often illegitimate, if not illegal. The institutionalised collection is supposed to have its objects kept out of the market mechanisms, while the collector is actively involved in them. He is also thought of as 'culturally displaced and in a morally ambiguous position' (Thomas, 1994: 116).

As a result, collections and collecting have not been the subject of detailed studies except for those cases where they have been 'sanctified' by having formed a museum,[1] as in the case of renowned collectors and donors (e.g. the Trandescants,[2] Sir Hans Sloane,[3] Joseph Mayer, Ashmole,[4] Payne Knight,[5] and, more recently, Franks[6]). Nevertheless, closer examination of museums and collections demonstrates that the study of the history of collecting lies at the heart of every attempt to understand the nature of museums and the shaping of contemporary society. Museums and collections have always been public in the sense that they were formulated according to public and social perceptions and ideas (Pearce, 1992: 89). Even though collecting depends very much on the personal motives of collectors and the way they perceive their society, it is true that 'the collections of a given country at a given time are, taken as a whole, the co-extension of that country's culture at that particular time. They incarnate and make visible to us its culture' (Pomian, 1990: 275). Thus, all aspects of collecting, and not only the formal ones, deserve consideration and can contribute significantly to the study of human society. It has been through this rationale that private collecting and museums have been drawn together in self-reflexive attempts,[7] like the People's Show,[8] as well as recent introspective exhibitions and seminars examining the relation between museums and collections, like those held in the Natural History Museum, London (1997),[9] the Booth Museum of Natural History in Brighton (1997),[10] the Walsall Museum and Art Gallery (1997),[11] or the multi-site exhibition[12] entitled 'Collected' in London (1997).[13]

Understanding of the role of the museum thus can be enhanced. Museums are not only holders of material evidence and related information concerning technology, economy, art and so on, but since museums hold collections and since these form the realisation of deeply rooted social beliefs and practices (Pearce, 1993),[14] museums are the holders of the state of mind which underlies the collections of which they consist. Consequently, the study of the history of collections, along with the historiography of museums, contributes to the museological discourse, and evokes the process through which the identity both of each museum separately, and also of the Museum as an institution, came into existence.

Historiography of Collecting

Since its very early stages, collecting practice has been accompanied by a heterogeneous body of literature, mainly written inventories, but also 'guides' for travellers, biographies of artists, descriptions of private and public museums, archives, and so on.[15] From the eighteenth century onwards, advice for collectors, monographs on collections and different categories of collectables, histories of specific collections and museums, as well as the first attempts to provide overviews became the pursuit of antiquarians, dealers, amateurs and dilettantes, historians and art critics. In most of these cases, the focus was on individual works of art, and the mass of literature thus created was characterised by art-historical methods (Pomian, 1990: 3).

More often than not the history of collecting had been closely associated with the sociology and history of taste. Gradually all the acquisitions of the collector(s), and even the physical environment in which they had chosen to live, were taken into account, with the result that the boundaries between collecting and decorating tended to disappear, and 'taste' became the overriding concern. This perspective emphasised the personal aspect of collecting rather than the social one, and meant that whatever could not contribute to the identification of taste faded into insignificance; thus, collections were isolated from notions of the past, from questions of scientific interest, ideas on religion and patriotism, differences in age, social background, ideological and political agendas. Taste thus was taken as a strictly personal characteristic, and collecting was reduced to a set of preferences according to certain artistic parameters and 'imprisoned in the aesthetic sphere' (Pomian, 1990: 3-4).[16] This approach characterises much of the discussion on Roman collecting, as we will see further in our literature review.

As a result, both the overviews and the more specific works on collections which have been produced until recently, have been written within the traditional paradigm, concerned with the choice of 'important' men (in the sense of their political, social and artistic influence) and 'significant' collections (in terms of the artistic treasures they hold) that were presented in an encyclopedic or art-historical way, which attempted to produce chronologically arranged narratives illustrating the continuous evolution from 'primitive' collections to modern museums (Murray, 1904; Bazin, 1967; Briggs, 1947; Alexander, 1979).

Nevertheless, collections are not solely 'guardians of works of art' and 'testaments to taste' (Pomian, 1990: 4). Collecting is a multi-dimensional phenomenon, which in order to be comprehended has to be studied in the light of questions which originate from theorising about the collection as an anthropological event. This realisation led to the publication since 1980 of important wide-ranging papers and books devoted to the study of collecting and of museums, that would go beyond the limitations described above. It is a well-known *topos* that the inauguration of the new perspectives was signalled by the publication of a collection of essays edited by Impey and MacGregor (1985), which resulted from an international conference held in Oxford. Interest now focused on collections of natural curiosities, scientific instruments or other objects with no self-evident aesthetic importance, while new qualities started to be appreciated. The political aspect of the creation of museums, sociological approaches, and cultural politics involved in the creation of public and private collections were brought to the forefront, in order to support a broader understanding of the phenomenon (DiMaggio, 1982; Poulot, 1985; Coombes, 1988; Sherman, 1989).

The new direction was underlined by the first publication in 1989 of the *Journal of the History of Collections*, which became the forum for the exchange of ideas and the application of new approaches to collecting (although both innovative and traditional approaches often co-exist in its pages). The inauguration of the new era in the history of collecting and museums is signalled also by the publication in 1992 of Hooper-Greenhill's thesis which studies Renaissance collecting under the influence of Foucault and by using the 'effective history' approach.[17]

In 1990 (English edition - 1987 French edition), Pomian published his own views on collecting. He suggests that the collection has to be seen as an institution co-extensive with man both in terms of space and time, and therefore as a very complex phenomenon whose history has to be discussed within geographical, political, religious, intellectual, artistic, economic, and social dimensions. He concluded:

> The collection is thus a unique domain, whose history cannot be consigned to the narrow confines of the histories of art, the sciences or history itself. It is, or rather should be, a history in its own right concentrating on "semiophores", or objects bearing meaning, on their production, their circulation and their "consumption" which most generally takes the form of mere viewing and does not, as such, involve any physical destruction. As the history of the production of semiophores it intersects with the histories of art, history and the sciences, as semiophores include not only works of art, but also relics of the past and objects found in the natural and exotic world. When the history of their circulation is examined, the history of economics cannot be avoided, especially when it comes to the evolution and development of the market in semiophores. Lastly, with the history of their "consumption", the history of the classification of objects and of the meaning vested in them, it comes into contact with intellectual history, while the history of those who place them on display and those who come and look at them intersects with social history. Placed at the cross-roads of several different currents of thought, the history of collections would seem to offer a valuable line of pursuit to cultural historians. (Pomian, 1990: 5-6).

The multi-faceted history of collections was emphasised also in a book edited by Elsner and Cardinal, where it is defined as 'the narrative of how human beings have striven to accommodate, to appropriate and to extend the taxonomies and systems of knowledge they have inherited' (1994: 2). To emphasise this, the edited essays of the volume adopt a variety of stances and methodological approaches to their subjects.

The sociology of taste and consumption acquired a new dimension in the work of Bourdieu (1974; 1984; 1987), who places emphasis on the 'economy of cultural goods' and the conditions in which this operates. In particular, he locates the parameters that create taste in the social sphere, by suggesting that cultural needs depend on upbringing, social origin and education, i.e. the 'habitus', the cultural inheritance and environment, that characterises different classes and class fractions. Material possessions then - and especially works of art - stand for more than financial capital; they represent the symbolic and cultural capital an individual possesses, and ensure his participation in a cultural élite. The actual, material possession of an artefact, along with the symbolic appropriation of it, i.e. the capacity to prove a genuine interest in its possession and an appreciation of its qualities, illustrate in the clearest way the 'internalisation of distinctive signs and symbols of power in the form of natural 'distinction', personal 'authority' or 'culture'' (1984: 282). In other words, the quality of the person who acquires the objects is affirmed by his capacity to appropriate an object of quality. It is interesting to note that Bourdieu suggests an equivalence between practices of exclusive appropriation of quality objects, collecting being one of them, with the ostentatious destruction of wealth, a characteristic of the gift exchange tradition (we will come back to this shortly), as sharing the notion that 'being' is inseparable from 'having' (1984: 282). Bourdieu's views provide illuminating insights into Roman collecting, as we will argue further in our book.

However, the most complete and innovative way of approaching the history of collecting is the one employed by Pearce (1995). She discusses collecting in its longevity in the European tradition, and aims to found it firmly in a cultural context. The annalist paradigm of historical time as dominated by three groups of processes, namely the long term structures (*Longue-durée*), the medium term forces (*Conjonctures*), and the short term events (*Evénements*), is employed profitably to argue for the continuous presence of the phenomenon of collecting in the European tradition, and its interrelation to all aspects of knowledge and life. The division of the history of collecting into phases which we mentioned at the beginning of the introduction finds its justification in this approach (see also Figure 0.1) (Pearce, 1995: 55).

Approaches to Collecting Theory

Early critical analysis of collecting dates back to the 1920s and 1930s, when essays were published by Adorno and Benjamin.[18]   Children also were discussed as collectors (e.g. Burk, 1900; Whitley, 1929; Durost, 1932; Witty, 1931) as early as the beginning of the twentieth century. Art collecting was the theme of a long series of publications (e.g. Rigby and Rigby, 1944; Rheims, 1959; Herrman, 1972; Saisselin, 1984; Baekeland, 1981; Alsop, 1982; Moulin, 1984), while popular collecting had to wait until well into the 1980s for a more equal treatment from the academic interest (Dannefer, 1980; 1981; Olmstead, 1987; 1988, Butsch, 1984; Bryant, 1989; Martin, 1996; 1997; 1999a; 1999b; Pearce, 1998).   Since then there have been many attempts to codify the phenomenon of collecting (Danet and Katriel, 1989; Belk and Wallendorf, 1990; Pearce, 1992; 1995; Elsner and Cardinal, 1994; Pomian, 1990), to discuss interaction between people and objects (Appadurai, 1986; Kopytoff, 1986), and to interpret the phenomenon of collecting from different perspectives. Prominent among these is the psychological aspect (e.g. Perret-Clermont and Perret, 1982; Belk, 1988b; Lancaster and Foddy, 1988; Dittman, 1991), the psycho-analytic perspective (Baekeland, 1981; Fanti *et al.*, 1982; Winnicott, 1953; Gamwell, 1996; Storr, 1983; Muestenberger, 1994), and the consumer research studies (e.g. Greenhalgh, 1988; 1989; Briggs, 1990; Belk, 1988a; 1988b, 1990; 1991; 1995, etc.).

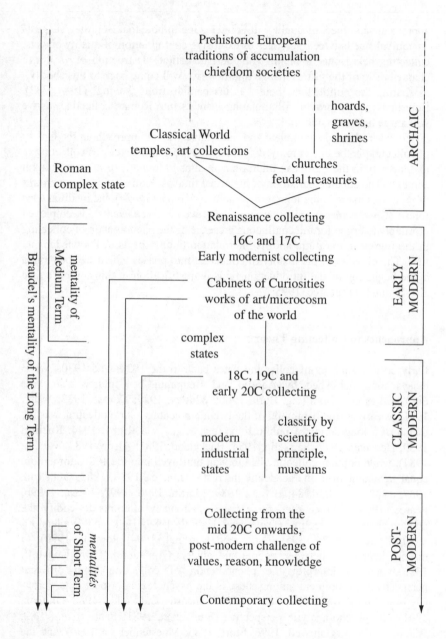

Figure 0.1:   The European historical sequence of collecting (after Pearce, 1995: 55)

Several attempts have been made to reach a definition of the phenomenon of collecting, and several characterisations have been attributed to collections. It would be interesting to start the discussion by offering some of those definitions, first for their own sake (since the attitude expressed by and through definitions has implications for the knowledge received on a subject - see also Bal, 1994); and second, as an initial step in order to present the basic characteristics of collecting, the motivation which lies behind collections, the different kinds of collecting and, finally, their relation to people and the past.

The first definition is one that dates back to 1932, often cited when referring to collections (Pearce, 1992; 1995; 1998):

> A collection is basically determined by the nature of the *value* assigned to the objects, or ideas possessed. If the *predominant* value of an object or idea for the person possessing it is intrinsic, i.e. if it is valued primarily for use, or purpose, or aesthetically pleasing quality, or other value inherent in the object or accruing to it by whatever circumstances of custom, training, or habit, it is not a collection. If the predominant value is representative or representational, i.e. if said object or idea is valued chiefly for the relation it bears to some other object or idea, or objects, or ideas, such as being one of a series, part of a whole, a specimen of a class, then it is the subject of a collection. (Durost, 1932: 10).

This is the earliest example of a series of definitions emphasising the same points: the 'value' and 'use' of the objects of a collection, their 'sequence', the relation between 'whole' and 'part', and the role of 'specimen'. Although it is clear that this definition refers mainly to the traditional collections of stamps or natural specimens, the parameters mentioned are present in almost all discussions of collecting. Baudrillard (1968), Stewart (1993), Pomian (1990), Pearce (1992), and Cardinal (1994), to name but a few, appreciate the importance of these factors to the creation and understanding of collecting, and devote much research in their attempt to define them and their interrelation to the creation of collections.

Pomian, for example, (1990: 9) has contributed to the discussion on value by suggesting that it is necessary for the natural or artificial curiosities forming a collection to be kept 'out of the economic circuit'. Thus, the objects can divulge their meaning (as 'semiophores'), which in its turn marginalises their usefulness, and lets the true value be revealed, i.e. the value to 'represent the invisible and therefore to have a share in the superiority and fertility it is unconsciously endowed with' (Pomian, 1990: 31). In other words, Pomian juxtaposes 'visible' and 'invisible' value, the former being monetary, and the latter one that is accrued only when an object is taken out of the economic circuit and acquires the status of 'priceless'. Collections rely heavily upon the latter, and collectors pursue it, in an attempt to grasp the 'invisible' and communicate with whatever exists beyond its borders. We will remember this juxtaposition when we discuss the case-studies, especially Pliny and Cicero, who base their views on collecting on issues of 'tangible' and 'intangible' value.

Stewart, on the other hand, believes that 'the collection represents the total aestheticization of use value' and therefore, 'the collection is a form of art as play, a form involving the reframing of objects within a world of attention and manipulation of context ... . Yet unlike many forms of art, the collection is not representational. The collection presents a hermetic world ...'. Furthermore, she suggests that 'aesthetic value is clearly tied to the cultural' (1993: 151-152; 154). Pearce reads value as mainly symbolic, and associates it with political considerations, regarding notions of aesthetics, knowledge, morality and societal structure, but also traditions of the long-term, and individual poetics (1995: 285-307). In her view, cultural value is assigned to objects that embody high technical ability and express cultural norms and ideal views about the self and the world; similarly, it accrues to objects that are seen as holders of knowledge and power to communicate with the depth of self, other people, and the divine. The assemblage and holding of these objects bring to the owner moral quality and power deriving from their intellectual prestige. These notions of valuation bear particular reference to classical collecting, as we will see further on (see Chapters 3 and 8).

'Seriality' has been another major issue in relation to collecting. Belk and his colleagues (1990: 8) defined collecting as 'the selective, active and longitudinal acquisition, possession and disposition of an interrelated set of differentiated objects (material things, ideas, beings, or experiences) that contribute to and derive extraordinary meaning from the entity (the collection) that this set is perceived to constitute.' We again can notice that the ideas of 'selection', 'set', 'meaning' and 'entity' are used in order to characterise and define collecting. Cardinal (1994: 71) also devised a similar definition: '(by collection) I mean a concerted gathering of selected items which manifest themselves as a pattern or set, thereby reconciling their divergent origins within a collective discourse'. Although Belk and his colleagues deal with collecting from the consumer research standpoint, while Cardinal does so from the academic art-historical point of view, it is obvious that they both agree on the importance of the same characteristics.

More of them are brought to the forefront through other definitions. Alsop (1982: 70) suggests: 'To collect is to gather objects belonging to a particular category the collector happens to fancy ... and a collection is what has been gathered.' This definition places the emphasis on the mentality of the collector and the subjective element in collecting. The same idea underlies the definition given by Bal (1994: 100): collecting is 'a process consisting of the confrontation between objects and subjective agency informed by an attitude'. A similar motif had appeared before in the definition given by Aristides (1988: 330): 'collection ... [is] an obsession organised'. This definition is further enriched with the idea of 'order'.

'Classification' and 'order' are two of the most important notions in collecting, and bear a series of implications for the formation of collections and our understanding of them. Collecting is the 'embodiment of classification' (Elsner and Cardinal, 1994: 2), and relates to the idea of 'completion'. Classification also marks the difference between 'collecting', and other forms of 'accumulating' and/or 'hoarding'. Collecting is an activity related to sociality and human relations (Baudrillard, 1968: 147-8).

'Completion' is another key issue of collecting. Danet and Katriel (1989: 266) offer five types of strategies that collectors pursue in order to reach 'closure/completion/perfection': 1. completing a series or set; 2. filling a space; 3. creating a visually pleasing, harmonious display; 4. manipulating the scale of objects; 5. aspiring to perfect objects. In this list lie the roots of a very interesting approach to collecting, which relates to psychology and psycho-analysis. Storr (1983), for instance, argues that the need to classify, to put order into chaos, to master material culture, to achieve the completion of a series, relates to human insecurity and is a mechanism through which people try to control themselves and their environment, to achieve ultimate satisfaction.

We can summarise the ideas presented above by underlining the close interrelation among sets/preferences, aesthetic/use value, subjective/social identity, and mentality/culture; and by providing an interesting definition (*in lieu*) offered by Pearce (1992: 50): 'ideas like non-utilitarian gathering, an internal or intrinsic relationship between the things gathered - whether objectively classified or not - and the subjective view of the owner are all significant attributes of a collection, together with the notion that the collection is more than the sum of its parts'.

The motives behind the formulation of collections have been the subject of much speculation and research. Rigby and Rigby (1944) tried to understand collecting within five parameters: physical security, distinction, immortality, knowledge and aesthetic satisfaction. Rheims (1959), on the other hand, expressed his view with four categories: the need for possession, the need for spontaneous activity, the impulse to self advancement, and the tendency to classify and regularise things. Belk (1988: 548-552; also Belk et al., 1991: 194-205) reached the following list of collecting motives: 1. collecting legitimises acquisitiveness as art or science; 2. collections serve as extensions of the self; 3. collections seldom begin purposefully; 4. collections tend toward specialisation; 5. addictions and compulsions pervade collecting; 6. post-mortem distribution problems are significant to collectors and their families; 7. profane to sacred conversions occur when items enter the collection; 8. there is a simultaneous desire and fear of completing a collection. Pearce (1992: 69-88) lists sixteen possible motivations for collecting: leisure; aesthetics; competition; risk; fantasy; a sense of community; prestige; domination; sensual gratification; sexual foreplay (these two may coincide); desire to reframe objects; the pleasing rhythm of sameness and difference; ambition to achieve perfection; extending the self; reaffirming the body; producing gender-identity; achieving immortality. Bal (1994: 103-4) notices the 'increasing urgency' of the above motivations and suggests that the underlying notion which connects them all is 'fetishism'.

This term has been used before by Stewart (1993: 164), and has a long and valid use besides the Freudian one (also, Gathercole, 1989; Ellen, 1988).[19] Having its origins in anthropology, this term connects the psycho-analytic narrative perspective, pursued by Freudians and now largely out-of-date (Baekeland, 1981; Muestenberger, 1994), with the Marxist-political critique (see also Pearce, 1992: 82-84). Possessions, and most specifically material ones, act as reminders and confirmers of people's identities (Pearce, 1992: 55; Martin, 1997; 1999b). This idea has been common to writers on collecting since Rigby and Rigby (1944) (see also Rheims, 1959; Stewart, 1993). The famous assertion by Clifford (1988: 218) '[I]in the West, however, collecting has long been a strategy for the deployment of a possessive self, culture and authenticity' expresses this idea, while it identifies the West, i.e. Europe and the societies influenced by it, as the core area which encourages that kind of collecting behaviour.

Cannon-Brookes (1992: 500-501) distinguishes between 'object-centred' societies, where objects are important in the transmission of cultural traditions, and 'concept-centred' societies, where the cultural traditions are transmitted mainly orally. Within the same anthropological perspective lies the attempt by Pearce (1993; 1995) to explain European-style collecting. She traces its origins to materiality, which 'is inherent in the long-term mentality of European society, because this depends upon the twin notions of personal effort and accumulation and the idea of evidence, arrived at by the processes of discrimination in time, space and form' (1993: 98; 1995: 57ff). In other words, Pearce interprets collecting within the framework of three long-term themes of European society. The first theme is that of the family system that produces many competitive individuals, who have to make their own fortune, because of the inheritance tradition that benefits the male first-born; they therefore have a special relationship with the material world, evident also in the Indo-European linguistic tradition, where the notion of possession is clearly expressed through language which connects people with objects. The second theme is the oath/ordeal paradigm, that produces a way of thinking which distinguishes clearly between people and things, 'true' and 'false', 'reality' and 'causality'. Oath is defined as 'a formal invocation to gods/men to witness the contested validity of acts or intentions' (quoted in Pearce, 1995: 76), whereas ordeal is ultimately the validation of the oath. The dichotomy between word and object, man and the material world, that the pair implies carries the seeds of a particular relationship between people and the material world, which is regarded as 'Other', and therefore provides an arena for the exercise of the analytical qualities just described. In other words, the oath/ordeal paradigm creates a society where one thing can be distinguished from another on the basis of truth and falsehood, with their companion ideas of 'reality' and 'causality'; the capacity for recognising these distinctions belongs not within a social group, but within each individual. Such a society is likely to see the accumulation, exchange and deposition of specially chosen objects as a prime way of creating relationships between men and men, and men and the divine (Pearce, 1995: 85). The final theme is that of the gift-exchange tradition, which within the above framework is a means of creating relationships between people, and people and gods. The implications of these themes in the discussion of classical collecting will be brought together later.

The motives for collecting have been organised into three types, each representing a category of collectors, firstly by Rheims (1959). He divided collections into those made by 'the dedicated collector', by 'the dilettante' and by 'the curio-hunter'. Pearce (1992: 68-88) also arrives at three types of collections (summarising her list of motives): systematic, souvenirs and fetishistic. Souvenir collections are those in which the objects take their relation unity from their association with either a single person and his/her life story, or a group of people, who function in this regard as if they were a single person. In fetishistic collections, emphasis is on the relationship between the objects and their collector. The collection plays a crucial role in defining the personality of the collector, who maintains a worshipful attitude towards his/her objects. Systematic collecting, finally, works by the selection of examples intended to stand for others of their kind and to complete a set. The emphasis is upon classification, in which specimens are extracted from their context and put into relationships created by seriality. Systematic collecting usually is considered a positive intellectual act designed to demonstrate a point (Pearce, 1992: 69, 78-84, 87). Unlike them, though, fetishistic collections have attracted the attention of psycho-analysts, who rather dismissively attribute collecting to notions of anxiety and tension (Muestenberger, 1994: 253), and provide the classic Freudian explanation that collecting relates to the tendency of the collector to direct his surplus libido to the inanimate objects, and that it corresponds to all three stages of his scheme of sexual development: oral, anal, and genital pleasures (Gamwell, 1996: 6). In this sense, collecting is related to childhood traumas and operates as an ego defense mechanism.

This is a very interesting approach, not for its interpretative merits, which are highly debatable, but because of the directions towards description and understanding of collecting that it provides. We can call the metaphors which Danet and Katriel (1994) have identified in the collecting discourse to our aid. By interviewing (directly or indirectly) collectors they have isolated a list of five metaphors that operate in their discourse: collecting is hunting; therapy; passion, desire; disease; supernatural experience. Interestingly, three out of five metaphors relate to the 'pathological' reference to collecting, to the dismissive view of it as unnatural, or too intense to be proper. These account for descriptions of collectors common from literature (Edgar, 1997), but they can also be related to classical sources and their views about their contemporary collectors.

Finally, one of the issues most commonly associated with collecting is its relation to the past. Collections have been characterised as a 'unique bastion against the deluge of time', and supposedly combine several themes: 'desire and nostalgia, saving and loss, the urge to erect a permanent and complete system against the destructiveness of time' (Elsner and Cardinal, 1994: 1). The nostalgic aspect of collecting has been also recognised by other researchers like Rheims (1959), Starobinski (1966), Stewart (1993), Danet and Katriel (1989), Belk (1988a; 1988b) and so on.   Benjamin and Adorno called collecting 'practical memory' (cited in Crimp, 1989).   As an extension of the same idea there is the desire for immortality, which is the peak of the motives mentioned above (Danet and Katriel, 1989: 272).

Finally, a post-modern approach to the phenomenon is that by Harvey (1989). He attempts a more radical reading of the personal world of collecting, and describes the home as 'a private museum ... to guard against the ravages of time space compression'.   His argument is that 'the personal collection, through metonymy and private classification, exemplifies the desire to fight the post-modern collapse of distance and temporality and "secure moorings" and "longer lasting values" in a constantly shifting world' (Harvey, 1989: 292, cited also in Duclos, 1994: 9). With this is connected the recently realised necessity to discuss the phenomenon of collecting as 'at once psychological and social that not only has its less than obvious material history, but is also a continuing contemporary presence' (Elsner and Cardinal, 1994: 5; also see Martin, 1997; Pearce, 1998).

Approaches to Roman Collecting

The study of the history of Roman collecting dates back to the nineteenth century. It has been a well-accepted fact that Renaissance collections were formed after the direct or indirect influence of the Romans, as part of both the general interest in the humanities and also the classical past that characterises that particular period, and the excavations in Rome and elsewhere in Italy, which had started long before to enrich private and public collections. However, the first history of Roman collecting as a separate phenomenon was published as late as 1867, by the chief curator of the Louvre, Edmund Bonnafé.

He studied in detail the ancient authors and some of the early publications concerning the amateur excavations at Rome, in order to make a list of the names of Roman collectors, and anecdotes about their preferences in collecting. Bonnafé claims that Roman collectors offered a major contribution to the contemporary art and culture of his time since they rescued important works of art for the successive generations. Part of his history is devoted to the desire to identify works of art housed in the Louvre with the ones which, according to

Latin authors, belonged to ancient personalities. This was the result of the romanticism of the writer, who took the works of the ancient authors at their face value, without examining them critically. Furthermore, Bonnafé worked at a time when archaeology was more of an art than a science, and thus he was more concerned with fiction rather than with facts (Taylor, 1948). In addition, the political circumstances of his era (the Napoleonic empire had represented itself as heir to the Roman Caesars) and the character of the Louvre ('the last magnificent example of a museum exhibiting a Roman character') could not but lead its chief curator to such an approach (Michaelis, 1908: 24-26; Jenkins, 1992: 24; Déotte, 1995). Nevertheless, the study of Bonnafé is of primary importance both as a source of reference for the information it provides on Latin authors writing on collecting, and as a source concerning the museological approach toward collectors and collections in the second half of the nineteenth century.

The subject of Roman collecting was discussed in part of the voluminous work by Friedländer (1865-1871; 1921), as well as in essays written by Blümner (1873), and Hermann (1855). All three attempts romanticise the phenomenon, and have to be seen within the romanticism of the revival of the humanist spirit which characterises the German academic tradition (Whitley, 1987). They all argue that the Romans did not develop a valid art sense (*Kunstsinn*), and that their collections were 'superficial' - assembled for their monetary value, and 'accidental' - the result of the Roman conquests and acquaintance with the luxurious and cultivated eastern way of life; they agreed, however, that subsequent generations should thank them for the preservation of Greek works of art that would have otherwise been lost. This debate over whether the interest of the Romans in art was 'real' or not, and whether this interest was enough to explain and justify collections, has been quite common in the discussion of Roman art and collecting from then onwards; and has thus largely defined the view toward classical collecting, limiting it to notions of taste and art historical appreciation. Naturally, the development of art history and the understanding of art plays an important role in art collecting. Nevertheless, it is not enough by itself to explain and justify the phenomenon.[20]

Since then, the history and nature of Roman collecting has been of interest to those attempting to produce an overview of the phenomenon, and universal histories of museums. Economou (1934), Rigby and Rigby (1944), Taylor (1948), van Salmon (1958), Rheims (1959), Bazin (1967), Holst (1967), Wace (1969), Alsop (1982), and even contemporaries like Belk (1995), devote part of their work to delineating the character of classical collecting, in an attempt to have a complete overview inclusive of the origins, supplemented with anecdotal perspectives. The Hellenistic and Roman periods usually form the prelude to the teleologically arranged development, so as to present the most 'primitive' of the appearances of the phenomenon of collecting, while ancient temples and Roman public buildings are thought of as the earliest museums. When their history is not discarded in a few lines, the appetite of the Hellenistic tyrants and the Roman *nouveaux riches* for Greek works of art, copies as well as originals is mentioned, and how they were prepared to go to extreme lengths in order to satisfy this, including plundering, looting and other criminal acts. The motives for the act of collecting are attributed more often than not to a 'philhellenic zeal', 'eastern luxury', 'political motives' or to merely the development of a 'world of refinement and culture'. Descriptive and generalised as these discussions are, they do not provide an insight into the real nature of Hellenistic and Roman collecting, or to its relation to the genesis of the idea of the museum.

From an archaeological point of view, interest in classical collecting has been limited to enquiries regarding ancient Greek and Roman sculpture and painting, and to the originality or provenance of works of art, as well as to their setting in public and private spaces of the Roman world (Bejor, 1979; Fuchs, 1987; Manderscheid, 1981; Marvin, 1983). Major attention was attracted by the Roman copies of Greek works of art, in an attempt to identify lost Greek originals, or the influx of Greek art and artists to Italy (Bieber, 1977; Stewart, 1979; Richter, 1982; Ridgway, 1984; Marvin, 1989). Even when the Roman creative spirit was recognised, collecting was understood as aesthetically defined, an excuse for the assemblage and creation of works of art, and never as a separate and independent phenomenon (see, for instance, Ridgway, 1984; Marvin, 1989; Strong, 1976). The influence of Greek art and civilisation thus was overemphasised in terms of the Roman 'admiration' for it; and at the same time more general patterns inherent in Greek thought, that might have found a continuation and flourishing in the Roman society due to the different social and historical circumstances or the social patterns inherent in the Roman world, were ignored. The most thorough studies on the Greek influence on Roman art criticism and taste are those by Jucker (1950) and Becatti (1951). On the same subject Pollitt has also contributed some interesting views (1974; 1978; 1983).

In 1975, Strong published an article entitled 'Roman museums' in an attempt to examine the similarities and differences between ancient public collections and contemporary museums, as well as to examine the reasons behind their creation. He comes up with two main reasons: public benefaction and religious dedication. Other researchers offer suggestions regarding the influence of Epicurean, Stoic, or Neoplatonic philosophy, singly or in combination, to the arrangement of art within Roman households, and the planning of decorative programmes in temples and houses. These usually result in establishing iconographic norms, and thus explaining the existence of particular works of art in particular settings, by referring to generalised, socially determined taste, and not to conscious personal decision-making. There is no doubt that some very interesting and thought-provoking articles have been written in that spirit, although far-fetched conclusions created in a very contemporary manner have also been reached (see, for instance, Vermeule, 1967; 1968; 1977; Pantermalis, 1971; Warden and Romano, 1994, Sauron, 1980; Grenier, 1989; Zanker, 1978 and Preisshofen, 1978). These attempts, though, do not really tackle the issue of classical collecting *per se*; they are just recognition of the presence of the phenomenon in the classical world. This book will challenge some of these elaborate attempts, by suggesting that maybe a number of the questions usually posed regarding the social role of works of art in the ancient world would be better understood and more adequately explained in the context of the discussion of the nature of classical collecting. We will endeavour not to impose contemporary views on the past, although contemporarily devised apparatus will be employed.[21]

The motivation behind collecting thus has been discussed in close relationship to questions on art criticism, taste and philosophy; and it also has often become associated with enquiries about iconographic and decorative programmes, or the social role of art. An interesting alteration to this pattern is provided in an article published by Bartman (1994), on sculptural collecting and display in the private realm. Although this is also confined to art collections, and indeed sculpture assemblages, it allows for the presence of more criteria that would permit a rather more personalised 'taste' to be expressed. The author lists five reasons that would have influenced Roman collectors' selection of statuary: appreciation of purely aesthetic qualities; appreciation of technical virtuosity; attribution of the work to a famous name; antiquity; (and the latter preferably combined with) distinguished genealogy. These parameters, despite their obvious limitations as far as the study of collecting as a social and personal phenomenon is concerned, provide a starting point for pursuing some interesting leads in our discussion of classical collecting.

The early collecting practices have been the subject of an important dissertation by Pape (1975). She is interested in the looting that occurred of Greek works of art and artefacts, and provides a complete list of all the material plundered from the Greek world during the Roman expansion. Pape distinguishes between the removal of works of art from the Roman provinces by the victorious generals, who had the 'right of the conqueror' to remove the artefacts and dispose of them, and the actual '*Kunstraub*', looting, which refers strictly speaking to the removal and extortion of works of art from the provinces carried out by the magistrates. She argues, though, that the latter, along with the '*Kunstsinn*', had received more attention than the former and the public display of art, and she therefore concentrates on the historical, cultural, civic, and religious law assumptions on the basis of which the accumulation of Greek works of art as war booty became known to Rome, and the importance of the public presentation of these objects for the political, religious, and cultural life of the Romans. Consequently, Pape limits herself to the study of the public assemblages of works of art, and does not discuss private interests and collecting.

Individual collections and collectors have also attracted scholarly attention. A brief attempt to discuss collecting in the Hellenistic Pergamon (Howard, 1986), for instance, addressed the questions of the formation of the Attalid art collection, the uses to which it was put, as well as the effects of these practices upon ancient and modern followers. Unfortunately, this is also a very art-historical oriented approach. A very good article, although written in the same spirit, is the one by Gualandi (1982) on Pliny and art collecting. Another attempt to deal with the issues involved in classical collecting has been the book by Chevallier (1991). Although his main interest is to present a social history of Roman art, he makes an important contribution to the study of Roman collecting, by posing questions as to the phenomenon. Lehmann has been concerned also with collecting as this has been presented through the ancient sources, and he published two articles on Martial, and reconstruction according to some of his epigrams of a public collection of sculpture in the temple of Divus Augustus (1945 - for discussion see Chapter 7), and on Philostratus (1941). Articles on the collecting activities of other personalities have also been published: on Cicero (Valenti, 1936); the 'museum' of Augustus (Reinach, 1889); Herodes Atticus (Neugebauer, 1934). Finally, a book published a decade ago by Neudecker (1988) combines archaeological and textual data and discusses in detail the sculptural finds of Roman villas in Italy. Undoubtedly interesting as they all are, these attempts have been fragmentary and largely descriptive; there has been no effort to put all the fragments together and to create a coherent picture of classical collecting, based on contemporary collecting theory, while firmly based on the information provided by the ancient world.

The only attempt to offer a comprehensive discussion of collecting and museums in the classical world is the recent book by Ruggieri Tricoli and Vacirca (1998); they start from an anthropological and a museological point of view and are interested in delineating, in Foucault's terms, an 'archaeology of museology'. Nevertheless, their effort focuses on museography and architecture as well as museology, and seeks to identify current design, architectural and museographical patterns with ancient ones. In this sense, their aims and stance are quite different than the ones we pursue and adopt in this book (see also next section and ideas on history in Chapter 1).

Aims and Justification

The subject of this book is the nature of classical collecting as this is illustrated by four Latin writers, Marcus Tullius Cicero, Gaius Plinius Secundus, Marcus Valerius Martialis and Titus Petronius Arbiter, who lived and wrote during the first century BCE and the first century CE.[22] Their selection as case studies, as well as the preference for this particular period of history, have been determined by a number of reasons. First, we should mention the need to fill a gap in the history and analysis of collecting, by discussing one of the earliest and most neglected appearances of the phenomenon.[23] Second, during the late Hellenistic - early Imperial period of Rome, broadly from the third century

BCE to the first century CE, crucial developments took place in the ancient Mediterranean world. The collecting modes of the previous phases were summarised, while new notions and collecting issues of the future were introduced. More specifically, the period under examination is the age of transition from collections as holy dedications and commemorations of triumphs, to collecting for its own sake as a social and intellectual phenomenon of indisputable status. Additionally, it is the age of attribution of new qualities to material culture, and inauguration of associated practices, as private art patronage, art market and art history. Furthermore, another innovation of this period is the active personal involvement in the formulation of collections. For the first time, individuals developed a wide range of collecting attitudes, according to personal, emotional and psychological motives, but also to social and ideological demands.

Elsner (1994a: 156) has summarised the importance of this period in his assertion:

> In suggesting that Roman Italy was constructed as the all-plentiful provider and the Ur-collection, I wish to address a dream lying wistfully behind the collecting impulse: namely the urge to evoke, even sometimes to fulfill that myth of a completion, a complete ancient world, which was once itself collected in the imperial splendor of Rome. For ancient Rome is more than just the supreme paradigm of collectors (its collections were and are our canon) and the ultimate exemplar for empires. It was these things not just because of its priority in the past of Europe but because (in the myth that it told to glorify itself) it succeeded. That myth, which brought fulfillment in the act of accumulation together with supremacy in the arts of government, may only have been propagated by the Romans and without total faith, but it was believed (and needed to be believed) by the myth-making collectors from the Renaissance to the Enlightenment whose activities have generated our cultural institutions, above all the museum.

Déotte, in his discussion of museological texts of the nineteenth century (Quatremère de Quincy) and the creation of the Louvre, also records the deeply-rooted belief that 'Rome was in fact the archetypal museum' (1995: 222). The reasons for that are identified with the assimilation of the aesthetic principle of the museum with pagan religion, the mere fact that Rome was (and is) a large, open-air repository of works of art and architectural remains, but also the view of antiquarians and dilettantes that in Rome they could see the interactive relationship developed between antiquities and objects of art, historical sites, mountains, roads, relative geographical features, memories of past local traditions, customs, and so on. In this sense, Rome has been considered a 'complete collection' of the natural and cultural world, brought together for the enlightenment of people (Déotte, 1995: 223). This view sounds remarkably familiar to the student of classical collecting, since its echoes are present in the Elder Pliny's work, who thus propagated his belief in the success of the Roman world by presenting Rome as a complete, and three-dimensional 'inventory' of the world. The implications of his attempts for the nature of classical collecting, and for collecting in subsequent periods, will be discussed in Chapter 6. However, this is not a study devoted to the early modern museum development in Europe, and therefore, a detailed comparison and discussion of the influence of the archaic tradition to that of the subsequent phases will not be undertaken here.

The reasons that this study has taken this particular shape and that these authors have been selected, relate to its aim, which can be described as being to focus on the motives behind the interest in collecting, and to provide some answers, more elaborate and analytic than the usual descriptive ones, to questions concerning the nature and character of the phenomenon in the classical world. The aim of this book, therefore, is neither to present another social history of Roman art, with collecting holding a secondary role, if any at all, or to present the interesting anecdotal incidents mentioned by ancient authors in order to suggest a fragmentary similarity with the general characteristics of collectors of successive phases.[24] Rather, the aim is to take a longer and more penetrative look at collecting attitudes in the classical world, and trace the seeds of this practice and mentality in a shared tradition that runs through European thought (in the light of Pearce's arguments: see 1993; 1995). Consequently, the views on collections and collecting expressed by the four writers mentioned at the beginning will not be considered in isolation. They will be incorporated into the Graeco-Roman tradition, and will be approached through the methodological aid of four parameters which have been identified as fundamental for structuring the collecting discourse: the first parameter is the notion of antiquarianism: this is defined as an inherent interest in the past, which takes shape in the systematic assemblage of artefacts, information, and anything else that can bring people closer to the past, to history, but also to accumulated knowledge. The second parameter is the gift-exchange tradition: this particular notion lies at the heart of collecting, as a parameter of valuation that responds to the need for objects to acquire genealogies, importance as bearers of value, and significance in a fetishistic manner. In addition, it is a mechanism of establishing connections between divine and human world. The third parameter is the notion of identity: people search to acquire a communal or individual identity through objects, to shape a model of themselves that they can hold onto and pass on to others. This is the notion which allows objects and collections to take part in the processes of defining the self and the 'Other'. In the particular period on which we have chosen to concentrate, collections illustrate the conflict between individual and communal valuation, and collecting is experienced as a constant debate between individual and communities, private and public. The fourth parameter is the notion of time and space. Objects are parts of the tactile world, they occupy space, and they

furnish an interesting relation with the notion of time: they literally help people
to accommodate themselves in temporal and spatial terms, to tame, appropriate,
define, and comprehend time and space. Within this framework, we aim to
avoid epistemological anachronisms expressed through attribution of the
phenomenon of collecting in the classical world to 'philhellenism' or the
'invasion of the eastern *luxuria*', that refer to historical symptoms more than to
motivation.

Finally, we will have to justify the selection of texts, and 'textual
collections', instead of archaeological data, for this research, as well as the
choice of the individual authors, and discuss in brief a few of the
methodological concerns that the decision to 'read' ancient texts as sources of
data imply. The four authors were selected according to the extent to which
their work survives, itself an indication of interest by subsequent generations,
to the wealth of information on collecting it provides, to the possibilities
offered in each of them to illustrate one or more of the parameters that we
presented above, and to their chronological proximity and inclusion in the
chronological limits set, as well as to personal preferences.

Naturally, any modern attempt to make sense of the ancient world inevitably
strikes against several problems. We have to admit, firstly, that all perception
and interpretation are culturally determined; and secondly, that we have limited
access to that ancient world, especially to its conceptual universe, since the data
available are often fragmentary and ambiguous. Therefore, there is a need for
the development of methodological tools, which will help us to make sense of
the ancient world, and overcome some, at least, of the delimitations that the
factors presented above pose. In this attempt we can benefit from the use of
cognitive discourses and disciplines concerned with the study of societies and
artefacts, as well as with the processes of perception, reading, making sense
and communication. These may be potential sources for the development of
helpful epistemological tools. Indeed, these discourses and their
epistemological principles can lead to the realisation that we need to place the
texts that we want to study in their social, cultural, economic, political,
religious and conceptual context, as well as to the construction of models of
'reading', which, despite their limitations, offer interesting insights. Finally,
they may lead to the understanding that certain modalities, such as, for
instance, the nature of the process through which the reader makes sense of a
text, brings into play the reader's prior knowledge and assumptions.

Following this line of thought, while insisting on notions quite contradictory
to it like 'reconstruction' and 'neutrality', Sourvinou-Inwood (1995: 6-7)
suggests two strategies for reading a text. The first involves the evidence being
studied in the most exhaustive detail possible, without preconceived notions of
what is important or representative, since such selections depend on *a priori*,
inevitably culturally determined, judgements. This was only partially possible
in my interpretation for several reasons: in order to comply with such a strategy
I thought it necessary to 'collect' the data for the research through an extensive

reading of the ancient sources (in translation and in the original) without having set in advance a certain set of criteria that would define my selection, but having the broad aim of assembling paragraphs relating to attitudes towards collectors/collecting or material culture. This resulted in quite an extensive range of material, not particularly uniform (in terms of length of paragraphs assembled, number of paragraphs from each author, content and so on); but I believe it to be quite representative. Nevertheless, the selection itself could not have been, and was not, free from culturally predetermined conceptions. Simply the fact that I had in mind a range of definitions regarding collections and collecting, was enough to suggest a certain bias.

The second strategy Sourvinou-Inwood (1995: 7) advocates involves the structuring of the investigation into a series of separate analyses. Besides the limitations posed by restrictions of length and time, the reasons I confined myself to the textual evidence were the beliefs that firstly, texts, despite their limitations (not being written to provide information of this kind, their fragmentary status, the problem of lost books, etc.) offer an insight into collections, since they are unrestricted by practical concerns, so in a way they offer a discussion of a wider range of collections; secondly, they offer people's (sometimes collectors') thoughts, feelings, receptions of/about collections/collectors, and therefore, confer a more coherent and comprehensive picture of the scene. Thirdly, material culture, and collections even more so can be and are read as texts; this similarity is explored further below. Finally, since to a considerable extent the textual evidence was largely available during the Renaissance, it provided the model upon which Renaissance collectors/collections shaped themselves.[25]

The development of epistemological and methodological tools for my research thus has been tripartite: firstly, it has been structured around the concern for the relationship between writer and audience, since this applies to the relation/perception of the writer's *oeuvre* both by his contemporaries and ourselves; furthermore, it deals with the issues of the 'original' meaning and its 'original' reception. Secondly, a model has been constructed which will give us a lead to an understanding of the text and will facilitate reading, although it is by no means a model *of* reading or *of* understanding (see Chapter 1). Finally, we have been concerned with if and how we can use documents, and particularly literary documents, to make sense of the past. Our assumption that collections 'operate like' documents is based on a long line of material culture research (for example, Hodder, 1986; Shanks and Tilley, 1987a; 1987b; Tilley, 1990).

Sourvinou-Inwood (1995: 9) suggests two basic ways of reading a text/picture: the first involves treating the text/image as a 'floating' artefact and thus reading it 'directly' and 'empirically'; in other words, we make sense of it according to our own assumptions and expectations. She finds this legitimate, but claims that since it produces different 'readings' in different circumstances, it 'fails to lead to the recovery of meaning, inscribed on it by its "creator" and "extracted" by his contemporaries'. The second involves anchoring the text in its historical context and attempting to recover the 'original' meaning. This is implicit in classical scholarship, and in order to be achieved it involves the reconstruction of relevant ancient assumptions and expectations, and the reading of the text through these filters. The impossibility, or rather improbability, of the success of such an attempt is acknowledged by Sourvinou-Inwood herself a few lines below: 'all reading and interpretation is a cultural construct, dependent on the assumption of the readings and interpreting culture' (1995: 10).

The first of the above 'ways of reading a text' refers to what can be called an 'empirical' reading/approach, one in other words which attempts to read the past as 'same', as readily accessible and easily intelligible. The second method refers to a past alien and dissimilar, that needs to be deciphered as such. In order to achieve this, the researcher has to neutralise herself and with a pure mind plunge into the unknown. Both these methods of approaching a text/image convey parts of the 'truth', but not the whole of it, and, as is usually the case, they need to be combined in order to achieve the most effective and rewarding way of approaching the past. In other words, instead of falling into the common humanistic (and specifically classicist) fallacy of rendering the past more up-to-date by seeking within it the direct confirmation of a contemporary interest, or instead of trying - albeit in vain - to 'purify' the researcher's conceptual and cultural universe, in order to achieve the closest possible to the 'original' - if that ever existed - reading of a text, this research takes the stance that the texts should be read in the light of the Analogue.[26] Besides the continuity that binds these texts to us, their substantial cultural otherness must be and is acknowledged too. In other words, without denying that the search for the notions of collecting/collections has been shaped by interests developed *a posteriori*, we are going to search for the archetypa of these, for the analogous notions, and read the ancient texts as referring to a 'similar' world (neither 'same' nor 'other').

Outline of the Book

The book starts with a discussion of the methodological strategies employed during our reading of ancient authors (Chapter 1), in order to provide a theoretical framework that will allow for the most rewarding 'reading' of the ancient texts, taking, of course, into account the limitations and concerns involved in the discussion of documents written so long ago.

After that, the book is divided into two parts, each of which consists of four chapters, that broadly correspond to each other. The chapters of the first part discuss the four parameters of collecting that we presented above, while the second part consists of the chapters devoted to the ancient writers.

Thus, Chapter 2 is a discussion of antiquarianism and the notions of the past that this implies. Objects, monuments and their use, as evidence in the ancient historiographic tradition, are examined in an attempt to suggest that this gave rise not only to one of the best known categories of collections, that of antiquities as usually understood, but also to the cabinets of curiosities, and the encyclopedic collections that we commonly attribute to other sources. The systematic assemblage of artefacts in order to amass a complete inventory of all knowledge available is a common motif for all students of collections from the Renaissance onwards. Similarly familiar is the notion of the 'book' accompanying the actual collection, or substituting it in the form of a 'paper museum' (see, for instance, Cassiano dal Pozzo[27]). In this chapter we aim to trace the origins of this notion in the development of antiquarianism in the ancient world, and follow the expressions of it in the work of Pliny (Chapter 6), which is an extensive discussion of the views and ideas on collecting presented by this author in his *Historia Naturalis*. The aim is to trace the relation between these two modes of thought within Pliny's own collecting activities, in addition to his major role as recorder of collections in the ancient world, and contextualise it within a broader philosophical and collecting discourse.

Chapter 3 refers to the gift-exchange tradition, as the origin of value assumptions regarding works of art and other artefacts. The discussion considers the nature of the tradition by presenting the vocabulary and institutions of gift in Homer and mythology, its appearance at the Geometric and Classical sanctuaries, and the institutions and vocabulary of value which were developed there, the notions that the collections assembled in them embodied, and their legacy. This chapter corresponds with Chapter 7, on Martial and his epigrams. It is argued that Martial's poetry, besides offering information on collectors and collecting and providing the most vivid and realistic picture of the Roman collectors in practice, contributes toward our understanding of the interrelation between people, material culture, and literature in the Roman world. The poet propagates a 'real' value of objects, which derives from the gift-exchange tradition, incorporates this concept in his poetry and in his perception of the social and material world.

Chapter 4 is devoted to the individual as a cultural category, and the implications of the understanding of this notion for collectors and collecting in the classical world. The Hellenistic period traditionally is associated with the 'rise of individualism'. Collections, and the introduction of privately initiated collecting during this period, have thus been interpreted as symptoms of this phenomenon. The thrust of this chapter's argument is to re-examine this view in the light of the recently developed scepticism regarding individual and communal ideals during this period, and to suggest that the creation of individual collections is the result of a much more complicated process. Collections actually embody the struggle during this transitional period between individualism and community-oriented ideals. Although they signal the victory of the individual agent over restrictions posed by communal morality, they also attest to the attempt of collectors to reach their individuality through participation in a group. This group is not now that of the city-state, but is that of the highly educated, intellectual élite, with strong associations to the ancient Greek past, which share the moral quality that the possession of art implies, and the intellectual prestige that knowledge entails. This ambivalent role of collections and collecting becomes evident in Chapter 8. This is a discussion of Petronius' *Satyrica*, a novel written during Nero's reign. The main pattern of the discourse on collecting in this work revolves around the role of the collections as methods of inclusion in the cultural élite and, therefore, power and 'cultural capital'.

The aim of Chapter 5 is to investigate the notions of time and space as these appear in the philosophical, the anthropological, and the mythical thought of the classical world, in order to trace their impact on notions of order, knowledge and assemblage of material culture. It is argued that objects were used, as they are today, to evoke a sense of time or place, but also to structure people's relations to ritual spaces, and notions of sacred, profane, individual, communal, present and past. Furthermore, the spatial understanding of memory, and the capacity of objects to act as *aide-memoires* is examined. This chapter is complemented by Chapter 9, which discusses Cicero's collecting discourse. It is interesting to note that the orator's personal 'reading' of collections and collecting revolves around their power to structure time and space, and to appropriate it for their owner.

Notes

1   For example, the book by Alexander that discusses the 'biographies-in-relation-to-their-museum-establishing-activities' of prominent Americans (1997).

2   For instance, MacGregor, 1983.

3   For example Brooks, 1954; MacGregor, 1994.

4   As in Hunter, 1983.

5   See Clarke and Penny, 1982.

6   For example, see Caygill and Cherry, 1997.

7   The very first of these self-reflexive attempts must have been the exhibition organised in the Musée d'Ethnographie, Neuchâtel, Switzerland, with the title 'Collections Passion'. The catalogue that accompanied the exhibition contains interesting essays discussing collecting (Hainard and Kaehr, 1982).

8   The 'People's Show' was the name given to an initiative of the Walsall Museum to display the private collections of the people of Walsall in the local museum; the objects in the collections ranged from toys and ties to pencil rubbers. The initiative was greeted with much interest and led to a 'People's Show Festival' which involved more than fifty museums throughout Britain. See also Digger, 1995; Lovatt, 1995; 1997.

9   The exhibition had the title 'Natural Mystery' and was an artist's view of the Natural History Museum; the artist in residence was Julian Walker (5 April - 19 May, 1997).

10   This exhibition had the title 'Things, collecting and the experience of the natural world'; artist Julian Walker was again responsible for an artistic reflection on museums and collections (10-15 June, 1997).

11   This exhibition was entitled 'Kissing the dust: contemporary artists working with collections'; the artists in residence were Ajamu Jane Grant and Michael Robertson (17 May – 6 July, 1997).

12   'Collected' had the sub-title 'Exploring the depth and diversity of the collection... from Egyptian antiquities via 18th century paintings to Marilyn Monroe memorabilia'. The venues were the Photographers' Gallery, the British Museum, Habitat, the Royal College of Surgeons, Hunterian Museum, Richard Lowe's flat, Selfridges, Paul Smith, the Wallace Collection, Sir John Soane's Museum, all in London. The exhibition was accompanied by a seminar held at the British Museum on 17 May, 1997. The duration of the exhibition was from 26 April to 21 June, 1997.

13   In the same self-reflective spirit we may include the exhibition 'Museum Europa' held in the Danish National Museum (1993), the exhibition on the 'Grand Tour' organised at the Tate Gallery (1997), and the exhibition on Sir William Hamilton and his collection at the British Museum (Jenkins and Sloan, 1996).

14   Martin (1996; 1997; 1999b) argues that museums need to start communicating with contemporary collectors and collectors' clubs if they want to keep in touch with contemporary society and the post-modern world.

15   Pliny's and Pausanias' works qualify for inclusion in this category; the same is true for the epigraphic archives of various sanctuaries.

16   See also the collecting theories discussed later in this chapter. For approaches to the history of collecting like those described above see Taylor (1948), van Holst (1967), Alsop (1982).

17   For an interesting review of literature on the history of collecting see also Herklotz, 1994.

18   For collection of their essays and discussion see Crimp (1989), Benjamin (1969; 1979), Adorno (1967).

19   The popularisation of the idea is attributed by Pearce (1992: 82) to Richard von Kraft-Ebbing (1892).

20   For a modern approach to the development of art history in the ancient classical world, and its implications for collecting, among other social and artistic phenomena, see Tanner, 1995; his approach is developed from a sociological and art historical point of view.

21   The article by Zanker (1978) presents a very interesting balance of these two aspects.

22   The use of classical texts in order to support an argument regarding the ancient world is not uncommon; nevertheless, this thesis is innovative in its attempt to group these texts together and discuss them in their internal cultural relationship along the lines of a new subject, i.e. the history and nature of collecting. For attempts similar in their approach, although different in their aims and subjects, see, for instance, Elsner (1995) and Flower (1996).

23   The need to study these deep origins of the phenomenon of collecting and of museums has been underlined by modern museologists; see Cameron, 1995.

24   While the thesis from which this book originates was in progress it became apparent that discussion of specific issues that we touch upon here, like the role of women in the collecting tradition of the ancient world, the early 'Museums' and their influence upon the institution of the 'museum' developed in subsequent periods, the implications of classical collecting for the development of collecting paradigms in the Renaissance and afterwards, and even classical collecting before and after the chronological limits that I had to choose for myself, deserve a full length discussion of their own, which unfortunately is beyond the scope of this work.

25   To these we should add the practical limitations regarding the survival of artefacts: even in the case of Pompeii and Herculaneum, where the context of catastrophe would be expected to produce undistrurbed by subsequent generations assemblages of artefacts, expectations have not been justified, since it seems that the inhabitants, having being warned of the catastrophe to follow, had taken their most valuable assets and run away; naturally, collections of small items must have been removed too (see Berry, 1997, and Pappalardo, 1990).

26   See discussion in Chapter 1, and Ricoeur, 1984.

27   For Cassiano dal Pozzo's 'Paper Museum', see the catalogue which derived from the exhibition held in the British Museum (*The Paper Museum of Cassiano dal Pozzo*, 1993).

Chapter 1

Reading Ancient Texts: methodological approaches to interpretation and appropriation

Introduction

Before we start the presentation of the arguments of this book, and since our discussion is based on literary, textual evidence, we need to consider in brief the methodological implications of our 'reading' of this evidence and the approach through which this 'reading' will take place.

The present chapter is structured around the paradigm that collections amassed during the Hellenistic and Roman periods will be treated as 'texts': the underlying idea being that material culture is a medium of thought, already an interpretation of reality, whereas collections are structures of the world (see Pearce, 1992; 1995; Tilley, 1991). Consequently, the classical texts that survive and have been selected to form the data for this book form the connotative level of a 'meta-language', that is the collections, of the world; the level, in other words, where the 'myths' of the world are created (see Figures 1.1 and 1.2, and discussion below). The climax of this paradigm becomes *our* interpretation, which cannot but be another derivative system, greatly indebted to and dependent on the chain of receptions through which their continued readability has been effected. This paradigm owes a great deal to Barthes' analysis of the fashion system (1990), and shares the main point of it, that societies display a continuous activity of signification and rationalisation, simultaneously contradictory and complementary, in their attempt to structure themselves and the world around them.

In order to justify the selection of the above paradigm, analyse it and employ it profitably, we will plunge into post-structuralism and hermeneutics. Firstly, therefore, we present a selection of ideas by Ricoeur and Barthes on the role of the material culture as text, the relations between single and multiple meanings, author and reader, interpretation and appropriation, the difficulties and restrictions of the endeavour to read 'readings', the past and its traces in the present. The relevance of those ideas is then indicated and their selection justified.

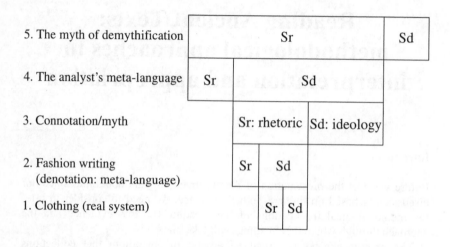

| 5. The myth of demythification | Sr | | | Sd |

Figure 1.1:   The 'rhetoric of fashion'; Source: Barthes' *The Fashion System*, figure 3.9, p.37 (after Tilley, 1990a: 174).

Ricoeur's Views on Interpretation

Ricoeur responds to what he considers the insufficiencies of structuralism, that is the dichotomy of *langue* and *parole*, the subordination of diachronic to synchronic and the emphasis on language as opposed to the 'real world' (Tilley, 1990a: 58-60), with the development of a hermeneutical approach which responds precisely to those points. It stems from a theory of language based on the sentence and on the fundamental distinction between system and discourse: 'The transition to the level of discourse creates the possibility of a genuine semantics of the sentence, as distinct from the semiotics of the sign' (Thompson, 1981: 11).

According to Ricoeur, all discourse is produced as an event, being thus the counterpart of language, but is understood as meaning (1981: 137, 167). Initially the notion of meaning may be analysed into two basic dimensions, comprising both an objective aspect, or that which the sentence means, and a subjective aspect, or that which the speaker means (Moore, 1990: 91; Thompson 1981: 11). Following Frege (1970), Ricoeur further distinguishes between two components of the objective aspect of meaning: the sentence has both an ideal sense and a real reference. It is only at the level of the sentence that language can refer to something, that the closed universe of signs can be related to an extra-linguistic world (Thompson, 1981: 11). 'The "objective" side of discourse ... may be taken in two different ways. We may mean the "what" of discourse or the "about what" of discourse. The "what" of discourse is its "sense", the "about what" is its "reference".' (Moore, 1990: 91). This distinction is directly connected to that between semiotics and semantics. As opposed to language, where signs refer only to other signs, discourse refers to the world. This dimension of discourse is further linked to creativity of language, and to the necessity for interpretation.

The polysemy of words inherent in any natural language is linked simultaneously in a process where ambiguity is reduced through interpretation, and in an expansion through metaphor. Ricoeur challenges the traditional idea which wants metaphor to be a type of trope, and argues that it is a semantic innovation, which takes place at the level of the sentence (Moore, 1990: 92). 'Metaphor is ... a contextual change of meaning' (Ricoeur, 1981: 170); not the actualisation of one of the meanings of a polysemic word, but a solely contextual action opposed to lexical changes (Ricoeur, 1981: 169). Thus Ricoeur's working hypothesis proceeds 'from metaphor to text at the level of "sense" and the explanation of "sense", then from text to metaphor at the level of reference of a work to a world and to a self, that is, at the level of interpretation proper' (1981: 172).

Ricoeur turns to hermeneutics with his concept of the text. The text is a work of discourse, and hence it is a *work*: a structured totality irreducible to the sentences whereof it is composed, with a codified form which characterises its composition, and produced on a unique configuration which can be called its style (Moore, 1990: 93; Thompson, 1981: 13; Ricoeur, 1981: 136). Unlike the 'logocentric' tradition criticised by Derrida (Tilley, 1990a: 63), Ricoeur does not give priority to the spoken discourse instead of the written; they are both alternative and equally legitimate. But being written discourse, text is characterised by four traits, the four forms of *distanciation*:

> i) the fixation of meaning as opposed to the event of saying, ii) the
> dissociation of meaning from the mental intention of the author, iii)
> the non-ostensive nature of the text's references and iv) the universal
> range of the text's audience. (Moore, 1990: 95).

These features provide the text with an autonomous status and determine Ricoeur's theory of interpretation.

According to the first two forms of *distanciation*, the 'objective' meaning of the text is different from the 'subjective' meaning of its author (Thompson, 1981: 14). Hence, 'the problem of the right understanding can no longer be solved by a simple return to the alleged intention of the author' (Ricoeur, 1981: 161). Furthermore, the other two forms lead to two attitudes toward the text: the first is that of structuralism, that is an attempt to explain the text through its internal relations; the second is to turn from 'sense' to 'reference' and to seek to understand the world toward which the text points. This is what Ricoeur calls 'interpretation' (Ricoeur, 1981: 153).

This line of thought leads to a series of important conclusions. Firstly, it means that Ricoeur does not exclude structuralism, but accepts its methodology, although not as being complete. Secondly, it bridges the contradiction between explanation and interpretation, which had been a very distinctive difficulty in the early hermeneutics. Thirdly, Ricoeur changes the emphasis, from the ability of the reader to transfer into the spiritual life of the writer, to the world which the work unfolds.

The culmination of Ricoeur's interpretation theory is his views on appropriation, which he defines as:

> ... the process by which the revelation of new modes of being ... gives the subject new capacities for knowing himself. If the reference of a text is the projection of a world, then it is not in the first instance the reader who projects himself. The reader is rather broadened in his capacity to project himself by receiving a new mode of being from the text itself. (quoted in Moore, 1990: 97).

As a result, and in conjunction with the aim of hermeneutics of struggling against cultural distance and historical alienation, interpretation is understood as a process of 'bringing together', 'equalising', 'rendering contemporary and similar' (Ricoeur, 1981: 185).

> To understand is to follow the dynamic of the work, its movement from what it says to that about which it speaks. Beyond my situation as reader, beyond the situation of the author, I offer myself to the possible mode of being-in-the-world which the text opens up and discloses to me. That is what Gadamer calls the "fusion of horizons" ... in historical knowledge. (Ricoeur, 1981: 177).

With this definition, Ricoeur does not aim to avoid the structure known in the Romantic hermeneutic tradition as the 'hermeneutical circle'. The thinkers of that tradition believe that the understanding of a text could not be an objective procedure, in the sense of scientific objectivity, but that it was determined by a pre-understanding on behalf of the reader producing a circle between self-understanding and text-understanding. Ricoeur embraces this idea, which he identifies with appropriation, but he disagrees with the idea that the 'hermeneutical circle' connects the subjectivities of the author and the reader on the grounds that 'the emergence of the sense and the reference of a text in language is the coming to language of a world and not the recognition of another person.' (Ricoeur, 1981: 178). Secondly, he disagrees with the idea that the projection of the subjectivity of the reading itself relates to the previous suggestion.

> To understand oneself in front of a text is quite the contrary of projecting oneself and one's own beliefs and prejudices; it is to let the work and its world enlarge the horizon of the understanding which I have of myself. ... Thus the 'hermeneutical circle' is not repudiated but displaced from a subjectivist level to an ontological plane. The circle is between my mode of being - beyond the knowledge which I may have of it - and the mode opened up and disclosed by the text as the world of the work. (Ricoeur, 1981: 178).

Consequently, interpretation encompasses both the apprehension of projected worlds and the advance of self-understanding in the presence of these new worlds.

Barthes's Deconstructive Reading

The interpretation of cultural production was Roland Barthes's primary aim. It was to this aim that he devoted the whole of his attention, by introducing the theoretical approaches of semiology and post-structuralism to a wider audience and by applying these to cultural objects other than literary and linguistic texts. He questioned the 'myths' of 'naturalness' and 'universality' with which bourgeois society used to rationalise and dress up reality. He was opposed to the traditional notions of 'author as producer' and 'reader as consumer' and questioned the 'mimetic function of writing as a representation of reality or a "dress to thought"' (Olsen, 1990: 163).

Strangely enough, though, and notwithstanding the fact that Barthes was first and foremost a literary critic and wrote extensively on writing and the literary text, the ideas examined here come mainly from his attempts to apply his methodological tools in wider areas and more particularly to what he calls the 'Fashion System'. Nevertheless, as he said in an interview: 'fashion exists only through the discourse of it' (Sontag, 1982: xxiii). Although the reason for such an idea is elsewhere explained in terms of economic and social reasons (Barthes, 1990: xi-xii), his idea is very close to the case of our texts about collections. For different reasons, having to do mainly with the time that has intervened since they were 'written', our collections exist only through the written discourse that has survived. Furthermore, there is a peculiar feature in both cases: discourse refers to actual objects and there is a very intriguing and characteristic transition from the 'real' to the 'written' (for a discussion about the 'real world' and the traces of it, see the following section).

As has already been stated at the introduction, the classical texts that survive for us to study correspond to the third level (see Fig. 1.2), the level of connotation/myth. We will thus start the discussion by presenting Barthes's ideas on myth, connotation, denotation and meta-language, and then we shall present his approach to the fashion system.

In the theoretical essay 'Myth Today' (1972), Barthes defines myth as part of 'semiology', the term used by Saussure to indicate the general science of signs. He claims that myth is a peculiar semiological system, since 'it is constructed from a semiological chain which existed before it: it is a second-order semiological system. That which is the sign in the first system, becomes a mere signifier in the second' (cited in Olsen, 1990: 168-9; Barthes, 1972: 114; Sontag, 1982: 99). Thus, 'myth' becomes what Hjelmslev called a *connotative* or *second-order* language. Barthes draws heavily on Hjelmslev from whom also he borrows the ideas of denotation (being the primary, direct or literal meaning), connotation (the mythical or symbolic meaning), and meta-language (Olsen, 1990: 169 and his fig. 4.1). The last concept especially becomes central in Barthes's studies. 'While the primary language (denotation) constitutes the plane of expression (signifier) of the second order language (connotation) it constitutes the plane of content (signified) in the meta-language' (Olsen, 1990: 173 and his fig. 4.2; Barthes, 1967: 150-151; 1967: 27-28). In other words, the meta-language is the one which 'speaks' *about* another language or system. Although Hjelmslev saw meta-language as neutral and scientific, opposed to connotations, Barthes rejected this neutrality by suggesting a political purpose behind semiology and by showing how a meta-language itself signifies by at least connoting 'science' (Olsen, 1990: 173).

Furthermore, Barthes distinguishes between the science of verbal signs, that is linguistics, and the science of object signs, that is semiology (1990: x). Thus Barthes inverts Saussure's classical formulation that linguistics is a part of semiology. The difference between linguistics and semiology is also located in the relationship between signifier and signified. In the linguistic sign the relation between the signifier and the signified is arbitrary, while in the case of the non-linguistic signs (objects, gestures, images) it is, at least partly, motivated (Barthes, 1990: 215-216; Olsen, 1990: 171).

Barthes analyses fashion as a rhetorical system (see fig. 1.1). He starts with the 'real' world (clothing/fashion/objects) with its signifiers and signifieds. Then this 'real' world is described by a meta-language (fashion-writing/written vestimentary code) which created a simulacrum of the 'real' object. However, this meta-language itself becomes the denotative level of a connotative (second-order or mythical) system, making it into the rhetorical expression (signifier) of its ideological content (signified). On top of this, the analyst (e.g. the semiologist) constructs a meta-language in which fashion as a rhetorical and mythical system is analysed. This does not end there; it is taken over by another level (the myth of demythification) and so on (Barthes, 1990: 36-37; 293-294; Olsen, 1990: 173): there is no 'truth', only further levels of meaning. Thus, the analyst cannot reach any external conclusions, but remains always based on the limits posed by his own social and historical circumstances. Barthes aims to use these ideas to show that society tends to establish signs, then naturalises them; this naturalisation in its turn becomes a sign, and so on, a continuous process of masking-unmasking... What we read is not a meaning, only the 'signifying of things' (Wasserman, 1981: 71).

Barthes is especially concerned with the text, the role of the writer and the role of the reader. He denies fiercely the tradition for the existence of the Author-God, who used the text in order to communicate a pre-conceived message. Instead, he argues that the role of the reader is more active since he brings to it areas and meanings far beyond the intentions of its author. The reader translates into the text the intervening history of economic and socio-cultural developments, and thus each text is a production of the present of the reader (Olsen, 1990: 179,181).

As with hermeneutics, Barthes believes that discourse begins beyond the sentence, and the text is what is created independently from any system. He proposes a structuralist 'science of literature' and searches for the universal nature of narratives. The most appealing part of his search has been the idea that a text is a multi-leveled, multi-dimensional space, open to different 'readings'; within the notion of 'inter-text',[1] there is a radical integration of readers in the production of texts (Olsen, 1990: 186). All these arguments aim to make possible the discovery of the idea of textual plurality, to destroy the unity and 'naturalness' of the text, and to reveal its polyvalence. Hence, Barthes introduces the deconstructive reading (Olsen, 1990: 187).

Documents and Historical Reality

The task of the historian is often defined as being to present the past 'as it *really* was'.[2] Archaeology and history depend upon evidence, the 'trace' of the past that survives in the present and constrains them. We are able to define the 'trace' as what is left by the past, and, therefore, what 'stands for it' or 'represents it' (Ricoeur, 1984: 1-3). The study of those 'traces', of the evidence, be then material or documentary, suffices to constitute history and archaeology as heuristic discourses different from the natural sciences. So powerful has been the impact of this documentary character of those disciplines, that positivism claims that we should allow the facts to 'speak for themselves' and that the ideal picture of the past would be the one that we could produce if we collected all the facts, or at least as many as possible to make it transparent and self-evident (Thomas, 1990: 18).

In recent years, archaeologists and historians alike have become more aware of their role and that history and archaeology are available to us only textually; and that in order to make sense of the past we have to create narratives and 'read' it (Thomas, 1990: 18). To achieve that, it is essential that the relation between narrative and trace is clarified, and that the nature of trace as a source of knowledge is researched.

The trace has been studied by the historian[3] in epistemological terms, in the sense of its value as proof, as evidence, rather than ontologically, that is in the sense of it being a source of a kind of knowledge with indirect referential character. This is an issue that needs to be further explored: what is the relation between the trace and the past as 'it *really* was'? What are the limitations that the adverb 'really' posits, and how does this delimitation influence our 'interpretation' of the past? These questions belong more to the area of philosophical enquiry rather than to historical investigation. We have been influenced mainly by Ricoeur in our understanding of these issues, and therefore it is in the light of his ideas that we are going to study the ancient texts as document-traces of the past, able to 'represent' it to us.

Ricoeur distinguishes between three tropes of historical writing: History-as-Same, History-as-Other and History-as-Analogue. Each of these is characterised by a particular understanding of the relation between past and present, or rather each attributes a different status to the written past (Thomas, 1990: 18). The first form, History-as-Same, is related to the re-enactment of the past in the present. It follows the idea of Collingwood (1993), and calls for a conception of the past as history's *absent partner* (Ricoeur, 1984: 5). By re-enactment, Ricoeur means the *rethinking* of events, and definitely not its reliving (1984: 8). In order to reach this conclusion Ricoeur posits the question 'of what are the documents the trace?', to answer it immediately: they are the traces of *thought*, as he calls the inside of events. Naturally, the physical action cannot be ignored, so Ricoeur suggests that the thought and the physical changes together form the *action*. The term 'thought' should be defined very broadly to include motivation, intentions, desires. Thus, the historian has to think of himself in action, in order to discern the thought of its agent. Thus, we are able to say that knowing *what* happened is knowing *why* it happened (1984: 7).

These limitations of the concept of historical evidence lead to the idea of re-enactment, which means re-thinking and incorporates the critical moment; this remains far from being a methodological tool. Re-enactment abolishes the temporal distance between past and present by rethinking what was once thought, and becomes the 'medium' of survival of the past in the present.

> One could say, paradoxically, that a trace becomes a trace of the past only when its pastness is abolished by the intemporal act of rethinking the event as thought from inside. Re-enactment, understood in this way, resolves the paradox of the trace in terms of identity; while the phenomenon of the mark, the imprint, and that of its perpetuation are purely and simply sent back to the sphere of natural knowledge. (Ricoeur, 1984: 11-12).

In opposition to re-enactment stands the concern with recovering the sense of temporal distance (Ricoeur, 1984: 15).[4] History in this sense attempts to make the past remote from the present and to produce an effect of strangeness. Thus, looking for the past becomes a sort of ethnological enquiry, at the service of the historian who attempts a spiritual decentring of our traditional Western history (Ricoeur, 1984: 15). Consequently, the idea of temporal distance is understood today in similar terms to the idea of the Other. This becomes the best analogue of historical understanding. Thus, the special characteristic related to the survival of the past in the present is eluded. Moreover, the otherness in this sense introduces the idea of difference, and we pass from the pair same-other to the pair identity-difference (Ricoeur, 1984: 17-18). The idea of difference may serve several uses. Ricoeur considers two of them: the question of individuality and the deviation. He argues that,

> in order for the individual to appear as difference (*sic*), historical conceptualisation must itself be conceived of as the search for and the posing of variants ... . The historical fact would then have to be grasped as a variant generated by the individualisation of those invariants. (1984: 18).

As far as deviation is concerned, it leads to a philosophy of history where the past is a 'pertinent absence' (Ricoeur, 1984: 23). But the question remains: 'how could a difference *take the place of* something which today is absent and lost, but once was real and living, being itself relative to an abstract system and as detemporalised as possible?' (Ricoeur, 1984: 24).

The difficulties inherent in both History-as-Same and History-as-Other can be overcome by History-as-Analogue. In order to define Analogue, we have a rhetorical theory of tropes, the primary position among them being held by metaphor (Ricoeur, 1984: 27). Ricoeur is concerned about the idea of re-construction of the past, and relies for his attempt to elucidate that on the efforts of White to present the 'representative' dimension of history through the theory of tropes (Ricoeur, 1984: 27; White, 1978). Ricoeur uses his ideas on History-as-Analogue to bridge the gap between his theories of narrative and metaphor. More specifically, in the *Rule of Metaphor*, he argues that metaphor makes an ontological claim and has a referential import (1978: 28). He hopes that the concept of the refiguration of time by narrative - i.e. the core of his mimesis III[5]- will be enriched by an enquiry into the role of figures in the constitution of the relation 'taking-the-place-of' or 'representing' (1984: 28).

According to White (1978), historical discourse has to comply with both the constraints related to the privileged type of plot and to the past itself, through the documentary material available at a given moment. The historian then has to render the 'narrative structure into a "model", an "icon" of the past, capable of representing it' (Ricoeur, 1984: 29). For this to be achieved we need to interpret discernible figures. In order to figure what happened in the past we need to *prefigure* as a possible object of knowledge the whole set of events reported in the documents (1984: 29). The tropes of rhetorical discourse offer a variety of figures of discourse for this prefiguration (metaphor-metonymy-synecdoche-irony). The most representative function among these belongs to metaphor (1984: 30). Thanks to the tropological frame of reference, the *being-as* of the past event is brought to language. Therefore, 'a certain tropological arbitrariness must not make us forget the kind of constraint that the past exerted on historical discourse through known documents, by demanding an endless *rectification* on its part' (1984: 33-34).

Although Ricoeur accepts White's ideas about the importance of metaphor and rhetorical tropes to the analysis of historical events, and believes that these offer credibility to his own ideas about the need for the succession through the Same and the Other to the Analogue, he cannot fail to notice that without the Same and the Other, White's ideas run the risk of erasing the dividing line between fiction and history (1984: 33). Thus, Ricoeur assigns to Analogue the role of fighting the prejudices that an historian's language should be transparent and that fiction can have no claim in reality. More specifically, Analogue presents the problem of the reality of the historical past with the solution of offering meaning to 'really' in terms of 'such as'. It holds within it the ideas of both re-enactment and distancing, in the sense that *being-as* is both being and not being. These ideas of Ricoeur do not aim to expose fully the relation of 'taking-the-place-of' or 'representing'. They are offered more as a contribution to what remains enigmatic in the pastness of the past as such (1984: 36).

Analysis of Texts and Collections

All the issues presented above concerning the nature of meaning, the relationship between language and what it describes, 'the capacity of words to exceed their allotted functions of argumentation, demonstration and proof' (Bryson, 1994: 282), and the different constructions of the historical past, present classical scholarship with a series of new epistemological tools, capable of more profitable and thought-provoking insights into the classical texts.[6] The main argument strives against the monolithic approaches to classical texts that classical scholars traditionally attempt,[7] and urges a more flexible appreciation of their polyvalence. The positivist and historicist approaches, which still dominate the study of ancient texts, can be, and are, severely criticised in the light of these epistemological advances.[8] The new 'readings', which come to replace the traditional ones, are based upon a greater self-awareness on the part of the reader/scholar. The notion of interpretation then acquires a further dimension than simply being a 'deciphering' of meaning; the appreciation of the status of the written past becomes more complex in terms of the philosophy of history, and the question of representation raises a number of important issues, the most timely among them being the rhetorical system of analysis.

Traditional approaches, in their search for the 'real' ancient world, invoke the notion of, and inscribe themselves within a discourse of, history, which seeks to ground itself in the actuality of the past (Kennedy, 1993: 7). Hence an artificial distinction is created - in the sense that it is projected as determining, whereas it is not - between past and present actualities, each supported in practice by historicism and textualism respectively. Historicism, on the one hand, aims to present the past as 'it really was' by constructing 'objective' representations of it. Thus, it leads to a presentation resembling the idea of the Same (in Ricoeur's terms), in the sense that the temporal distance between past and present acquires the leading role and the historian gestures towards a non-perspectival objectivity. Textualism, on the other hand, asserts that historical events are discursively selected, shaped and organised under a teleological shadow, and therefore, history is an accommodation of the past in the present interests (Kennedy, 1993: 7). Kennedy (1993: 7-13) therefore argues that the distinction created between these two modes of thinking about the past and its texts, far from being determining, is enabling. Following literary criticism and the renewed concern with representation in all its forms, from which stems the idea of language and textuality as operative metaphors for cultural production, he denies the existence of any world of objective facts to which language provides unobstructed access; instead he supports the notion that systems of representation always problematize and obfuscate the real as much as they reflect it (see also Dougherty and Kurke, 1993: 5). Therefore,

> in order to depict and argue for the multiplicity of representations, it is necessary to project "representation" as a foundational term of transhistorical validity, a preoccupation "present" in the texts of the past; in order to argue for "differences" it is necessary to posit sameness or identity, and *vice versa*. A discourse of "representation" provides a set of terms which enable and determine the articulation of issues of reality, identity, control etc. (Kennedy, 1993: 13).

'Representation' thus becomes a key issue in the study of classical texts due to its consequences. First, it provides a more accurate way of thinking about the past as Analogue, that is by substituting the 'real' with the 'such as' and thus combining History-as-Same and -as-Other; it consequently becomes the enabling aspect of the distinction. Second, as a discourse it opens up the way towards a rhetorical system of analysis, providing a new epistemological tool. Third, in representation as a discourse the key trope becomes metaphor, which not only is a very useful epistemological tool, but also leads to a different appreciation of interpretation. Finally, in the light of this interpretation the single meaning is questioned. If we approach the past in terms of representation, the meaning of the past cannot be single and unique. Each of those points is important for our understanding of the ancient texts.

The three signs of historical writing that Ricoeur distinguishes offer a methodological tool towards the understanding of the approaches to the past devised by ancient authors. Naturally, having mere fragments of their works delimits the possibilities of comprehension. Nevertheless, it will still lead to some rewarding and thought-provoking insights into classical thought (undeniably a comment inspired by re-enactment). Furthermore, the categories of Same, Other and Analogue serve the ideas on interpretation that we chose to follow in this analysis.

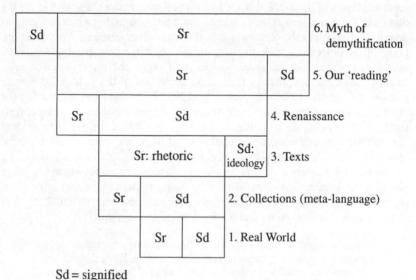

| | | | 6. Myth of demythification |
| Sd | Sr | | |

Sd = signified
Sr = signifier

Figure 1.2:   Model of analysis of texts and collections.

Ricoeur defines interpretation as an activity culminating in the act of appropriation. These terms and ideas are closely interwoven (and therefore in accordance with the need for a 'reading' which combines both the Same and the Other). The classical texts have been used as sources of information. It would therefore be self-refuting to suggest that interpretation means anything else than an opening towards which the text points. As Ricoeur has argued, interpretation does not merely mean the projection of one's own world to the text. The deconstructing ideas of Barthes and Derrida concerning the open-endedness of the text diminish the role of the author too much for the aims of this thesis. Certainly, this does not mean that the text had/s an 'original' meaning, pre-conceived and intentionally pre-addressed to us. The writers of the texts wrote them with different aims in mind. Therefore, our task today is very different to theirs. Appropriation, as defined by Ricoeur, bridges this gap between the reader and the world of the text, and leads to the 'making of one's own something that was initially alien and distant' (1981: 159; Moore, 1990: 96).

Furthermore, the rhetorical connotations of appropriation with their emphasis on metaphor, make the point of multiple meanings very firmly. Metaphor extends the original meaning in both semiotic and semantic terms. Therefore, collections and texts can be pictured as extensions of each other and of the world from which they originate. Metaphor thus 'works' at multiple levels, and as a safeguard of multiple meanings. The 'texts' of the collections are related metaphorically to the world, whereas the paragraphs of the ancient authors are metaphors of the texts of the collections. Consequently, we need a rhetorical system in order to understand and analyse our paragraphs and texts.

This rhetorical system (set out in Figure 1.2) is based on the one that Barthes devised for his analysis of the fashion system. We start with the 'real world' (objects/material culture) with its signifiers and signifieds. Then this 'real' world is described by a meta-language (collections), which creates an 'ideal' world, as this is the projection of the 'real'. However, this meta-language itself becomes the denotative level of a second-order system, making collections the rhetoric of its ideology. On top of this, subsequent generations (be it ours or that of, for example, the Renaissance) construct a meta-language in which collections as a rhetorical and mythical system are analysed. This does not end there; it is taken over by another level (the myth of demythification) and so on. For Barthes, there is no 'truth', only layers of meaning, and the analysts can not reach any external conclusions, as they depend on the limits imposed by their own circumstances. This cannot be but wholly true for the classical world and collections. We cannot reach the 'real' world through the means that are available to us. What we can reach is interpretations of this world, or perceptions of the interpretations of this world. In other words, what we have available to us is a second-order system, which is possibly even more rewarding than the first could be, for, although it does not offer to us either the 'real' or the 'ideal' world, it does offer the reception of these and the ideology based or modeled upon them. It is this ideology - the nature of which will be discussed later in the chapters on the individual authors - that was undertaken by subsequent generations, was interpreted according to the socio-cultural and economic circumstances, and gradually led to contemporary perceptions of museums and collecting.

Notes

1   The notion of inter-text has been borrowed from Kristeva and is a way of expressing the plurality of the text. It refers to the transportation of one text into another within the matrix of all texts (see Kristeva, 1986: 11; Olsen, 1990: 186).
2   'Wie es eigentlich gewesen' (Ranke, 1830s, quoted and discussed in Carr, 1986: 3).
3   I use the term historian from now on to include archaeologists and all those whose interests lie in the past.
4   The destruction of the notion of historical time is the disadvantage of re-enactment.
5   Mimesis is a central idea in Ricoeur's theory of history, time and narrative. Narrative leads to the creation of a new work of synthesis: a plot. Plots mimic action, through a

poetic refiguring of action. The dynamic of emplotment is central in the understanding of the relation between time and narrative. Emplotment consists of three moments of mimesis: mimesis 1, mimesis 2, and mimesis 3. Mimesis 1 involves the realisation that to imitate or represent action is first to pre-understand what human action is, in its semantics, its symbolic system and its temporality. Mimesis 2 has a mediating function which derives from the dynamic character of the configuring operation known as emplotment. Mimesis 3 marks the intersection of the world of the text and the world of the reader; that is the world configured by the plot and the world in which real action occurs and unfolds its specific temporality. The transition from Mimesis 2 to Mimesis 3 is brought about by the act of reading (Moore, 1990:102-105).

6   For contemporary literary theory see Suleiman and Crosman, 1980 (esp. pp. 3-45) and Fish, 1980.

7   For contemporary literary hermeneutics and the interpretation of classical texts see Kresic, 1981; Galinsky, 1994; Martindale, 1993; de Jong and Sullivan, 1994 (where also extensive bibliography, see pp. 281-288), as well as the volumes of the journal *Arethusa* devoted to the subject, mainly, 7 (1974: Psychoanalysis and the Classics), 8, (1975: Marxism and the Classics), 10 (1977: Classical Literature and Contemporary Literary Theory), 16 (1983: Semiotics and Classical Studies), and 19 (1986: Audience-oriented Criticism and the Classics).

8   At least when they are used as historical evidence. Nevertheless, alternative approaches have been, and are currently being, developed as the examples cited above display.

PART I

Notions of Collecting in the Ancient World

Chapter 2

Collecting Material Testimonies: antiquarianism and notions of the past

thesauros oportet esse, non libros (Pliny, *H.N.*, Praef. 17)

Introduction

The 'past' is largely defined by what interest people develop in it. In studying the growth of a particular society's historical awareness, it is necessary to pay close attention to the intellectual trends in the present that give rise to the awareness of the past. We should, therefore, ask questions like 'what are these trends, what forms do they take, what part of the past attracts their attention, to what purpose and to fulfill what functions, what is the role people have in the historical structure, how is this supported?', and so on (Finley, 1986b). People turn to past for a series of reasons: they seek to reaffirm and validate their present, to identify individual existence with what is memorable and, thus, give meaning, purpose and value to themselves, to receive guidance for the future, to enrich and lengthen their lives by acquiring links with events and people prior to themselves, to find alternatives to an unsatisfying or unacceptable present (Lowenthal, 1985: 41). Objects and material possessions form a means through which these aims are pursued. They are the material bridges that join the intellectual, spatial and temporal gap between people and their past. They are used as mnemonic tools to create, store, and retrieve a sense of the past, that is by itself instrumental in managing social and individual identity (Belk, 1991: 114).

The aim of this chapter is to examine the first of the four parameters associated with classical collecting, that is, the notion of material culture as evidence in the ancient Greco-Roman world, and the relation of the ancient society with its past through its collecting activities. The starting and finishing point of this enquiry is the major importance that antiquity seems to have had in the eyes of the Hellenistic and Roman collectors. As a result, and following the kind of enquiry introduced mainly by Momigliano (1950), and worthily continued by Haskell (1993) and Schnapp (1996), we try to see how the ancient Greeks and Romans related to their past, in terms of their understanding of the role of objects and documents in the creation and appreciation of historical narratives. I argue that the notion of material culture as evidence existed and was firmly defined during that period, and that the intellectual trends concerning the past had a predilection toward monuments and objects, whose importance as sources of knowledge, although not pursued to its full extent, never ceased to be appreciated. This appreciation provided the motive and, perhaps, the most influential intellectual justification for the Roman collectors. Major evidence of this comes from Pliny's, Pausanias' and other minor antiquarians' and *periegetes'* 'collections' of information on works of art and monuments; as Pliny explicitly asserted in the *Praefatio* to his *Historia Naturalis* (paragraph 17) Romans (or at least, some of them) seem to have believed that '*it is not books but store-houses that are needed*'.

There are two broad areas where intellectual trends concerning the past can be located: historiography and philosophy. We are going to be concerned with historiography, since it is with this particular trend that we can associate ideas surrounding material remains more directly. Traditionally, Western historiography's mainstream is concerned with the development of the historical narrative as a literary form, an intellectual problem and a social instrument. But this is only part of what concerns historiography, which can be more fully described as representing 'a complex series of relationships between members of a society in the present and the traditional and documentary evidences of its pasts... [It is imperative] to assert that these relationships cannot be confined to those which exist with its "histories", in the limited sense of its inherited narratives of events in its past' (Pocock, 1962: 213). It becomes, therefore, clear that a society's relationships with the past is mirrored in the kind of historiography this produces and *vice versa*, since it is a continuous two-way process.[1] The role of art and of material culture is not of less importance, but again it is defined by the space that historiography (in the broader sense of the term) offers to it. This chapter, therefore, examines the creation and development of Greco-Roman historiography as a discipline. It also attempts to distinguish the role of historiography in the study of the recent and distant pasts, as well as the ideas that led to the invention of the methodological approach which insists on truth and evidence.[2] All the above support my hypothesis that the notion of material culture as substantial witness of the past and the present, self and 'Other', same and different, is familiar to Greek thought, enough to support collecting in its early formative stages. The development of historiography - and of antiquarianism in particular - is the most rewarding way to follow in our attempt to support this argument. Antiquarianism, besides being a kind of historical research immediately associated with collections, is also a strategy of definitions (of self and 'Other') and appropriations (see also Stewart, 1993; and discussion below).

Origins of the Notion of Evidence in Historical Thought

Long before the need for 'history' as a discipline was realised, the past was taking shape through the 'art of memory', the major expression of which was myth and epic poetry. Herodotus introduced a radically new way of dealing with the past when he began his *Histories* with the phrase *Herodotou Halicarnasseos histories apodexis* - 'What Herodotus the Halicarnassian has learned by enquiry is here set forth' - and he presented as his aim 'the memory of the past not to be blotted out from among men by time, and that great and marvelous deeds done by the Greeks and foreigners and especially the reason why they warred against each other not to lack reknown' (*Histories*, I.I).[3] This novel way of accounting for the past is important for a series of reasons: firstly, the past is not seen as relating to only a few people, but it becomes a common enquiry - for Greeks and foreigners alike; secondly, history is introduced as a discipline and a new genre of writing, that has nothing to do with dedicatory and foundation inscriptions, or annals - as history was meant in the Eastern monarchies - or the timeless myth presented in poetry. Finally, a new notion acquires importance: this is *apodexis* (setting forth, publication, proof).[4] It is through this notion that the transference from the art of memory to history is accomplished. Instead of a discovery or narration of the past based on mystic enunciation from gods and divine mediators (priests and royals), Herodotus introduces a text whose authorship he retains for himself (*Herodotou Halicarnasseos*) and which is a product of reflection, experience and human labour (Schnapp, 1996: 43-45). Herodotus mediates between the epic tradition and history. The term *apodexis* implies oral publication (see Hartog, 1988: 276, nt. 57; also Thucydides, I.97),[5] and being in the preface of the work denotes the aim of the historian to both invoke the epic tradition and to rival it.[6] The balance is now transferred from somewhere out of the man (the Muse as in *Il.*, 1.8 and *Od.*, 1.3) to the man himself, and the protagonistic role is given not to the heroes of the past, but to contemporary people, Greeks and foreigners alike (Hartog, 1988).

Writers before Herodotus had been λογογράφοι (logographoi), writers-down of current stories; Herodotus chose for his work the term *histories* (ιστορίαι), which means enquiries or investigation. The notion of enquiry was firstly introduced by the Ionian philosophers, together with their scepticism about myth. Although initially used in cosmography and metaphysics, Herodotus linked it with historiography. Therefore, he set out to pose questions and investigate in order to find out the 'truth'. It is this investigative process, (and this commitment) implicit in the word 'histories' that make Herodotus 'the Father of History' (Cic., *De Leg.*, 1.5).[7] Furthermore, by defining the subject of history as 'the deeds of men', Herodotus introduces a humanistic approach to the past, distinct from mythical and theocratic ones. He is interested in what humans do, but also in the reasons behind their actions. This definition, which also relates to the epic tradition (*klea andron*), with some expansion relating to the treatment of notable individuals, remained standard thereafter. History after Herodotus was *res gestae* (Fornara, 1983: 92, 96).

According to Collingwood (1993: 18-19) history has four characteristics:

> (a) that it is scientific, or begins by asking questions, whereas the writer of legends begins by knowing something and tells what he knows; (b) that it is humanistic, or asks questions about things done by men at determinate times in the past; (c) that it is rational, or bases the answers which it gives to its questions on specific grounds, namely appeal to evidence; (d) that it is self-revelatory, or exists in order to tell man what man is by telling him what man has done.

Herodotus introduced three of these characteristics (a, b, d), while the fourth (c) is taken up by Thucydides, who, by giving to it a central role in historiography, establishes one of the most important notions in the study of the past.

Although Herodotus was not unfamiliar with the idea of evidence (he used tradition, usually oral and epic, and visual remains, such as the pyramids),[8] Thucydides was the one who emphasised the necessity of definite sources. He viewed them as signs or 'positive proofs' (*semeia - tekmeria*).[9] Sometimes, he used a form of argument that allowed him to reach probable conclusions by an appeal to *eikos* or *eikota*, which, for the most part, represent the probabilities of human behaviour (Hunter, 1982: 93). To summarise Thucydides' methodology we can recount his vocabulary: probability (*eikos*), evidence (*semeion, martyrion*), reasoning (*eikazein*), and examination (*skopein*) (Marincola, 1997: 97). The central place, however, is given to *autopsy*, as the only real source of data. As a result, Thucydides regards as certain only events at which he himself was present; those which his contemporaries observed or could have observed themselves he accepts only when their report stands up to examination. This does not mean that the experience upon which historical knowledge (*saphos eidenai*) is based relies solely on sight, but that it is organised on the basis of the evidence that the latter procures (Thucydides, 1.1; 1.21; 1.22.2; 1.73.2). This had a major consequence for history in the strict sense of the term. If this methodological principle is applied to the letter, the only history possible is contemporary history (Hartog, 1988: 265-266). And this is what Thucydides and those historians following his tradition (e.g. Xenophon, Ephorus, Sallust, Polybius, Livy, Tacitus and others) suggest. In Finley's words (1986a: 31) 'serious Greek historical writing was about contemporary history', and according to Momigliano (1977), the most important historians are attracted by, and practice, this sort of history, which is the most innovative. Equally, this is used by orators and politicians to provide *exempla* drawn from the recent past.

History and Antiquarianism

In the middle of the fifth century BCE, two distinct types of history can be identified. The one had developed from the Herodotean and Thucydidean tradition, was interested in the recent past, i.e. in something that we can call contemporary history, and became the basis of the political science. In the other, the authors of local history, chronography, genealogy, erudite dissertations, and ethnographical works were interested in the distant past, and in the history of cities, institutions and private life. Their approach was descriptive rather than analytical, and aimed to serve the erudite man and the scholar rather than the politician (Schnapp, 1996: 61). Momigliano called the practitioner of the second kind of history 'antiquarian' and described him as

> a student of the past who is not quite a historian because: (1) historians write in a chronological order; antiquaries write in a systematic order, (2) historians produce those facts which serve to illustrate or explain a certain situation; antiquaries collect all the items that are connected with a certain subject, whether they help to solve a problem or not. The subject-matter contributes to the distinction between historians and antiquaries only in so far as certain subjects (such as political institutions, religion, private life) have traditionally been considered more suitable for systematic description rather than for a chronological account. (1950: 286).

Historical research in its antiquarian form was also distinguished by the extensive use of lists, inscriptions and monuments. Historians interested in contemporary history, though, from Thucydides to Polybius, and from Fabius Pictor to Tacitus, very rarely availed themselves of archives, and even more rarely did they quote *in extenso* the documents they happened to have found there; writing a history by a systematic search of the documents never became part of their methodology. The assemblage of documents became the business of the erudite men, the φιλόλογοι (Momigliano, 1990a).

Although history acquired its name right from the start, erudition had to wait longer. The most important word describing this sort of enquiry was the term 'archaiologia' (αρχαιολογία) which firstly appeared in Plato's *Hippias Major*. It was put in the mouth of the sophist Hippias, who in his discussion with Socrates proudly asserts that nobody is indifferent to his services, not even the Spartans; they do not show any interest in the subjects he mainly specialises in (that is, astronomy, geometry, arithmetics, rhetoric, or language), but they are interested in the genealogies of heroes and men, traditions about the foundation of cities, and lists of eponymous magistrates - all those parts of a science called 'archaiologia':

> Socrates: Well, just what is it they love to hear about from you, and applaud? Tell me yourself; I can't figure it out.
> Hippias: The genealogies of heroes and men, Socrates, and the

settlements (how cities were founded in ancient times), and in a word all '*archaiologia*'- that's what they most love to hear about. ... So because of them I have been forced to learn up on such things and to study them thoroughly.
S.: Good lord, Hippias, you're lucky the Spartans don't enjoy it when someone lists our archons from the time of Solon. Otherwise, you would have had a job learning them. (*Hippias Major*, 285d).[10]

This new word, the creation of the sophist movement - although perhaps not devised by Hippias himself - is not intended to describe a new discipline; rather it is a new term, devised in order to include all those descriptions of origins, of Antiquity as a period and the antiquities as objects of knowledge. In this sense, the term reveals an interest in the past which is less determined by the explanation than by the description (Schnapp, 1996: 61). Unfortunately, tradition has not preserved for us the contemporary works that could bear the title 'archaiologia': Περί Ἐθνῶν (On Nations), Ἐθνῶν Ὀνομασίαι (On the Names of the Nations), Κτίσεις Ἐθνῶν καί Πόλεων (On the Building of Nations and Cities), Νόμιμα Βαρβαρικά (Laws of the Barbarians) by Hellanicus, Ἐθνῶν Ὀνομασίαι (Names of the Nations) by Hippias, Περί Γονέων καί Προγόνων τῶν εἰς Ἴλιον Στρατευσαμένων (On the Parents and Ancestors who went to Troy) ascribed to Damastes or Polus, and others (Momigliano, 1950: 287).[11]

After the fourth century BCE the term 'archaiologia' is not generally used. The notion was expressed, with a certain vagueness, by terms such as κριτικός (kritikos), φιλόλογος (philologos), πολυΐστωρ (polyistor), γραμματ ικός (grammatikos), *doctus, eruditus, literatus*. During the Hellenistic and Roman times 'archaeology' was used to indicate a work on archaic history, or a history from the origins. Dionysus of Halicarnassus' *Roman Archaeology,* for instance, is an archaic history of Rome, and Flavius Josephus' *Jewish Archaeology* is a history of the Jews from their origins to Josephus' own times. A work by King Juba, who wrote in the age of Augustus, was called either *Roman History* or *Roman Archaeology*. A poem attributed to Simonides on the origins of Samos was retrospectively given the name of the *Archaeology of Samos*, and even the *Atthis* of Phanodemus (fourth century BCE) was later called *Archaeology* because it dealt mainly with the archaic history of Athens. The term 'archaiologia' was even used to describe the first book of Thucydides' *History of the Peloponnesian War*. Thus, in the Hellenistic age the word 'archaeology' lost the meaning we find in Plato.

But the failure to create a permanent terminological distinction between history and other types of research does not imply that the distinction was forgotten, or felt only vaguely. According to Momigliano (1990a: 60-62) antiquarian research (or 'archaiologia') was of practical importance. A better chronology was established for the Greek world, based on the lists of the winners of the Olympic games prepared by Hippias, or the lists of the priestesses of Hera at Argos and of the winners of the Carnaean games at

Sparta compiled by Hellanicus. Furthermore, the issues raised or implied by many antiquarian studies, like the origins of the cities, the comparison between foreign and Greek laws and customs, the search for the inventors of arts and crafts, were of great theoretical importance. They provided the necessary material for an evaluation of human nature and civilisation; antiquarianism was, therefore, nearer to philosophy and an interest in the origins of culture than to any other subject. The systematic character of erudition was in tune with the systematic character of philosophy. It seems that sophists used their antiquarian research to buttress their political and legal views as well (Momigliano, 1990a: 63-64).

Philosophical research and erudition remained connected throughout the fourth century. Plato, although uninterested in history in the Thucydidean sense, encouraged research in customs and laws, to judge from his own work on the *Laws* and from the encyclopaedic activities of his pupil Heraclides Ponticus. The third book of Plato's *Laws* (which is an examination of the origins of civilisations according to the principles laid down by the sophists) and the books by Heraclides, '*On the Pythagoreans*' and '*On Discoveries*', are typical examples of antiquarian research. 'Discoveries', *heuremata*, became a typical subject for systematic erudition, and many examples survive (see, for instance, Ephorus) (Momigliano, 1990a: 64).

Naturally, it was in the school of Aristotle that erudition and philosophy combined most closely. Aristotle's methods were in accordance with the Ionian tradition and practice of 'history', that is, enquiry into things as well as into events.[12] He based all his conclusions, especially those on politics, on extensive systematic surveys and empirical knowledge. The close connection, for instance, between topography and historical interpretation is illustrated in his *Athenaion Politeia* (the only surviving from his 158 *Politeiai*). Aristotle was also responsible for a number of historical works, such as a List of Victors at the Pythian Games, the List of Olympic Victors, the *Nomima* or *Nomima Barbarika*, the *Dikaiomata* or *Dikaiomata Poleon*, and the *Hypomnemata* (published under the name of Theophrastus) (de Ste. Croix, 1975: 53 and 57). Aristotle used what we would call antiquarian methods in his work. Coins, weights, measures, and inscriptions all served as evidence for historical purposes. Thus, he explained why the god Ammon and the vegetable silphion appeared on the coins of Cyrene (Frg. 528 Rose); he discussed the peculiar denomination of Himeran and other Sicilian issues (Frg. 510 Rose) as well as the use of the λάγυνος (laginos) by the Thessalians (Frg. 499 Rose), and quoted from an inscription in the *Tegeate Politeia* (Plut., *Quaest. Graec.* 5; Arist. Frg. 592 Rose). He may also have used 'archaeological' evidence if he had actually examined the discus upon which, according to Plutarch, the name of the Spartan Lycurgus was written, in order to synchronise the chronology of Lycurgus with other events (Frg. 533 Rose; FGrHist 6f2; *Politics*, 1271b25-26) (also Huxley, 1973: 281-2). In other worlds, Aristotle and his pupils[13] used antiquarian methods: topography, examination of artefacts, attention to numismatics, reading of inscriptions, interest in material evidence, and an attempt to discuss historical research as a necessary condition for the study of their own society (de Ste Croix, 1975).

Greek and Roman Antiquarians

The historical tradition of antiquarianism, supported by philosophical interest, prospered during the Hellenistic period, while the Thucydidean tradition declined. As Momigliano (1990a: 64) has suggested, antiquarianism prospers especially during periods of intellectual doubt. This is logical, since it is especially at these periods that people seek the consolation of the past and feel nostalgia. We are going to present in brief some of the Greek and Roman antiquarians, so that we can appreciate their interest in the past and the methods they employed. Our discussion is by no means comprehensive and the antiquarians mentioned are not the only ones.

Among the most celebrated Greek antiquarians was Dicaearchus of Messene (347- 287 BCE). He was the author of an important work entitled 'Βίος της Ελλάδος', which was an attempt at a history of civilisation, tracing the 'life of Greece' from the dawn of history to the age of Alexander. It included an account of the geography and history, as well as the moral and religious condition of the country (Sandys, 1921: 98-100). He distinguished between primitive life and civilised life, and discussed at length the features of primitive life. In his accounts of more recent times he displayed a lack of interest in chronological order and a preference toward a systematic approach (Rawson, 1985; Cole, 1967).

Polemon of Ilium (early second century BCE) was also an important figure for antiquarianism. He wrote a work on the treasures of Delphi and was made a *proxenus* of that area in 177 BCE by Attalus in recognition of his work. He was a prolific writer on Greek topography, and his diligence in collecting, copying and elucidating inscriptions led to his receiving from an adherent of Crates in a later age the title of *stelokopas*.[14] Polemon was however more widely famous as a *periegetes*. His works were quoted by Didymus and Aristonicus, and by Strabo and Plutarch, the latter of whom eulogises his learning and his vivid interest in Hellenic matters. He devoted four books to the Votive Offerings on the Athenian Acropolis alone; the question how far Pausanias is directly or indirectly indebted to Polemon has been much discussed.[15] His interests were not limited to topography; he also studied literary forms as, for example, the Greek Comedy (Sandys, 1921: 154-155).

The late second-century Romans were acquainted with the Greek antiquarian work, especially that of Aristotle and his followers, but also of other scholars. This acquaintance is attested in all three types of historical research developed in Rome during the first century BCE. The first of these was the traditional annalistic history, which usually started with the foundation of the city by Aeneas. This kind of enquiry had started much earlier, at first as an extension to diplomacy and gradually as an attempt to prefigure the domestic problems of the second century BCE. During the first century annalistic history became the subject of second rate writers who did not have the scholarly interest or the seriousness of purpose that the previous ones had had. The second type of historical research dealt with recent and contemporary history. Very important in this tendency was the influence of Polybius, who followed the Thucydidean tradition of writing on recent political and military history, which should explain and judge, rather than merely record events. This second type attracted the most prominent figures. Finally, antiquarianism developed separately, more closely related to *grammatica* rather than to rhetoric, and found its peak in the work of Varro, *Antiquitates* (Rawson, 1985: 217-218; see also below).

Well before Varro, Greek scholarly techniques like etymology and aetiology (the finding of origins-stories for surviving monuments and institutions) were employed. Junius Gracchanus (a friend of Gaius Gracchus) wrote a lengthy *De Protestatibus* on the traditional, and therefore proper, powers of the different magistracies. L. Aelio Stilo Praeconicus (c. 154-74 BCE) was characterised by Cicero (*Brutus*, 205) as a man of the profoundest learning in Greek and Latin literature, and as an accomplished critic of ancient writers and of Roman antiquities in their intellectual as well as in their historical and political aspects. Stilo's legal and antiquarian pursuits were noticed by Cicero in his *De Oratore* (I.193). His grammatical, and mainly his etymological enquiries were partly inspired by his devotion to Stoic philosophy (Sandys, 1921: 175-177; Rawson, 1985: 234).

The great annalists on the whole assume no very great change throughout the centuries in the Roman way of life, although they often refer to it as simpler, poorer and more virtuous (Rawson, 1985: 235). There were men in Rome, though, who did not encounter any difficulty in understanding the past as something really different, strongly contrasted with the present, either for good (causing admiration) or for bad (causing contempt). This contrast with the past took shape and substance through material remains. Atticus' sense of the past, for instance, was formed in the house of his uncle, which he refused to alter after this uncle's death because of its *sal*, its character (Cornelius Nepos, *Atticus* 18.1; 13.2). In fact, Rome was an antiquarian's 'paradise', since, despite the natural disasters (floods, fires) that changed the appearance of the city, ancient remains were generally protected. It was a similar case in the old towns of Latium. Whatever the local stimulus, however, the antiquarian standards owed a great deal to the Greek traditions, too. Cicero and Atticus at least knew and admired Dicaearchus of Messene, whom they mention with enthusiasm in their work (*Tusc. Disp.* 1.77; *Ad Att.* 2.2.2; 12.4; 16.3; 6.2.3) (Rawson, 1985: 235).

M. Terentius Varro (116-27 BCE) was Stilo's most famous pupil. Cicero characterised him a '*diligentissimus investigator antiquitatis*' (*Brutus*, 60), and Quintilian (x.1.95) a '*vir Romanorum cruditissimus*'. Being a prolific writer, with wide interests, Varro wrote 620 books, which belonged to 74 separate works. Among them there were 41 books on *Antiquitatum rerum humanarum et divinarum*, with other antiquarian works *de vita* and *de gente populi Romani*, a book of 'origins' called *Aetia* (like the *Aitia* of Callimachus), and a treatise on Trojan families and on the Roman tribes (Sandys, 1921: 177). Varro was greatly respected by his contemporaries.[16] He was a collaborator of Pompey and a correspondent of Cicero, who addressed his book *Academica* to him. In the dedicatory letter, Cicero expresses his admiration and respect in the following words, which also reveal an interesting association of Roman people and material remains initiated by Varro:

> for we were wandering and straying about like visitors in our own city, and your books led us, so to speak, right home, and enabled us at last to realise who and where we were. You have revealed the age of our native city, the chronology of its history, the laws of its religion and its priesthood, its civil and its military institutions, the topography of its districts and its sites, the terminology, classification and moral and rational basis of all our religious and secular institutions, and you have likewise shed a flood of light upon our poets and generally on Latin literature and the Latin language, and you have yourself composed graceful poetry of various styles in almost every metre, and have sketched an outline of philosophy in many departments that is enough to stimulate the student though not enough to complete his instruction. (Cicero, *Academica*, I.III.9).[17]

No Roman writer before him had collected so much historical evidence and had presented it in such a logical way. Varro's contribution was important for his data accumulation and the erudition this involved, but also, and mainly, because he suggested through his work that there is the possibility of acquiring positive knowledge about past societies. Social types, places, circumstances, material or immaterial constructions of previous generations are all capable of being organised as a kind of progressive and complete knowledge, and then the relation between human and divine things can assume a rigour close to that of the sciences of nature. Undoubtedly, this brings forth a novel way of looking at the past (Schnapp, 1996: 60-65).

Varro used for his work early poets and recorded traditional stories; but above all, he studied ancient documents, religious and legal. He even quoted from some of these at considerable length. Varro also studied inscriptions (Rawson, 1985: 236-237). As Momigliano (1950: 288) observes, no other Hellenistic antiquarian scholar seems to have been so broad and systematic in his scope; his impact on Rome was profound (it has been said that the Augustan restoration is inconceivable without him). Besides his shortcomings (he is criticised as not being original enough in his approach, or as critical as others), Varro certainly did stimulate antiquarianism in others (e.g. Fenestalla, 52 BCE-19 CE, Verrius Flaccus, fl.10 BCE, and so on) (Sandys, 1921: 200).

Other Genres of Erudition: Biography

The decline of Thucydidean history in the third century BCE put the erudite scholars at the centre of historical research. There are broadly five main lines in Hellenistic erudition, which can be summarised as: the editing of and commenting on literary texts; the collection of early traditions about individual cities, regions, sanctuaries, gods, and institutions; the systematic description of monuments and copying of inscriptions; chronology; and, finally, the compilation of biographies (Momigliano, 1990a: 67).

The predilections of Greek biography were much the same as those of antiquarianism. Biography appears to have developed within the context of erudite research, reflecting its interest in phenomena apart from mainline Greek politics. The earliest known biographers, Skylax of Caryanda, Xanthus of Lydia, Ion of Chios and Stesimbrotus of Thasus, were older contemporaries of Herodotus. Although Herodotus labeled them λογοποιοί (logopoioi) and Thucydides considered them among the λογογράφοι (logographoi), the pioneer historians, these writers actually share the logographers' preoccupation with mythographic treatises, geographical travelogues, and cultural histories of non-Greek civilisations; this places them rather in the antiquarian camp. Though some form of biographical writing thus is attested early in the fifth century BCE, the genre was not distinguished by receiving a name until the Hellenistic period. Scholarly attempts to find out the obscure genealogy of ancient Greek biography have credited both the Academy and the Peripatos with the invention of the genre (Cox, 1983: 6-7; Tarn, 1952: 289; Momigliano, 1993). Central to the development of biography is the notion of βίος (vios - life), which could be applied either to individuals, or to whole nations (Momigliano, 1990a: 67-68).

Dicaearchus' *Life of Greece* belongs to this tradition and so does the biographical information that the librarians of Alexandria included in their tables or guides, *Pinakes*. The biographical form we find in Suetonius and Diogenes Laertius is certainly in keeping with Alexandrian antiquarianism. As far as the collective biographies are concerned, Varro's *Life of the Roman people*, and perhaps another *Life of Greece* attributed to Jason, imitate Dicaearchus (Momigliano, 1990a: 66; 1993).

An interesting by-product of the systematic and erudite biography is the work by Varro, *Imagines or Hebdomades*, in which seven hundred portraits of Roman and non-Roman famous men, from kings to statesmen and philosophers, historians, poets and so on, were collected, each accompanied by a short epigram characterising the man in question. Discussions in prose seem to have accompanied the poetic parts.[18] A similar attempt is recorded for Atticus, and both attracted the praise of Pliny, to whom we owe this piece of information[19]:

> The existence of a strong passion for portraits in former days is
> evidenced by Atticus the friend of Cicero in the volume he published

on the subject and by the most benevolent invention of Marcus Varro, who actually by some means inserted in a prolific output of volumes portraits of seven hundred famous people, not allowing their likeness to disappear or the lapse to prevail against immortality of men. Herein Varro was an inventor of a benefit that even the gods might envy, since he not only bestowed immortality but despatched it all over the world, enabling his subjects to be ubiquitous, like the gods. This was a service Varro rendered to strangers. (Pliny, *H.N.*, XXXV.II.11).[20]

This kind of erudition has to be placed within the Roman aristocratic tradition of '*imagines maiorum*' and the '*tituli*' of the ancestors. Varro and Atticus, however, revolutionise this tradition by extending it to include personalities from the Greek, as well as from the Roman world, and non-aristocrats, as well as members of aristocratic families. Augustus' decision to erect busts of great men with appropriate inscriptions in the Roman Forum and in other public places in Italy was probably inspired by these compilations; Suetonius' *Lives of the Caesars* and the Renaissance collections and displays of portrait-busts can also be traced back to this kind of erudition.

Ideas about the Past

The distant past formed the centre of a considerable attempt by poets and philosophers alike, to answer two basic questions relating to the origins of culture: how did the human race come into existence, and how did it acquire its present cultural status? (Blundell, 1986: 1). Discussions of Greek thought concerning these questions usually distinguish two currents: the myth of Golden Age and the myth of human progress. The first - Hesiodic fantasy - is closely related to the cosmogonical myths which derive from sources dated as early as the eighth century BCE and as late as the fifth century CE, while the second relates to Ionian science, and from the mid-fifth century BCE acquired the leading role in offering explanations in this subject (Cole, 1967: 1).

The first current is a rather pessimistic approach that sees man falling from an original divine, or semi-divine, status to human. The Hesiodic vision of a Golden Race that lived at the beginning of man's history and descended gradually, through silver and bronze, to Hesiod's own race of iron is quite characteristic of this approach (*Works and Days*, 106-201). Homer, on the other hand, although his references on the subject are sporadic and very brief (e.g. see *Il.*, 1.272; 5.304; 12.383; 12.449; 20.287) glorifies a heroic age of power and splendour, vanished in his times. Other categories of thinkers sharing similar ideas with Homer and Hesiod are the primitivists, who also put the apex of human felicity somewhere in the remote past - although their motives are closely linked with nostalgia for a simpler way of life, as well as with those suggesting a cyclical view of history (Blundell, 1986; Cole, 1967).[21]

The Golden Age theory was soon surpassed when Ionian philosophical thought started to replace the mythological. Since then, and starting with Thales, almost all writers express their personal ideas on the subject, although the ones who present a systematic and full-length treatise are few. Among them, the most important place is occupied by Plato's *Laws* (book III) and Lucretius *On the Nature of Things* (*De Rerum Natura*) (book V). Plato's account treats the origins of culture and society as a preface to the political history of Peloponnese, Attica and Persia, and offers a combination of technological and social history (Lovejoy and Boas, 1997: 155-168). Lucretius' attempt, on the other hand, is very much indebted to Epicureanism (Cole, 1967; Lovejoy and Boas, 1997: 222-242).

It is not the aim of this chapter to discuss in detail the ideas of each of those writers. We need only say that civilisation was seen as a process of constant improvement in the practical spheres of life - the ethical ones should be discussed separately since there was no unanimity on that aspect: progressivists suggested that the continuous evolution extended to all aspects of life, while the primitivists asserted that, despite the physical difficulties, life in the past was more simple and innocent, aspects lost with technical improvements (Blundell, 1986: 105).

Nevertheless, two important points concerning the scope of this book can be made. Firstly, since this area of interest is the common ground between both philosophers and antiquarians, the relation between the two disciplines is better understood. Most of the treatises on this subject have been written by antiquarians - unfortunately now lost or fragmentary. The most ambitious of these, Dicaearchus' *Vios* (Frg. 47-66 Wehrli), schematised prehistory in three successive phases: food gathering, herding and farming (Cole, 1967: 4). Writers of universal history started sometimes with a piece on *Kulturgeschichte* (e.g. Diodorus Siculus, 1.8), and so did ethnographers and local historians. Sophists also composed cultural histories, and fragments from many pre-Socratics suggest that this was one of their principal interests. Further information about ancient theories on cultural origins comes from passages of an aetiological character (Cole, 1967: 7-9).

Secondly, the material/technological aspect of previous civilisations is the centre of interest, together with language, ethics and social norms. Antiquarians like Ephorus (*FGrH* 70T33d; F2-5, F104-106), Heraclides Ponticus (Frg. 152 Wehrli), Theophrastus (Diogenes Laertius, 5.47), Strato of Lampsacus (Frg. 144-147 Wehrli) and others tried to study different aspects of it, from the elementary ones (clothing, fire, and so on) that made possible man's survival, to more advanced aspects on which a complex civilisation depends (Cole, 1967: 5). Although this interest did not lead to an archaeological (in the contemporary sense) practice (see Schnapp, 1996: 68-73),[22] it undoubtedly offered the belief that objects, in the sense of technological expertise, indicate the level of civilisation of a society and can be a testimony to that (see Plato, *Laws*, III.677e-678a; Lucretius, *De Rerum Natura*, 925-962; 1011-1027; 1091-1104). In that sense, this idea is vital for the creation of collections.

Objects and Monuments

Tangible remains provoke a sense of curiosity since they speak equally to reason and imagination (Schnapp, 1996: 13). They add emphasis to memory and history, help to assure us that there *really* was a past, and are essential bridges between then and now. Certainly, they have their limitations as informants, since they require interpretation, and are static and subject to destruction. Nevertheless, they symbolise or memorialise communal links over time, and provide archaeological metaphors that illuminate the processes of history and memory (Lowenthal, 1985: xxiii; Belk, 1991: 121). As Vygotsky (1978: 51) asserts: 'It has been remarked that the very essence of civilisation consists of purposively building monuments so as not to forget. In both the knot and the monument we have manifestation of the most fundamental and characteristic feature distinguishing human from animal memory'. Monuments, therefore, are especially important in preserving aggregate memory.

Ancient Greeks and Romans could not have been indifferent to the attraction of objects and monuments. As we have already seen, technical evolution and materialism have been at the centre of the theories on the origins of humanity and the progress of civilisation. Objects and monuments have often been described in detail by poetry and literature, for instance the description of Achilles' shield by Homer, and the heroic tradition of exchanging objects as part of a complex social system lies at the heart of the large collections of offerings in the Greek sanctuaries (Schnapp, 1996: 56). But what were the roles that the objects and the monuments held in the mind and the heart of ancient Greeks and Romans? And more specifically, what was their role as sources of knowledge about the past and metaphors of it?

As we have seen previously, both Herodotus and Thucydides used the observable vestiges as a source of data. Herodotus, as an early *periegetes*, had examined with care the monuments he had seen, which were ascribed into his narrative as a history. When it came to the pyramids of Egypt, for example, Herodotus made them stand for their period and dynasty, the embodiment of the great men who had built them. As Elsner (1994b: 233) has put it: 'The *monumenta* function as a material and present link ... to a past which might have been lost but that it can be evoked through them. The pyramidal evocation is more than a link to famous persons, it is a link to stories about these persons'. Similar is the case with other incidents where Herodotus verifies the actuality of a fact, or disproves it, by referring to particular objects and monuments; for instance, when he discusses Croesus (*Histories*, 1.50) he refers to his offerings to Delphi, compares these with the actual objects in the sanctuary, but also relies on witnesses to disprove the evidence offered by an object. Herodotus used the monuments as icons in order to define both the 'Other' (i.e. what was remote in time and space) and through it the 'self' (Elsner, 1994b).

Although Herodotus used monuments as metaphors, Thucydides was the one who observed the visible traces in the soil, and put them in relation to tradition, in order to analyse them materially, functionally and stylistically (Schnapp, 1996: 51). Thucydides used monuments - as well as inscriptions (Hornblower, 1987) - as a source in order to argue about the distant past, when ordinary cross-questioning and autopsy were inappropriate or impossible. Twice in his narrative Thucydides used objects and monuments to reach archaeological conclusions. The best known of these paragraphs is the one concerning the purification of Delos:

> for Carians inhabited most of the islands, as may be inferred from the fact that, when Delos was purified by the Athenians in this war and the graves of all who had ever died on the island were removed, over half were discovered to be Carians being recognised by the fashion of the armour found buried with them, and by the mode of burial, which is that still in use among them. (Thucydides, I. VIII.1).[23]

Although contemporary archaeology is well aware that these tombs were Geometric (ninth-eighth centuries BCE), Thucydides's methods were undoubtedly well in advance of his period. In order to analyse these tombs he employed a typological and comparative approach. In this sense, by moving the focus from the objects (or monuments) as signs of power to objects as elements of history, proper archaeological thinking was introduced (Schnapp, 1996: 27).

The second paragraph describes the ruins of Mycenae:

> And because Mycenae was only a small place, or if any particular town of that time seems now to be insignificant, it would not be right for me to treat this as an exact piece of evidence and refuse to believe that the expedition against Troy was as great as the poets have asserted and as tradition still maintains. For if the city of the Lacedaemonians should be deserted, and nothing should be left of it but its temples and the foundations of its other buildings, posterity would, I think, after a long lapse of time be very loath to believe that their power was as great as their renown. (Thucydides, I.X.1-2).[24]

Once again Thucydides examines the ruins, compares sources, establishes levels of similarity, and thus reaches conclusions. His method suggests beyond everything else that observations acquire validity only through careful consideration, and that material evidence gets its value through a constant dialectic between imagination, reason, past, present and future perceptions, knowledge and critical ability (see also Schnapp, 1996: 49).[25]

After Thucydides, the study of the archaeological and epigraphical evidence was never again part of the business of the ordinary historian. By way of compensation, the old type of geographical description, the *periegesis* (introduced by Hecataios' *Periodos Ges*) was transformed to satisfy the needs of antiquarian research on monuments. The geographer became an antiquarian. In the second century BCE, Polemon probably called himself a *periegetes*. The antiquarian monograph could be so narrow as to include only the monuments of the Athenian Acropolis, or so wide as to embrace the whole of Greece - which is what Pausanias did later. Polemon went even beyond Greece and wrote on Carthage and Samothrace. Local histories became full of antiquarian details, and the greatest of the local historians of Athens, Philochorus, was also one of the most active writers of monographs on Attic inscriptions, religious institutions, and other antiquarian subjects (Momigliano, 1990a).

We have so far concentrated on objects and monuments used by historians and antiquarians to support their historical views, but we have not been concerned at all with the methods they developed in order to acquire these tangible proofs, or tokens of the past, for their purposes, and the implications these entail for the understanding and appreciation of material culture. The active pursuit of material remains is illustrated in a few paragraphs that have survived down to our days. Herodotus, for instance, records:

> In this former war with Tegea the Spartans had continually the worst of it, but by the time of Croesus, under their kings Anaxandrides and Ariston, they had got the upper hand. This is the story of their success: after a long series of reverses in the war they sent to Delphi and asked of which god they should beg favour in order to ensure their conquest of Tegea, and the Priestess promised them victory if they brought home the bones of Orestes, Agamnemon's son. Unable to find the tomb of Orestes, they sent again to inquire where the body lay, and the messengers received this answer: ... .
> They searched everywhere; but all in vain until Lichas, who was one of the Spartan special agents called 'Agathoergi', or 'good-service men', solved the riddle. ... Taking advantage of the better relations which existed at this time between the two towns, he went to Tegea and entered a forge where he watched some iron being hammered out, a process which caused him great surprise. The smith, seeing his astonishment, paused in his work and said: 'Well, my friend, your surprise at seeing me work in iron would be nothing to what you'd have felt, if you had seen what I saw. I wanted to make a well in the yard here, and as I was digging I came on a huge coffin - ten feet long! I couldn't believe that men were ever bigger than they are to-day, so I opened it - and there was the corpse, as big as the coffin! I measured it, and then shoveled the earth back.' Lichas turned over in his mind the smith's account of his discovery, and came to the conclusion that the oracle was fulfilled and that this was the body of Orestes. ... Then he dug up the grave, collected the bones and took them away to Sparta; and ever since that day the Lacedaemonians in any trial of strength had by far the better of it. They had now subdued the greater part of the Peloponnese. (Herodotus, *Histories*, 67-68).[26]

A similar story has survived through Plutarch:

> And after the Median wars, in the archonship of Phaedo, when the Athenians were consulting the oracle at Delphi, they were told by the

Pythian priestess to take up the bones of Theseus, give them honourable burial at Athens, and guard them there. But it was difficult to find the grave and take up the bones, because of the inhospitable and savage nature of the Dolopians who then inhabited the island. However, Cimon took the island, as I have related in his Life, and being ambitious to discover the grave of Theseus, saw an eagle in a place where there was a semblance of a mound, pecking, as they say, and tearing up the ground with his talons. By some divine ordering he comprehended the meaning of this and dug there, and there was found a coffin of a man of extraordinary size, a bronze spear lying by its side, and a sword. When these relics were brought home on his trireme by Cimon, the Athenians were delighted, and received them with splendid processions and sacrifices, as though Theseus himself were returning to his city. (Plutarch, *Life of Theseus*, XXXVI).[27]

The same motif of the sacred relics unearthed and carried to the homeland of the hero (or heroine) is also present in Plutarch's *Moralia*, 577-78 (the tomb of Alcmene).[28]

Although these paragraphs do not imply that the Greeks or the Romans had any sense of archaeological curiosity, they are important because they testify the tendency to pursue and appreciate objects, not merely because of their role as historical sources in the epistemological sense, but mainly as symbols and reminders of an event, a personality, a specific action, and as sacred talismans that would protect them individually or as a community. These paragraphs are not only indicative of the use of archaeological methodology, but of a thinking that relates material remains with the past (glorious heroes of the past can be touched - literally and metaphorically - when their relics are brought forth), and according to which objects are evidence of that past, prove the divine provenance, or divine will, and deserve as such to be preserved and honoured;[29] this again is a notion related to antiquarianism and collecting. Schnapp (1996: 56) relates these approaches to ideas about the sacred, and argues that they imply an immediate connection to the objects collected in sanctuaries. He attributes these to the social role of the sanctuary, that has its origins in the tradition of 'presents' which is so familiar to Homer. The objects that heroes used have acquired a long history and the list of their proprietors is inseparable from their intrinsic quality. In Greece, where social distinction depended upon genealogy, the exchange of objects was part of a complex system of giving among heroes, kings and nobles. Thus, a genealogy of objects emerges, as important as the genealogy of people. This is where the importance of the *periegetes* and the antiquarian, who are the people to thesaurise this type of knowledge, comes from. The treasuries of the temples function as repositories of knowledge and collective memory and inheritance; they exhibit objects whose quality, rarity, antiquity and genealogy form reasons for their admiration by the people (see discussion of the gift exchange tradition and the treasuries in Chapter 3).

In Rome none of these uses of objects and monuments was unfamiliar.

Early Roman historians used largely monuments 'from the so-called tomb of Romulus in the *comitium* to the *tabulae triumphales* of victorious second-century proconsuls' (Wiseman, 1986: 88; 1994). During the early period, they were used as foundations for aetiological stories. Among the monuments, Wiseman (1986) mentions the tombs of Romulus, Faustullus, Hostus, Hostilius and other early heroes of Rome. Probably accurate knowledge about the true nature of such monuments did not survive to the time of Fabius Pictor, Cincius Alimentus or any of their successors. The stories about them must be part of an 'expansion of the past', an elaboration that the writers developed in order to have a 'detailed history' (Wiseman, 1986: 89). Gradually a methodological change took place, and by the time of Livy, antiquarian material (monuments, objects, toponyms, etc.) instead of being invested with legendary associations so that they acquired historicity, as was the case in the past, were used as documents, whose very presence guaranteed the credibility of legends or stories (e.g. Livy, I.25.14; 26.13-15; 36.5; 48.6-7; II. 10.12; 13.5; 13.11; 14.9; 40.12, etc.; Gabba, 1981: 61).

The active search for objects described in the previously mentioned paragraphs is only one aspect of the search for real tokens of the past. Strabo offers another insight into the same phenomenon when he describes the foundation of an Augustan colony in the first century BCE on the site of ancient Corinth, in these words:

> Now after Corinth had remained deserted for a long time, it was restored again, because of its favourable position, by the deified Caesar, who colonised it with people that belonged for the most part to the freemen class. And when these were removing the ruins and at the same time digging open the graves, they found numbers of terra-cotta reliefs, and also many bronze vessels. And since they admired the workmanship they left no grave unransacked; so that well supplied with such things and disposing of them at a high price, they filled Rome with Corinthian 'mortuaries', for they called the things taken from the graves, and in particular the earthenware. Now at the outset the earthenware was very highly priced, like the bronzes of Corinthian workmanship, but later they ceased to care much for them, since the supply of earthen vessels failed and most of them were not even well executed. (Strabo, *Geography*, 8.6.23).[30]

Similarly, Tacitus refers to Nero's 'treasure-hunting' approach to material remains of the past (*Annales*, XVI, I-III).

We can therefore testify to an active involvement in the creation of this past, not mediated through prophecies and oracles but initiated by people. The underlying principle of object valuation remains more or less the same: objects are evidence that can bear information about the past, parts of the past that can be touched and owned. The emphasis, though, has been transferred from objects being markers of power, as was the case in the Eastern monarchies, or historical evidence, as in the case of Thucydides and those mentioned above, to becoming antiquities in the Augustan age that could be collected and exchanged (Schnapp, 1996: 28). The same attitude is developed toward monuments, which also become objects that could be collected to form part of the inventory of the Roman domination (Elsner, 1994b: 241). Pliny's encyclopaedia (see discussion in Chapter 6), Diodorus *Library*, Pausanias *periegesis* are the products of this novel way of dealing with them. They share the role of recorder of art and history, and use monuments as a frame through which to explore and represent in some depth the identity of Roman self.

Stewart (1993: 140-143) argues that antiquarianism always displays a functional ambivalence: 'either a nostalgic desire for romanticism or the political desire of authentication. Thus the antiquarian seeks both to distance and appropriate the past'. In order to do so, he must alienate his culture by making it 'Other' - distant and discontinuous. The Roman antiquarians, therefore, motivated by this, sought to define themselves through the past, which is Other - Greek and distant in time - but also self, since now they have conquered Greece and own, literally, but still not metaphorically, its relics. Monuments and objects thus become tokens of that distant past, which need to be appropriated in order for the past to be appropriated, too. Tangible remains are, consequently, metaphors of this past for the present, and thus a medium through which to define the Roman self.

Conclusions

Antiquity, as a notion which turns objects into desirable collectibles, is a recurrent theme in the ancient Greek and Latin authors. It was therefore felt necessary to attempt to throw some light onto the ideas of ancient Greeks and Romans on what constitutes antiquity and the past, how they placed themselves within it and what was the role of objects and monuments in their attempts to understand and define it.

In order to answer the first of those questions we examined the historiographical tradition, which mainly reflects the ideas and feelings of a society to its past. We discerned two different kinds of past: the recent and the distant. The first attracts the major attention, by the most celebrated historians: the reason for this preference is confined to the development in the mid-fifth century BCE of the idea that only the past for which personal testimonies acquired through autopsy can be collected deserves to be studied. As a result, only the recent past can form a legitimate subject for the serious historian. It is used to provide *exempla* to politicians and orators and is at the heart of the development of political thought.

Nevertheless, the distant past had its students as well. These are the erudite men and the antiquarians, who study the past systematically and collect all the available data that relate to it. They use lists of archons, winners, priests, other individuals, monuments, inscriptions, and archives. Their inquiry is also connected to philosophy, which denounces political historiography as dealing with the mundane and the particular, instead of with general truths. The philosophical interest in the origins of humanity and culture thus presents double interest for our enquiry. Not only does it legitimise erudition, but it also supports this by suggesting that the technological aspect of civilisation, i.e. arts and crafts, is an infallible indication of the level of civilisation, be it descending, from Gold to Iron, or ascending, from food-gathering to farming.

Another interesting point arising from the study of antiquarianism is the development of the erudite genre of biography. It became the archetype for the creation of the discipline of physiognomy, which in its turn influenced greatly the portrait collections of the Renaissance (Haskell, 1993).

All these ideas determined the values attributed to objects. The first in the series is the notion of evidence. Objects and monuments are not exactly the sort of evidence on which the initiators of this notion, Herodotus and Thucydides, put their emphasis. Nevertheless, by introducing it, they created the prerequisites for such a use. Material remains are, hesitantly at first, to be used as sources of information and knowledge. Gradually, they are used more and more as reminders of events, personalities and actions, and metaphors of a lost past.

During the Roman period the material remains acquired primary importance. Being ancient was a proper quality (see Arafat, 1992 on Pausanias) as such. But it meant more than merely that. Objects had acquired the unique role of being used as indications of both the 'Other' and the self. Defining the 'Other' is a major step toward defining self. The Romans of the imperial period had conquered almost the whole world known to them; thus, to find another way of defining this new self of theirs, they had to search for the 'Other' in the past. Objects and monuments then become a poetic metaphor of the 'Other' of the past, in the present, in the self. Consequently, they become of unique importance for the definition and understanding of Roman identity. As Pliny has put it, as early as the first century CE, it was not books that the Romans needed, it was store-houses. If books help people to learn the unknown, objects help them to re-know things more deeply (Hubbard, 1984).

Notes

1 To the Greco-Roman world the term 'history' was not synonymous with an aspect of time; therefore 'past' and 'present' were equally related to 'history' (Fornara, 1983: 91-92).

2 This idea is related to the oath/ordeal paradigm, see discussion in Pearce, 1995.

3 Translated in Loeb CL, by A. D. Godley, vol. 1, 1946.

4 For a recent view that connects Herodotus' vocabulary of evidence and proof with late fifth-century Presocratics and early medical writers, see Thomas, 1997.

5 The word belongs to the oral tradition since its first meaning is 'showing forth, making known, exhibiting', all these implying oral presentation, see Lidell-Scott, 1966 edn, pp. 195-196, s.v. αποδειξις.

6   For a discussion of the oral tradition and orality in Greece and Rome, see Thomas, 1992 and Beard, *et al.,* 1991 respectively.

7   The role of Herodotus in the development of the historical enquiry has been the subject of many and fierce discussions: for an account of the feelings and ideas on Herodotus see Hartog, 1988, part 2.

8   The main difference between the two historians' notion of evidence is that Herodotus relates to the oral tradition, or rather he is in a transitive stage between oral and written culture. In this sense, Herodotus has evidence in his mind as this is understood in orality, i.e. orally transferred information is more valid, or as valid as written information, or other tactile source (monument, document). For that reason, in Herodotus, 'I have heard' and 'I have seen' have the same importance. Herodotus was not readily prepared to accept all evidence that objects or documents bring along (and he is willing to exchange the information they provide with that of oral witnesses, who tell the truth the monuments, or documents conceal (see for example, 1.50; 1.93; 2.106; 2.125) (also Hartog, 1988: 279-280; 283ff).

9   In the first two books of Thucydides, where the major part of his methodology is presented, the terms '*semeion*' (sign), '*tekmerion*' (evidence), and '*martyrion*' (testimony) appear quite often. According to the rhetorical handbooks, there are differences between these terms: 'semeion' is a sign which may be fallible, pointing to a result. A '*tekmerion*' is an indication that the result will necessarily occur. Other terms used by Thucydides are: '*paradeigma*' (proof), and the phrases '*kata to eikos*' and '*os eikos*' (as usual/ as natural); also, the word '*abasanistos*' (untested), used to describe the methods of careless researchers. For a detailed discussion on the terminology of evidence in Thucydides see Hornblower (1987: 100-107).

10   Translated by Woodruff, 1982.

11   For a detailed discussion of the use of the word 'αρχαιολογία' in the ancient sources, and subsequent generations, see Papaioannou (1997).

12   Aristotle's ideas on political history have been the subject of much debate (Fornara, 1983: 90-98). In *Poetics* he defines history in opposition to poetry (*Poetics*, 1451b). He disapproves of political history, since he finds that dealing with particular facts instead of general truths, does not contribute enough to human progress.

13   His pupils Theophrastus and Dicaearchus developed their views on religion and civilisation on the basis of antiquarian research. A famous example is Theophrastus' survey of offerings and sacrifices to the gods (Diogenes Laertius, 5.47). One of the notable features of Aristotelian scholarship is the combination of antiquarian research with textual criticism and editorship (Momigliano, 1990a: 64).

14   Στηλοκόπας is a noun, meaning tablet-glutton; it is also an epithet atrributed to Polemon, who copied the inscriptions on public documents (στηλαι), see Herodic. ap. Ath. 6.234d (Liddell-Scott, 1966 edition: 1644, s.v. στηλοκόπας).

15   The indebtedness of Pausanias to Polemon of Ilium is completely disproved by Frazer (1898), the major translator and commentator of Pausanias in English.

16   And the following generations too; see for instance the mixed feelings of St Augustine, *City of God*, VI.3.

17   Translated by H. Rackham, in Loeb CL, 1951.

18   Aulus Gellius mentions a discussion in the chronology of Homer and Hesiod (3.11).

19   For Atticus, see also his biography by Cornelius Nepos; the assemblage of portraits is mentioned in paragraphs 18.5-6.

20   Translated in Loeb CL, by H. Rackham, 1952.

21   Primitivism is discussed in detail in the book edited by Lovejoy and Boas, 1997.

22   Wace (1969) suggests that the Greeks and the Romans had no real intellectual curiosity as regards ancient monuments or works of art. They were apt to regard them as curiosities and practically never indulged in any examination or discussion of them. They were never involved in scientific research in art history or archaeology.

However, it seems that by contributing the idea that technological expertise indicates the level of civilisation, ancient Greeks and Romans created the basis for contemporary archaeological thought.

23   Translated in Loeb CL, by C. Forster Smith, vol. 1, 1951.

24   Translated in Loeb CL, by C. Forster Smith, vol. 1, 1951.

25   We have seen above the views of Herodotus about objects as evidence, and we have discussed it, alas in brief, in relation to orality (see above, nt. 7). Here we can close our argument, by comparing it with Thucydides' views: the latter comes from a written tradition, and he has placed the emphasis on tangible evidence in a way that Herodotus was not prepared to do. Therefore, in his paragraph on Mycenae, Thucydides has to warn his readers about the 'traps' that material evidence *per se* includes. He argues that these have not to be taken at face value, but have to be compared with other information and critically discussed.

26   Translated by A. de Sélincourt, revised by A. R. Burn for the Penguin Classics, 1972 (originally published 1954).

27   Translated in Loeb CL, by B. Perrin, 1914.

28   This practice is associated with the hero cult by Boedecker (1993); there are many other examples as well, see for instance, Pfister (1909: 196-208) and Rohde (1920: 122 and notes). Another very interesting example is mentioned elsewhere by Herodotus (5.77- 81): when Thebes requested some help from Aigina, the latter complied with it by sending the Aiakids; we do not know exactly how this was possible, but the idea of 'borrowing heroes' must be related to the transference of relics (Boedecker, 1993: 173, nt. 7). Solon is also associated with 'excavations' of tombs in order to prove arguments (Diogenes Laertius, 1.48). See also discussion in Higbie (1997).

29   Boedecker (1993) and Huxley (1979) discuss the incident about Orestes' bones recorded by Herodotus in social and political terms. It is interesting that both agree that the possession of the bones, although it did not provide some kind of general right to hegemony over their neighbours, offered to the Spartans 'the power to defeat Tegea' (Boedecker, 1993: 167).

30   Translated by H. L. Jones, in Loeb CL, vol. 4, 1954.

Chapter 3

'Gifts-to-Men and Gifts-to-Gods'[1]: defining (collecting) values

Telemachus: Stranger, you say these things out of a friendly heart, like a father to his son, and I shall never forget them. But come now and stay on, although you are anxious to be on your way: after bathing and enjoying yourself, you will return to your ship with a gift, rejoicing in your heart, a very fine and precious gift, which shall be an heirloom from me, such as dear friends give to friends. Athena, the grey-eyed goddess, answered: 'Do not detain me, as I am eager to be on my way. The gift, which your heart bids you give me, you will offer it to me on my return to take home. Choose a very beautiful one, and you will get an adequate one in return.

Homer, *Odyssey*, I, 306-18[2]

Kokkale: La! Kynno dear, what beautiful statues! What craftsman was it who worked this stone, and who dedicated it?
Kynno: The sons of Praxiteles - only look at the letters on the base, and Euthies, son of Prexon, dedicated it.
Ko.: May Paeon bless them and Euthies for their beautiful works. See, dear, the girl yonder looking up at the apple; wouldn't you think she will swoon away suddenly, if she does not get it? Oh, and yon old man, Kynno. Ah, in the Fates' name, see how the boy is strangling the goose. Why, one would say the sculpture would talk, that is if it were not stone when one gets close. La! in time men will be able even to put life into stones. Yes, only look, Kynno, at the gait of this statue of Batale daughter of Myttes. Anyone who has not seen Batale, may look at this image and be satisfied without the woman herself.
Ky.: Come along, dear, and I will show you a beautiful thing such as you have never seen in all your life....
Ko.: Only look, dear Kynno, what works are those there! See these, you would say, were chiselled by Athene herself - all hail, Lady! Look, this naked boy, he will bleed, will he not, if I scratch him, Kynno; for the flesh seems to pulse warmly as it lies on him in the picture; and the silver toasting-iron, if Myllos or Pataikiskos, son of Lamprion, see it, won't their eyes start from their sockets when they suppose it real silver!

And the ox and its leader, and the girl in attendance, and this hook-nosed and this snub-nosed fellow, have they not all of them the look of light and life? If I did not think it would be unbecoming for a woman, I should have screamed for fear the ox would do me a hurt: he is looking so sideways at me with one eye.

Ky.: Yes, dear, the hands of Apelles of Ephesus are true in all his paintings, and you cannot say that he looked with favour on one thing and fought shy of another: no, whatever, came into his fancy, he was ready and eager to essay off-hand, and if any gaze on him or his works save from a just point of view, may he be hung up by the foot at the fuller's!

. Herodas, *Mimes*, IV, 20-40, 56-78[3]

Introduction

Lavishly decorated gold and silver vessels, bronze tripods, chryselephantine statues, xoana,[4] clay figurines, marble statuary groups and reliefs, paintings, arms and armour, luxurious vestments, but also curiosities, they were all treasured in the ancient Greek and Roman world for reasons related to their intrinsic qualities. Most importantly though, it appears these objects were carriers of more profound value, ineradicably associated with their noble genealogy and skilled craftsmanship. Myths, the Homeric epic poetry, inventories chiselled on stone in Hellenic sanctuaries, along with collections of facts and images created by antiquarians and *periegetes*, like Polemon, Strabo and Pausanias, all argue for a hierarchy of values imposed on material culture, which transforms it from mere commodity to inalienable possession worthy of treasuring and appreciation.

Revealing this hierarchy and its relevance to collecting/treasuring of artefacts is the main aim of this chapter. Despite the bulk of publications devoted to specific archaeological or architectural concerns (e.g. the architectural details of buildings,[5] the spatial organisation of the *temenos*,[6] the identification of certain works of art mentioned by ancient authors with specific fragments that have survived,[7] the organisation of chronological and typological sequences of artefacts and so on[8]), or behavioural patterns related to ritual and religious aspects,[9] there are very few hermeneutical discussions, reconstructing behavioural patterns, vocabulary, objects and institutions of value in their unity.

'Museum' is a term often attributed to ancient sanctuaries (Wernicke, 1894: 103; Kent Hill, 1944: 353; Wace, 1969: 204; Alsop, 1982: 197), but the attribution refers, more often than not, to the functional aspect of being repositories of *objets d' art* (at least as they are categorised by contemporary scholars) and arms (Snodgrass, 1980: 63). This chapter shares the stance most explicitly argued by Pearce (1995: 406), that there is a more profound relationship between ancient sanctuaries and museums. They are both historical - in the long-term - manifestations of the idea of the communal shrine, where communal treasure is 'set aside' as a means to create relationships with the 'sacred' and thus reinforce and legitimise the community's own judgements about aesthetics, knowledge and history. In other words, they are both repositories of collections.

Lifting objects away from the world of common commodities into a world of special significance' is a fundamental characteristic of the collecting process (Pearce, 1995: 27). This notion has its root in archaic ideas about objects serving to create and perpetuate social relationships with other men or the gods, as well as in the idea of 'sacred' as it emerged in the early European languages and links with the oath/ordeal paradigm, and kinship relations. Gift exchange in particular, as a means of creating social relationships, Pearce argues, helps us to understand the role of collecting within the whole social fabric. The emotional values connected with gifts are embraced in modernist capitalist societies by collections (1995: 406-407). The aim of this discussion is to utilise this wide-lensed approach of the *longue durée* employed by Pearce, but to focus on the *conjoncture* of the classical world (Braudel, 1973). More specifically, this chapter aims to pursue further and elaborate on the argument that the (collecting) values of the classical world - as these are revealed in the ancient literary sources discussed in this book - stem from the tradition of gift exchange and its specific character in the early Hellenic world.

Although the existence of gift exchange as inherent in the structure of Homeric society is very well documented (e.g. Finley, 1979), the full implications of this argument for the classical world have only recently began to be appreciated by scholars. Schnapp (1996: 56), for instance, mentions:

> This social role of the temples finds its origins in the tradition of presenting gifts, so often found in Homer. The objects which the heroes used - the arms of Achilles made by Hephaistus; the helmet of Odysseus which came to him from his uncle, the magician Autolycus; the bow of Philoctetes which was a gift from Apollo - all had a long history and the list of their owners was inseparable from their intrinsic qualities. In Greece social rank was linked with fame, a fame which attached to each weapon and each precious object. The exchange of objects was part of a complex gift-exchange system between heroes, kings and nobles. Thus there emerged a genealogy of objects just as important as that of men. From this grew the importance of the work of scholar-travelers and antiquaries who were the repository of knowledge of this kind.

Following this line of thought, this chapter will discuss the role of gift exchange in the classical world, the values to which it gave rise and how it shaped the mind-set that resulted in the creation of the public and private collections of the classical world.

In order to argue the above, we will firstly present in brief the main principles of gift exchange, and how they have been broadened in the study of the archaic Greek tradition. Then, we will present and discuss the vocabulary and institutions of gift in Homer and mythology. In the next two sections, the focus will be on sanctuaries and the institutions and vocabulary of value there, the notions that these collections embodied and their legacy. Then, we will draw all the above together and discuss the hierarchy of values and its implications for subsequent collecting practices.

Main Principles of Gift Exchange and the Archaic Greek Tradition

Mauss' *Essai sur le don* (1925; English translation 1970), the now classic study of gift exchange, argued that exchange in primitive societies consists not so much of economic transactions as of reciprocal gifts, and this is what he calls *prestation totale* (a total social fact), in other words an event which has a significance at once social and religious, magic and economic, utilitarian and sentimental, jural and moral (Lévi-Strauss, 1969: 52). This system of exchange was contrasted with the European economic tradition, that is a system of commodity exchange, as this was developed mainly by Marx. Marx defined commodity as an alienable object that can be exchanged between transactors in a state of reciprocal independence (1867: 91). This definition of commodity exchange, implied what Mauss verified, that non-commodity exchange (that is, gift) is 'an exchange of inalienable things between transactors who are in a state of reciprocal dependence' (phrased as such in Gregory, 1982: 19).[10] It follows, therefore, that whereas commodity exchange establishes a relationship between the objects exchanged, gift exchange establishes a relationship between the subjects. Gift economy is an economy of indebtedness, where accumulation is only meaningful when it aims at 'de-accumulation'. The transactors do not aim to 'pay off' their debts, but to preserve them, and acquire, instead of maximum profit, as many gift-debtors as possible (Morris, 1986: 2).

Mauss (1970; also in Morris, 1986: 2) places societies in a three-stage evolutionary scale: total prestation, gift economy and commodity exchange:

> At first it was found that certain things, most of them magical and precious, were by custom not destroyed, and these were endowed with the power to exchange... In the second-stage, mankind having succeeded in making these things circulate within the tribe and far outside it found that these purchasing instruments could serve as a means to count wealth and make it circulate. The third stage began in ancient Semitic societies which invented the means of detaching these precious things from groups and individuals and of making them permanent instruments of value measurement - universal, if not entirely rational - for lack of any better system. (Mauss, 1970: 94).

Sahlins (1972) and Gregory (1980; 1982; 1984) pursued this further and agreed, quite wrongly as was later proved, that clan-society is where the gift-economy predominates, whereas class-society is where the commodity thrives.

Gregory in particular elaborated on that and introduced instead of a bipolar opposition, a continuum of related forms of technology, distribution and exchange; he suggested that the movement from the clan system of organisation at one end of the continuum to the capitalist system at the other end, is a movement from 'equality and unity to inequality and separation' (1984: 37; also in Morris, 1986: 3).

Morris (1986) assessed this distinction in the light of the earliest Greek literary sources and argued that there is no reason to believe that gift can be a primary mechanism only in kinship based, non-state societies. Ancient Greek and Roman societies cannot fit on a simple-complex, natural-political economic scale, like that presented by Gregory. Both kinship and class were active in defining the character of the ancient world. The references to the importance of gift exchange are very clear in the literary sources.

> The Archaic Greek case, then, suggests that in a political society gift exchange can flourish as a primary exchange form even within a state system. As the scale and complexity of the state grows, the relative position of the gift and commodity are likely to change, but personification of transactors and the transacted objects through long term social relationships and the gift is not purely a primary feature of clan societies. (Morris, 1986: 7).

Gift exchange entails a competitive aspect as well. Mauss argued that in societies with a rigid hierarchical structure, the exchange of gifts tends to be absent (1970: 91, nt. 68), whereas it flourishes in societies with an unstable clan hierarchy. Gregory (1982: 20) reasserted that point in his observations on the societies of Papua New Guinea. Morris similarly saw gift exchange phenomena as expressions of social and economic instability (1986: 13). Gift exchange as an expression of relations of indebtedness and power has been discussed by Leach (1982a) who summarised his points in the following formulae:

state of indebtedness	= social relationship
payment of debt	= manifestation of relationship
nature of payment	= nature of relationship
reciprocal equal	= equality of status; absence of power flow either way
asymmetrical patterns	= inequality of status; power flow from 'higher' to 'lower'

Figure 3.1:   Gift exchange as power and indebtedness, after Leach, 1982a: 59).

Each of the above equations is reversible.

Two other characteristics of the gift exchange tradition should be discussed in relation to the above: the notion of reciprocity and the inalienable quality of the gifts. The 'norm of reciprocity' was seen as the connecting principle of the gift exchange economy. This though has been recently challenged by Weiner (1992) who saw the norm of reciprocity as an ideal projected by the nineteenth century evolutionary beliefs. Therefore, she argued that the social actions are far more dense that the reciprocity rule entails.[11] Consequently, she searched for the social dynamics of 'keeping-while-giving' and how they influence gift exchange. She argued that cosmologies are the cultural resources that societies draw on to reproduce themselves. But these resources are not merely ideologies, located outside the production of material resources. The traditional dichotomy between cosmology or superstructure and the material resources of production and consumption leaves little space to explore the cultural constitutions by which the reproduction of the authority vested in ancestors, gods, myths, and magical properties plays a fundamental role in how production, exchange and kinship are organised. To emphasise and overcome this problem, Weiner uses the term 'cosmological authentication', to amplify how material resources and social practices link individuals and groups with an authority that transcends present social and political action. Because this authority is lodged in past actions or representations and in sacred or religious domains, to those who draw on it, it is a powerful legitimating force. As Beidelman pointed out 'one must understand the cosmology of the people involved so that one has some idea of what they themselves believe they are doing' (quoted in Weiner, 1992: 4-5).

Consequently, Weiner suggested that what motivates reciprocity is the inalienable character of gifts, that is the 'paradox of keeping-while-giving', 'the desire to keep something back from the pressures of give and take' (1992: 43). Mauss had already considered inalienability as a paramount characteristic of gift exchange (1970: 9-10, 18, 24, 31 etc.). Inalienability means that 'the objects are never completely separated from the men who exchange them; the communion and alliance they establish are well-nigh indissoluble' (1970: 31). Weiner pursued this point further and suggested that these objects 'are imbued with the intrinsic and ineffable identities of their owners which are not easy to give away' (1992: 6). Inalienable possessions have a subjective value which is above their exchange value, and thus they serve for the 'cosmological authentication'. Consequently, inalienable possessions, by having a unique character, generate and confirm power and difference. They produce an arena of heterogeneity rather than homogeneous totality. The possession of an inalienable object authenticates the authority of its owner and affects his other transactions. The ability 'to keep' that object empowers the ability to attract other important gifts. In other words, 'things exchanged are about things kept' (1992: 10).

The inalienable possessions as sources of difference and hierarchy, and as retaining for the future memories of the past, are representations of how social identities are constructed through time. 'The reproduction of kinship is legitimated in each generation through the transmission of inalienable possessions, be they land rights, material objects, or mythic knowledge.' (Weiner, 1992: 11).

The anthropomorphic quality of gifts has also to be related to that aspect of inalienability (Mauss, 1970; Gregory, 1982: 20). According to Mauss, the goods transacted were thought to be persons or pertain to a person; in exchanging something one was in effect exchanging part of oneself. The bonds created by things were thus bonds created between people, since they were parts of the people exchanged through things. One gives away part of his own substance, and receives part of somebody else's nature. This part needs to be reinstalled in his own clan/family/owner; it is not inert. In other words, it is inalienable, cannot be separated from its owner, even though it has been given away (1970: 8-10). (For attribution of the properties of living organisms to objects see also Ellen, 1988: 223ff.)

According to Leach (1982a), pre-eminence in a gift-economy is achieved when asymmetrical patterns in object exchange lead to power 'flowing' from 'higher to lower' (see above). Mauss (1970: 4-5) suggested that the total prestation has an agonistic character. 'Essentially usurious and extravagant, it is above all a struggle among nobles to determine their position in the hierarchy to the ultimate benefit, if they are successful, of their own class.' This agonistic character defines the contexts in which gift exchange appears. The primary contexts seem to have been marriages (for the conceptualisation of marriage itself as a part of the gift exchange tradition, see Lévi-Strauss, 1969), funeral games, and guest-friendship arrangements, but also the many other occasions that provide a pretext for prestations.

Destruction of wealth is the occasion *par excellence*. Gregory (1982: 60-61) assumes that the destruction of wealth is the simplest strategy available to an individual who wishes to achieve pre-eminence in a gift society. The most characteristic expression of that is 'potlatch' where men who rival each other in generosity destroy precious objects. This concerns not only them and the objects involved, but also 'their spirits of the dead which take part in the transactions and whose names the men bear; it concerns nature as well' (Mauss, 1970: 12). Mostly this notion concerns what we call 'sacrifice'.[12] 'Sacrificial destruction implies giving something that is to be repaid' (Mauss, 1970: 14). Mauss further justifies the idea: 'Among the first groups of beings with whom men must have made contracts were the spirits of the dead and the gods. They in fact are the real owners of the world's wealth. With them it was particularly necessary to exchange and particularly dangerous not to; but, on the other hand, with them exchange was easiest and safest.' (Mauss, 1970: 13). Grave goods[13] and sanctuary offerings therefore form destruction of wealth in this sense (Morris, 1986: 9).

To summarise the above points and illustrate the character of gift exchange we can draw the following formulae:

commodity economy	: gift economy
commodity	: gift
alienable	: inalienable
temporary alliance	: perpetual interdependence
relationship between the	: relationship between the subjects
objects exchanged	exchanging them
equality	: assertions of domination and control
objectification process	: personification process
(things and people assume	(things and people assume the social
the social form of objects	form of persons in a gift economy)
in a commodity economy)	
alien transactors	: related transactors
use value	: symbolic value
profane	: sacred

In other words, the gift exchange tradition (the right column above) defines value and gives material culture a certain character. Firstly, it assumes for material culture the possibility of creating relationships between subjects, of asserting domination and control and of having a symbolic character. Secondly, it assumes that objects can be inalienable, personified and have a symbolic value. Therefore, it is in the gift exchange tradition that we come across the seeds of what we could call (collecting) values, and of what made objects worthy of collecting. We can also deduce from the above that the context of collections is the context of gift exchange and also one (at least) of the associations/creations of the notion of 'sacred'. Gift exchange is therefore at the heart of the collecting process, since it endows material culture with certain qualities that remain, in substance, the same.[14] It is in gift exchange that objects are endowed with the power to relate people, to be prizes, to be vehicles of memory, to relate people with the 'Other', remote in time or in space, and so on.

Vocabulary and Institutions of Gift in Homer

We are now going to turn our attention to the vocabulary and institutions of the gift-exchange tradition as these appear in the Homeric epic poetry. We will have the opportunity to search for some of the fundamental notions regarding gifts, their value, and the context where the gift exchange occurs. We are therefore going to examine the social aspect of gift exchange in the Greek world. Many methodological problems surround the Homeric epics. Scholars do not have a uniform view on the subject: some think of them as being representative of the society during the tenth and ninth centuries BCE (Finley, 1979); some others argue for them being an ahistorical melange of elements of the traditions from the thirteenth to the eighth centuries BCE (Snodgrass, 1974). Another suggestion has been that the poems cannot be treated as direct evidence for a particular period, but they are a rather complex transformation of actual facts together with mythological and traditional elements (Morris, 1986). Oral poetry is composed through a long period of time and with a complex system which connects tradition with personal talent, and particular events with 'mythological' ones. Therefore, it needs to be treated with care; nevertheless, Homeric poetry presents a world-view which might not correspond to a particular historical period. It does though, provide a reliable picture of the world of Archaic Greece.

The gift exchange system was the basis of all social interaction in the *Iliad* and *Odyssey*, and it operated among strangers and friends, men and gods (Finley, 1979; Langdon, 1987: 109; von Reden, 1994). Heroic/aristocratic life was accompanied by an important circulation of prestige goods. Gift giving was part of the network of competitive honorific activity. One measure of man's true worth was how much he could give away in treasure. Heroes boasted of the gifts they had received and of those they had given as signs of their prowess. Metal objects, chariots, horses, and women were all objects that changed hands as a result of war or other social circumstances.[15] Their 'participation' in those events added to their intrinsic value, constituted their importance and gave them the status of 'honourable gifts of imperishable fame'. When Telemachus refused Menelaus' offer of horses, the Spartan king countered with the following proposal:

> Of the gifts, such as are treasures lying in my house, I will give you
> the one which is finest and most valuable. I will give you a skilfully
> wrought bowl; it is all of silver, finished with gold on the rim, the
> work of Hephaestus. The hero Phaedimus, king of the Sidonians,
> gave it to me. (*Od.*, IV. 609-619).[16]

A trophy with such a history obviously shed greater glory on both donor and recipient than just any silver bowl, as the armour of Hector was a far greater prize to his conqueror than the arms of one of the lesser Trojans. Status was the chief determinant of values, and status was transmitted from the person to his possessions, adding still more worth to their intrinsic value as gold or silver or fine woven cloth. The possession of these objects of worth, on the other hand, transfered their status to the owner (Scheid-Tissinier, 1994). It was this honourific quality that distinguished the wealth of the heroes, and their almost overpowering accumulative instinct, from the materialistic drives of other classes and other ages (Finley, 1979: 120-121).

Finley (1979), following the traditional ideas about reciprocity, suggested that wealth meant power and direct material satisfaction to Odysseus and his fellow-nobles, and that equation was never absent from their calculations. Apparently, this conclusion is not precise. Recompense for the Homeric heroes was conceived in terms of honour and reinforcement of the network of obligations rather than tangible material profits (see also Weiner's views above). A similar pattern determined relation with the gods. The Homeric gods could mediate for the attainment of humans' goals, if humans in their turn were ready to observe the correct rituals which would stregthen the network of obligations. The poems often echo the belief that good fortune can be obtained through prayers and sacrifice (*Il.*, XXII. 259-261), but also that evil befalls those who fail to maintain their balance with the gods (*Od.*, IV. 351-353). A deity often would initiate the contract (*Il.*, I.212-214), by offering to the mortal material gain (Langdon, 1987: 109; Finley, 1979). The aim was to maintain a social and psychological equilibrium.

From the religious parallel we can reach another point: that of the morality of the material wealth, associated with those noble activities. Objects that have been through this network of exchanges and have been acquired as a result of a social relation with either a human or a god, were obviously fortified with moral value, that in turn was transferred from the owner to the object and *vice versa*. The reverse was also true, so that when the objects were products of unfair, incomplete, or non-noble transactions, their accumulation was equated to an illicit and punishable act.[17]

Enquiries into the vocabulary used to denote riches in the epics can illuminate what these objects were and what exactly it was that made them valuable. There are two kinds of riches: κειμήλια καί πρόβατα (keimeilia kai provata) (*Od.*, II. 75). The word 'keimeilia' derives from the verb κειμαι (*keimai* - to rest) and designates durable and storable valuables only, whereas 'πρόβατα', which comes from the verb προβαίνω (to walk, to proceed), means movable property, i.e. slaves, cattle or any kind of livestock (Benveniste, 1973; also van Wees, 1992: 244). *Keimeilia keitai* (rest) usually (*Il.*, VI. 47; *Od.*, IV. 613; XV.101; XXI.10) in the *thalamos* (θάλαμος) of the palace. The frequent presence next to the word *keimeilia* of the words πολλά καί ἐσθλά (polla ke esthla - many and good of their kind[18]) denotes the abundance and richness of these treasuries, as well as the importance that the possession and keeping of these objects had for the owner as indications of wealth and distinction. A common formula when these objects are discussed is that they are made of gold, bronze or iron[19] (*Il.*, XVIII.289). Symbols of wealth, then, these objects frequently qualify as ἄγαλμα (*agalma*). This term means the object which offers pleasure both to the person who gives it as well as to the person who takes it (*Od.*, XVIII. 300; XIX. 257; IV. 602; *Il.*, IV.144ff) (for discussion see Gernet, 1981; Scheid-Tissinier, 1994: 42-43). In its most ancient usage this word implies the idea of value. It can refer to all kinds of objects, even humans, as long as they can be considered 'precious'. Most often it refers to aristocratic wealth (horses are *agalmata*). Its etymology from the verb '*agallein*', which means both to adorn and to honour, is indicative; applied especially to the category we have been examining, it refers to personal objects and furnishings. We should add that in the classical period the verb regularly refers to the offerings to gods, especially such objects as statues of divinities (Gernet, 1981: 77).

Another word used to describe these objects is the word κτήματα (Scheid-Tissinier, 1994: 45). This derives from the verb κτάομαι (to acquire), and thus it accentuates the idea of 'acquisition', that is of things acquired as a result of war, games, or gift-giving - never that of commercial gain (Gernet, 1981: 76). Κτήματα also include women *(Il.*, V. 480-1; *Od.*, XVIII. 144; XXIV. 459). These κτήματα are found in the *thalamos*, the most secret and sacred part of the house; they are the prestige objects that belong to the warrior and indicate his rank and wealth. They constitute, according to Gernet, 'un trésor royal, dépôt de richesses, dépôt d'agalmata' (1981: 96-97 and 129-130). They are the very objects that accompany the warrior in his tomb (Scheid-Tissinier, 1994: 48).

The word *thalamos* itself is indicative too. Besides being the treasury of the palace,[20] the same word is used for the women's quarters.[21] Sometimes the word denotes the young girl's room before her wedding (*Od.*, VII.7), sometimes the nuptial chamber or couch (*Il.*, XVIII.492; Pindar, *Pythian Odes*, 2.60), whereas the verb θαλαμεύω (thalamevo) means to marry (Heliodorus, 4.6). Vernant (1983: 149-150) discusses the use of the word in his presentation of the dichotomy between interior and exterior space. He argues that women are associated with the accumulation and storing of goods, and the men with acquiring them. In Xenophon's *Oeconomicus* (7.20-21, 25, 35-36; 7.33) the model wife is compared to the queen bee who dwells in the hive watching over the honey collected in the honeycombs (also called *thalamos* or *thalame*) (see pages 85-86, where discussion of the word θησαυρός). Other similar associations regarding the role of women and material culture include the assimilation of the *thalamos* with woman's lap, or even a stomach (as in Hesiod, who presents the woman as seated inside, storing the riches that the husband brings directly in the depths of her stomach - *Theogony*, 598-599) (Vernant, 1983: 149).[22]

Thalamos has also a series of other meanings revealed in the discussion of mythology (see Gernet, 1981). It is represented as an underground chamber, and the legend of Danaos has preserved its mythical connotations (Sophocles, *Antigone*, 947). The same implications are true for the *thalamos* of Aietes (Pindar, *Pyth.* IV. 160), the keeper of the Golden Fleece. For Mimnermus (frg. 11.5ff) there is a golden *thalamos* 'in which the rays of the sun repose'. Euripides (frg. 781) speaks of a *thalamos* where the king, the alleged father of Phaethon, keeps his gold locked up, and where the body of Phaethon himself (in reality, the son of the Sun) is placed at the tragedy's conclusion. The queen, according to Euripides, has the keys to it. In a parallel fashion, Athena, Zeus' daughter, has the keys to the treasury where Zeus' thunderbolt is kept (Aeschylus, *Eumen.* 826-828). The idea of royal treasury is based on a belief in protective sacra, which are kept in a secret corner, guarded by a mythical king or king-god (Gernet, 1981: 101). The same term is also used for the funeral chamber of the tomb (Scheid-Tissinier, 1994: 48; Vernant, 1983: 148ff).

Another term associated with precious objects is γέρας, which means prize object. It is often accompanied by the verbs 'ἀπηύρα' and 'ἄγετο', meaning 'to carry away', to indicate the fact that they are trophies (e.g. *Il.*, XXIII.560; XXIII.800; XXIII.808; XXIII.829). The terms appear in contexts of honourable competition, be it war or games. The γέρας is the prize the hero gets, the symbol of his prowess and part of the honour bestowed on him because of his success. Thus there is association with the competitive aspect of gift exchange, and the social context where this tradition appears (Scheid-Tissinier, 1994: 60).

It is possible to distinguish, therefore, the following three categories into which objects should belong in order to be valuable and in consequence to deserve to be treasured (Scheid-Tissinier, 1994). The first depends on the rank of the persons in whose hands the objects circulated (e.g. *Il.*, VII. 149; XI. 20-23; XV. 532; XXIII. 745; *Od.*, IV. 125-126; IV. 617-618; XXI. 31-33). This gave to objects a similar status to that of their proprietors; they were personified, they acquired an almost civic status (the one the proprietors had).

The second category consisted of objects which descended from a god. This meant prestige for the family, which was thus supposed to have divine origin and, consequently, be in special relationship with the divine. Therefore, in this case the emphasis lies on the political aspect of gift exchange, as well as on the competitive character of it (e.g. *Il.*, V. 266; XVI. 381 and 867; XXIII. 277-278; II. 827; VII. 146; XVIII. 84; XXIV. 74-75).

> Then among them lord Agamemnon uprose, bearing in his hands the sceptre which Hephaistus had wrought with toil. Hephaistus gave it to king Zeus, son of Cronos, and Zeus gave it to the messenger Argeïphontes; and Hermes, the lord, gave it to Pelops, driver of horses, and Pelops in turn gave it to Atreus, shepherd of the host; and Atreus at his death left it to Thyestes, rich in flocks, and Thyestes again left it to Agamemnon to bear, that so he might be lord of many isles and of all Argos. (*Il.*, II. 100-107).[23]

This was another aspect of the prestigious genealogy, and had to do with the relation with the 'Other'; furthermore, this was a way of legitimatisation for the dominant families, and a medium of practising power over people. The linear syntax used to express the change of hands of objects also indicates a long line of prestigious ancestors.

The third category belongs to the most interesting notion of γέρας (prize object). This is also related to the competitive aspect of gift exchange, and is indicative of the social contexts for the exchange of gifts. Furthermore, immediately related to the above is the category that can be described by the notion of μνῆμα, which means vehicle of memory (remembrance, memorial, but in modern Greek also tomb). This relates to the inalienability of gifts as bearers of individual and communal identity (e.g. *Il.*, XXIII. 619) - also:

> Lo, I too give thee this gift, dear child, a remembrance of the hands of Helen, against the day of thy longed-for marriage, for thy bride to wear it. (*Od.*, XV. 126-127).

> This bow (the one that Iphitus gave to Odysseus) goodly Odysseus, when going forth to war, would never take with him on the black

ships, but it lay in his halls at home as a memorial of a dear friend, and he carried it in his own land. (*Od.*, XXI. 38-41).[24]

Another important aspect of this is the possibility inherent in objects, that they serve as exemplars - especially in the case of the arms which were booty of war and could serve to commemorate the ancestors' glorious deeds as examples for new generations.   This again relates to inalienability and the creation of identity.

Consequently, these objects which were qualified as prestige items, are, on the one hand, preserved in the palace treasury, and on the other, 'are used', in the sense that they 'take part' in events that constitute the life of heroes, they circulate.   It was precisely this circulation in violent or peaceful events that gave them a prestige which took them to another dimension.   It was the will to circulate and become vehicles of memories and of the myths that gave these objects their value.   In other words, the objects in this sense are also considered to be in a position to legitimise and materialise events and relations.

Vocabulary and Institutions of Gift in Mythology

The above discussion aimed to highlight the social value attributed to objects when they participated in the social contexts of gift exchange, as these appear in the Homeric world. Now, our interest will focus on another 'kind' of value, similar but not quite identical with the symbolic one that we have associated with gift exchange, the one that Gernet has termed 'mythic value' (1968; English translation 1981).

He defines this not as an abstract and measurable notion that rests on economic criteria, but as a 'preferential value embodied in certain objects, a value that not only predates economic value but is its very precondition' (1981: 77).   It has to do with an object of respect, even fear, with the source of interests, attachments, or pride. It also presupposes or signifies a psychological tone more elevated, more diffused, than in our human nature (1981: 73). Gernet believes that the mythical notion of value tends to be total, and it touches the 'whole ensemble of economy, religion, politics, law, aesthetics' (1981: 101). It is his belief that the concept of value is mythical in its mode of thought, a creation of imagination (also Pearce, 1995: 255).

Gernet chooses to discuss myths as a mediating factor of value. He assesses myths to be general representations that belong to a society, contribute to its definition, and constitute for it the necessary framework of all its thought. In addition, Gernet believes that myths can be particularly useful for the study of the function of symbols (1981: 74). Myths convey both the symbolic value of the objects and their mythic value. Values are constructed as parts of social mechanisms designed to enhance specific social groups' dominance. They are neither 'revealed', nor 'natural' (Pearce, 1995: 304 and 307).   Myths are used to legitimise that dominance, to persuade one of those values' 'natural' and 'self-evident' importance; they are used to conceal the game of domination and control. Gift exchange, therefore, being a social phenomenon, with special reference to notions of domination and control, initiated value assumptions, which were legitimised through myths. This is where social values are becoming norms (see Chapter 1 on theoretical approaches and Barthes[25]). On the other hand, myths are the natural habitat of mythic concepts, which humans find difficult to apprehend, or which they need to mediate their encounter with the supernatural.

Gernet, therefore, employs myths in his attempt to divulge the origins of value. The myths that he considers all reveal similar patterns: (a) the tripod of the seven sages: brings forward the notion of award, the pattern of successive ownership of the object, the importance of the object as a product of luxurious human industry, but also with religious connotations (possibly due to the very fact that it is a product of the luxurious human industry), its role in relations of antagonism (relations of power); (b) the necklace of Eriphyle reveals the talismanlike nature of object, its role in transfer and installation of royal power, but also the mythic notion of danger associated with it; (c) the ring of Polycrates underlines the role of certain objects as symbols of wealth (the seal ring is particularly so in Myceanaen Greece, as the archaeological discoveries from tombs also emphasise), while it makes the point about objects having a necessary relationship with the world beyond and arising from it - with this seems to be related the idea of throwing precious objects into the water, whose re-emergence might be a bad sign. Finally, (d) the myth of the Golden Fleece brings forth the idea of the protective sacra guarded by a king or king god, along with the need of holding certain objects as essential symbols of power and royal control.

Treasure therefore, is a social reality, but also a mythic reality (Gernet, 1981: 100). The social reality is governed by rules of conduct deriving from the gift exchange tradition. Consequently, the objects can be distinguished between those which can be termed commodities, and those that are valuable, not related to profane, ordinary activities, but associated with the 'noble commerce'. They are objects given as 'prizes' in different circumstances: customary gifts, gifts of hospitality, ransoms, offerings to the gods, funeral offerings, and objects placed in tombs of leading men. These objects circulate in contexts of competitive (agonistic) gift exchange - and thus are categorised differently and contrasted with the 'inferior' category of commodities. These valuables - the products and means of social events - are κτήματα, i.e. strictly speaking property, that may follow the owner to the tomb (Gernet, 1981: 75-76); in other words, inalienable.

In purely economic terms, these objects, due to the technical skills required in their manufacture and the extensive trading links that they presuppose, characterise classic chiefly, redistributive economies which centre on god-descended princely families and their immediate retainers. They live all together in the royal hall, where the objects themselves are hoarded and distributed, and where everything of importance takes place. The royal hoard is constantly depleted as gifts are given away, and can be replenished only by constant warfare against similar royal houses; political fortunes, therefore, flow with the ability to attract substantial numbers of warriors and keep them fed and rewarded, and consequently, power is in a perpetual state of flux. In this kind of community, therefore, together with kinship, honourable gifts constituted perhaps the most significant social bond (Pearce, 1995: 71); this answers the question of why particular objects seem to be chosen in order to participate in these transactions.

In parallel with this social character, the valuables also have a mythic reality. They are full of magical properties, they function as talismans, and they relate with the 'Other', the world beyond, often directly. The idea of royal treasury, of the storehouses of riches and *agalmata*, is based on the belief in protective sacra. The earth is generally considered keeper of treasure - possibly in relation to the burying of the dead,[26] but also in association with religious practices related with chthonic religion. Direct association with the earth and the chthonic deities who live there can be dangerous or beneficial. Placing a child on the ground may cause death or immortality. There were two practices with which immortality could be bestowed on a child: by 'hiding' it in fire, and in the earth (as Medea did: κατακρυπτεία - katakrupteia).[27] It is obvious that the two rites correspond to each other and are in contrast, exactly as were the two forms of funerary deposition that the Greeks used. In the Greek world, the dead are sometimes 'hidden in the fire' (incineration), sometimes in the ground (internment). In both cases, they have to disappear from this world, so that they can pass to the other world (Vernant, 1983: 154). A similar practice, which supports this belief (along with the personification of objects, and the transference of the practices that we are discussing from the private context to the sanctuary, public context) is the burial of the 'old' votives of a sanctuary, to dispose of them.

Sea, similarly, is whence precious artefacts usually derive. When the object is a tripod - as, for instance, in the myth of the seven Sages - the standard theme is that it was discovered in the sea and brought back in a fisherman's net. The sea is also where the god is carried or cast up, the dead man is raised to the status of hero, the child hero and the chest where he is placed travel ... (Gernet, 1981: 80). A common motif of myths is also that the object is a gratuitous gift from the world beyond; or that the object is divine in origin and has been fashioned by Hephaestus. *Agalmata*, furthermore, may be in contact with cult instruments and thus acquire prestige. For instance, the cup in legend is usually a *phiale* (libation cup), or garments, which have a very ancient role to play in religion (1981: 102-103). Nevertheless, the relation between religious value and intrinsic value is also reversible: it is not only because an object has a religious use that it has value; it is also because it is precious that it can be consecrated (1981: 103). Classic examples of this attitude are the *larnax* (chest where infant heroes or gods were exposed,[28] now holding *agalmata*) and the tripod.

The votive tripod had a continuous presence since the Mycenaean terracotta versions, through to the bronze forms that became common during the Geometric period (Snodgrass, 1980). The bronze tripods with ring handles that survive from earlier periods come from domestic and tomb contexts, not shrines (there are ten examples known, see Langdon, 1987: nt. 4). In the Homeric poetry, bronze tripods are very prominent gifts; they appear as the first prize in the funeral games of Patroclus, as the guest-gifts taken home from Odysseus, and as the appeasement offered to Achilles by Agamemnon. Tripods began as cooking pots, utilitarian, scarcely decorated artefacts; they soon acquired prominence through their presence in feasts, where they were expected to grace the table. The feasts were usually accompanied by games, and the tripods became convenient prizes and therefore the symbol of athletic victory. However, since a tripod's shape was awkward, and not easy to carry away, dedicating it to the local sanctuary was a simple and honourable way to dispose of it without actually losing it completely (Benton, 1934-1935: 114-115).[29] This practical interpretation of the transition from the utilitarian role of the tripod to the ritual one, can be complemented with a symbolic aspect as well. Participating in the ceremonies of the heroic world, the tripod acquired a direct linkage with their values and social practices, which eventually made it the most appropriate category of object to operate as a transitional medium, through which the social rituals of the aristocratic world were transferred to the social organisation as this changed shape in the following periods. The impetus thus was both political and religious: on the one hand, being a familiar practice, the gift exchange to the gods reassured the social security, status, legitimacy, proof of class, and claims to power. On the other, it was a custom based on the secular past, and as such familiar and socially acceptable.

Having this double identity, the social and the mythic, *agalmata* are particularly important for those who claim religious or political authority. Tyrants, especially, who need to appropriate mythical thought to bolster their authority, are particularly concerned about objects. They need them to justify their role and relation to the 'Other', the source of power (see also the Chapter about Cicero and Verres).

To illustrate the double role of the object and its relation to value, Gernet uses the adjective *timeeis*. The complex notion of *time* (τιμή) (honour, social prerogative, religious quality) is concentrated on the specialised notion of the 'precious'. Therefore, this represents a turning point: the same object is charged with mythical potential, but also represents what might be called external signs of wealth. From its origins and constant associations, however, it reveals a mode of thought in which the objects mentioned above are not merely signifiers of wealth; they have a mysterious power embodied in them as well (1981: 103-104).

We can present the practice which resulted from this mind set (evident in myths) regarding objects as follows:

precious objects	: ordinary objects, like cattle, cows, corn...
gold/bronze/precious stones, etc.	: organics and iron
inorganics dug out	: organics growing up
Athena/Hephaistus/Demeter	: Persephone[30]
divine	: mundane
death (dead)	: life (living)
sacred/royal power	: ordinary people
larnax (which can be used as a coffin)	: open storage
valuable	: not very valuable
enduring	: consumable
keimelia	: *provata*
sacred	: profane
collections	: non collections

We can summarise the above by structuring the parameters of value we have been discussing into two axes, the gift : commodity axis and the sacred : profane axis. The four quarters that these create structure the ancient (but also the amazingly contemporary) ideas and hierarchies of value. In the gift/sacred quarter are included objects that serve as *agalma;* tripods, jewellery, *phiale*, collections, in other words objects that appear both in the mythic reality and in the social context of gift exchange. In the gift/profane quarter belong objects like horses, and women; in other words, precious in the sense that they can be exchanged between nobles/kings and serve to retain social relationships, but which do not claim divine origins and canonistic value. The sacred/commodity quarter is where the 'ordinary' votive offerings can be located: clay figurines, for example, or objects that can be purchased around the sanctuary, made locally, without claims for prestigious genealogy, sanctity, or antiquity, but merely tokens of piety. Finally, in the profane/commodity quarter all the objects intended and appreciated for their 'use' are included. Here we can find all sorts of vessels, even tripods, when they were merely cooking-pots, cattle and cows, organics, in other words 'ordinary objects' (Figures 3.2 and 3.3).

This structure can be taken one step further in Figure 3.4. There the persons involved in each of the valuations we discussed in the previous figures can take their own place on the two axes. We reach therefore some very interesting equations. In the gift/sacred quarter we find gods, who have direct access to the sacred, the divine and the dead, the valuable, the objects with mythic value; king-warriors and king-gods, who have the power to safeguard the prestigious items of mythic value; the dragon or snake, who protects the sacra; and the collector, who safeguards the collection, for good or for bad, as a warrior-king or a dragon himself. In the gift/profane quarter nobles and heroes find their place, that is people who participate in the social dimension of the gift exchange but do not have direct access to the sacred. In the sacred/commodity quarter, pious people and priests have direct access, whereas in the profane/commodity quarter all the other, ordinary people, are included.

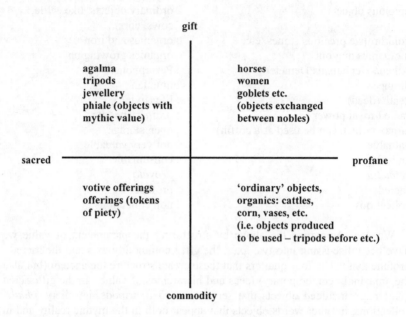

Figure 3.2:   Structuring the parameters of value according to the gift:commodity and
               sacred:profane axes, I.

Sanctuaries: Treasures in Treasuries

Having discussed the institutions and vocabulary of value as this was shaped in
the Homeric epic poetry and the mythological tradition, we are now going to
focus on the development and survival of these notions in the Geometric
sanctuaries of Greece. The princely *thalamos* that Homer has described for us
was gradually replaced by other forms of the same notion, communal treasuries
in the new centres of Hellenism and power.

A mixture of art and historical material was arranged in and around the
buildings of the sanctuaries, devoted (donated) by people who wanted to
commemorate their deeds and their names, and thus legitimise the social
hierarchy that (was) supported (by) them. The construction in Panhellenic
sanctuaries in the eighth century BCE onwards of large monuments is related
to a process of institutionalisation of religion empowered by the creation of
city-states (see de Polignac, 1995; also Morgan, 1990: 5).

Sanctuaries, therefore, became the arenas where practices and ideologies of the
aristocratic world were transferred, as a result of changing circumstances. The
holdings of the sanctuaries came to represent frozen an immobile wealth, to be
admired but not consumed; a kind of conspicuous consumption, expected to be

'repaid' in terms of status, legitimacy, proof of class and of claims to rule and domination (see also Pearce, 1995: 90; Burkert, 1987: 49).

Figure 3.3:   Structuring the parameters of value according to the gift:commodity and sacred:profane axes, II.

Snodgrass (1980) analyses the deposits of bronze goods in important sanctuaries from the eleventh century to the eighth century and reported a considerable increase in bronze dedications which coincided, as Morris' research suggested, with a decline in grave goods in many areas, where the city-state was gaining precedence, around 700 BCE (Morris, 1992). Morris further argued that this transition, which is evident in the archaeological record, is a clear example of change from gifts-to-men to gifts-to-gods, in the context of destruction of wealth. He associated this with the need of aristocratic competition to be represented as having a wider communal value at a time of great social stress, i.e. as the result of a profound structural change in society, empowered by the creation of the *poleis* (Morris, 1986). The arguments that Morris offered to support his thesis are two: firstly, the word *agalma*, which from being a term denoting the 'precious' in the gift exchange tradition of the Homeric society, is transferred in the context of sanctuaries to mean the offering in general from the fifth century onwards (and gradually in modern Greek it came to mean simply the statue); secondly, the inscriptions found in abundance in sanctuaries made sure that the donors' names would be commemorated, serving, that is, the need to impress and to compete, but also to assure the return of the gift.

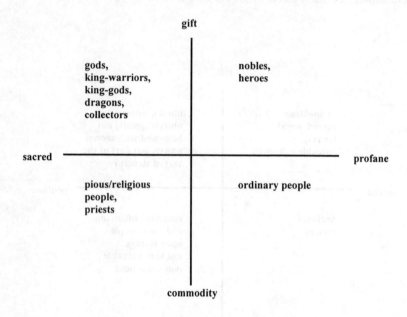

Figure 3.4:   Structuring the parameters of value according to the gift:commodity and sacred:profane axes, III.

Indeed, these are not the only arguments that can be put forward to support this thesis. The building of treasuries within the sanctuary enclosures make the same point and even elaborate it for the purposes of this chapter; we can argue that treasuries are expressions of the tradition of gift exchange, in so far as they are also associated with mythic values and concerns. Treasuries monumentalise the transition from gifts-to-men to gifts-to-gods and bear both the social/political set of values of gift exchange, as well as the mythic parameters of value, i.e. qualities that people cannot comprehend and thus attribute to mythic/religious spheres.

The treasuries were small scale, temple-like buildings, with a porch and an inner room of similar width behind (Plates 3.1 and 3.2). Most (but not all) had porches consisting of two (usually but not always Doric) columns between the forward continuations of the side walls. In Delphi, we have examples of more elaborate buildings, like the Siphnian treasury, which had two Caryatids at the entrance (Plate 3.3).

In Olympia the treasuries stood on a low terrace which was raised above the general level of the sanctuary along its northern end and placed between the temple and the approach to the stadium (Figure 3.5).

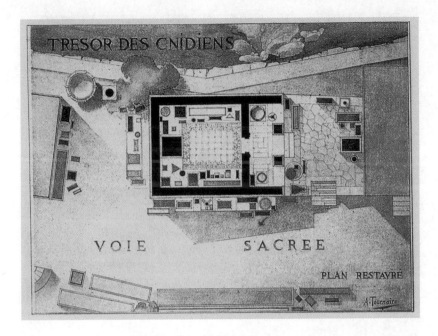

Plate 3.1: Ground plan of the treasury of the Cnidians in Delphi (as reconstructed by Tournaire, 1902).

Archaeologists uncovered remains of twelve treasuries, but Pausanias mentions only ten, possibly because by his time two of them already had been demolished (to make way for a new road leading from the Altis to the Hill of Cronus). Ten of the twelve treasuries have been identified. They are all Dorian (Drees, 1968). The three oldest were dedicated by Greek colonies in the west, two from Italy (Sybaris and Metapontium), one from Sicily (Gela). The other sixth-century examples were built by Epidauros, Cyrene, Selinus and Megara. The row thus was almost completed by the end of the sixth-century; of the later treasuries, that of Byzantium was placed in an apparently vacant space between that of Epidauros and that of Sybaris; the other two (Sicyon and Syracuse) were placed at the beginning of the line. One more dated from the sixth century, the seventh in the sequence from east to west, which is of unknown dedication. Although archaeologists disagree about the identification and the exact date of each of the treasuries,[31] they agree that their date ranges from the seventh to the sixth centuries BCE. The treasuries were depleted by the time Pausanias saw them in 173/4 CE. Then, in the third century CE, when the Altis was reduced in size, they were demolished, and the stones and rubble used to build a new wall to protect the sanctuary against the assaults of the Heruli. Consequently, only the foundations were discovered by archaeologists (Drees, 1968: 120-121), and nothing of their contents.

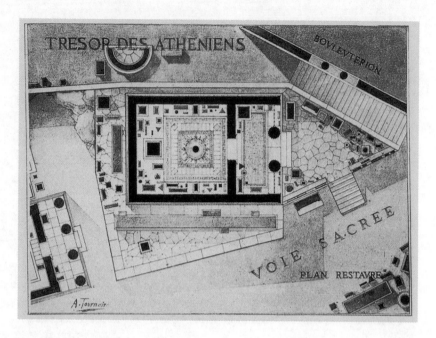

Plate 3.2:   Ground plan of the treasury of the Athenians in Delphi (as reconstructed by
                 Tournaire, 1902).

Ancient sources attest to thirteen treasuries at Delphi: those of Sicyon,
Siphnos, Thebes, Athens, Knidos, Potidaia, Syracuse, Corinth, Brasidas and the
Akanthians, Clazomenai, Massilia and Rome, Agylla (Caere) and Spina.[32]
Within the walled boundary of the sanctuary though, excavators found twenty
three possible treasury foundations, and two more in the sanctuary of Athena
Pronaia. Of these the identification of only one - that of Athens[33] - has never
been challenged or doubted. In antiquity the Delphian treasuries were famous:
they attracted offerings even by 'barbarians', such as the kings of the Lydians,
Gyges and Croesus (Herodotus, I.14; I.50-51; also Parke, 1984). They were
mentioned by Euripides (*Andromache*, 1092-1095), and Strabo (9. 419), who
associates the greatness of the sanctuary with them.   They were built in as a
conspicuous place as possible, along the Via Sacra. They also date to around
the sixth century BCE (Rups, 1986: 92-93) (Plate 3.4 and Figure 3.6).

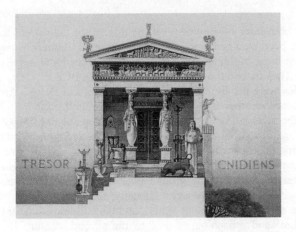

Plate 3.3:   Graphic reconstruction of the façade of the Treasury of Cnidos, with
                  Caryatids, Delphi (after Tournaire, 1902).

Delos is a very well documented sanctuary since many of the sanctuary
inventories were found *in situ*. In a number of these records, buildings called
'oikoi' are listed. Some of them bear the name of cities and seem to be
treasuries. They are the 'oikoi' of the Naxians, of the Karystians, of the
Delians, and of the Andrians (Rups, 1986: 172). An 'oikos' of the Lydians is
also mentioned in inscriptions (Couch, 1929: 70). There are two main
problems related to these buildings and their identification as treasuries: firstly,
since we have here no record like that by Pausanias, the identification of
certain ruins and inscriptions with certain buildings and the determination of
their nature becomes difficult; this is more so since the remainder of the
treasury-like buildings do not bear the names of cities, but are identified
according to their contents or location: the oikos with the paintings by Colotes
(Picard, 1946), or the oikos near the Diadoumenos, and so on. Secondly, the
use of the term 'oikos', instead of treasury, opens up the buildings to other uses
and possible explanations (there is extensive discussion on this by Dyer, 1905).
As far as the contents of these buildings are concerned, the oikos of the
Andrians, according to the inventories, was a mere storehouse (with scrap
metal, utensils, minor votives and building material listed as deposited in it),
rather than a museum as we would imagine. Rups (1986: 180-185) offers two
possible explanations for this: either that the 'oikos' did not belong to the
Andrians any more (the inventories date to the third century BCE) - due to their
losing power - and, therefore, their treasury was used by the sanctuary
authorities as a common store-house; or that all treasuries were like that, but
ancient writers and *periegetes* only mention the most impressive of the items in
them. Dyer (1905) on the other hand, offers another alternative suggesting that
the role of the treasuries was not to hold material, but also - or mainly - to be
the meeting place of citizens of certain *poleis*, in a way to serve as embassies.

Of course, both lines of argument can be true, since the role of the treasuries might have been changed since they were originally built. In any case, it is unlikely that these buildings were temples in the functional sense (Tomlinson, 1976: 74). They date to the seventh or sixth century BCE. [34]

Treasuries were not limited to Olympia, Delphi, and Delos. Archaeologists have uncovered at other sites buildings that share the *templum-in-antis* ground plan, and the size and/or the conspicuous location we usually associate with treasuries, and have accordingly but hesitantly labelled them as such. We lack any background information about these structures, and do not know who dedicated them, or why. Moreover, it would be very daring to associate every building that conforms to the ground plan we have come to associate with treasuries with, indeed, a treasury.[35] Usually, the discussion of the treasuries includes the sanctuary of Hera at Samos, and the buildings that Strabo (14.637) calls 'naiskoi' and arhaeologists date to the seventh century BCE.[36] Also, Nemea[37] (Rups, 1986: 214; Miller, 1978; Miller, 1990), where a row of nine buildings along the south side of the sanctuary have been called 'oikoi', but do not match the typical ground plan; the sanctuary of Artemis Laphria in Kalydon and several small buildings found there; the 'οικήματα' in the Hecatompedon on the Athenian Acropolis (Dinsmoor, 1947); and a building of the sixth century in the sanctuary of Hera at Foce del Sele in Lucania (Rups, 1986: 223).

The archaeological evidence about the contents of the treasuries is so scanty as to be almost non-existent. Very few pieces of information can be confirmed archaeologically. At Olympia, for instance, the foundations of the Sicyonian treasury were strengthened, presumably to support the weight of the bronze *thalamoi* we know it contained (see Pausanias' description); there is a base in the Geloan treasury, presumably for the statues Pausanias reported had been there; another base was found in the Selinountian treasury, possibly intended for the chrycelephantine Dionysos. Similarly, we can be sure about the existence of some objects in the treasuries when they are related to the actual building of it, as, for instance, the linen breastplate dedicated after the battle of Himera, and the statue of Zeus in the Syracusan treasury, since this was built to commemorate that victory (Rups, 1986: 232). But other than that, we can tell with certainty only that which Polemon lists, or Pausanias mentions, was there in the second century BCE, or in 173/4 CE respectively, and not when the treasuries were originally built.[38] Nevertheless, it is not the contents of the treasuries that interest us, at this point at least, but the buildings themselves.

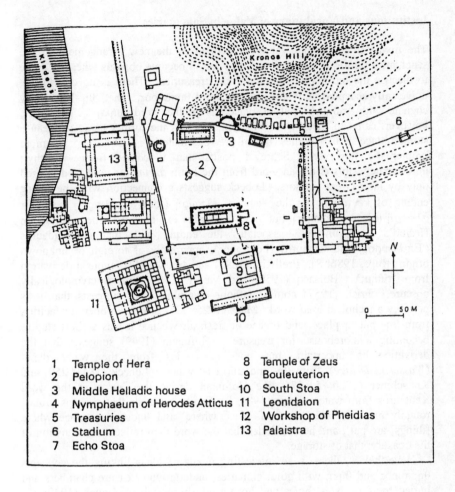

1	Temple of Hera	8	Temple of Zeus
2	Pelopion	9	Bouleuterion
3	Middle Helladic house	10	South Stoa
4	Nymphaeum of Herodes Atticus	11	Leonidaion
5	Treasuries	12	Workshop of Pheidias
6	Stadium	13	Palaistra
7	Echo Stoa		

Figure 3.5:   Ground plan of the archaeological site of Olympia (after Morgan, 1990: 27).

Institutions and Vocabulary of Value in Sanctuaries

The mythical and social values embedded in the new arrangement of the sanctuaries during the early Geometric period become obvious when we come to discuss the terminology used for the treasuries. There is no conclusive, universally accepted derivation for the word θησαυρός. The 'θη–' is clearly cognate with 'τίθημι', 'put or place' as in the word 'θήκη'. The latter, however, came to mean tomb or crypt, whereas the former came to mean a storage place, not of bodies, but of precious material. The '-αυρος' is more problematic however. Schrevel posits that it comes from 'wealthy'; unfortunately, this is a loan word from the Latin *aurum*, or gold, and is used only by later Greek authors. Lobeck suggests a connection with the αυρος ending of κένταυρος or the –ωρε of ἐλπωρή (form of ελπίς = hope) or ἀλεωρή (place of shelter), but gives no further explanation. The scholiast on Hesiod's *Theogony* 832 associates the ending with that of Epidauros (Ἐπίδαυρος) and Galauros (Γάλαυρος), apparently of foreign or unknown origin (Rups, 1986: 8). Prellwitz (1892) and Juret (1942) favour a derivation from 'τίθημι'. Boisacq (1950) and Meyer (1901) find it etymologically obscure. Frisk (1957) comes without etymology, but suggests that it is possibly a technical loan word. Maas (1925: 235) offers 'an open air facility, from θη- put or place, and breeze or fresh air whence it was a short step to becoming a storehouse for treasure'. Hofmann (1949) suggests that the derivation is uncertain, but possibly comes from the water depot (*Wasserniederlage*), from θη- and αὖρα (= water). Lobeck (1843: 259) and Kretschmer (1920: 51-57), like Hofmann derive the -auros in the word Kentauros from water. Rups (1986: 8), finally, suggests that perhaps -αυρος roughly means 'place, place of, place where' and θησαυρός, 'place where [things] are put', and he concludes that the word then reflects one function of the treasury: that of storage.

Nevertheless, there is an interesting nexus of ideas linking the concepts θησαυρός and θήκη with gold, granaries, underground treasure chambers and buried treasure, bees, hives and honey, and immortality. Couch (1929: 13) brings up the possibility that θησαυρός is also cognate with σιρός, granary, and σορός, funeral urn, which would fit the pattern of tombs / gold / honey / immortality (see also Ziehen, 1936). Although there is not a universal agreement on these ideas either (Rups, [1986: 8], for instance thinks that this is the sort of *gestalt* that is fascinating to speculate upon with examples from Greek and Roman literature, but this cannot be proven), the use of the term in literary sources allows us to notice some interesting points. It needs to be said that the same term is used to denote offertory boxes and θησαυροί in the monetary sense, which is not of interest here. Moreover, the term was gradually used to denote storehouses of other, non-valuable objects as well (Couch, 1929). However, there are aspects even in these uses which can be of interest in this discussion.

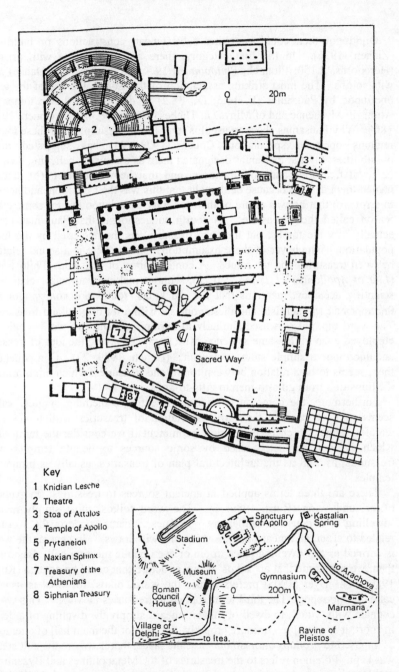

Key

1 Knidian Lesche
2 Theatre
3 Stoa of Attalos
4 Temple of Apollo
5 Prytaneion
6 Naxian Sphinx
7 Treasury of the Athenians
8 Siphnian Treasury

Figure 3.6: Ground plan of the archaeological site of Delphi (after Morgan, 1990: 128).

Θησαυροί then could be either subterranean constructions or buildings (Ziehen, 1936). In the first category, there are associations with prisons (Herodotus, II.150; Plutarch, *Philopoimen* 19 - also the prison of Danae) and with tombs. The most striking association of this sort is the use of the term θησαυρός by Pausanias (II. 16.6; IX. 38.2) to discuss the tholos tombs of Atreus in Mycaenae and of Minyas in Thebes (Ziehen, 1936; also Couch, 1929: 18ff). Why Pausanias chose to use this term for the description of these tombs remains open to speculation. Couch (1929: 23) has suggested three possibilities: (a) that Pausanias designated them as treasuries, believing them to be royal treasuries and nothing more, and that he was correct; (b) that he named them as such because he thought that this was their function, and he was in error; (c) that he was aware of their funerary association but for some other reason called them treasuries. A fourth suggestion is that Pausanias never actually saw the tombs, but the term treasury was the one used by the local population. Whichever of these assumptions is true, there is a sound relation between treasuries and the tombs. A contemporary of Pausanias, Philostratus (*Life of Apollonius of Tyana*, VII.23), without making Pausanias' claims to scientific accuracy, mentions that the old kings' tombs are πολύχρυσοι καί θησαυρώδεις (poluchrisoi and thesavrodeis - with a lot of gold and treasures). The word θήκη also is used similarly to θησαυρός. The two words could be employed even in the same sentence, with θήκη conveying the idea of treasure and θησαυρός a simple store or deposit[39] (Couch, 1929: 27). Consequently, there seems to be a relation between tombs and treasuries, which might mirror the transition from gifts-to-men to gifts-to-gods.

Furthermore, the common motive of protecting something of great value seems to have ensured the early association of treasuries with tombs and temples, a fact which becomes more prominent if we consider the term ναός which is indiscriminately used by some sources to denote temples and treasuries, as well as the architectural plan of treasuries, usually as miniature temples.

There are three terms applied in ancient sources to treasuries: θησαυρός, οἶκος, and ναός (Rups, 1986: 6). The word 'oikos' most simply means 'dwelling' - a house or settlement. Ioannes Zonaras suggests the word is related to εἴκω, and means that to which one withdraws.[40] In general the word is defined as any dwelling place, room or even public meeting hall. Basically, then, we can argue that an 'oikos' is any structure that could be entered (Rups, 1986: 11). Dyer (1905) prefers to use the word 'oikos' for what is usually called a θησαυρός. The third term applied to treasuries is 'ναός'. This word, cognate with 'ναίω', to dwell or inhabit, means simply the dwelling of a deity. In short, it is a temple - or more properly, the cella or the main hall of a temple, as opposed to *pronaos* or *opisthodomos*: the place, that is, where the cult statue was kept. Polemon refers to the treasuries of the Metapontines and Byzantines at Olympia as ναοί, making no distinction between treasury and the Heraion mentioned in the same passage.

Polemon at any rate, or whoever is the author of the book entitled *Of Hellas*, when discussing the temple of Metapontines at Olympia writes as follows: The temple of the Metapontines, in which are 132 silver saucers (*phialai*), two silver wine-jugs, a silver vessel for sacrifice, three gilded saucers. The temple of the Byzantians, in which are a Triton of cypress wood holding a silver *kratanion*, a silver Siren, two silver *karchesia*, a silver cylix, a golden wine-jug, two horns. In the old temple of Hera there are thirty silver saucers, two silver *kratania*, a silver pot, a gold vessel for sacrifice, a golden mixing bowl - a votive offering of the Cyreanaens - a silver saucer. (Athenaeus, *Deipnosophistai*, xi. 480).

Plate 3.4:   Graphic reconstruction of the ancient site of Delphi (as in Tournaire, 1902).

Polemon was a man acknowledged, at least by Plutarch (*Quaest. conv.* V, 675B), as an expert on treasuries. Dyer (1905: 306) therefore reasons that, if this ancient scholar used the word ναός for the Olympian treasuries, it was because this was the term officially used at Olympia. At Delphi, Polemon uses the word θησαυρός for the treasuries in the temenos of Apollo. Pausanias refers to the entire row of buildings, including two treasuries, at the Athena Pronaia sanctuary at Delphi as ναοί, but he seems genuinely to suppose they were all temples: he makes the point that the second ναός, (identified by archaeologists as either treasury 6 or 8), was empty of *agalmata*, or cult statues, as well as *adriantes*, or secular statues. Strabo uses the word 'ναίσκοι' (naiskoi) when he describes the sanctuary of Hera at Samos, but what these actually were remains to be found.[41]

Beyond the architectural similarities between temples and treasuries, it is also their function as θησαυροφυλάκιο (thesaurophilakio) that it is common to both buildings. As has been indicated above, temples were used to store and display vessels and other ceremonial objects, items of historical interest, votive offerings, and art.[42] We know, for instance, that the Erectheion contained gold and silver vessels in the early fourth century, or a folding stool made by Daidalos, the breastplate of Masistios, and the sword of Mardonius in Pausanias' time (I. 27.1; also Arafat, 1992; Harris, 1995). Twenty-five bronze shields for the armoured race and a bronze tripod once used for carrying the victory wreaths were kept in the Temple of Zeus at Olympia, along with the throne of Arimnestos, king of the Etruscans and the first non-Greek to be allowed a dedication at Olympia; and wreaths, presumably of gold copying the wild olive branch wreaths, dedicated by Nero. Strabo informs us that the Heraion of Samos was actually turned into a *pinacotheke* (9.3.7-8). The range of items known to have been in temples is precisely the one we find in treasuries: for instance, at Olympia, the gold and silver vessels listed by Polemon, the bronze discuses of the pentathlon, the linen breastplates from Himera, the Myronian *thalamoi*, the various statues, and so on (Rups, 1986: 243). The Heraion at Olympia as well, whatever its original function in Pausanias' time at least, was a repository for works of art, most of them valuable for their antiquity and their material (Kent Hill, 1944: 354-355; Wernicke, 1894 [see, also Figure 3.7]; Arafat, 1995: 29).

Nevertheless, treasuries were not temples. A temple contained a cult statue and was a religious centre for the community around it. It was build by this community for the god, and bore that god's name. A treasury contained no cult statue, it bore the name of its dedicators, and these did not form part of the surrounding community. A treasury was a votive itself, as well as the container of votives (Rups, 1986: 247). Unlike the other, simpler votives, which one might refer to as 'passive' because, once dedicated, they remained static, treasuries were active, inasmuch as they also contained objects that could be added to or removed (Rups, 1986: 248).

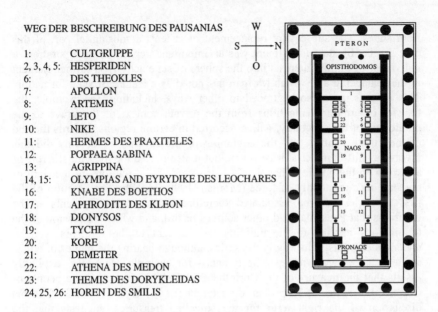

WEG DER BESCHREIBUNG DES PAUSANIAS

1:	CULTGRUPPE
2, 3, 4, 5:	HESPERIDEN
6:	DES THEOKLES
7:	APOLLON
8:	ARTEMIS
9:	LETO
10:	NIKE
11:	HERMES DES PRAXITELES
12:	POPPAEA SABINA
13:	AGRIPPINA
14, 15:	OLYMPIAS AND EYRYDIKE DES LEOCHARES
16:	KNABE DES BOETHOS
17:	APHRODITE DES KLEON
18:	DIONYSOS
19:	TYCHE
20:	KORE
21:	DEMETER
22:	ATHENA DES MEDON
23:	THEMIS DES DORYKLEIDAS
24, 25, 26:	HOREN DES SMILIS

Figure 3.7   Possible arrangement of the statuary decoration in the Temple of Hera at Olympia (after Wernicke, 1894: 114).

The associations of *thesaurus* with religion, the underground and temples, as well as its origins in relation to the protective sacra is most interestingly attested by the transference of religious symbols from temples to treasuries and vice versa. Impressively, the snake is pictured as the guardian of the temple, for the serpent is likewise presented as the protector of the treasury (Eustathius, *Od.* I.357; schol. on Arist. *Lysist.* 759; also discussion and references in Couch, 1929: 67 and Ziehen, 1936).

The political motivation behind the building of treasuries is more or less evident and falls within the generally accepted role of the sanctuaries as arenas for competition - which took every possible form, from literary and music contests to athletic games and arms dedications (Marinatos, 1993; for arms dedications see Jackson, 1991, 1992). According to the sources, treasuries were mainly dedicated as spoils of war (Strabo, 9.3.7-8), to commemorate a victory, or to display a city's prosperity, as in the case of the Siphnian treasury (Pausanias 10.11). Another reason was the display of the piety to the god (Pausanias, 10.11.4). As monuments erected to celebrate the wealth, achievement and civic pride for individual states, they were striking and innovative artistic creations, lavishly decorated,[43] that could not be matched by the buildings related to the sanctuary as a collective entity (Morgan, 1990: 18).

During the eighth century, activity at sanctuaries outside state borders rested primarily upon investment from individuals or prominent families, rather than from states. The subsequent replacement of at least a substantial part of this élite display by state investment was an important step in the incorporation of individual or family interests into the sphere of state activity, a further element in the 'balancing act' which Morgan has noted as a feature of state formation. This process may also be traced in other ways, including, for example, the transfer of armour dedications from the private context of the grave to the public one of the sanctuary, which occurred in certain regions towards the end of the eighth century and the beginning of the seventh. Not only did this involve a shift in material investment, but it also placed the individual's role as a warrior in the public rather than the private domain, reinforcing the right of the state to a monopoly of force (Morgan, 1990: 16-17). The erection of the first treasuries can be associated therefore to these developments. The traditions that Pausanias and other sources record, and which discussion of the terminology applied to the building has brought to the forefront, can be understood in this light. Early treasuries, although bearing the names of cities, are also associated with specific tyrants - for example, Herodotus explicitly asserts that the treasury of the Corinthians at Delphi was not of the people of Corinth, but rather of Kupselos, their tyrant (I.14). Dyer (1905: 310) in his discussion of the right term for the so-called treasuries, suggests that the multiplicity of terms associated with these buildings relates to their role and nature as well as their founders. When they are built, or supposed to be built, by tyrants, they are called θησαυροί, whereas when they are built by cities, they are called 'oikoi'. This point supports the arguments about the mythic origins and associations of treasuries, and about their role as expressions of the destruction of wealth practice, i.e. of gift exchange.

In Olympia, for example, the first treasuries built by Doric colonies of the West and cities of the Isthmus area have to do with the fact that they were small *poleis* with well-defined territories, relatively fewer problems of integration or border definition, and an early transition from the oligarchic government to tyranny. Colonists, in addition, had to ensure their own rights and obligations as citizens, and also to ensure the survival of their colony in alien territory. Furthermore, Olympian treasuries were dedicated mostly by Dorian Greek communities, emphasising the role of the sanctuary at a relatively early stage in its history to this particular group of Greeks. Rups' (1986) practical argument about their need to have a permanent foothold in the sanctuary, or to keep these ritual implements protected from the risk of travelling whenever they were needed, does not alter the thrust of the argument.

Furthermore, the difficulty of explaining why the custom of building treasuries died out, is thus overcome. Tomlinson (1976: 59) has argued that a possible explanation could be the development of sculpture, and the custom of dedicating statuary and other outdoor monuments which is typical of the fifth century BCE and later. A further factor has been suggested in the disappearance of the *polis* system itself: once the old *polis* system was no longer prevalent and the individual treasury-dedicating cities had diminished or disappeared, the treasuries became, in many cases, glorified storage sheds (Rups, 1986: 63). This argument, correct as it is for associating the treasuries with their political role, seems to advocate their rather early decline.[44] But if we conceive treasuries as expressions of the early gift-exchange tradition, and survivals of mythical associations, then their rise and decline, their initial and subsequent names, and their individual or communal role, seem to fit very well together.

Without diminishing the importance of any of the above reasons for the dedications of the treasuries, I would like to argue that the notion of treasury relates to the mythical past and the gift exchange tradition. For political reasons obviously these traditions have changed context, exactly as Morris has argued. I would like to further argue that obviously the valuation parameters of objects remained the same. This is evident not only from the vocabulary, but also from the treasuries themselves: the way they are built, their decoration, their placement in the sanctuary, are all meant to underline the sacred character of the assemblages, to be conspicuous and prominent. The messages they were giving to their contemporaries were undoubtedly about zones of influence, political dominance of certain groups and persons (e.g. Athens was, or wanted to be, the dominant power in the Aegean), and the transition to the city-state; they reflected political instability (as Mauss has argued), and generally were the 'arena of heterogeneity' (in a new context, of course). Simultaneously, they were complying with the mythical and religious tradition not only as far as objects as such are concerned but also in practice, since they employed techniques of competition familiar from the previous traditions. Furthermore, they reassumed (or continue to assume) characteristics like the power of objects to create relations of perpetual dependence, of being in a position to satisfy religious concerns, of objects being inalienable (devoted but not supposed to be parted from their donors), of objects being media of competition exchangeable with morality and divine aid, and so on.

The development of panhellenic sanctuaries after the ninth/eighth centuries BCE initiated a transformation in the tradition of gift exchange: instead of destroying the conspicuous gifts to the gods, 'setting them up high for display' (ανατιθέναι - anatithenai, or ανάπτειν - anaptein) became the norm (Burkert, 1987: 49ff). Herodotus records this transition when he mentions that Croesus, the king of the Lydians, both destroyed artefacts in a conspicuous sacrifice, and offered others for display as a visible perpetuation of his generosity, and, consequently, power:

> Of every kind of appropriate animal he slaughtered three thousand; he burnt in a huge pile a number of precious objects - couches overlaid with gold and silver, golden cups, tunics, and other richly coloured garments - in the hope of binding the god more closely to his interest; and he issued a command that every Lydian was also to offer a sacrifice according to his means. (I. 49).

He also caused the image of a lion to be made of refined gold, in weight some five hundred and seventy pounds. ... This was by no means all that Croesus sent to Delphi; there were also two huge mixing-bowls, one of gold which was placed on the right-hand side of the entrance to the temple, the other of silver, on the left. ... In addition Croesus sent four silver casks, which are in the Corinthian treasury, and two sprinklers for lustral water, one of gold, the other of silver; ... There were many other gifts of no great importance, including round silver basins; but I must not forget to mention a figure of a woman, in gold, four and a half feet high, said by the Delphians to represent the woman who baked Croesus' bread. Lastly, he sent his own wife's necklaces and girdles. (Herodotus, I. 50-51).[45]

The power of the great king of the East is exemplified though the display of his wealth. He could afford to sacrifice huge amounts both of living creatures and artefacts - the list of which sounds very familiar to the students of ancient collections - either by destroying them, or by taking them out of circulation in a conspicuous display, the reasons for which are obvious: to exchange these with the favour of the god, who would thus agree to bestow him his wishes (about sacrifice, see Vernant, 1991a; Detienne and Vernant, 1989; Burkert, 1983; Hubert and Mauss, 1899).

Echoes of this tradition survive in tragedy as well. The motif of the virgin, herself an *agalma*, offered as a sacrifice to the gods is often present in Greek tragedy; her loss is equated with the waste of precious objects (*agalmata*), a practice which came to be considered impious, since complete destruction was not the best practice for conspicuous consumption anymore. The socially approved practice was to dedicate the *agalmata* to the gods, (*anatithenai*) (Aeschylus' *Agamemnon;* Euripides' *Hecuba;* for the implications of these in tragedy, see Scodel, 1996; Crane, 1993). The issue of display then becomes central to the notion of conspicuous consumption, a fact which eventually influenced collections and their setting.

Naturally, the tradition of gift exchange did not disappear in later periods. Philip's methods of dealing with his subjects, friends and allies complied with it: he continued the practice of offering presents in order to win loyalty, and retain status for himself and his state. Similarly, Alexander was well known for his gifts, and continued this practice, so fitting to monarchs (Mitchell, 1997: 149, nt. 6 and 167ff). Parallel methods are described for the Hellenistic kings: for instance, Ptolemy Philadelphus in Alexandria and Antiochus Epiphanes in Daphne displayed their wealth to demonstrate their power through the material artefacts they possessed (Alexandria, Kallixeinos, FGrHist 627 F2; Frazer, 1972: 231-232; Polybius, 30.25-26). Roman triumphal processions with the plunder from the East were public displays of power. It is from this tradition that the difference between 'good' collections and 'bad' collections stems: the former are the ones where the *agalmata* are properly used to secure communication with the gods, and circulate in the social sphere; the latter involve destruction of objects through improper use, i.e. hiding them in the house.

Both these dimensions are 'mythologised' - and therefore in the myths we find both elements: objects help and reassure interpersonal relations, whereas they also assure, they seal, the mythic character of facts. Consequently, values are parameters of stability, reassurance of the social and individual identity, as well as of the social order and hierarchy.

Notes

1   The first part of the title is inspired by an article written by Gregory (1980).
2   Translated in Austin and Vidal-Naquet (1977).
3   Translated by Knox (1922).
4   Wooden carved statues, see Donohue (1988).
5   See, for instance, Herrmann (1992), Daux and Hansen (1987), Audiat (1933); for a collective bibliography on the ancient treasuries see Østby (1993).
6   See, for instance, Doxiades (1972); Bergquist (1967).
7   A characteristic example is Kent Hill (1944).
8   For example, see Rolley (1977) in FdD; similar publications in the other major series of publications of sites.
9   See, for instance, van Straten (1981; 1990).
10   As we are going to discuss later as well, 'inalienable' things are those from which the owner is not parted even if he gives them away; the very act of giving them away as gifts reassures their continuous presence.
11   This answers the arguments posed by Hooker (1989), who argues that in Homer gift-exchange is just a polite custom, and the phenomenon is not institutionalised as for instance in other epics of later times, like *Beowulf* or *Nibelungenlied*. He bases his argument among others on the lack of reciprocity that he detects in many incidents in Homer. Obviously this is not the case, because the mechanisms of gift exchange are more complicated than the simple equation 'I give, you give' would describe. For a full critique of all the points made by Hooker, see Seaford, 1995: 14-15, nt. 59.
12   For a discussion of the notions of offering, sacrifice and gift, see van Baal, 1976.
13   Other explanations have been offered for the grave goods as well. For example, Rosenblatt et al. (1976: 67-76) suggest that grave-goods serve to 'break ties... and facilitate establishment of new patterns of living' (p. 68). Discussion of the same issue can be also found in Firth (1965: 344-347).
14   Whether it will be statues or plastic frogs that are collected is of minor importance; what is more important is the fact that objects are considered to be in a position to form interpersonal relations, to be vehicles of memory, to have a symbolic value and so on.
15   For a discussion of the role of women as property and in the Homeric gift exchange tradition see von Reden, 1994: 49-55.
16   Translated by Finley, 1979: 120.
17   We see again the origins of a pattern that we will come across further when discussing the attitude towards collectors and collecting. The method of acquisition of the material culture assembled remains of vital importance and determines the acceptance or the denunciation of the collection.
18   The translation of ἐσθλά is from Liddell-Scott, edn 1966, p. 696, s.v. ἐσθλός, -ή, -όν. It is very interesting to note that the one of the translations offered for the word when referring to people is 'morally good'; it would be interesting to associate this with the ideas of the objects being products of noble social interaction, as mentioned earlier.

---

19   For metal-working in Homer see Gray (1954).

20   As in *Od.*, XXI.8ff, where Penelope goes down to the depths of the *thalamos* to find
        among the among riches stored there, the bow to be used in the competition of the
        suitors. Also discussion and description of *thalamos* in *Il.*, VI.288-295 (Hecabe in
        Priam's *thalamos*); XXIV.191-192, 228-235 (Priam fetches precious objects from his
        thalamos); *Od.*, II.337-355 (Odysseus' *thalamos*); XV.99-119 (the *thalamos* of
        Menelaus).

21   For instance, *Od.*, XXIII.41ff. It is interesting to note the role of women: as wealth,
        sacred and connoisseurs' items: this reminds one of more recent collectors, e.g. Lord
        Hamilton; see also Edgar (1997) about collectors in popular fiction.

22   Is it from such kind of associations that passionate collecting, storing, and hiding the
        artefacts of the collection are considered indications of effeminate behaviour? Is it
        from here the collector is in the same part of the equation as women? We are going to
        take up this subject further.

23   Translated by A. T. Murray, in Loeb CL, 1954.

24   Translated by A. T. Murray, in Loeb CL, 1953.

25   Barthes in *Myth Today* undertakes the task of showing how modern society applies
        myths to naturalise socially determined meanings and thereby to eternalise the present
        state of the world in the interests of the bourgeois. Everything which claims to be
        universal and natural turns out to be cultural and historical (Olsen, 1990: 166).

26   Whether we mean the burial of the dead body or the burial of the ashes after the
        cremation of the body. For a discussion of burial customs in Greece see Kurtz and
        Boardman (1971): 'cremation had been by no means unknown to Greece before this.
        There are a very few possible cremations from the Middle Bronze Age and scattered
        examples from the earlier Mycenaean period. The extensive Mycenaean cemetery at
        Perati has yielded both chamber tombs and cremation graves, some of which can be
        dated by the presence of seal-stones and scarabs.   Cremation was an established
        practice in parts of the Near East and its appearance in Greece in association with
        objects of Levantine origin is not altogether surprising. The introduction of cremation
        to the Greek mainland seems to have been gradual. At Argos, Perati, in the Athenian
        Kerameikos and on the island of Salamis some cremation was practised concurrently
        with inhumation without any apparent distinction rites. The association of cremation
        graves with eastern trade has been noted and links with Troy VI have been suggested.
        It is however important to bear in mind that at approximately the same time
        cremations were replaced with inhumation in barrows throughout central Europe'
        (1971: 25-26).

27   Pausanias, 2.3.11; also Vernant, 1983: 172-173, nts. 147-148.

28   For the motif of the hero or hero-god who was exposed as a child and the objects that
        were left with him, see Huys, 1995, esp. pp. 198ff.

29   For the significance of tripods see Benton (1934-1935), Schweitzer (1971), Snodgrass
        (1980), and Rolley (1977), where also there is a bibliographic review of the subject.

30   Nagy (1981) in a very interesting article on the deceptive gift in the Greek mythology,
        considers the myth of Persephone and Demeter, and argues that Persephone has in the
        myth the status of a gift, that creates obligations and relationships between the
        celestial and the chthonic realms, between Zeus and Hades. Demeter, on the other
        hand, is a giver of gifts and a gift herself, that makes people obligated and initiates a
        relationship between people and the goddess, which she receives through the
        establishment of her cult (1981: 197-198).

31   Dörpfeld dates the treasuries at Olympia in part using a system based on the height of
        the ground level beneath their foundation, using the east stylobate of the temple of
        Zeus as zero level (Rups, 1986: 20). By applying these criteria, Dörpfeld suggests the
        order in which the Olympic treasuries were built: XII (ca. 610-600); X; XI (last
        quarter of the sixth century); VII, VI, and V (just before 550); IX (late sixth century),

IV (shortly after 550); II (480), III, and I (Rups 1986: 21). Mallwitz (1961; 1972), finally, bases the dating of the treasuries on archaeological and stylistic grounds. The oldest would also seem to be the largest: those of Sybaris (V), Metapontium (X), and Gela (XII), in the first half of the sixth century. The second group is composed of smaller buildings: the proto-Sicyonian treasury, and those of Epidamnos (III), Selinous (IX), and Cyrene (VI or VII); the roof terracottas assigned to these buildings date them to between 540 and 520. At the end of the sixth century comes the treasury of Megara (XI), while those of Syracuse (II) and Byzantium (IV) were probably built in the beginning of the fifth century, as was the second Sicyonian treasury (I) (Rups, 1986: 21-22).

32   Sikyon: Pausanias 10.11.1; Polemon (ap. Plutarch *Quaest. Conv.* 675 B)- Siphnos: Pausanias 10.11.2; Herodotus 3.57- Thebes: Pausanias 10.11.4; Diod. Sic. 17.10.5-Athens: Pausanias 10.11.4; Xenophon *Anab.* 5.3.5- Knidos: Pausanias 10.11.3-4-Potidaia, Syracuse: Pausanias 10.11.4- Corinth: Pausanias 10.13.5-6; Herodotus 1.14, 50, 51; 4.162; Plutarch, *De Pyth. Orac.* 399F, 40F; *Sept. Sap. Conv.* 164A- Brasidas and the Akanthians: Plut., *De Pyth. Orac.* 400F, 401D; *Lys.* 1.18.3- Klazomenai: Herodotus 1.51- Massilia and Rome: Appian 2.8, Diod. 14.93- Agylla (Caere) Strabo 5.220- Spina: Strabo 5.214, Polemon (ap. Athenaeus 606 B), Pliny, *HN*, III.129.

33   The Athenian treasury has been reconstructed and now has a prominent place in the ancient site (Bommelaer, 1991). It is a small Doric building, built at about the turn of the sixth century as an offering to Apollo in gratitude for victory (which victory depends on the precise date of the building, which in its turn depends on the subjective evaluation of its architectural forms and the carvings of its metopes; either the double victory over Chalkis and Thebes in 506, or, more likely, the battle of Marathon and the resounding defeat of the Persians in 490). The building as it now stands is reconstructed, mostly from the original material which was discovered by the French excavators of Delphi, scattered over the hillside below. It is interesting that Athens was able to achieve such a dominant position for its treasury; since it was built after the downfall of tyranny, and at a time when Kleisthenes was either in control of Athens himself or had died only recently, this might bear out the stories of the influence he had secured there. The present dominance of the Athenian treasury is enhanced by its relative completeness; in the sixth and fifth centuries many others were built, of which only the foundations survive *in situ*. Of these only reconstructions on paper are possible. The Athenian treasury would have been much more crowded in by those other treasuries in antiquity; nevertheless, its position is an excellent one (Tomlinson, 1976: 67).

34   The oikos of the Karystians could have been built either before the Persian wars or after 480 BC (see Rups, 1986: 186 for discussion).

35   Indeed it would take another book to examine the buildings uncovered in ancient sanctuaries and associate them with treasuries.

36   Walter (1976) disagrees with this identification, whereas Kyrieleis (1993: 133) supports it.

37   Marchand (in Miller,. 1990: 117ff and 160ff) suggests that there are similarities in the arrangement and building plan of the treasuries with those at Olympia, but the evidence for other uses of the buildings is stronger: therefore, she suggests that they were embassies, meeting halls, and so on. She thus confirms the ideas presented by Dyer (1905).

38   The main methodological issue which emerges when we discuss this issue relying on Pausanias, Strabo or Polemon, is that we 'reconstruct' ancient sanctuaries as they were centuries after the original depositions of the offerings. Consequently, what we are dealing with is the sanctuaries as they were from the third century BCE to the second century CE - (from Polemon to Pausanias respectively). Nevertheless, this does not change the argument of this thesis, mainly because it is based on the concepts

more than the actual findings; in other words, the argument is not to prove that certain objects were appreciated during certain periods, but only that the echo of the gift tradition determined appreciation during subsequent periods as well.

39   For a detailed discussion of the subject and references in ancient authors, see Couch, 1929: 26ff.

40   Oikos seems to be cognate with the old Indic 'vicati' and Avestan 'vissiti', 'to go in' or to 'enter' (Rups, 1986: 11)

41   See note 14 above.

42   The discussion of the material wealth stored in actual sanctuaries is beyond the scope of this chapter (and this thesis), whose aim is not to offer a complete listing of the contents found in sanctuaries during excavations, or known to be there through the literary sources.   For detailed accounts of the contents/offerings in specific sanctuaries, see for example Harris (1995), Linders (1972 and 1975), IDélos (1972; 1926; 1929; 1935).

43   Many treatises have been written on the symbolic and other meanings of the decoration of treasuries. See for instance Brinkmann (1994) for the frieze of the Siphnian treasury at Delphi; also FdD series, and many articles published in different academic journals. For a bibliography see Rups (1986). Almost all attempts to analyse the selection of the subjects favour a political explanation.

44   The intention of Rup's thesis was to gather the evidence on treasuries into a convenient form so that conclusions could more easily be drawn, and to provide some insight into these so-called treasury buildings. In order to do this, he examined the archaeological, architectural and inscriptional evidence, the extant literary sources, and, in so far as it was relevant, the historical context of both the buildings themselves and those who dedicated them (Rups, 1986: 2). Furthermore, Rups limited his study to the remains of treasury buildings in Olympia, Delphi, and Delos, whereas he mentions the ruins of a few other sites, where we can talk about treasuries with some reasonable certainty. The reason for this limitation is that, as Rups explains, although there are remains of buildings elsewhere which conform with the ground plans to the treasury patterns, the information we have is not enough to include them as treasuries with certainty. Nevertheless, this does not limit the scope of the present discussion. Rups' work is interesting as being a collective approach to the treasury building, but it still leaves a lot to be desired. Besides other, mainly methodological shortcomings, the conclusions that he reaches, i.e. that 'a treasury is not only a building to hold votive, it is itself a votive, dedicated as simpler votives were, by individuals or by states' (p. 255), is only partially satisfactory. Furthermore, although he discusses in detail the literary sources and posits interesting questions related to the motives behind the building of treasuries and the dedications, he fails to put the questions into a wider context.

45   Translated by A. de Sélincourt, revised by A. R. Burn, in Penguin Classics, 1972: 58-59.

Chapter 4

The Concept of the Individual as a Cultural Category: its implications in classical collecting

Material symbols, then, can bring private experience into the social world, and social experiences into the private world (Pearce, 1995: 166).

Introduction

Individualism is implicit in any discussion concerning the nature of collecting. Collections are one of the main expressions of the conflict between the cultural structure of commoditization and the individual's attempts to bring a personal value order to the universe of things (Kopytoff, 1986: 76). The application of this principle in the case of classical collecting can be very illuminating.

Individualism is a nineteenth century word (Lukes, 1973: 1), often used to describe preceding phenomena in an attempt to legitimise the value which the term actually refers to and which holds a dominant part in Western thought. Its origins are usually sought in the ancient Greco-Roman world - the absolute source of legitimisation of the West and the origin of the majority of Western values and ideas. Thus, we often come across different versions concerning the 'rise of individualism'.[1] The individual

> was discovered by the lyric poets, we are told; or in Athens, at the end of the fifth century; or by Plato, with his portrait of Socrates; or in the Hellenistic age; or by the Roman poets; or by the Antonines; or by Augustine. Perhaps he had been there all the time, lurking in Homer's Achilles and Odysseus. Still, he had evidently fled away again by the early Middle Ages, only to be rediscovered first in 1050-1200; then, according to Burckhardt's famous analysis, in Renaissance Italy; then, again in the sixteenth, or seventeenth, or eighteenth centuries. (Pelling, 1990: v).

In each of these cases a different phenomenon is described and a different set of values is implied. Historical scholarship often confounds the social acknowledgment of individuals and concern with their well being, with the appreciation of individual values more than the collective ones (Martin, 1994: 119). The same term is also used indiscriminately to denote self-consciousness, introspection, or awareness of decision-making and responsibility (Pelling, 1990: v). Therefore, searching for the origins of individualism means first of all defining the term.

During the Hellenistic[2] period the social and political frame, along with the conditions of artistic production and consumption, changed and a new cultural context was created. Among the phenomena which played a prominent role in the development of this 'new culture', a distinct place is occupied by the genesis of art theory and collecting. According to the traditional approach, which suggests that the 'rise of individualism' coincides with the origins of collecting, the argument would run as follows: in the city-state identity was collective and, therefore 'collections' were held in public places, sanctuaries, whereas when identity became a matter of the individual (due to the socio-political changes resulting from Alexander's conquest of the East), the first private, or privately initiated, collections were formed.[3]

The traditional approach regarding individualism has been based upon arguments deriving from philosophy, religion and the artistic expression of the period, mainly sculpture, portraiture and biography. Attempts to reconsider the issue of individualism (and therefore for our purposes to put on a different basis the above argument regarding collecting) are not new, although in their majority they are not as explicit as the article by Luther Martin entitled 'The anti-individualistic culture of Hellenistic ideology' (1994). He employs arguments from the same fields in order to argue that the conclusion that individualism is a characteristic phenomenon of the Hellenistic age is arbitrary, and was coined along with the term 'individualism' itself during the nineteenth century, exactly when the 'Hellenistic period' was 'discovered' by historians.[4] He thus attributes the issue to a mis-reading of ancient data, due to the common phenomenon of employing and projecting contemporary ideas to the past.

The present enquiry supports neither the traditional nor Martin's approach. It will be a critical discussion of the arguments offered by both approaches in the light of definitions of the individual and individualism given by historical anthropology. The fact that private collections were first formed during this period, means undoubtedly that the individual has 'won' (in a way) the conflict with society,[5] and that is now in a position to enhance the value of objects by adding elements of personal valuation in the social order of things. On the other hand, and by using information deriving from collections (objects in them, the reasons behind their formulation and so on), I would like to argue that the recent assertion by Goldhill (1994: 198) that during the Hellenistic period the frame of the fifth-century *polis* was replaced by the frame of the Museum within the Alexandrian city-scape, even though asserted in connection with the artistic production, acquires an even wider application. At least the dominant classes of the Hellenistic world, which have to be identified with the 'collecting classes',[6] needed to be, and were, members of a wider community, the community of the (Alexandrian) 'Museum'. This leaves us with a double-edged issue: individualism, on the one hand, is a philosophical, social and economic issue, which according to the ideas of Kopytoff and other social anthropologists as well as collecting theorists, forms the backbone of collecting. On the other hand, collecting can, and must, be used as an argument toward the definition of individualism and phenomena of identity during the Hellenistic and early Roman periods. This chapter will argue that collecting activities are not necessarily and in a monolithic way associated to individualistic concepts; on the contrary, ancient writers seem to suggests an attempt by the ancient collectors to be 'rationally' and 'not individualistically' predisposed against collections, as well as an effort to enter through them to a social group, to which they may, or may not, actually belong.

The discussion will begin by comparing and contrasting definitions of 'individualism' given by historians and anthropologists, in order to reach a working definition of the term. Then follows a presentation of the common beliefs about the individualistic character of the Hellenistic period, and a critical discussion of each category of arguments, i.e. philosophical, moral and political thought, religion, and material culture. Finally, some conclusions are drawn together regarding the nature of collecting during the Hellenistic and early Roman periods.

Definitions of Individualism

As Pelling (1990: v-vi) has asserted, everything depends on what we mean by the terms 'individual' and 'individualism'. Many attempts have been made by scholars of different disciplines to define them before they express any ideas about them, and we have to start by presenting some of those definitions, involving assumptions about the early origins of the phenomenon. An 'analytic' definition is given by Pelling (1990: v-vi) who suggests that the term 'individual' may refer to many different notions (he lists five): it may refer to self-consciousness, 'a clear awareness of one's own or others' identity as something which will involve definitions of social role, status, and responsibilities, but - at least in the Greek and later European context - will not be *exhausted* by those definitions'. It may refer to 'something a little different, more clearly introspective: a person's capacity to describe or analyse psychic events, or simply a readiness to accept some sort of "responsibility" for those decisions, and a normal obligation to bear the consequences'. A third option would be to 'be concerned with describing accurately the characters of oneself or others.' The term may refer to 'mark how a figure belies normal expectations - a process of "individuation"'. Finally, one may mean 'the discriminating self-awareness, one's duty or license to be true to oneself, to follow and realise the implications of one's character rather than acquiesce in society's fixed norms of conduct - a form of "individual*ism*"' (Pelling, 1990: v-vi, emphasis in the original).

Dumont (1982: 2) adopts a sociological approach and defines 'individual' as both an object and a value:

> Comparison obliges us to distinguish analytically these two aspects: one, the *empirical* subject of speech, thought, and will, the individual sample of mankind, as found in all societies, and, two, the independent, autonomous, and thus essentially non-social *moral* being, who carries our paramount values and is found primarily in our modern ideology of man[7] and society. (emphasis in the original).

Starting from this definition and with reference to the latter (rather than the former) aspect, Dumont defines 'individualism' as having a double meaning: first, as opposed to 'holism', i.e. as the ideology that valorises the individual and neglects or subordinates the social totality. 'Where the individual is a paramount value I speak of individualism. In the opposite case, where the paramount value lies in the society as a whole, I speak of holism.' (Dumont, 1982: 2). Secondly, individualism in the above sense is a major trait in the configuration that constitutes modern ideology, which Dumont defines as individualistic, 'individualistic ideology' or 'individualism' (Dumont, 1983: 264).

In order to trace the origins of individualism and explain the transition from holism, i.e. the appreciation of the *empirical* individual, to individualism, i.e. the *approbation* of the particularity of its unique existence, Dumont borrows a hypothesis that derives from his study of Indian society (1970). He thus suggests that there are two opposite forms of the notion of the individual. The first is the individual-outside-the-world, in the sense of the Indian renouncer, who could achieve individual spirituality only by leaving the community and renouncing the world. The second is the individual-in-the-world in the sense of the modern person who affirms and lives his individuality within the world, and the community where individuality is a dominant value (Dumont, 1983: 35). The extra-worldly individual, Dumont further suggests, is the first step toward the worldly individual. Therefore, Dumont attributes to Christianity the genesis of individualism in the West, since he suggests that it was its conception of 'man' as an extra-worldly individual, an individual-in-relation-to-God, that became the starting point for the understanding of the individual as a worldly conception. Yet, he argues, since Christianity could not succeed in the long run unless it had firm grounding in the pagan past, the extra-worldly individual was a notion already known to Hellenistic philosophy; it was the notion of the 'sage' that Hellenistic philosophy had introduced. Although this idea might seem to contradict well-established conceptions about the rise of the phenomenon of individualism, it only modifies them. It is a well-known and well-argued issue that the transition from the philosophy of Aristotle and Plato to the Hellenistic philosophy shows a great gap, i.e. 'the surge of individualism'. The great difference is the transition from the idea of self-sufficiency as an attribute of the *polis*, to self-sufficiency as an attribute of the individual person. Dumont further argues that although the middle and later Stoa assumed heavy duties in the world for their followers, the primary idea was the self-sufficiency of the individual, even if he acts in the world. The genesis of this philosophical individualism is not attributed by Dumont to the destruction of the *polis* and the unification of the world under Alexander, since he postulates that 'this tremendous historical event can explain many traits, but not, to me at least, the emergence of the individual as a value, as a creation *ex nihilo* (Dumont, 1982: 4). The reason has to lie with philosophy itself:

> Not only have Hellenistic teachers occasionally lifted out of the Presocratic elements for their own use, not only are they heirs to the Sophists and other currents of thought that appear to us as submerged in the classical period, but philosophical activity, the sustained exercise of rational enquiry carried out by generations of thinkers must by itself have fostered individualism, because reason, universal in principle, is in practice at work through the particular person who exercises it, and takes precedence, at least implicitly, over everything else. (Dumont, 1982: 5).

The Hellenistic philosophers set a superior ideal, that of the 'sage' against man as a 'social being' as presented by Plato and Aristotle. Obviously, the vast political change and the universal empire that was created undoubtedly favoured this movement. Dumont also suggests that there might be influences, direct or indirect, from the Indian model - although the data that would prove such an influence are insufficient.

Foucault (1986: 41-42), on the other hand, distinguishes three notions in order to describe 'individualism':

> (1) the individualistic attitude, characterised by the absolute value attributed to the individual in his singularity and by the degree of independence conceded to him vis-à-vis the group to which he belongs and the institutions to which he is answerable; (2) the positive valuation of private life, that is the importance granted to family relationships, to the forms of domestic activity, and to the domain of patrimonial interests; (3) the intensity of the relations to self, that is, of the forms in which one is called upon to take oneself as an object of knowledge and a field of action, so as to transform, correct, and purify oneself, and find salvation.

Although these three notions can be interconnected, their connection is neither constant nor necessary. Foucault suggests that the presence of only one, or even two, of them does not necessarily mean that 'individualism' is a dominant value.   Therefore, when it comes to discuss the origins of individualism he argues that in a traditional military society, for instance, the warrior is invited to assert his self-worth by means that set him apart from the group to which he belongs.   Alternatively, there are societies to which private life is highly valued but the relations to self are largely undeveloped.   Finally, there are societies, such as the early Christian society, where although the relations to self receive extreme interest, the same does not happen with the values of private life and the person's independence from the group to which he belongs.   When it comes to the Hellenistic and Roman periods, then, Foucault suggests that, although civic and political activity might have changed their form, they nonetheless remained an important part of life, especially for the upper classes.   Existence was led in public in ancient societies, and everybody was situated within a strong system of local relationships, family ties, economic dependencies and relations of patronage and friendship (Foucault, 1986: 41).

Based on the ideas of both Foucault and Dumont, Vernant discusses the role of the individual within the city-state in his article (originally published in French in 1987; English translation 1991b), where he proposes and applies a different classification, within the perspective of historical anthropology:

> (a) The individual *stricto sensu*. His place and role in his group or groups; the value accorded him; the margin of movement left to him; his relative autonomy with respect to his institutional framework. (b) The subject. When the individual uses the first person to express himself and, speaking in his own name, enunciates certain features that make him a unique being. (c) The 'ego', the person. The ensemble of psychological practices and attitudes that give an interior dimension and a sense of wholeness to the subject. These practices and attitudes constitute him within himself as a unique being, real and original, whose authentic nature resides entirely in the secrecy of his interior life. It resides at the very heart of an intimacy to which no one except him can have access because it is defined as self-consciousness. (1991b: 321).

In order to discuss the first of the above categories, he further delimits it as: 1) the individual's valorisation, in his singularity; 2) the individual and his personal sphere: the domain of his private life; and 3) finally, the emergence of the individual within social institutions that, by their very functioning, afford him a central place from the classical period onward (Vernant, 1991b: 322).

Vernant takes as a starting point Dumont's arguments and his suggestion that traces of individualism exist already in the Greek world and the Greek philosophy; he therefore examines the city-state in order to locate exactly those traces and disprove the validity of Dumont's distinction.   Following his definition he examines the Greek city-state and the role of the individual within it, only to reach the conclusion that in Greece the individual had a role, and a very prominent one, but it was not conceived as extra-worldly. He recognises the Hellenistic era as the period when a major change occurred regarding the role and value attributed to the individual, but he still denies any relation with the extra-worldly type.

Finally, Morris (1994) giving an anthropological perspective, distinguishes between three inter-related but distinctly different conceptions, to form the core of individual /individualism. He asserts that the term 'person'[8] should be used to refer to several conceptions. Firstly, the individual as a human being (as a generic human), meant to derive from empirical, rather than cultural knowledge.

> The person as a human being thus represents a realist perspective on the world shared by all humans: it is part of the basic or 'first order' cognitive dispositions which conceives of living beings in the world as material 'essences' with underlying natures. Such dispositions are prior to, and form the basis or grounding of social representations. (1994: 11).

This first category coincides with Dumont's understanding of the individual as 'object'. Secondly, there is the individual as self, that is, as a psychological concept.[9] Although the category of self is a universal category, it acquires its unique character within a specific social context, and has been the subject of a vast literature in both philosophy and psychology. 'The self is in essence an abstraction, created by each human person, and refers to a process rather than an entity' (Morris, 1994: 12). Finally, there is the individual as a 'cultural category', expressed in a specific community, in its ritual context and ideological construction. This category owes a lot to the early writings of Mauss (1979), and Hallowell (1953), who distinguish between social praxis and cultural representations, as well as between the self, seen as a self-aware, socially constituted human agent at both a generic and a psychological level, and the person, understood as a cultural conception (category, according to Mauss) of a particular community.[10] However, it needs to be noted that since cultural representation is embedded in the practical constitution of everyday social and material life, it is misleading to see cultural classifications as separate from lived experience (1994: 12). In order to make his argument clear, Morris brings as an example the case of a society based on slavery. There, a class of people, although treated as human beings at an empirical level, are defined as property, not as persons.

Hellenistic Culture and Individualism

Ever since its invention in the nineteenth century, the Hellenistic period has been characterised as the period when individualism and cosmopolitanism go hand in hand (Pollitt, 1986). Both these tendencies are interpreted as a by-product of the conquests of Alexander and the consequent political internationalism, which generated the conditions for the failure of the city-state. 'Man as a political animal', Tarn (1952: 79) suggests, 'a fraction of the *polis*, or self-governing city-state, had ended with Aristotle; with Alexander starts man as an individual'. Therefore, in order for this individual to meet the needs of belonging and of acquiring new standards by which to lead its life in a changing world, there had to be two developments, it is alleged: the philosophies of conduct, on the one hand, which aimed toward 'an inward search in the private recesses of human mind and personality', and thus to make self-sufficiency an attribute of the individual instead of *polis*, and the notion of human brotherhood, on the other, that is 'an outward search toward *oikoumene*' (Pollitt, 1986: 7).

Scholars have elaborated their theses for and against this basic argument. Griffiths, for instance, supports this approach, and elaborates it by suggesting that a sense of personal insignificance engendered by the conquests of Alexander had as a result to throw 'the citizens back on their own spiritual resources so that their concerns as individuals counted correspondingly by more' (1989: 238). Pollitt supports this and adds: 'in the Hellenistic world no standard of society, even of an utopian society, was more important than what the individual did, thought and experienced' (1986: 7-8). Green also agrees with this: 'cities and empires had become too vast and heterogeneous to give adequate psychological support to inheritors of the old, local *polis* tradition: their society was no longer integrated or manageable.' Therefore, the individual 'was thrown back on himself' (1990: 587).

In contrast to the above, more recent scholarly work attempts to disprove this approach and to replace it with a less schematic and more realistic one. Most explicitly Martin (1994), but also Foucault (1986), Gill (1995) and others, suggest that far from being 'individualistic', the attitude of the Hellenistic era, never stopped being influenced by the communal ideals, which are characteristic of the Greek thought. Their argument is three-fold: political, ethical and methodological, exactly as the 'traditional' argument is structured. In the political sphere, it is suggested that although the political and social changes were significant, the ideal of living within a community and in mutually beneficial relationships was not replaced, either in the political or in the ethical theory. Greek thought continues to hold this idea even when it faces the 'failure' of particular types of community; it only replaces those with ideal communities, since man can live only within a communal schema. As far as the ethics are concerned, it is argued that the internalisation of ethical attitudes and ideas, which the traditional approach equated exclusively with Hellenistic philosophy, is as old as Homer and had been a recurrent theme in Greek philosophy from his time onwards (Gill, 1995: 2-3). Martin emphatically suggests that 'although the cultural transformations that marked a Hellenistic age may have occasioned a heightened awareness of the empirical individual, any valuing of such an existence ... was imputed by the modern values of a nascent historical discipline which periodized a Hellenistic era in the first place' (1994: 121).

Notions of 'Individualism' in Hellenistic Philosophy: Community vs. Individual

We are now going to discuss the doctrines of the major Hellenistic philosophical schools, namely Cynicism, Stoicism and Epicureanism, in order to argue that despite the common view that these did advocate 'individualism', this is not as straightforward as has been suggested. The major political changes that the fourth century brought to the Hellenic world influenced social and philosophical beliefs, and altered the relation of the citizens to their societal structures, the old city-state (*polis*). Nevertheless, my argument continues, they did not result in 'individualism'; only in alternative societal structures, that the philosophical thought of the period was willing to fortify in ideological terms. In this section, we are going to focus on the notion of the individual living within or outside the community; then we will discuss the moral and ethical aspect of individual as this is presented in Hellenistic philosophy.

According to the traditional approach, Hellenistic individualism is mainly embodied in the Cynic philosophers, who had as their goal the achievement of *autarkeia* (self-sufficiency), through a life of discipline and austerity. For this they did not hesitate to 'drop out' of society (Pollitt, 1986). Although the model of the Cynic philosopher was too extreme for the average person in the Hellenistic era, there have been exemplars of this type like, for instance mercenaries (Griffith, 1968). The other dominant philosophies of the period have also maintained an individualistic perspective. Both Epicureanism and Stoicism aimed at the satisfaction of practical needs and the happiness of the individual. Furthermore, they both treated the universe as composed of something material, and adopted physical explanations: Epicurus that of Democritus, and Zeno[11] that of Heraclitus. The concept of 'cosmopolitanism'[12] was also grasped by them. The term itself was introduced by the Cynics, whereas Zeno's ideal state was characterised by its universalism (Pollitt, 1986; Tarn, 1952: 327-328; Bryant, 1996).

Before we start discussing these traditional arguments, we should note that there is something Socratic about the Hellenistic ethics, and this is not only the doctrinal inheritance - although this is central in the case of the Stoics. More than this, it is the particular idea about what ethics should be concerned with: the removal of fear and uncertainty, the ordering of priorities in life and around the soul's health, the question of convention, the 'cultivation of the self' (Long, 1993: 141). The common emphasis of all Hellenistic philosophers on an alternative world and on the acquisition of a new self is characteristic of this same attitude. The happy and virtuous self that Hellenistic ethics attempt to define is at its most distant from ordinary attitudes and satisfactions in the area of needs and motivations (Long, 1993: 150). Therefore, it seems possible to argue that the modern anthropologists' conception of self and its interest and needs as a social construct is not that far away from the Hellenistic philosophers. Indeed, it seems clear that they have a strong urge towards this notion. Hellenistic philosophers aimed to transfer the authority to decide on the *telos* and the goals towards it, from the city/community to the person (Hossenfelder, 1986: 247). Possibly the example of the Hellenistic monarchs and generals, together with the vicissitudes that these figures experienced, helped to advocate the alternative paradigm, the transfer of external characteristics, such as power, leadership, control, to the inner self. Its power now consisted of 'an inversion of monarchical appurtenances, minimal possessions, minimal material needs, hierarchical subordination of conventional interests to a controlling rational outlook, and adaptability' (Long, 1993: 152).

Cynicism is usually considered the protagonist in the play of the rise of individualism during the Hellenistic age. Although not a philosophical system, but rather a practical approach to life, it provided the basic framework for the 'invention' of the individual as a separate entity, whose well-being in accordance with his natural endowments, should be the major aim of life. Cynics maintained that the virtue of the wise man makes him self-sufficient (for the possessions of everyone, even the gods, belong to him - Diogenes Laertius, 5.11a). Therefore, they rejected all conventions of civic and social life and pursued a bohemian lifestyle. The influence of the self-sufficiency doctrine has been pervasive in Hellenistic ethics, and, along with the interest in the 'nature' that the individual shares with humanity at large, they formed the two major characteristics of the Hellenistic philosophy. Stoics, especially, have structured a central part of their ethical philosophy around these two major themes. 'The city thus recedes in the background, and man's inner resources and his rationality can provide the basis for a tranquil and happy life' (Sedley, 1980: 5; also, Long, 1974: 4).

Yet Cynics' emphasis on the individual does not lead to concern about his personal value or rights as such. The sage, being free from his community, holds in contempt those who are weaker than him, or who still hold some hope for the community, and he is not interested in advocating any general theory of rights or of value. In other words, the individual in this sense presents great similarities to the extra-worldly model, as defined by Dumont. Furthermore, Cynicism became fashionable during the middle part of the fourth century, well before the dawn of the Hellenistic age. Therefore, although its influence in Stoicism, Epicureanism and Scepticism should be taken seriously into account, it should not be considered as directly relevant (in the reason-result sequence) to the genesis of individualism (Long, 1974: 3; Rist, 1982: 147-148).

Stoic philosophy, on the other hand, introduced the understanding of the empirical individual, and initiated what is called the 'philosophy of the self' (although it did not lead to an ethical individualism). Stoic philosophy preserves the Cynic principle (which has a Socratic origin) that virtue is self-sufficient and the only source of happiness, whereas it found an integral role for social values, such as prosperity, public honour, health which have been regarded as the raw material for the correct actions (*kathekonta*) out of which a virtuous disposition can be achieved (Sedley, 1980: 7; Bryant, 1996: 427ff).

Central to the Stoic philosophy of the self is the idea of 'representation' (*phantasia*), which means the way the individual human beings perceive themselves, or what it is for them to have the first person outlook on the world, or a first-person experience. In this sense, self is something essentially individual - a viewer and interlocutor uniquely positioned, a being who has interior access of a kind that is not available to anyone else (Long, 1991: 103). The term '*phantasia*' (representation is only one of the words that we can use to translate it[13]) was firstly introduced as a Platonic term of art meaning the different perception that one and the same entity can generate to different observers. *Phantasiai* therefore are individual experiences, appearances to individuals (Long, 1991: 104). Consequently, all post-Platonic philosophers who wished to refer to an individual experience already had the term to do so: *phantasia*. In Stoicism this term acquires a much greater role than it had in Platonism. According to the Stoic philosophers, it is one of the two main 'forces', together with impulse (*horme*) that move man and animals alike in the world (Origen, *de Principiis* III.1.2-3; see also Watson, 1994: 4772ff).

Stoics analyse the pre-rational impulse in terms of the idea of what may be called a 'subjective viewpoint'. This has two aspects: firstly, the viewpoint is *subjective* in the sense that it is based on the agent's awareness of its own self. Hierocles, a Stoic of the Roman Imperial period, argues at length that the first object of an animal's (man included) *aisthesis* is not anything external to its body, but the animal itself. Self-awareness, he argues, is the pre-condition of perceiving externals; hence, Stoicism introduces the idea of the empirical individual (and initiates what Mauss and other sociologists or anthropologists argued much later). Secondly, the *viewpoint* is a perspective from which things are seen, i.e. the 'representation' (*phantasia*). Therefore, Stoic analysis of impulse (desire, *horme*) depends on first, the awareness of individual identity and second, the belief about the 'constitution' of the self according to the chosen perspective (Engberg-Pedersen, 1990: 121 and Long, 1991). Thus, any representation becomes part of man's experience, according to whether he gives or withholds his 'assent', which for Stoics is an essential faculty of the human soul (Long, 1991). Man has the right to 'assent', or not, to a decision - and this right resides in the *hegemonicon* (i.e. the governing-principle of the soul), which thus provides the Stoics with the concept of a unitary self, actively engaged as a whole in all moments of an animal's experience (Long, 1974: 171; 1991: 107).

The faculty-assent (*prohairesis*) is the essential self. Epictetus[14] conceives of this as the bearer of personal identity. '*You* are not flesh or hair, but *prohairesis*: if you get that beautiful, then *you* will be beautiful' (III 1.40; emphasis on the translation by Oldfather, 1946). A person's *prohairesis* is the moral character (moral purpose), a function of reason, a state of the soul's 'commanding part'. Yet, since the role of reason is the individual's autonomy and responsibility, Epictetus identifies himself with the practical application of reason in selecting the right goals and values, so as not to extend it beyond control. Thus, Epictetus identifies himself with something personal and personified (Long, 1991).

But the self has certain constrains: the contents of the 'subjective viewpoint' are public and accessible to rational discourse. Although the Stoics stressed so much the notion of self, they did not allot to it any ineradicably subjective content (Engberg-Pedersen, 1990). The Stoic view is that humans are bound to the world and so is human reason. Stoics did not pursue the points leading to a high evaluation of individuality within a particular group as related to the specific nature of the group to which the individual belonged. This interesting implication derives from the fourth of the Stoic *Categories* (Long, 1974), the 'relative disposition', which classifies properties which one thing or animal possesses in relation to something else. In Stoicism, this idea of inter-relation is vital: man needs to be related in a certain way to Nature or God. The Stoic philosophy of Nature provided a cosmic orientation for personal identity, which makes human relationships implicit in life, according to reason: 'The good of a rational being consists in communal association' (V.16) (Long, 1974: 163; also, see Bryant, 1996). Nature unites mankind in a civic association, since it implants an impulse toward familial and social relationships (Cicero, *De Fin.* iii.6; *De Off.* 1.12). This forms the basis of Stoic ethics. Therefore, the starting point for the Stoics is *oikeiosis*, meaning that moral development is the recognition that community life and virtue are pre-eminently things which belong to human nature (Long, 1974: 191). As a result, we cannot fail to notice two inconsistencies here, which are worked by the Stoics: first, the use of nature as both an objective and subjective factor, and second, the rational assent which may give independent decision capability (subjective consciousness), but is objectively determined by the necessary sequence of cause and effect (or *logos*) (Long, 1974: 207).

In Stoic political, but also ethical thinking (it is hard to distinguish), there are two strands, or phases, related to the idea of 'a community of sage'.[15] The first is presented in Zeno's (now lost) *Republic* and suggests - as far as we can say - a radical, 'natural', property-held-in-common society. Although we do not know whether this was an actual political ideal, or the discussion of an utopia, we can rely on the most important and certain thought, that there is real community only among the sages and virtuous people; all the non-wise communities are not real ones (full wisdom meaning sharing the ethics and 'natural' understanding and appreciation of the Stoics). The second strand is far more conventional, and is represented by Cicero (e.g. see *De Officiis*): this suggests that the social and political structures of conventional states constitute the framework in which people can practise the *kathekonta*[16] that provide the means toward full wisdom and virtue. Relevant issues are discussed in Panaetius' theory[17]of four roles (*personae*) which includes the idea that specific people should shape their lives in the light of what is appropriate to their specific talents and interests. But taken in the context of the communal framework, Panaetius' idea does not lead to a more radical ethical individualism, such as that we find in Nietzsche or Sartre,[18] but these ideas ('community of the wise', 'city of gods and humans') figure as normative ideas, providing an objective and ultimate framework to ground ethical life (like Zeno). The idea of benefiting others seems to be standard in both strands, beyond the immediate relations (family, friends and city); but although for the radical strand this is a negation of the social and political structures, in the more conventional it is more a normative ideal (more about Panaetius' theory of the four *personae* in section IX) (Gill, 1995: 58-60).

As a result, we could summarise this brief presentation of the Stoic ideas[19] by saying that Stoics did not pursue the point of seeing grounds for a high evaluation of individuality *within* a particular group. Perhaps, as Rist suggests, the reason is that for the Stoics, as for Plato and Aristotle, 'perfect being is finite being, and a theory that would associate perfection with individual uniqueness might seem to compromise that principle of finitude' (1982: 150).

In Epicurean philosophy human beings are seen as chance products of a world which is itself the mechanical product of atoms moving in an infinite void. Epicurus was a dedicated admirer of Democritus, and it is on his atomic theory that he rests his own. Nevertheless, humans share free will. Although this does not mean that he introduces anything like the modern theories of free will (Annas, 1991), some things do depend on human agents (they are not *eph' hemin* - up to us - they are *para hemas* - depend on us) (Annas, 1991: 90). He uses the term development (*apogegennemenon*) for the way people evolve, and tends to identify the self with development, contrasting it with the 'constitution'. Epicurus argues that people 'advise, combat and reform another, as having the cause in themselves and not only in the original constitution and in the necessity of what environs us and enters into us spontaneously' (LS 20c (2), and in Annas, 1991: 89). Therefore, to the extent that something depends on us, it depends on something developing, self-moving, not merely a series of mechanical responses to stimuli. The way actions depend on us is explained chiefly by our rationality; thus, our actions can be flexible and sensitive to circumstances and hence, allow for the development of dispositions and character to take place (Annas, 1991: 90).

Human agents' morality refers to one goal that we all naturally seek, pleasure. This lies in freedom from anxiety, an end to which all philosophical research must be geared (Sedley, 1980: 9). The Epicurean way of life, therefore, requires an external environment that will be capable of satisfying people's natural and necessary desires of pleasure and freedom from pain. Although he recognises that to a certain extent his contemporary citizens and societies have the accumulated cultural experience, intelligence and wherewithal to secure food and organise security, mainly by legal means, and although they are already utilitarians in their pursuit of aims, misconceptions about what constitutes a pleasurable sentiment and mutual benefit restrict them from having an 'ideal' community (Long, 1986: 313). Epicureans, consequently, founded 'alternative' communities (Epicurus' own Garden was the first), and had the material means to live utterly self-sufficient lives, with their spiritual welfare secured by the master's teaching (Long, 1986: 286). Therefore, Epicurus rejects the idea that a *polis* is essential for human flourishing. Thereby, his ideas were understood to imply that each person is just concerned with himself and consequently, the Epicureans came to be thought of as radical individualists (Long, 1986: 290).

Yet this does not correspond to the truth. Epicureans simply advocate a different, 'alternative' kind of society, and they do not reject it altogether, neither in a moral nor a political respect. Epicureans discuss human individuals in terms of possessing various types of value-producing qualities, but there is a striking lack of concern about what we would call a 'unique' aspect of individuality; in Epicurus' world even gods are numerically different, but qualitatively identical. The question of uniqueness is thus left aside (Rist, 1982: 148).

In political terms, on the one hand, Epicureanism has theories about justice in conventional, non-Epicurean societies. This is reflected in Lucretius' poem (marking the summit of the curve of Epicureanism in the first century BCE) *De Rerum Natura*, where he presents a three-stage development of human civilisation.[20] On the other hand, in the Epicurean communities such as Epicurus' own Garden, all members lived in harmony reassured by the fact that they shared the Epicurean ethical standards of friendship or virtue. As a result, Epicureans, just like one strand of Stoic thought, take the view that the only real kind of community depends on philosophically-based understanding (Gill, 1995: 60; Frischer, 1982). Epicureans thus are very much like the rest of the Greek philosophical schools, at least as far as a communal ideal is advocated, even though they base their community on a very different ground.

To conclude this brief discussion, we should add that Hellenistic philosophy is far from the cultivation of 'individualism', as defined by Dumont, i.e. the approbation of the individual's unique identity and existence in the world. As far as the independence of the individual from the group to which he belongs, (the first category of Foucault), this also remains unsatisfied (only the third category of Foucault is covered). Although the individual should set his own goals, he is not conceived as living outside a community, although the values of the community, and the community itself, has and should be reconsidered. In other words, the individual is conceived of as a person, i.e. as agent-in-society, socially constructed, but in need of reconsidering this society and its values that determine him, and of reshaping them on a philosophical and virtue-defined basis.

Notions of 'Individualism' in Hellenistic Philosophy: ethic philosophy

The second strand of the above argument leads us to enquire about the individual as a moral, ethical agent, with personal responsibility for his *telos*. The traditional approach seems to advocate a developmental process from a relatively primitive understanding of human agency toward a conscious human being responsible for his decisions during the Hellenistic period. Snell (1953), for instance, claims that since in Homer there are no words that could be translated by our 'mind' or 'soul' man is not presented as a concrete individual, and since he is presented as acting under the influence of external (or quasi-external, like *ate*) forces, he is not experienced as isolated or autonomous; man is absolutely embedded in a social unit. The same is also true, he continues, for Greek tragedy, e.g. Euripides *Medea* (see esp. 1021-1080). Others, like Dodds (1951) and Adkins (1970), associate the understanding of human agency in Greek poetry with the influence of a 'shame-culture', or a society where people are judged according to their actions and not their intentions; therefore, the social status is more important than their individual or internal motives. In Vernant (1991b), these patterns have been combined with a structural approach; he suggested that there is a development (tragedy represents the transitional point) from the stage where responsibility was shared between himself, one's household and the divine powers, to the stage where the individual undertakes personal responsibility. All those explanations have been based on the assumption that a decision is personal only when the one who makes the decision regards himself as a unified 'I', a personal centre of self-consciousness and will; and they reflect influential philosophical ideas of the seventeenth and eighteenth centuries, especially those of Descartes and Kant.

These ideas have been recently challenged strongly by scholars such as Williams (1993), MacIntyre (1985), and Wilkes (1988).[21] Williams has suggested that the picture of human psychology that is presented by the ancient Greeks is very close to modern understanding of human experience, and especially to two ideas central to modern psychology, used extensively by him, that is, 'agent regret' and 'moral luck', which means that people accept responsibility for actions they perform without being able to assent to them completely. Insofar as the psychology and ethics of early Greek poetry and philosophy express these ideas, they reveal a profound response to human experience, rather than a primitive picture of human agency and responsibility. Therefore, even though in Homer, and in Plato, Aristotle and some other Greek accounts too, human psychology is pictured as the interplay between parts or functions, this does not mean that individuals do not undertake responsibility for their actions, and therefore, that they are not ethically responsible; the picture of the ethical human being presented as such has many similarities with the individual as presented by modern functionalist psychology, e.g. see Dennet (1979). Another parallel that can be also drawn is that between Aristotelian and Stoic motivation and modern 'action theory' (see Gill, 1995: notes 12-17).

Furthermore, another Kantian idea that can be traced behind the traditional approaches is that a properly moral response involves a combination of a distinctively individual stance with the recognition of the universal application of moral principles. According to Kant, a moral response involves 'autonomy', that is, binding oneself to universal laws, as opposed to principles which apply to a particular context or class. As a result, Dodds (1951), like Adkins (1970), Snell (1953) and those following the traditional approach in general, associates the idea of 'shame' (αιδώς) with early Greek thought, and relates it to an ethical framework that stresses the social status of one's acts rather than the individual or internal motives. Williams (1993) argues that these ideas are used to mark a distinction between a cultural framework in which ethical standards depend on social judgements, and one in which they are based on the individual's inner sense of what is right and what is wrong. This distinction is typically connected with the assumption that the second type is more mature and developed than the first. This reflects the Kantian belief presented above (that is, that each individual should bind himself to universal laws rather than relying on the ethical framework of its society). Similar ideas have been expressed by Cairns (1993) and MacIntyre (1985). Cairns also argues that shame (αιδώς) does not function as a moral force only due to external influences, but also depends on the *internalisation* of the ethical judgements of a community by an individual, so that these become 'its own' as well as part of the discourse in society. MacIntyre, moreover, argues that moral thinking has no validity unless it is grounded in the attitudes and institutions of a particular community and culture. He also criticises the prevalent modern idea that the role that the individual plays in the community and the web of roles and practices that make up his shared life in it do not have to be taken into consideration when defining the moral life and status of an individual. Thus, MacIntyre suggests that Homeric thought is extremely valuable, since it presents the proper way of living within a community, and he commends Aristotle's thoughts about virtue, which is again exercised within a communal schema (1985: chs. 1-8, 14-18; Gill, 1995: 26; Gill, 1996: 7-8).[22]

The ideas presented by Julia Annas (1992), are very interesting indeed; she stresses that the starting point of Greek ethical theory is reflection about one's life as a whole, particularly about its overall goal (*telos*). This is *eudaimonia*, uniformly accepted as the primary aim of man's life, but fiercely debated as far as its content is concerned by the Greek philosophers. Nevertheless, Annas stresses, even though Greek philosophers give a central role to *arete* (virtue) in their account of happiness, they allow scope for other-concern. This point is taken up by Gill (1995: 29), who further underlines that ethical reflection is conceived in Greek philosophy as a shared debate, rather than as individual reflection, concerning a shared human happiness instead of a personal life. He also stresses that 'this debate is conceived as partly extending and partly counteracting, the guidance about goals of action and life contained in pre-reflective discourse between people and within communities'. These two points contribute to what he sees as a dominant image in Greek thought: that of human beings as situated in three inter-connected types of 'dialogue' (or discourse): reflective debate, interactive exchange, and 'dialogue' with other parts of the personality (see Gill 1995: 29, also chpt. II, notes 19-25 and 27-31 - examples from ancient Greek literature - and chpt. VI, notes 6-12; also Gill, 1996).

I will not go into further details about Greek ethical notions, which after all, are not the main focus of this chapter. However, I will keep these ideas in the background of this discussion, to reinforce my argument that we do have to conceive of the 'individual' and 'society' notions of the Greeks and Romans in their own terms, and not through nineteenth- or twentieth-century lenses.

To conclude this strand, the idea of the traditional scholarly work that the individual was not 'present' in the early Greek thought and only came to the forefront as a moral and ethical agent in the Hellenistic period, has to be reconsidered in the light of contemporary ideas about moral and ethical philosophy. Even if we do not adopt those, we cannot fail to reflect on them and realise that the ideas about what constitutes an 'individual', and therefore, when and under what circumstances this notion was first introduced, have been biased and pre-determined. Consequently, conclusions deriving from them need to be reconsidered.

'Cultivation of the Self'

Before we change the area of enquiry, we should also discuss, briefly, the issue of the 'cultivation of the self',[23] which arises in relation both to philosophy and religion (as we will also see in section VIII). Martin (1994) structures part of his arguments referring to Hellenistic thought around the philosophical proverbs *'gnonai eauton'* and *'epimeleisthai eautou'*, which have been fundamental in the Socratic philosophy, and are based upon the axiom (documented by Herodotus, 5.29; Thucydides, 2.40.2; 6.9.2; Plato, *Prot.* 318 E and so forth) that those who take good care of their own affairs, will best take care of the affairs of the city. Therefore, even these most 'individualistic' assertions, Martin argues, have a communal rather than personal character. During the Hellenistic age, the argument continues, 'the Socratic notion of communal care became extended from being the concern of a young man' (as in the case of Alcibiades and Alexander - since these assertions have been especially used in connection to these two individuals), 'to being considered a permanent duty throughout one's life, and from political relationships to encompass all human relationships' (Martin, 1994: 124). But although it was taken up by philosophy and placed at the centre of the 'art of existence' that philosophy claimed to be, it never became an expression of individualism, not even during the Roman Imperial period when it reached the peak of its popularity, but always carried social connotations.

Philosophy, the main source of cultivation, was not an exercise in solitude, but a social praxis. Consequently, it found support and its social basis not only in the philosophical schools, but also in relation to customary links of kinship, friendship and obligation. It was also closely related to medicine and science. Furthermore, personal and social self-knowledge occupied a considerable place. The theme found its highest philosophical development in Epictetus: 'the care of the self is a privilege-duty, a gift obligation that ensures our freedom while forcing us to take ourselves as the object of all our diligence' (quoted by Foucault, 1986: 47). As a result, we would suggest that the cultivation of the self was part of the art of self-knowledge, which also took the form of exercises in poverty, self-examination, labour of thought with itself as object, and conversions to self. Consequently, the cultivation of the self became part, not of the development of individualism, but of certain modifications relating to the formative elements of ethical subjectivity (Foucault, 1986).

The 'City-state' in the Hellenistic World

In this section, we will deal with the refutation of the arguments concerning the decline of the city-state during the Hellenistic period. The dichotomy between individual and community had never been as sharp as it is usually accepted, and the individual in the Greek world acquired his individuality by his inclusion in a social network. Similarly, the transition from an arrangement where the city-state held a prominent position to one where that position had drastically changed has been the product of a long process, which exceeds the limits of what we have termed the Hellenistic period.

In numerical terms, the Hellenistic period coincides with a vast expansion of the *polis*. Many cities were founded by Alexander and colonised by Macedonians (Jones, 1940). In qualitative terms though, it is generally held that the Hellenistic period is a period of decline for the city-state (Gauthier, 1993). It has been widely admitted that Philip II and Alexander the Great were responsible for its decline and fall, that after Chaeronea the Greek *polis* ceased to exist or to be the frame in which Greek civilisation achieved its perfection, and therefore that the Greek ceased to be a citizen of his city and became a citizen of the world (Giovannini, 1993: 283).

Whether this picture corresponds to an objective point of view or not, depends solely on the starting assumptions. If we take the traditional view that the Greek *polis* was an independent and by definition individualistic city-state, then our conclusions would not differ much from the above. Similarly, if we take the 'sociological definition' (more of economic character, in fact) by Runciman, that there are two conditions for a *polis*: (a) a distinction between citizens and non-citizens and (b) autonomy in the monopoly of means of coercion; then it is obvious that the *poleis* which survived and flourished during the Hellenistic period are *poleis* only in name, that is urban communities with a life of their own and not 'citizen-states' (1990: 348).

If, on the other hand, we see the city-state as 'a partnership in living well' (Giovannini, 1993: 283), a community of a particular kind, and the characteristic expression of the collective consciousness of the Greeks (Murray, 1990: 19-20), then we reach rather different conclusions. It appears, then, that during the Hellenistic period the city preserved its role and identity better than ever. Giovannini (1993: 283) has argued that the *Gymnasium* and theatre, the symbols of the Greek culture and education continue to adorn the cities and serve both their practical purposes and their symbolic/metaphoric ones. Furthermore, the cities continue to provide their citizens with identity, and this do not cease to be so not even under the Romans or Parthians (Dihle, 1993: 290).

It will all become coherent if once again we reconsider the issues related to the 'independence' of the Greek state in sociological and philosophical terms. First of all, we should note that the Greek cities never in their history were isolated or individualistic, but were operating within a large(r) community consisting of the Greek commonwealth. Greeks were not members of that as individuals, but through their families, clans and, ultimately, cities. The *polis* had to send delegations to the panhellenic festivals and support a network of interhellenic relations (Giovannini, 1993: 285). The leagues (*koina*) that seem to predominate in the Hellenistic period, and the undertaking of leadership by those leagues and the successors of Alexander (and later the Romans), do not introduce so much of an innovation for the Greek world as may seem at first sight. This is so not only because the civic institutions continue to function - the official domination takes (at least at the beginning) the form of beneficiaries and the citizens keep being involved in the running of their own municipal affairs, protection of public buildings, religious affairs and so on - but even more importantly because this sort of 'independent-dependency' relation was already familiar to most of them.

Most information known about the Greek *polis* comes from Athens (due to the number of Athenian writers). But this seems to obscure the fact that the majority of Greek *poleis* were before Alexander organised in leagues, the Greek cities of Asia Minor were under the Persians (from 545 to 480 BCE and then from 386 to 334 BCE), while in the mainland smaller cities were subject to Athens, Sparta or Thebes (Gauthier, 1993: 217). Furthermore, and due to the religious aspect of the city as mentioned above, the Greeks did not face the community that was 'wider' than their city for the first time, and they were not uncomfortable about having multiple identities (concentric circle identities), in being for instance Athenian, Dorian (or, Ionian ...), or Greek (see also Hammond, 1951).

Furthermore, another point that should be made is that the Hellenistic period offers an inversion of the classical facts, i.e. we are very well informed about the hegemonic cities of the classical period, the smaller ones (that Aristotle mentions in his *Politics*) are unknown to us and therefore were merely part of the *decor*, while in the Hellenistic period the situation is inverted. Although the sources are by no means sufficient to fully bring to our knowledge hegemonic cities, for instance Rhodes, the epigraphical evidence available brings alive the smaller cities and offers an invaluable insight into the political and social cells of ancient society (Gauthier, 1993: 217).

In terms of political theory, there are two interesting points: firstly, the Hellenistic monarchs as well as the Romans after them, needed the city-state in order to retain their control over the Greek world, which was organised in this way. Therefore, they displayed a respect (even if superficial) for their status (a respect varying according to their geographical position, their political environment, size, resources, prestige, status and so on) (Gauthier, 1993: 212). At the same time, the Peripatetics (who founded the Alexandrian Museum) and the Stoic and Epicurean philosophies, as we have already discussed, perpetuated the 'orthodoxy' of the organisation in a city-state as ideal (although they changed the necessary bond for such a connection). There was no satisfactory substitute for the theory of community, and although leagues were quite successful (e.g. the Achaean survived from 280 to 146 BCE) there were no attempts to justify federation on philosophical basis (Hammond, 1951: 50).

The city-state was not a monolithic association; on the contrary it developed a network of associations (the ties of kingship by blood, matched with the multiple forms of political, religious and social groupings, companionship for a purpose (whatever that would be) that created a sense of community (Murray, 1986). As far as individual freedom is concerned within this group, it is worth quoting in full Murray in the *Oxford History of Classical World*:

> In such a world it might be argued that multiple ties limited the freedom of the individual, and there is certainly an important sense in which the conception of the individual apart from the community is absent from Greek thought: the freedom derives precisely from the fact that the same man belongs to a deme, a phratry, a family, a group of relatives, a religious association: and, living in this world of conflicting groups and social duties, he possesses the freedom to choose between their demands, and so to escape only particular forms of dominant social patterning. It is this which explains the amazing creativity and freedom of thought of classical Athens: the freedom which results from belonging in many places is no less a freedom than that which results from belonging nowhere, and which creates a society united only in its neuroses'. (1986: 209-210).

Society and Individuals in Religion

Religion in the Hellenistic age has been thought to illustrate most clearly the 'discovery of individualism'. Mystery cults in particular have been treated as the major testimony of the need of individuals to find personal salvation and establish a personal communication with the divine element. Burkert (1987), in his monograph on the subject, suggests that the traces of the early appearance of both mystery cults and individuals all date back to the sixth century BCE and reach their peak at the Hellenistic period. Moreover, Fortune (*Tyche*) becomes a dominant figure among both traditional and new deities, thus signifying, it is said, the same need for establishing a personal destiny and for enduring an individualistic life.

Contrary to this traditional view, Martin (1994) argues that although the classical perception of collective identity undoubtedly was challenged during the Hellenistic era, the social basis of identity was never challenged at all. 'Rather it produced alternative strategies of social inclusion, strategies defined not by place of birth but by inclusion in a newly defined international plurality of social groupings in which membership was conferred by invitation and instruction' (1994: 130). Nowhere is this idea concerning Hellenistic culture in general more easy to prove than in Hellenistic religion.

Martin supports his view with a series of arguments; he refutes (briefly) Burkert's assertion presented above (discussed earlier) with reference to Sophocles' *Oedipus at Colonus* and Aristotle's *Politics* (1253a), which both clearly suggest the impossibility of life out of a social group, to return to Hellenistic religion, and its survival and continuation in the Roman period, and particularly to the only surviving document which describes mystery cults, i.e. the second-century CE novel of Apuleius *The Golden Ass* or *Metamorphoses*. The novel's basic theme is the 'miserable wanderings' of Lucius (11.20) (the hero) in his attempt to find salvation, that is to re-join humanity, after having been turned to a beast (ass) due to his 'individualist assertions'. Socially excluded, he wanders desperately until he joins, after invitation, the society of Isis (one of the most prominent of the Hellenistic societies). Thus, Lucius acquires a new collective identity and he re-joins humanity.

This issue, besides the obvious argument against life out of a community, needs to be discussed further, since it brings to light the issue of religious community. In the classical period, the fundamental framework for Greek religion has been *polis*. Each *polis* was a religious system, autonomous and at the same time part of the more complex world-of-the-polis system. The *polis* mediated its citizens' participation in panhellenic religion, and the individual is perceived as participating not on its own behalf, but on behalf of the group, of the *polis*. This does not mean that Greek religion was a 'group religion' in the sense that group worship was the norm and individual cultic acts were exceptional; it was the individual who was the primary cultic unit in *polis* religion and not a unit like, for example, the *oikos*. Nevertheless, the *polis* regulated all religious activity, not only the cult of polis' sub-divisions, for instance the *demos* cult, as well as cults which we would consider private, like the *oikos* cult (Sourvinou-Inwood, 1990).

In the Hellenistic era that model changes, it is argued by the traditional approach, due to the weakening of the city tie. Risking contradiction the argument continues, with religious communities being created in order to meet the need of the individual lost in the vast new world, to belong to a group (Tarn, 1952). These religious communities took the form of clubs, primarily social and religious bodies grouped around the worship of some god; possibly the more purely religious ones were called *thiasoi*, while the *eranoi* were primarily social bodies. Most of the clubs were very small - a membership of 100 was quite unusual. About 200 BCE, family associations appear, founded by some individual to perpetuate their family's memory. Every club had its temple and coped with its perpetual financial difficulties either by letting it, or by the contribution of some wealthy member who was afterwards honoured accordingly. The clubs modeled themselves on the city organisation (they had officials with similar names and passed resolution like city degrees); they became so much the standard model that the most diverse forms of activity - the philosophic schools, the Museum at Alexandria, the Dionysiac artists, Ptolemy's garrison troops - all adopted the same form of organisation (Tarn, 1952: 93-95).

The individuals in the clubs remained independent, especially on the economic level, and fully integrated into the complex structures of family and *polis*; they contributed, of course, interest, time, influence and part of their private means. This independence, along with the fact that these societies were not friendly societies in the sense of economic or other co-operation among their members (Burkert, 1987: 32), support for the poor and so on, led some scholars to suggest that ancient mystery cults did not form religious communities, reserving this term for the communities created by Judaism or Christianity. Undoubtedly, they did not form such communities; yet, this does not mean that they advocated some sort of individualism; quite the opposite, because they were very much influenced by the ancient city model, which itself served as a sort of religious community. *Ekklesia* undoubtedly indicates a different level of involvement, and it is offered as an alternative society model. Nevertheless, it operates more or less on a similar to the city-state basis, as an intermediary between the individual and the deity. Naturally, neither the Hellenistic clubs nor, of course, *ekklesia* in the Christian or Jewish sense, were substitutes of the city-state. They simply followed the 'essential communal' nature of religion in antiquity (Griffiths, 1989: 238). Christian ideology is particularly characteristic of this sort of attitude, evidence of which offers both the commandment 'love your neighbour as yourself' and the story of the Good Samaritan, where the proverb *'epimeleisthai eautou'* takes a more communal character and is addressed to the others (Martin, 1994: 129-130). Green (1990: 588), risking self-contradiction in his turn, concludes that religion during this period represents the 'urge to retreat from the self-determination, to seek authority outside the self'. In other words, salvation was at base a social position confirmed by membership to confer status (Martin, 1994).

The second issue about religion that should be discussed is Fortune, *Tyche* and its undeniable popularity during the Hellenistic period, attested mainly by art. In order to discuss this subject fully we should extend the chronological limits of our enquiry to the full Hellenistic period in religious terms, meaning the twilight of pagan religion, that is until the fourth century of our era. The Hellenistic notion of Fate had its origins in the classical Greek assumption of a natural or cosmic order of things, expressed by *Moira*. *Moires* (three), although they did not belong to the Olympian Gods, were among the most ancient deities, and their power was considered greater than that of the other gods. The issue of Fate was brought forward during the Hellenistic period, probably as a consequence of the 'individual's loss'; nevertheless, this idea needs to be seen in the light of Ptolemaic cosmology. The novel ideas it introduced about the cosmic order and chaos, which are guided by forces far beyond the individual's control and understanding, along with the actual internationalism deriving from Alexander's conquests, led to new ethical questions about individual existence. During the Hellenistic age, the traditional structures about *Moira* were reconsidered, along with the new cosmological enquiries, and provided a new systemic basis for the religions of the Hellenistic world. Mystery religions particularly distinguished between *Tyche*, as a personification of the Ptolemaic view of deficiency in the terrestrial realm, and *Agathe Tyche*, the personification of a cosmic order of things. *Agathe Tyche* was able to intercede on behalf of humans in the face of a capricious fate. With the Ptolemaic differentiation of the bounded cosmos, and the consequent immigration of the traditional along with the newly naturalised deities to the celestial realm, access to a divinely sanctioned but new distinct order was perceived as an even more fortuitous and individual affair (Martin, 1987: 160). This whole attitude was addressed through and by mystery religions, which appealed to a broad spectrum of social situations and provided support for everybody, 'establishing socio-political identity for all individuals, whether 'rural' (Eleusinian), or urban (Isaic), male (Mithraic) or female (traditional Dionysiac), ethnic (Jewish) or catholic (Christian), ecstatic (Dionysian) or bureaucratic (Mithraic), or exclusive (Jewish, Christian) or non-exclusive in some combination or juxtaposition' (Martin, 1987: 161). Mysteries therefore reintegrated the individual into some sort of ideal, spiritual society.

Material Culture

It has been argued that, just as the perceived prevailing individualism of the Hellenistic period dominated philosophy, so did the visual arts and literature genres.[24] This has been understood to stem from the interest of artists and craftsmen in exploring the inner experience and nature of the individual. The most striking development in this direction is usually considered the revolution in portraiture, as well as a new interest in the artistic world for novel subjects: grotesque figures, passionate subjects, theatrical elements, interest in the exotic and in realism (as opposed to the classical idealism) are some of the new trends in Hellenistic art allegedly suggesting an individualistic and cosmopolitan attitude (Pollitt, 1986: 10; Tarn, 1952: 316).

Portraiture in particular has been associated with the development of biography, and therefore, with the intellectual history that produced an inward-looking disposition and a preoccupation with the life of the individual. Thus, the ground was fertile for art to pursue the inner nature of the subjects, rather than the social, public façade (Pollitt, 1986: 64). Furthermore, portraiture, emphasising the personality of individuals, was argued to be inimical to the group-orientation of the Greek city-states. Therefore, the fact that the first realist portraits were created under the Persian rule (Robertson, 1975; Pollitt, 1986: 64), that is where the typical Greek restraints upon individual ambition and power did not exist, seems absolutely reasonable. But, no matter how attractive this suggestion might seem, it is not strictly correct, since attempts toward more realist portraits (and not only 'role portraits') also occurred in the Greek world, at an early stage of the fourth century BCE. The fourth century sculptor Demetrios of Alopeke, for example, was remembered for the remarkable realism of his portraits even in the Roman period (Pollitt, 1986: 64).[25] Roman 'Republic portraits' were influenced by the busts and wax masks of the renowned ancestors of prominent families which were kept in the *atria* of patrician households. Their existence is evidenced by Polybius in the second century BCE (6. 53). That means that they were related to household, and therefore, 'group' tradition, rather than individual choice.[26]

Votive figurines, on the other hand, have also been perceived as expressions of individualism (Uhlenbrock, 1990). Martin (1994) discussed that argument in the last part of his article, and suggested that far from being highly individualistic, these figurines – found in tombs and sanctuaries – are expressions of an ideology of self-inclusion, as designating techniques to establish 'right relationships' with other humans and deities. Thus he suggests that they were used to establish bonds between the person who offered them and the other devotees, as well as to support and sustain the class that depended on them to make a living (i.e. craftsmen, shopkeepers and so on). Furthermore, they were supposed to present tangible and enduring evidence for the successful strategies of piety. These works of art were seen as memorialising a collective piety that would re-establish 'a sense of place, an enduring spatial framework in which a community might distribute its richest ideas and images with respect to specific locations and sanctuaries' (Martin, 1994: 133). Besides the material links between the new social formations and cult sites that the figurines established, Martin contends, their use as funerary offerings ensured that the redefined locative definitions of social existence endured over time.

Therefore, he continues, these figurines should be considered material tokens of inclusion and membership in an enduring sub-culture, rather than indications of any personal or individualistic enterprise (Martin, 1994: 133-134).

Clear and satisfying as the above explanation is, however, it probably treats only part of the argument. The figurines' style and subject, no less than their use can classify them as bearers of individualism. The interest in human beings, in their individuality (attested by the presentation of grotesque, or extraordinary and exotic figures, for example deformed, aged people, and so on) forms an interesting indication of the concerns artists developed in searching for other, more contemporary and less idealised, areas of life. Nevertheless, we should note that the fact that there is this new trend and that interest does not suffice to prove the 'rise of individualism', since this is just a part - and a small one - of what is needed in order to characterise art as bearer of individualism. The individuality may lay with the subject, with the style, or, with the creator (artist) signing his work, employing methods of making his identity separate and easily discernible. In this last sense, individual artists have made their identity known already in the sixth century BCE, when they first started inscribing their names on the bases of statues along with the names of the dedicators (as had been the older custom) (Snodgrass, 1980: 186). Furthermore, the transition from one artistic style to the next (be it from the archaic to the severe, from the severe to the classic and so on) presupposes some artists developing a similar exercise of individualism and a similar kind of intellectual and moral courage.

Collections and collecting activities during this period offer one more, extremely important insight into the notion of individualism, as this applies in the Hellenistic period. Hellenistic collections (like the Roman ones) were formed indiscriminately by works of art that belonged to different periods and were made by different artists. Attalus I, for instance, assembled a comprehensive collection of statuary, where examples of famous artists from all periods of Hellenic culture were represented. From the draped Graces by Bupalus of Chios, dated to the sixth century BCE, to copies of famous works made by contemporary artists, they all found their place in the Hellenistic collections, assembled by kings who were more interested in establishing themselves as patrons and successors of Alexander's panhellenic ideal, than in establishing their individuality.[27] Most importantly, originality of the work of art (although appreciated) was not a necessary condition for the inclusion of an object in a collection. Copies were acceptable, and even these were limited to a certain number of sculptural models, that became the norm for the Roman collectors.[28] Instead of being monotonous and unimaginative, this had only positive connotations, since it assured social acceptance for the owners, and 'a sense of cultural belonging, of *romanitas*' (Bartman, 1994: 78). The only quality which was important for these collectors was the Greek origin or style of the objects. As a result, we can argue that the majority of collections formed an attempt to provide their owners/creators with an identity, to help them recreate either only for themselves, or for their people, an ideal community to which to belong. Collecting is not an exercise in solitude - at least not at this particular period, but also perhaps generally - but an attempt to make the collector part of a wider community, to provide a communal identity for him. The origins of the phenomenon, therefore, coincide with, and correspond to, such a need.

Consequently, we can support the suggestion we made in the introduction of this chapter, concerning the possibility of belonging to many but different communities during the Hellenistic period. Thus we can maintain that when the city-state was dominant, collections were held in local temples and panhellenic sanctuaries, such as Delphi, and were initiated by the city-state because as a collective body it could, and should, take action on behalf of its citizens to secure their Hellenic (or Ionian, Dorian etc.) identity. In the Hellenistic period onwards, this initiative belongs to different 'bodies'. At first there were monarchs, who undertook the role of the city and initiated in their turn the assemblage of collections in sanctuaries and temples, but also created their own identity-sanctuaries, in order to reinforce the group-identity and, through it, their own. Then came prominent citizens, who having been in a position to 'take care of themselves', were in a position to take care of the affairs of their fellow-citizens (however widely this is perceived) and to supply an identity for them by, and through, creating an identity for themselves. In other words, despite the major political developments, changes in the political structure and universalism, people still felt the need to belong in a wider group; therefore, instead of advocating heautocratism/individualism, they simply searched for a new 'community' to which to belong.

To support this claim further, we can return to Panaetius' four *personae* theory that has reached us through Cicero, and that forms a kind of middle-ground where Hellenistic philosophy and Roman culture meet. In this theory we encounter the justification of at least one mode of collecting during this period, and a clear presentation of the relationship between creating identity and collections. In *De Officiis*, Cicero declares that the individual should behave according to four considerations that he calls *personae*: the first two are the nature people share with all humans, and the individual nature of each separately. The third is the *persona* arising from circumstances imposed by chance and time, while the fourth depends on personal choices, according to judgements about the life each person wishes to lead (de Lacy, 1977: 163). Much ink has been spilt on attempts to define *persona* (e.g. Gill, 1988, where also bibliography); and so, we will not concentrate on this. Instead, we will focus on a notion that the four *personae* theory shares with Roman collecting: *decorum*. The development of the former (I. 107-121) is part of the section devoted to the latter (I. 93-151), and it is obvious that there is a close interrelation between the two doctrines. *Decorum* is presented as the outward aspect of moral excellence, and the four *personae* are part of Cicero's advice of how his readers can achieve this moral excellence. It depends on acting according to nature and in an appropriate manner as humans and individuals. Interestingly, the notion of individualism is four-fold: it has what we should call a 'natural component' - human nature, the same for everybody - two individual(istic) parts, the very personal character of each individual and the personal choices for which everybody bears complete responsibility, and finally, an outward parameter, i.e. circumstances. All these, however, form part of a social frame, and the practice of individuality falls within the borders shaped by social concerns. Cicero understands individuality in a highly conventional way, where being an individual responsible for their own choices does not contradict, but instead reinforces the fact of belonging in a social group, that of the Roman élite. Individuality, therefore, is part of the social role everyone is called to undertake, and acting as a conscious individual is as much part of appropriateness as is decorating one's house according to one's position and social standing.

> In his *decorum* theory, then, Panaetius articulated a widely held assumption: that if a person was to 'play' his social role well, and in a way that would enable him to 'shine' in his society, he had to adhere to certain accepted patterns of speech, movement, and style of life in general. (Gill, 1988: 195).

In other words, to 'acquire' individuality ('shine in society') means going through the social network, which in order to be maintained had to include a certain set of attitudes, central among which was the 'decoration' of one's house in an appropriate manner. We can see, therefore, that the pursue of individuality goes through behaving and living according to social patterns, and that material culture, as well as personal behaviour and composure, is a means toward this pursuit.

This view is in accordance with the Stoic philosophical belief that the acquisition and possession of private property is part of human nature, and so is the interaction of individual human beings with one another as property owners (Long, 1997: 15).[29] Property ownership and legal accumulation of it were considered functions of a morally good person, and gained part of their justification in their contribution to the well-being of society. More specifically, material possessions, although they had no moral value for the Stoics, had instrumental value, for they allowed 'living in agreement with nature' (LS 58m). Stoics did not perceive any inconsistency between belief in private ownership and in the community of reason and justice they advocated (Cicero, *De Fin.*, III.67). On the contrary, Stoic philosophy understood and justified holding material possessions and treating them with respect and affection, as part of man's *oikeiosis*, that is the process of accommodating himself in the world. They actually defined society's role as being to safeguard private possessions (in a manner that resembles Locke's, and other eighteenth century philosophers' claims - Cicero, *De Off.*, II. 73). This belief, however, did not lead to placing individuals above society. On the contrary, the Stoics treated 'the disposition to choose material property as a natural and rational extension of self-love and of human identity as a social animal' (Long, 1997: 29). The Stoic position regarding material possessions then can be interpreted as follows: the appropriation of private property is a natural human tendency, that helps the individuals to establish their identity and place in society. In this sense, collecting expresses exactly these views. They offer to the collector an opportunity to establish his personal identity, to appropriate the world, and also to acquire, or construct, his place in the social sphere.

Conclusions

The aim of this chapter has been to discuss the role of the individual in the nature of classical collecting. Starting from the assumption that collections are parameters to shape identities and to define the self, as well as attempts to reconcile the citizen (individual) with the centres of power and aid his claims for a position as an independent agent within them, we set out to explore the interrelationship between individuals and material culture in the classical world. For that purpose, it was thought necessary to examine the widely approved view that relates an alleged 'rise of individualism' during the Hellenistic period with the formation of the first private, or privately initiated, collections, which also occurs during this time. This chapter has maintained the view that collections in the classical world, while signifying an advanced role for the individual, cannot be associated with the 'rise of individualism'. On the contrary, collections have been ways by which the classical collectors aimed to create a niche for themselves in the social sphere, by acquiring access to a community of culture and prestige that the assemblage of Greek works of art and artefacts signified. Thus, we argued that collections of the Hellenistic and Roman worlds were part of a social game between the individual and the community. Far from being a medium of isolation, in the sense of setting the individual aside, and creating an original and unique identity for him (as the aim of individualism is often defined) they were attempts to prove the membership in a tradition of excellence, which would transfer to the owner the prestige and qualities implied in belonging to such a community. In this sense, collections of the Hellenistic and Roman eras have the specific aim to prove their owners' participation among the élite, and therefore their capacity to take part in the decisions made by this élite. They do not aim to set the owner apart as a unique or original personality, but to help him gain individuality through the perfect accomplishment of his social role.

   To support our argument, we had first to reach a working definition of individualism and individual. We distinguished between the empirical individual, which has always been inherent in humans, and the cultural individual, i.e. the one who is historically and socially developed and constructed, and which forms the category with which we are currently dealing. Then, we had to discuss the traditional views regarding the flourishing of individualism at exactly this period critically, and to consider the existence of a social base deeply embedded in all the expressions of the Hellenistic thought. The first area of discussion was the philosophical concepts as developed in the Hellenistic world after Plato and Aristotle. Cynicism, Stoicism, and Epicureanism are traditionally considered the carriers of the individualistic ideology, and the philosophical justification behind similar ideas. We presented their views on issues about individuals and communities, and concluded that despite a phenomenal encouragement of individual tendencies and the care of the self, Hellenistic philosophy displayed a remarkable faith to the traditional community schema, although of course it redefined it for the purposes of the changing world. Instead of the traditional *polis*, Hellenistic philosophies advocated alternative communities, based on different and more profound values, that is share of interests, ethics, and reason, instead of financial, religious, or other bonds that had been present in the old city-state. A person could become self-fulfilled only through a community of people, which also defines his code of conduct. It is in philosophical thought that we find the seeds of what we discuss as a common social view in the Roman world, i.e. the notion of *decorum*. In Cicero's *De Officiis*, the discussion of the four *personae* is part of the *decorum* theory. It is a strong argument, which discusses the individual's responsibility to comply not only with his internal nature, but also with the circumstances into which he is placed. To achieve preeminence as an individual, in other words, means that one has to acquire an active social role too. Collections are part of this social role, and form indispensable parameters for such a pre-eminence.

Then the argument continued with the notion of the city-state, and its 'destruction' during the Hellenistic era. We maintained that the idea of the city-state remained strong in principle, besides the presence of new political and social arrangements. The idea of the community remained alive, even vital, in the Hellenistic world. Similar conclusions are drawn from the discussion of religion, where again the Hellenistic period is considered of vital importance, as a transitional period from communal religion to individualistic ones. Still, the concept of community pertains there as well, although, naturally, the arrangement of these communities alters. Interestingly, these refer to the ones of the city-state. Finally, material culture brings alive the same argument. Art production has been considered a most explicit testimony for the 'rise of individualism', since this is the era when idealism gives its place to realism, portraits and biographies are created, and so are collections. Although there can be no doubt that certain developments have their origin in the new social and political circumstances, and that the monarchy, for instance, has been an important parameter for defining these new developments, I argue that the collections and the other expressions in material culture are the means through which these power games are played, and not their results.

The community of the city-state was thus replaced by the community of the (Alexandrian) Museum in the Hellenistic period, and from then onwards to the Roman period. The collections were understood as, and actually were, means through which individuals tried to cast themselves as members of a cultural élite, so as to underline their culture and pursue a role in the decision taking through their participation in that cultural society (see Bourdieu, 1974; 1984).

The notion of individualism takes many forms and shapes. That of the Hellenistic period was not one where the individual identity acquires preeminence over community; it was just an attempt to redefine social and individual character in a new, changing, and expanding world.

Notes

1   The term is borrowed from Snodgrass' book *Archaic Greece*, chapter 5 (1980).

2   With this term I mean the period from the death of Alexander (323 BCE) until the naval battle at Actium (31 BCE), as it is usually the chronological span of this period. For the history of the period see Austin, 1981; Cary, 1951; Delorme, 1975; Rostovtzeff, 1941; Wallbank, 1982; Will, 1979.

3   This argument leaves out the 'collections' held in tombs and brings to the forefront the issue of whether those were collections or not, whether these were public or private, how do we know that and so on; although I cannot examine tomb 'collections' [offerings' collections] as case-studies, due to the size of material, I cannot ignore the fact that there is an issue which I have to take into account. Of course, maybe this supports my argument even better, in the sense that the Hellenistic collections might not have been the first private collections, and therefore, one more reason to suggest that we are not talking about individualism.

4   He actually mentions one historian, Droysen, who started the first volume of his three-volume *Geshichte des Hellenismus* (1836) with the famous words: 'Der Name Alexander bezeichnet das Ende einer Weltepoche, den Anfang einer neuen'.

5   If what has been said above about tomb collections is true, then this might not be like that; maybe the private aspects of collecting were one way of acquiring private existence during a period when this was a difficult thing to achieve.

6   Or, at least, with the 'collecting classes' that we can have information from; whether or not members of lower social classes were collecting other things is beyond our knowledge.

7   The non-inclusive language of many of the quotations is due to their age.

8   Harris (1989) differentiates the concepts of 'individual' as member of the human kind, 'self' as locus of experience, and 'person' as agent-in-society. These distinctions are slightly different from those made by Morris (1994), although both mirror the tripartite division which anthropology prefers when it refers to individual and individualism.

9   Morris (1994) puts this category third, but I have changed the order since the first and third categories are understood as closely related and in opposition to the second.

10   For a new translation of Mauss' text, and a series of articles replying to it and, offering explanatory and alternative readings of it, see Carrithers, Collins, and Lukes, 1985.

11   Zeno of Citium was the founder of the Stoic school. (Fourth century BCE.)

12   For Diogenes' cosmopolitanism see Schofield, 1991, esp. appendix H, pp. 141-145.

13 The term 'representation' is the one that Long prefers (1991: 105, note 6), while in LS the term 'impression' is used; other modern suggestions include 'appearance' or 'presentation'.

14 Epictetus was a Stoic philosopher, c. 55-c. 135 CE; his lectures were written down by his pupil Arrian.

15 We can define sage as the ideal, virtue-defined and virtue-oriented person, like Socrates or Cato.

16 On *kathekonta* see LS 59; also Kidd, 1971.

17 Panaetius was head of the Stoic school from c. 129 BCE (c. 185-c. 110 BCE). For his four- *personae* theory discussed by Cicero in his *De Officiis*, I. 93-151, see Gill, 1988; de Lacy, 1977; Long, 1983; Gill, 1994. For a discussion of Cicero's own contribution to the shaping of this theory, as opposed to the views of Panaetius himself, see Brunt, 1973.

18 For modern ideas on individual and individualism see for example Taylor, 1989; Lukes 1973; MacIntyre, 1985; Wilkes, 1988, Carrithers, Collins, and Lukes, 1985; for a presentation of the Western conceptions of the 'individual' see Morris, 1991.

19 For the personal identity in Stoic thought see also Kerferd, 1972.

20 See especially *De Rerum Natura* 5, 925-938, 9539-61, 1011-1027, 1105-1157; for further bibliography see Gill, 1995: 66, note 96.

21 For a detailed presentation of the ideas of each of those writers in relation to ethical issues of the ancient Greek and modern Western philosophy see Gill, 1995.

22 For a discussion of MacIntyre and his views, as well as their influence, see also Long, 1983.

23 For an extensive discussion on the 'cultivation of the self' and the 'technologies of the self' as Foucault terms the notion, see Martin et al., 1988.

24 Biography and autobiography are the genres most related to the issue of individualism; we have mentioned the development of these in Chapter 2, as part of erudite literature. For a more detailed discussion, see for instance, Momigliano, 1993; 1985; Baslez *et al.*, 1993.

25 For an interesting discussion of the civic portrait in classical Athens, and an argument against individualism as expressed through these portraits, see Tanner, 1992.

26 For the art of portraiture, its origins and development, see Breckenridge, 1973; 1981, where also bibliography; Zanker, 1979b; Schweitzer, 1948; Hiesinger, 1973; Toynbee, 1978.

27 About Hellenistic collectors, see Fränkel, 1891: 48-60; Hansen, 1971: 316ff, 353ff, 366ff; Howard, 1986; Neudecker, 1988: 6-8.

28 For the role of copies in Roman art see the fundamental Lippold, 1923; also Jucker, 1950; Pollitt, 1978; Ridgway, 1984; 1989; Bieber, 1977; Marvin, 1989; Vermeule, 1977; Landwehr, 1985; Gazda, 1995; Zanker, 1974; 1978.

29 Stoicism was the first philosophical school to actually support property ownership and involvement in financial affairs. Unlike the aristocratic beliefs of Plato and Aristotle, who claimed the pre-eminence of communal property (city property) over individual one (e.g. Plato, *Laws*, V. 739), and the unsuitability of commerce and money-making as activities for the male citizen (e.g. Aristotle, *Pol.*, I.8-9; II.5, 1263b1-4), and the indifference for private ownership that Epicureans and Cynics assumed (Long, 1997: 17-18), the Stoics developed a theory that can be extended to include individual human beings' relation to themselves, and other human beings. For a discussion of these views and further bibliography, see Long, 1997.

Chapter 5

Collecting in Time and Space in the Classical World

The stream of a lifetime slides smoothly on and is past before we
know, and swift the year glides by with horses at full speed.

Ovid, *Amores* I.viii.49-50[1]

I come to the fields and spacious palaces of memory, where are the
treasures of innumerable images, brought into it from things of all
sorts perceived by the sense. There is stored up, whatever besides we
think, either by enlarging or diminishing, or any other way varying
those things which the sense hath come to; and whatever else hath
been committed and laid up, which forgetfulness hath not yet
swallowed up and buried. When I enter there, I require instantly what
I will to be brought forth, and something instantly comes; others must
be longer sought after, which are fetched, as it were out of some inner
receptacle; others rush out in troops, and while one thing is desired
and required, they start forth, as who should say, 'Is it perchance I?'
These I drive away from with the hand of my heart from the face of
my remembrance; until what I wish for be unveiled, and appear in
sight, out of its secret place. Other things come up readily, in
unbroken order, as they are called for; those in front making way for
the following; and as they make way, they are hidden from sight,
ready to come when I will. All which takes place when I recite a
thing by heart.

Augustine, *Confessions*, X.8.[2]

Introduction

Time and space belong to the most universal properties of things (along with
number, cause, personality, etc.), what philosophers call 'categories of
understanding' (Durkheim, 1915: 9).[3] They are in a dialectical relationship
with society, since they derive from it, but they also dictate to it ways and
methods of comprehension (Gell, 1992). The individual can hardly liberate

himself from them, and is often represented at the point where the vertical axis of time and the horizontal axis of space, as they are schematically presented in the Western tradition, cross each other. Similarly, it is impossible to think of objects that are not set in temporal and spatial terms.

Collecting as a classification process *par excellence* which involves individuals, societies, and material culture[4] is immediately associated with these two coordinates. This dimension of collections is frequently highlighted in the collecting discourse: '...the sphere of material objects is *ordered* in ways upon which we rely for a *sense of continuity* and as *markers of temporal change*'; '[w]hen *put aside* or *gathered into* collections...[objects] can be used to *evoke a sense of their time and place*'; they may be 'removed from their *temporal and spatial context*'; and 'serve as *reminders* or as a *focus for recalling time* ... or ... *places*' (Radley, 1990: 46, 47, 50, 51; emphasis added). According to Stewart (1993: 162)

> there are two movements to the collection's gesture of standing for the world: first, the metonymic displacement of part for whole, item for context; the second, the invention of a classification scheme which will define space and time in such a way that the world is accounted for by the elements of the collection.

In other words, collections are by definition based on the capacities of objects to define a spatial and temporal context, and be defined by it, to evoke the sense and essence of this context when they are placed (*sic*) elsewhere, to establish a relationship with time as reminders of the past, as points signifying temporal change, or as media towards a sense of continuity, and, finally, to order the world in an intelligible way for the collector. Collections aim at a comprehensive appropriation either of space and distance, or of time (past, present, and future), or of both. In addition, they are expected to furnish (in both meanings of the term) the world of the collector, to define his own context, create an environment for himself, and help him make sense of it. On the other hand, perceptions of time and space define the way collecting patterns develop and influence individual and communal views about the world.

The aim of this chapter is to trace the notions of time and space as these appear in the philosophical, the anthropological, and the mythical thought of the classical world, in order to appreciate their interrelationship and their influence in the creation and the origins (*sic*) of the above notions related to collecting. We will thus discuss firstly the classical perceptions of time and space, and the impact of these on notions of order, knowledge and assemblage of material culture. Then we will examine the relation between space and objects and how this leads to different conceptions about what constitutes a place devoted to or appropriate for certain people and activities, and not for others. In the next part, we will focus on the use of objects to evoke a sense of time or place, and the impact of this on the architecture, decoration and furnishing of Roman houses. Finally, we will argue that the ritual aspect of museum visits (Duncan, 1995), where a transference into a different place and time is expected and/or experienced, relates to ancient notions of memory, and the capacity of objects to remind us of things and words.

Perceptions of Time and Space in Classical Philosophy

Ancient Greek and Roman philosophers invested considerable energy in their attempt to define space and time. They developed elaborate theories to account for those two qualities that could not be dealt with in isolation, and that could not but influence and define concepts like universe, God, eternity, and so on, themselves holders of spatial and temporal implications. The present discussion, far from being comprehensive, will be a brief review of ancient philosophical thought regarding time and space, in an attempt to indicate some of the most widespread views on the issue, and thus approach, in a way, the beliefs of the Roman élite.

Plato defines time as the 'image of eternity' (*Timaeus*, 37d).[5] He attributes time's creation to God and believes that it was created along with the universe, and is inseparable from it (38b). He therefore describes the 'genesis' of time as follows:

> ... when the Father that engendered it [the universe] perceived it in motion and alive, a thing of joy to the eternal gods, He too rejoiced;[6] and being well-pleased He designed to make it resemble its Model still more closely. Accordingly, seeing that that Model is an eternal Living Creature, He set about making this Universe, so far as He could, of a like kind. But inasmuch as the nature of the Living Creature was eternal, this quality it was impossible to attach in its entirety to what is generated; wherefore He planned to make a movable image of eternity, and, as He set in order the Heaven, of that eternity which abides in unity He made an eternal image, moving according to number, even that which we have named Time. For simultaneously with the construction of the Heaven He contrived the production of days and nights and months and years, which existed not before the Heaven came into being. And these are all portions of Time; even as "Was" and "Shall be" are generated forms of Time, although we apply them wrongly, without noticing, to Eternal being. For we say that it "is" or "was" or "will be", whereas, in truth of speech, "is" alone is the appropriate term; "was" and "will be", on the other hand, are terms properly applicable to the Becoming which proceeds in Time, since both of these are motions; but it belongs not to that which is ever changeless in its uniformity to become either older or younger through time, nor ever to have become so, nor to be so now, nor to be about to be so hereafter, nor in general to be subject to any of the conditions which Becoming has attached to the things

which move in the world of Sense, these being generated forms of
Time, which imitates Eternity and circles round according to number'.
(*Timaeus*, 37c-8b).[7]

In other words, time came into existence with the ordering of the universe.
According to Callahan (1948: 18) 'we should look upon time as somehow
resulting from the activity of mind in the created order; for time does not
belong to that which is not created'. Time is an aspect of change, and this is its
chief difference from the eternal nature. But time bridges this gap, since it does
not belong to becoming as such, but to becoming that has been set in order by
mind in accordance with an eternal model. The sun, the moon, and the planets
were fashioned to distinguish and guard the numbers of time in order for the
creation of time to be accomplished (*Timaeus*, 38c). Consequently, time is an
image proceeding according to number, and thus it has to be numerable or
measurable.

Measurability is structured around two different circles (forms) in the
universe, that of the Same and that of the Other. The motion of Same
represents in a way the self-identity of the universe. The notion of Other
expresses the diversity of the universe as a consequence of its being in the
order of becoming (Callahan, 1948: 19). These two circles have been
discussed already in *Timaeus* as the compounding parts of the soul and the
universe (36c-d) (Same, Other and the mixture of the two) that provide it with
the ability to pronounce identity and difference, and thus to possess truth
(Callahan, 1948: 13). The movement of the universe, which arises from the
soul also is structured around two revolving circles, those of the Same and the
Other. (Both, of course, have the Same and the Other in their constitution).
The circle of the Same has predominance over that of the Other, since it is
single and undivided, whereas the latter is divided into seven orbits. The
bodies of the 'instruments of time' (sun, moon and planets) are put into these
seven orbits made by the revolution of the circle of the Other. Time, therefore,
has a special reference to the circle of the Other, which ensures the diversity of
number that gives time its measurability, but it is also governed by the circle of
the Same which reassures the uniformity and regularity (Callahan, 1948: 21).

The existence of a coherent theory of space in Plato has been disputed
(Algra, 1995: 73ff, where also bibliography). Plato seems to had been
committed to different and often incompatible concepts of space, as it is
obvious from *Timaeus* (48e-52d). In particular, there seems to be a certain
inconsistency in the association of the receptacle with matter and/or space in
Plato's thought, which is further obscured by the inconsistencies in the use of
terms like *hedra* (ἕδρα), *chora* (χῶρα) (52a), and of expressions of everyday
language in the discourse, like 'to occupy a place', 'to be in place', 'to be in
something', and so on. Nevertheless, if we agree to read Plato's text accepting
his inconsistencies, or associating the receptacle with space rather than matter,
then we can distinguish a sharp division between the Platonic concepts of time

and space. The latter existed before the creation of the universe, and consequently, time; although there is not an immediate 'generative' relation between the two (that is time does not arise from space, nor space from time), and they clearly belong in two different orders, the two are related in the sense that time is sensible only insofar as it involves motion in space. Nevertheless, time holds the pre-eminence, since it does not merely exist as space does, but it is an attempt to be more than becoming (52b) (Callahan, 1948: 192).

Unlike Plato's metaphysical and moral discussion of time (and space), where analogy and metaphor often caused inconsistencies and ambiguities, Aristotle deals with the issue on a physical level, and uses fixed terminology with literal meaning. Aristotle defines time within the framework of motion and magnitude: 'the number of a motion with respect to the prior and the posterior' (*Physics* IV, 219b-220a).[8] This does not mean that time *is* motion, but that it is something which belongs to motion (κινήσεώς τι). Motion as motion is the actualisation of the potential. But the notion of prior and posterior (before and after) associated to motion is something different. Time is related not to motion as such, but to motion as having in it the distinction of prior and posterior, which arises from spatial difference. This distinction of prior and posterior, as long as it is numerable, is time. In other words, to understand time, a soul has to recognise that there have been two 'nows' (moments), one prior, the other posterior, and an interval between the two. The perception of motion as such is not recognition of time; we need a perception of the prior and posterior in motion and a numbering process based on these (Callahan, 1948: 48-50, 194).[9] Consequently, time is the numerable aspect of motion (*Physics* IV, 219b2). Aristotle calls time a number because its parts have not a definite position (θέσις) with respect to one another, as a line does. Moreover, time has a certain order (τάξις), since one part is prior and one posterior. The parts of time are related to others not by position but by order; they do not exist all together, but are related to each other by the order of prior and posterior. Consequently, 'time may be called the numerable aspect of motion, for motion is reckoned by means of successive nows, inextended like number and having among themselves the order that is possessed by number' (Callahan, 1948: 53). That which distinguishes time as prior and posterior is 'now': this can be understood as the subject which has as attributes the events which take place in it. If events happen in the same now, they are simultaneous, and happen at the same time (also 220b5-8). 'Now' is in a sense always the same (when it is considered as substrate), but in another sense different (when considered in relation to the moving body). Therefore, the moving body at two different places is the same moving body, but is different in position (Callahan, 1948: 55) (also 219a31-32). 'Now' is the unit of number in a way (219b33). Callahan summarizes the above points as follows: 'motion has a numerable aspect, which we call time, because the mind can perceive these indivisible phases that exist not all at once but in a certain order, and number them by means of discrete nows' (1948: 57, as in *Physics* IV, 220a12-220a21).

Aristotle distinguishes time as the number of motion, but also as a continuum (Callahan, 1948: 63; also 220a25). Movement is continuous, because the spatial magnitude is continuous, and time is continuous because movement is so (1948: 193; Owen, 1979: 156). Time may be called the measure of motion (since both time and movement are continuous), or the number of motion (since there is in time a sequence of moments that provides a series of numbers analogous to an abstract numerical series). We may speak of many or few days, numbering by means of regularly recurring nows, or as long or short time, thinking of it as continuous measure (Callahan, 1948: 64). Time, though, is not abstract number, but that which is numbered. In this sense, any ten men or ten horses are the same, but not any ten days: although any ten days are of the same length, they will not be the same period, because one is posterior, the other prior. And although it may seem that the same time can recur (for example, year, summer) this is not true because numerically the years are different (Callahan, 1948: 66, 220b12). Magnitude, motion and time correspond to one another as continuous and divisive quantities (1948: 67).

Since time is the measure of motion, it is also the measure of rest (1948: 68-69). It measures the quantity of the motion (either something moves or has the potential to but does not) (1948: 69-70). The 'now' is a link of time, for it connects past and future time, but it is also a limit, since it is the beginning of one part and the end of another. The 'now' divides time potentially, and as dividing the 'now' is always different. It connects time since it is the end of one part and the beginning of another, and as connecting it is always the same (1948: 70-71).

Time is the measure of a continuous and uniform motion, that is the circular motion. This is prior to all other movements, since it is the only one that can be eternal (the others are interrupted by an interval) (265a24-27). Consequently, circular motion is the primary kind of motion, and as such it is the measure of time above all. By means of it, all other motions are measured as well (265b8-11) (Callahan, 1948: 87).

Aristotle builds on spatial order to define time, and although the discussion about the preeminence of temporal order or of spatial order has not reached definite conclusions, what is important here is that Aristotle finds a general parallel between time and space, and goes through it to account for the incorporeality of time (Owen, 1979: 158).

Aristotle approaches the notion of space from different angles: in the *Categories*, he classifies place as a quantity, coextensive with the body that occupies it (6, 5a8-14). In *On the Heavens*, Aristotle stresses natural place. He argues that the notion of 'natural place' (each element to its own place - fire at the top, earth at the centre, water and air in the middle) explains the natural movement of the elements; he says that such movements show that place has power (*dunamis*) (*Cael.* 4.3, 310b3; also *Physics*, IV.8, 214b12-17; IV.1,

208b11). In biology, Aristotle defines up and down, front and back, left and right in terms of biological function.[10] Up relates to the intake of food, so that the upper parts of a plant are its roots. Right is defined by the initiation of motion, and front by the direction of the gaze. These ideas are equally applied not only to humans and animals, but also to the cosmos as a whole. We will return to these ideas later in our discussion. Lastly, in the *Physics*, Aristotle defines place as a thing's surroundings. 'A thing's immediate place is the inner surface or boundary (*peras*) of the body that surrounds and contacts it, as the air surrounds and bathes a person' (Sorabji, 1988: 187) (*Phys.* IV.4, 211a24-b4; 212a2-7; 212a29-30; IV.5, 212b19). The classical Aristotelian definition of *topos* is the one in *Phys.* IV. 212a20: τό τοῦ περιέχοντος πέρας ἀκίνητον πρῶτον: 'the first unmoved boundary of the containing body' (Algra, 1995: 125).[11] He thus rejects, in this book, the three-dimensional extension or interval (*diastema*) that he has approved in his *Categories*, in favour of a two-dimensional surrounding surface. Thus, he justifies the choice of the term 'place' (τόπος), instead of space (χῶρα - *chora*) that he is using (about these words see Algra, 1995: 31ff).[12] Furthermore, his requirement that some thing's place should be equal to its size (*Phys.* IV, 212a2; a27-29) indicates that he is not interested in the position only, but also in the space and the objects that fit into it (Sorabji, 1988: 187).[13]

Epicurean and Stoic philosophers developed their own views on time and space.[14] Lucretius, for instance, who popularized among the Romans the philosophy of Epicurus, defined time as follows:

> Time as such does not exist *per se*: it is from things themselves that our perception arises of what has happened in the past, what is present, and further what is to follow next. It should not be conceded that anyone perceives time *per se* in separation from things' motion and quiet rest. (Lucretius, I. 445-82).

Time, in other words, cannot be discerned by itself but only in relation to certain bodies' accidents like motion and rest. It is something self-evident, but still in order to be understood we have to resolve to 'analogy': firstly, to draw directly on experience to collect an appropriate set of accidents, then to isolate time as the common measure of these all (Epicurus, *Letters to Herodotus*, 68-73). Demetrius of Laconia (c. 100 BCE) attempted to extract a precise metaphysical status for time from Epicurus' definition of it as an 'accident of accidents', associated with days, nights, hours, motions and rests, plus their own status as accidents of the body (Sextus Empiricus, *Against the professors* 10.219-27) (also Long and Sedley, 1987a: 36-37).[15]

Epicurean views on place evolve to cope with conceptual difficulties raised already by Aristotle. To start with, they take for granted that only that which exists spatially does actually exist: 'For whatever will exist will have to be in itself something with extension, whether large or small, so long as it exists'

(Lucretius, I. 419-444). But Epicureanism fails to distinguish between void and place, that is space unoccupied by body, from space occupied by body. Already from *Physics* IV, Aristotle had argued that a place can be empty or filled, and that 'void', 'plenum', and 'place' all denote the same thing (Long and Sedley, 1987a: 29-30). Epicurus, who accepts 'void' as a primary conception, and has to explain what happens to it when a body approaches, invents the name 'intangible substance':[16] this is the term he uses to denote space in general. 'Void', 'place' and 'room' (*chora*) are the terms by which he refers to it in specific contexts: 'void' when it is empty, 'place' when occupied, and 'room' (*chora*) when bodies move through it. Epicurus says that the difference between 'void', 'place' and 'room' is one of name (Aetius, 1.20.2). Bodies and space, being mutually exclusive, are also the only two orders of reality required to account for the universe. All other candidates (namely properties, time, facts, etc.) are mere parasitic properties of body (see also Lucretius, I. 445-482). Space, on the contrary, cannot be written off like that because it exists when and where the body does not (also Long and Sedley, 1987a: 27-30).

According to the Stoic ontology, void, place and time are three (out of four) incorporeals[17] (Sextus Empiricus, *Against the professors*, 10.218). Unlike Epicurus, the Stoics did not treat place and void as different aspects of the same concept. The void is always external to the world, and infinite. Place is what the body actually occupies, and is finite. The Stoics probably used the term '*chora*' to denote space which combines place and void. They followed Aristotelian determination not to accept the existence of void within the world: 'They [the stoicizing pneumatic doctors] think there is no such thing [as empty space] in the world but that the whole substance is unified with itself' (Galen, *On the differences in pulses*, 8.674, 13-14). The infinite void merely surrounds the world providing the spatial condition ('room' - *chora*) for its changes of volume (Long and Sedley, 1987a: 162-164, 293-297).

The Stoics approached the question of time from more than one point of view.[18] Many definitions are offered: according to Zeno, time is 'the dimension of all motion without qualification' (Simplicius, *On Aristotle's Categories* 340, 15-16);[19] or, in the words of Apollodorus:

> Time is the interval of the world's motion; and it is infinite in just the way that the whole of number is said to be infinite. Some of it is past, some present, and some future. But the whole of time is present, as we say that the year is present on a larger compass. Also, the whole of time is said to belong, though none of its parts belongs exactly. (Stobaeus, I.105, 8-16).

Posidonius, on the other hand, declares that '[s]ome things are infinite in every respect like the whole of time. Others in a particular respect like the past and the future. For each of them is limited only by reference to the present.' He therefore defines times as the '...dimension of motion or measure of speed and slowness'. He thus holds that time which is thought of in terms of 'when' is partly past, partly future, and partly present. 'The last consists of a part of the past and a part of the future, encompassing the actual division. But the division is point-like. Now and the like are thought of broadly and not exactly. But now is also spoken of with reference to the least perceptible time encompassing the division of the future and the past' (Stobaeus, I. 105, 17-106, 4 Posidonius frg. 98). Similarly to Aristotle, the Stoics established a relation between time and motion, but unlike the Peripatetics they did not insist on number and the soul as a counter (*Phys.*, IV 14.223a25). Time depends solely on the existence of motion, just as place depends on being occupied by body. Chrysippus located one movement and the existence of everything in time (Stobaeus, I.106, 5-23). God, the world's active principle, is not a timeless being but a continuously self-moving agent. Past and present are 'parts' or 'constituents of time' (Stobaeus, as above; Plutarch, *On common conceptions* 1081c-1082a), infinite on one side and 'limited' by the present on the other (Stobaeus, I. 105, 17). Chrysippus claimed that no time is exactly present, as any stretch of time consists of both parts of the past and of the future. It is also recognized that the temporal discourse is unavoidably imprecise and varies according to the context (Stobaeus, I. 105, 8-10). Finally, even though time is incorporeal, day and night and longer durations of time are bodies (Plutarch, *On common conceptions*, 1084c-d; also, Long and Sedley, 1987a: 306-308).

A discussion of Stoic conceptions of time could not be complete without a brief mention of their views on the everlasting cycle of world-order and conflagration. Being infinite and the dimension of the world's motion (Stobaeus, I. 106, 5-23), time could not but be linked to a kind of clock, like the succession of days and nights. Chrysippus clearly declares '... it is evidently not impossible that we too after our death will return again to the shape we now are, after certain periods of time have elapsed' (in Lactantius, *Divine institutes,* 7.23). In other words, he contends that there is an everlasting sequence of worlds and conflagrations, and that an individual and his actions in one world are exactly the same as those in any other of the worlds (Nemesius, 309. 5-311.2). This means that the Stoics understand time not as a linear concept, but rather as a cyclical one (also Eusebius, *Evangelical preparation*, 15.19.1-2). A similar view can be read in Cicero's *De Divinatione,* where his brother Quintus defends Stoicism and suggests that 'the passage of time is like the unwinding of a rope, bringing about nothing new and unrolling each stage in each turn' (I. 127). This cyclical view of time was not exactly new for the classical world, since ideas about endless recurrence have been attested for Anaximenes (ap. Eusebius, *Praep. Evang.* 1.8.1), Anaximander (Simplicius, *Phys.* 1121; in *Cael.* 293-4; 307), Heraclitus and Empedocles (Arist., *Cael.* 1.10, 279b13-17; also frg. 17, II.11-13);[20] circular time has also been sustained by Aristotle and Plato (see before).[21] The circular notion of time has been attributed as a general characteristic to the Greek thought, and it was meant to differentiate the classical world from Christianity and the changes the latter introduced

(Momigliano, 1969; also Fabian, 1983: 2). It is not the place and time (*sic*) here to deal with this issue and develop at length arguments for and against these views (see Sorabji, 1983; 1986; 1988). Nevertheless, we have to note that linear time was not an unknown option for the ancient Greek and Roman world. The common view of modern commentators that the Greeks presented time as circular, has been argued by Sorabji (1988) to have a much less drastic meaning than it seems at first. It could mean merely that events repeat themselves in linear time. Of course, the heavens could be seen as a kind of clock, where the longest period is marked by all the planets returning to their original alignments, and consequently, time comes to an end at the end of their cycle, and then starts all over again. Nevertheless, the word 'again' itself reveals a concept of time that does not end, but continues indefinitely in linear fashion (Sorabji, 1988: 182).[22] Finally, we should add that the Romans emphasised the idea of linear time, and they attributed the success of the Roman empire to a long line of ancestors during their past (Walsh, 1992: 10).

Other Roman attempts to define time also include Quintus Ennius (third century BCE) who affirmed that time is 'an objective manifestation of the universe under certain fixed laws' (*Annales* 8. 294). Varro materialized time as 'the division of movement in the universe' (*L.L.*, VI.2.52). Cicero, undertaking the conception of Plato, considers time as 'part of eternity that we determine with the words year, month, day, night...' (*De Invent.* I.26). Seneca reactualises the ideas of Plato, of Aristotle and of the Stoics on the time conceived as '...primary cause of the creative principle in nature', and confirms that 'without time nothing can be done' (Seneca, *ad Lucil.*, LXV) (also Baran, 1976).

To summarise, we have discussed the philosophical views on time and space developed by the four major philosophical schools of the ancient world, namely the Academics, the Peripatetics, the Stoics, and the Epicureans. In all four, time and space are necessary qualities for their discussions of ontology, physics, and epistemology. Time is related to motion and rest, it is measurable and numerable, and it can be used to arrange events in a prior/posterior order. Space, on the other hand, besides being the container of body/matter, and absolutely necessary in order to perceive the existence of everything in the world, is also an idea related to biological function, quantities and natural place. Furthermore, space has the capacity to provide the conditions for existence. In this sense, time and space are necessary determinants of knowledge, and as such define and order human life.

Mythical and Anthropological Perceptions of Time and Space

We saw already in the previous part how important language has been in defining space and time. We also discussed, albeit briefly, the interrelationship between the two qualities, as well as their association with ideas of arrangement and order. We are going to turn our attention now to the anthropological aspect of this discussion, and consider the dialectical relationship between language and deeply-rooted cultural beliefs on the one hand, and localisations of time on the other. The discussion will rely on Bettini's research (1991). But instead of arguing for the cultural construction of time as he does, we are going to focus on the implications of the relation between culture, time and space. In other words, we will discuss a number of oppositional sets through which time 'takes place', their similarities and correlations, at both the level of signifiers (more than one set expresses one and the same opposition), and the level of what is signified (one and the same category conveys several cultural contents) (Bettini, 1991: 193). Thus, we are going to put forward our argument that the way people perceive time and space can influence their personal, as well as the communal, construction of the world order, knowledge, material culture and memory.

Incorporeality of time renders it necessary for people to make out time as space, when it becomes an object of discourse.[23] Implications are arranged 'near' or 'far' ('*iuxta*' and '*longe*'), 'before' or 'behind' ('*ante*' and '*post*'), 'above' or 'below' ('*superiora*' and '*inferiora*') (Augustine, *Cat.* 10).[24] The individual either proceeds towards various temporal points, or awaits the advancement of time, which will bring (or has brought) happiness or trouble. A careful examination of the language used reveals not only the spatial conception of temporal notions, but also people's responses to these qualities.

One of the best-known adjectives associated with time, for instance, is '*antiquus*' (ancient), deriving from the word '*ante*' (before). Although we are used to understand the term as having a mere temporal meaning (that of antiquity, past), it is definitely a word with spatial connotations that imply arrangement. Examples from Latin writers[25] bring this meaning alive: 'that which is preferable is commonly called senior [*antiquius*]' (Fronto, 162.9 Nab.); 'Nor do good citizens hold anything senior to the common safety' (Varro, *Rerum humanarum* 20); 'It behooves to hold nothing senior to the laws' (Cicero, *De invent.* 1.142); 'he held nothing earlier [*prius*] or further before [*antiquius*] than...' (Velleius Paterculus, 2.52.4). Apparently, although the link of the adjective with its etymological root '*ante*' and consequently its positional value is largely lost for us, it was quite alive with the Romans. In this sense, the word '*antiquus*', and its comparatives *antiquior, antiquius,* imply hierarchy and order, and are associated with notions like 'senior' (and 'junior'), and 'first' (and 'then'). We can argue, therefore, that in the pair 'ante(rior)/post(erior)', 'first' is linked with what comes 'before', and 'then' is linked with what comes 'behind' (also 'senior/junior': 'before/behind') (Bettini, 1991: 117) (Figure 5.1).[26]

antiquus > ante > past > senior > before > first

ante	:	post
past	:	future
senior	:	junior
before	:	behind
first	:	then

Figure 5.1:   Spatial and temporal notions in linguistic terms.

This relation, however, changes when we start to think in terms of 'past/future'. 'Past' is commonly related to events and things that are 'behind', whereas 'future' is related to events that are 'in front of, before'. In this case then, the spatial representation is reversed, and instead of the equation 'anteriority/posteriority: first = before, then = behind', we reach the one where 'past/future : first = behind, then = before' (Bettini, 1991: 122) (Figure 5.2).

past	:	future
behind	:	before
first	:	then

Figure 5.2:   Linguistic associations between time and space: the 'absolute model' that contrasts past and future.

The Latin authors provide an abundance of examples illustrating these two new equations. Lucretius, for instance, speaks about it in these words: 'For when you look back [*respicias*] at the whole past space of immeasurable time...' (3.854); or Cicero asks 'how much further can my mind look back [*respicere*] the space of past time?' (*Pro Arch.* 1). Seneca also offers a wealth of examples: 'Nor do these who are busy have leisure to look back at what has given before' (*De brev. vit.* 10.2); 'No one gladly... twists himself back toward the past' (10.3).[27] In other words, to look at his past, the individual has to turn around, look behind. This is a way of establishing contact, and that is exactly what ought to be avoided with the world of the dead (Plautus, *Mostellaria*, 523). On the contrary, looking back is a useful thing for those who have reached the peak of their careers, since this is a way to maintain contact with mortal nature. Generals celebrating their triumphs were often advised to look back and remember that they were only humans (e.g. Tertullian, *Apol*. 33.4). The future, on the other hand, is placed in front of individuals. Death, which is the future event *par excellence* for all humans is usually located ahead.[28]

Another point that relates to time as past and future and its countenance with people is that of movement.[29] This is initiated sometimes by the individual, who 'runs toward' the future, sometimes by time itself that, as a personified figure, moves towards the subject. This is quite a popular picture drawn by Latin authors: 'Time will come, when...' (Virgil, *Geo*. 1.493); 'The years coming bring many advantages with them; going take many away' (Horace, *Ars Poetica*, 175); 'The present time is very brief, ... for it is always on the run; it flows and falls away' (Seneca, *De brev. vit.* 10.6). Consequently, the idea of time meeting the individual can be schematically presented as in Figure 5.3a.

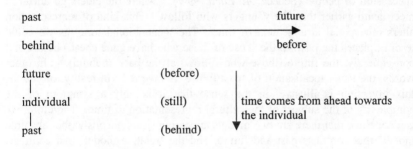

Figure 5.3a: Time 'meets' the individual.

On the other hand, the individual can be 'on the way' toward the future. Seneca, for instance, alerts his readers: 'Consider the shortness of this space, through which we run so very fast' (*Ad Lucil.* 99.7). In this case, the model is the same; it is the initiation, and the direction of movement, that alter (Figure 5.3b). Although in terms of spatial and temporal relations, these two models remain in principle the same (future = before, past = behind), they do influence people's views of the world in time and space, as well as of the individual itself.[30] In this sense, the spatial formula 'He goes and goes ...' and the temporal formula 'one day goes by and then another, and then another ... ' have homologous uses, since movement through space is movement through time, but they definitely imply a more static or dynamic context, and a different direction of time (from ahead to behind, and from behind to ahead) respectively (Bettini, 1991: 141)[31].

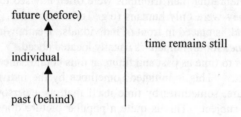

Figure 5.3b: The individual 'meets' time.

The association of space and time with movement can be a key point in understanding the concept of generation(s). Life can be represented as a long succession of people (Seneca, *Ad Lucil.* 99.7),[32] where the elders go ahead to meet death earlier than the youngers who follow. This kind of representation alters our spatial arrangement of time. The 'generational time' as we could term it, places the past (in the sense of those who have gone ahead) before and consequently, the future (those who follow) at the back (behind).[33] In other words, the usual localisation of 'past/future' is inverted. In reality, of course, this inversion is illusive, in the sense that it is only a symptom of the complexity of the subject of the cultural representation of time. Therefore, we can conclude that there are two models appearing simultaneously: the 'absolute model' that contrasts past and future, and the 'relative model' that contrasts before and behind (anterior and posterior) (also Bettini, 1991: 142-143) (Figure 5.4).

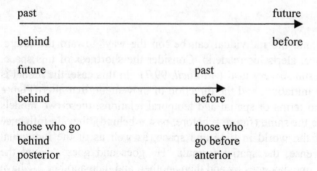

Figure 5.4:   Spatial and temporal relations: the 'relative model' that contrasts before and behind (anterior and posterior).

Besides the individual's role across time and the consequent spatialisation of it, as well as the individual's position (spatial and temporal) in line (θέσις and τάξις - see the distinction of Aristotle, previous section), knowledge defines its own time and space arrangement and is defined by it. In order to argue for this, we are going to turn to Roman religion and mythology. Janus, the two-faced god, bears temporal and spatial associations. He was the god of the beginning of the year (Ovid, *Fasti*, 1.65) and the source of the year's flow. But he also 'ruled' the end of the year (1.163), in what seems to be a cyclical perception of time (beginning and end coincide). But Janus had spatial powers too: he was the god of 'passings',[34] and the passageways were called *'iani'*.[35] The god, therefore, was associated with both 'going out' and 'coming back', both looking 'ahead' and looking 'behind', both 'future' and 'past' (Bettini, 1991: 127-128). In a paragraph by Macrobius we get a description of these beliefs:

> [Janus] is believed to have borne a twin countenance so that we might see what was before and what was behind his back: which undoubtedly must be explained as referring to the foresight and diligence of the king, who is to know what has passed and foresee what will be. Just so, the Romans worship Antevorta (Fore-turned) and Postvorta (Back-turned), certainly the most fitting companion of Janus. (*Sat.* 1.7.20).[36]

The word order here renders it explicit that to see ahead (*ante se*) is equated with knowledge of the past, whereas to see behind (*post*) is equated with foreseeing the future. The goddesses who accompany Janus are also mentioned in Ovid (*Fasti*, 1.631-636):

> If thou hast any love of ancient rites, attend the prayers offered to her: you shall hear names you never knew before. Porrima and Postverta are placated, whether they be thy sisters, Maenalian goddess,[37] or of companions of thine exile: the one is thought to have sung of what was long ago (*porro*), the other of what should come to pass hereafter (*venturum postmodo*).[38]

These goddesses are indications of this association: Porrima (or Antevorta), the goddess who is ahead, (*porro*) can speak about the past, whereas Postvorta (or Postverta), the one who is behind, knows about the future. Similar associations are true for Janus: the face that looks ahead symbolizes his knowledge of the past, and the face that looks back symbolizes his knowledge of the future. In other words, when knowledge is involved in the past and future, localisations are inverted, the 'cognitive model' of time becomes: past = front (ahead), future = behind (at the back) (Bettini, 1991: 151-157).

To the pairs that we have isolated and discussed so far (past/future, before/behind, anterior/posterior), we can also add one more: that of 'high/low'. Time is not only horizontal, in the sense that it does not receive spatial expressions only in the pairs 'before/after' (Figure 5.5). It can also be represented in a vertical manner as 'high/low', in which case we have a schema like that in Figure 5.6. The most characteristic example of this kind of representation is the genealogical tree/*stemma*, the characteristic figured version of the kinship system, arranging spatially the temporal relationships between the members of a family (Pearce, 1995: 265).[39]

before	after
ante	post

Figure 5.5:   Time as a horizontal notion.

Roman noble families prominently displayed in their *atria* representations of their genealogy.[40] This is a custom associated with the funerary portraits of ancestors kept in cupboards, and brought out for ceremonial occasions (Flower, 1996; Gazda, 1994: 26-27). In order to make the idea of prestigious genealogy, expressed through the possession and display of these portraits, visible and explicit, the same room was also often decorated with the names of the forebears linked by a complicated network of lines, the *stemmata* (Pliny, *HN*, 35.6; Polybius, *Histor.* 6.53). The 'high' position in these was held for the earlier times, whereas the 'low' position for subsequent ones. This orientation is in line with the 'future at your back' one we noticed earlier; in other words, time is inverted in order to express cultural values that overpower and dominate over mere localisation of time (Bettini, 1991). It thus becomes the medium for the expression of these values - but also in a way, it has influenced their creation.[41]

So far we have discussed a number of oppositional pairs and their role as signifiers of temporal localisations. We have argued that although all these sets express more or less the same opposition, they can convey several cultural contents. These acquire their significance as a result of cultural practice, and in their turn project back their hierarchies so that they create new and more complicated cultural valuations. To be more precise, the pair 'before/behind' corresponds with the pairs 'first/then', and 'high/low'. The first parts of these sets are apparently the stronger ones. This becomes obvious by both linguistic and other cultural examples: 'before', for instance, in Latin is expressed through a wealth of words/phrases, whereas 'behind' is very poorly represented. Similarly, when war ethics are involved, wounds that are 'before' (in front) are indications of bravery and decency, but those 'behind' are humiliating indications of cowardliness. 'Highest and lowest', to take another set, is an expression used to distinguish the dominant from the dependent classes, (e.g. *summi infimique* in Livy, 3.34). The same value is expressed with terms like '*humilis*' meaning 'lowly' both in position and in cultural terms, or '*fastigium*', which means both the 'upper part' of something and the 'height' of power (see again Livy, 6.38.13), and so on. The reason for their pre-eminence over the second parts derives from notions originating from the projection of the plan of the body.[42] In Aristotle already space had a biological dimension: just as in a person the principal organs and the head (the sovereign part, as the Stoics called it) reside in the higher and front part,[43] and the secondary or less important ones exist at the lower part and behind, so it is in metaphorical terms as well. 'Before' (in front of) is more important than 'behind', 'high' than 'low' and so on. The pair 'left/right' belongs here as well. Therefore, localisation does not merely mean a placement of time in space. It also involves the setting of cultural hierarchies; it acquires signification power, and cultural significance. In this sense, what comes 'first' may be considered the cause of what follows (comes 'then'), it can contain its grounds, constitute a precedent to be imitated and so forth.

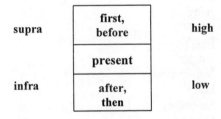

Figure 5.6:   Time as a vertical notion.

The pair 'past/future' acquires different values according to the circumstances. In personal terms, the past is linked with 'behind' and the future with 'before'. So the future (which is the personal 'then') gets cultural preeminence over the past (which is the personal 'first'). Instead of an objective model here (where 'first' is more important than 'then'), we have what we can call an 'existential' one. Life lived is put behind, whereas life that is yet to be lived is put in front. This personal 'past/future' relation cannot be considered an objective one, however, and it carries individual along with cultural investments in time (Bettini, 1991: Chapters 8, 12).

In 'absolute' terms, on the other hand, the past comes 'first' and the future 'then'. So it does when knowledge is involved: what we know (the past) is in front ('before' us), but what we cannot see (the future) is 'behind' (at the back). In this sense, the past is more important than the future. This idea can be further explored in relation to the next set, that of 'first/then : high/low'. We have seen this equation mainly in association with the genealogical *stemma*. There, the elders were at the top (high) and the youngers at the bottom (low). An additional indication of this hierarchy is the terms used: in Latin the ancestors are called *maiores* (greater) and the descendants *minores* (lesser). In between there is space for the a*equales* (the equals, of the same age). Of course, there is an immediate relation between these terms and the 'high/low' equation. What comes 'high' is more important than what comes 'low', and consequently, what is 'first' more than what is 'then'. This 'high/low' set is recognized by the Romans as an inversion of the 'natural' order of the tree, where the most important parts are 'low' and the less vital ones are 'high'. It does correspond though to the most important natural association of space, that of the human body. The case for 'before/behind'is similar: in humans all the vital parts are 'up' and 'front', all the lesser ones are 'down' and 'back'. We thus reach the following set of cultural significations for the pairs that we have discussed and some of the values they convey:

High	:	Low
Before	:	After
Front	:	Back
Noble	:	Ignoble
Refined	:	Vulgar
Human	:	Non-human
Right	:	Left
Important	:	Secondary
Brave	:	Cowardly

It is in these equations that we find the roots of concepts that determine our views about the world and our appreciation of values. It is from here that temporal statements often acquire their relation to causality; that we tend to impose models based on the past and ancestral customs; that those who can boast of remote origins acquire social and cultural predominance; that the origins of people and of cities are important; that men are proud of their autochthony, since having no predecessors means that the foundations of history and time can be touched; that *ab origine* people are more authentic; that the original thing (as opposed to the copy), and the antique (as opposed to the newly-made) are more desirable. It is obvious that personal and communal notions of the world order, of knowledge, and of the assemblage and arrangement of material culture, along with the value of memory, are determined by notions originating in the perception of temporal and spatial dimensions (Bettini, 1991).

Relation between Space and Objects

Space and time interact with other social actors, namely people and objects, in order to construct social organisation. Many of the abstract notions we use when referring to space (in particular, but the same can be said of time as well), for instance sacred, profane, public, private, male, female, and so on, in reality are defined as such because of the interaction of people and objects with spatial and temporal parameters. A variety of markers determine the classification and use of a certain space (or time), and signal to people the divisions and the role of space (or time)[44] according to social distinctions. Naturally, this relation becomes reciprocal, since social organisation also is reflected through the arrangement of space (or time). In the words of Goffman: 'the division and hierarchies of social structure are depicted microecologically, that is, through the use of small-scale spatial metaphors' (1979: 1).

In her discussion of the structuration principles that could be used to analyse architecture, as the process of organising unbounded space and human beings, Donley-Reid distinguishes three categories, people, spaces, and objects, and she examines five sets of reflexive relationships among them, as a means to see how symbolic values are created and how they are associated to power relationships (1990: 116). These are the following: '1. People-space': People tend to behave according to the room or the area they are in. Perceptions of space along with the environment (in the spatial sense) impose and shape views and behaviour. On the other hand, the presence of people determines the nature of a space. As Ardener (1978: 32; 1993: 18) has put it: 'The Court is where the King is'. In this sense, people define space. '2. People-objects': Objects as tangible parts of culture and tangible means of communication and thought (Douglas and Isherwood, 1979: 82) have the capacity to hold (and illustrate clearly) values attributed to them. In this case as well, the relationship is reciprocal since value is directed from people to objects, but also the other way around. '3. Objects-objects': this set means to describe the interrelation between groups (collections) of objects, where value is attributed due to, and in association with, objects being parts of the same group (collection). '4. Objects-space': the social value of an object affects the value of the space it occupies and vice versa. And finally, '5. Space-space': the social significance of a space actively participates in determining the value of related areas.

Material culture bears a very explicit reciprocal relationship with space.

> Objects are thought to structure the environment immediately around themselves; they cast a shadow, heat up the surround, strew indications, leave an imprint, they impress a part of themselves, a portrait that is unintended and not dependent on being attended, yet, of course, informing nonetheless to whomsoever is properly placed, trained, and inclined. (Goffman, 1979: 1).

Objects are also affected by the place in space of other objects: not only their presence but also their absence, or their 'negative presence' (Ardener, 1987: 3). We have come again across another reciprocal relationship: material culture acquires its value in relation to the value of other objects (in their presence or absence), according to the relative place of other items, but also according to their contexts.   A space is defined clearly by the 'selection' of objects occupying it (or not): a mere look at a room's or area's contents is enough for people (belonging to the same cultural group or having the means to decodify them) to let them classify it as private, public, sacred, profane, inner, outer, and so on.[45] Similarly, the inclusion of an object in an environment that is known to be (or has been classified as) any of the above, is enough to transmit the same quality to the object.

In the classical world, all the above parameters were clearly part of the mind set operating and dictating power relations and the setting of values.   The definition of space and its interrelationships can be discussed using the five points set by Donley-Reid (1990) and briefly presented above.   The most characteristic example of the relationship between people and space can be traced in Vitruvius' allocation of domestic arrangements, according to the social status of the owner (*De Architectura*, VI.v.2). His social role has to be, and was, reinforced by the appropriate spatial determinants that reassured a reciprocal suitability (and appropriateness).   In this category of 'markers' belong the size and complexity of buildings, room arrangement, decoration, and so on. (see also George, 1997: 305).[46]

In the second category (people-objects), collections are included. People use them to define or give social status and symbolic value to themselves or others. Inappropriate relationships of this sort are ridiculed among others in Petronius' *Satyrica* (see also Wallace-Hadrill, 1994: 3).   As for objects defining other objects (third set), we know that the relative position of artefacts was particularly important in the Roman world. Varro, for instance, argues that the principles of similarity and contrast work hand in hand in house decoration (as they do in language).[47]   Thus, a *triclinium* with three dissimilar couches is considered inappropriate, and the shortcoming should be corrected by analogy (*L.L.* 9.9). Similarly, different rooms are expected to be distinguished by the use of different furniture,[48] and the setting of silverware on the *abacus* (sideboard) to be arranged so that some pieces form matching pairs, while others contrast (*L.L.* 9.46) (Wallace-Hadrill, 1994: 14-15).[49]

This and the next relationship (objects - space) relate to notions of 'essential objects' and oppose to ordinary objects. The former are set apart for special use, they have sacramental associations and partake of the quality of the 'sacred'. In this sense, the placing of these objects helps the organisation and use of the physical space, the interplay of 'sacred' and 'profane'. Thus, objects of everyday life are permeated by sacred qualities, and thus are transformed, and also transform their surroundings.   Consequently, certain objects are appropriate for certain settings and others are not. For instance, when Cicero complains to his friend Fabius Gallus about having purchasing statues of Bacchantes for him, his rejection of the statues was based partly on their price, but partly too on the notion of them being inappropriate objects for the orator's space - he did not know where to accommodate them, they did not 'fit' into his surroundings (*ad Fam*. VII.23). Similar notions define, for instance, the opposition to the plundering of artefacts and the transference of them to individuals' space, or the regret expressed by most writers for those collectors who loved their objects so dearly that they kept them in the *cubicula*.[50] Space and objects bear a close interrelationship which holds a wealth of symbolic messages. Objects carry the capacity to evoke the sense of their time and place, which Romans knew and appreciated.

We can now proceed to our next section, where the impact of this knowledge and appreciation of the architecture, decoration and furnishing of Roman houses will be considered. We are going to limit the discussion to the Roman house, and leave out the Greek residencies, for two reasons: firstly, because the Roman house was the *locus* for the collections that we are going to discuss in the next part of this book; and, secondly, because Roman domestic space and architecture has attracted scholarly attention at a greater extent than the Greek ones,[51] and consequently, there is a wealth of evidence and of analytical approaches available that will facilitate our discussion.

Use of Objects to Evoke Sense of Time and Space: the impact on architecture, decoration and furnishing of Roman houses

The domestic context of ancient Rome offers the possibility to explore some aspects of the dialectical relationship between social and spatial behaviour. In addition to detailed and thorough publications regarding the physical evidence from excavations, recent years have seen a number of studies discussing social approaches to the subject (e.g. Zanker, 1979a; Thébert, 1987; Clarke, 1991; Wallace-Hadrill, 1994; Gazda, 1994, etc.). Naturally, the stance of this discussion is different, since, instead of placing emphasis on the social reasons for, or implications of, decorative programmes, and rather than establishing arguments for the interdependence of claims for social status and appropriate settings, we are going to underline the evocative power of objects. For the sake of this argument, mural decoration will be treated as belonging to the category of objects.

Two underlying factors have been particularly characteristic in Roman houses: the symbolic elements that were attached to and reinforced by the identity of the occupants and their relationship with the world around them, and a range of practical considerations deriving from both social concerns (they had to adapt space to suit the needs of social responsibilities), and broadly speaking, environmental requirements (weather, location, etc.) (Nevett, 1997: 289). Symbolism was largely responsible for the decoration of the house; we are thus going to try to illuminate (as far as this is possible) the motives behind the selection and arrangement of these decorations, not in order to argue for a conscious collecting motive behind every single case, for we cannot argue that every individual or family group who decides to decorate the living-room is collecting. Rather, it is mainly to argue for the power of objects to evoke a sense of their place and time, and the appreciation of this by the Roman élite. In other words, the Romans were conscious of how they could use objects to bring distant places and times closer, to appropriate them and the culture from which they derived (see also Stewart, 1993).

The central area of activities in the Roman *domus*[52] was the atrium: a large rectangular hall, onto which a series of symmetrically arranged rooms opened. This was the place of the hearth,[53] the site of the shrine (*lararium*), and the place devoted to *mos majorum*, the traditional, patriarchal arrangement of the Roman household (Dwyer, 1994). The atrium was there to impress visitors, and its effect was enhanced by sculptural and painted decoration, along with wax portraits and the family *stemma*.[54] It was also where the continuity of the family was projected, and the 'public' image of the household was constructed (about private versus public see below). The lavish nature of some of the items furnishing the atrium (for instance gold and silver vessels,[55] couches decorated with gold, silver and ivory[56]) further underline the importance of the room for impressing 'outsiders' with the wealth, power and importance of the household members (see also Nevett, 1997: 290). On each flank of the hall, two or three doors concealed small rooms, called *cubicula*, used for rest, but also for reception of intimate friends, clients or business associates (e.g. Apuleius, *Metamorphoses*, 1.23; Cicero, *Pro Scauro* 26.4; Pliny Younger 5.1.6; 5.3.1, etc.) (see also Dwyer, 1994; Riggsby, 1997). At the back of the hall was the *tablinum*, the sanctuary of the master of the house, where he received the *salutationes* from his clients, and others who were indebted to him. The place of the *tablinum* at the end of a longitudinal axis, slightly higher than the rest of the rooms, conveys familial and social messages about the role of the paterfamilias in Roman society, as well as the capacity of architectural space to enhance and reveal complicated social constructions (Dwyer, 1994: 27).

At this point, we should note that notions such as private and public are culturally determined and were very different in the Roman world than they are now. The Roman house was primarily public, open to the outside world, with the aim of having almost everything happen in the open, before everybody.[57] Although there were spaces where an invitation was necessary in order to enter (for example, in the *cubicula*), the Roman house was a much more public space than we are used to thinking of houses today (Nevett, 1997: 297-298; Wallace-Hadrill, 1994; Elsner, 1995: 76-77). The division of space served as a reminder of social hierarchy, and imposed on visitor and owner a certain set of behavioural rules, culturally ingrained and understood (George, 1997: 209-301; Riggsby, 1997). The discussion of Wallace-Hadrill (1994: 8-9) also reminds us that in the Roman house there were neither gender nor age spatial differentiation.[58]   The main division had to do with social hierarchy, and notions of public and private (George, 1997: 309; Wallace-Hadrill 1994: 10ff).

At this point we can choose only a few aspects of the huge variety of themes open to the student of the social implications of Roman interior and garden decoration. The first point to be mentioned is the transference of the language of public spaces to the domestic context, to give the illusion of a public space to the visitor. In this sense, forms that in Greece were used to enhance public space were translated by the Romans into the domestic context. Similarly, symbolisms associated with this kind of architecture crossed the line between public and private (Wallace-Hadrill, 1994: 10). Thus, Greek public building types were emulated by Roman architects and owners. This was not confined in architectural terms only (scale is one of the architectural parameters usually involved, use of columns is another),[59] but was extended to include the arrangement and the 'filling' of space, that would evoke a different feeling which would refer to Hellenistic notions of culture, and would eventually lead to the appropriation of whatever was considered important in that culture. Consequently, the Roman villas came to have their own *gymnasia* and *porticoes*, their *pinacothecae* and *palaestrae*, and resemble (in the sense of having absorbed) palatial and sacred buildings of the Hellenistic past.

According to contemporary theoretical views on architecture and society, the individual conceptions of 'places' in the built environment seem to be founded on specific value judgments and expectations defined by the world view (Sanders, 1990: 45-46).   Within a cohesive group, conceptual attitudes resulting from cultural conventions are incorporated in future decisions about the built environment (Canter, 1977; Sanders, 1990).   In this sense, a continuous interactive relationship is being built among culture, architecture, behaviour and decoration. According to Rapoport, 'Buildings and settings are ways of ordering behavior by placing it into discrete and distinguishable places and settings, each with known and expected rules, behaviors and the like. ... Built environments thus communicate meanings to help serve social and cultural purposes; they provide frameworks, or systems of settings for human action and appropriate behavior;' (1980: 300) (see also the same about time: Rapoport's system of activities, 1990).

The above discussion finds its best expression in the Roman notion of *decor*. In scholarly literature it has been emphasized that the choice of works of art for the Roman collector was determined by their theme, according to the notion of appropriateness, and we know how important this was for Roman artistic thought (Pollitt, 1974). Although current research has shown that this principle alone was by no means the only one that dictated the selection and arrangement of collections in the classical world (far from that - the burden of this book is a long argument against such exclusivity, and an advocate of a wider resonance), there can be no doubt that it was indeed a very important one (see also Bartman, 1988; 1994). This principle dictated the placement of images of athletes in the *gymnasium*, and portraits of the Muses in the library.

Cicero offers the best documentation for this kind of principle when he writes his letters to Atticus and Fabius Gallus: he exhorts Atticus to purchase for him statues that would be appropriate for the *gymnasium,* and he refuses Gallus' purchases on the grounds of their inappropriateness for the image of himself he wants to create in his own domestic context, using works of art as a medium. Just like books, he was constantly reminding Atticus, were necessary for the formation of a library, so were the statues and herms for the evocation of the feeling of the *gymnasium* (see Chapter 9 on Cicero). Cicero was nostalgic for his golden days in Athens, and he wanted to have the memory of those days in his domestic environment (Marvin, 1989). For this reason, he was keen to acquire a collection that would allow such an appropriation of space and time.

Similarly, we know both from literary sources and archaeological evidence that the Romans enjoyed the recreation of geographical or mythological spaces in their properties. Scholars have associated these with the 'decorative programme' of different villas, and elaborate attempts have been made to account for some of the most coherent and best surviving recreations. Vitruvius advises his readers to decorate walkways with a variety of landscape settings, which copied the most characteristic features of specific places [*a certis locorum*]. Other famous examples include the villa of the Papyri at Herculaneum, where statuary (and possibly other objects) were diplayed in harmonious settings to evoke an elaborate message (Lafon, 1981),[60] and Hadrian's villa at Tivoli, which was decorated with a *lycaeum,* an *academia,* a *prytaneum,* a *canopus,* a *poecile* and a temple (*Scriptores Historiae Augustae, Hadrian,* 26.5).

We have tried here to read the ideas about decorative programmes developed in ancient Rome, as an attempt to recreate through objects a certain spatial metaphor, to evoke and appropriate the distant in time and space. We are now going to look at another aspect of this notion: Romans developed further the mnemotechnics that Greeks had devised, and gave a tangible and corporeal dimension to it. In addition, the Roman house, with its decoration, became one of the major areas for depositing and retrieving memories. In this sense, it incited the notion of the rituals involved in visiting collections in public or private settings.

Role of Objects in the 'Art of Memory'

Wallace-Hadrill recently encouraged scholars to treat the Roman house 'as a coherent structural whole, as a stage deliberately designed for the performance of social rituals, and not as a museum of artifacts' (1994: 60). Although this assertion is justified, since archaeologists tended until recently to treat excavation material from ancient Roman contexts as devoid of any value other than aesthetic, it is unjustified when it comes to an actual comparison between the Roman house and a museum. Both share the common characteristic of being places where artefacts are used to appropriate distant space and time, and a social ritual of remembrance and transference into another spatial and temporal context is performed. In this section, we are going to discuss classical notions of memory, in order to suggest a profound equivalence between the Roman *domus* as a setting for collections and subsequent settings.

Spatial arrangement was associated with memory already in the Greek world. The invention of a mnemonics technique based on spatial arrangements was assigned to Simonides of Ceos[61] (Cicero, *De Oratore* 2.351-354) in an anecdote concerning the guests at a banquet (Yates, 1966: 1-3). Roman writers rendered this system a basic feature of rhetorical education, that reflected the highly elaborate capacities of the verbal and visual culture the Romans fostered. Three descriptions of this system survive today, one by Cicero (*De Oratore*, 2.86.351-360), one by the anonymous Auctor ad Herennium (once attributed to Cicero too) (*Rhetorica ad Herennium*, 3.16-24), and the last by Quintilian (*Institutio Oratoria*, XI.2.17-26).

The Sophists developed some kind of a memory system in order to provide general arguments of discussion, or lists of cities, genealogies, and so on (see for instance, Plato's *Hippias Major*). But the first to provide a full description of the system of memorizing through places was Aristotle (*Topica* 163b.24-30). He also wrote a treatise on the subject of memory (*De memoria et reminiscentia*), based on the theory of knowledge he expounded in his *De Anima*. Aristotle recommends a method of memorising based on his views about knowledge and imagination (it is impossible to think without a mental picture created in the mind),[62] and suggests memorising in sequence, because it is easier to remember things in an order.[63] Similarly to Simonides, Aristotle recommends a permanent set of places (*topoi*), where a number of different pieces of information can be stored; each set of information has its own group of vivid images associated with a single set of places. Aristotle encouraged the placing of arguments (or parts of them) in numbered *topoi*, which would enable the philosopher, or any other person, to recall a list of arguments, items, rules, and so on, in any order (Yates, 1966: 31-35; Small, 1997: 87-94). Aristotle and the Greek thought retained the system as a purely mental construct with no physical aspects (Small, 1997: 94).[64]

The Romans extended this system from a mental construct into a physical embodiment, where '*topoi*' became actual settings or buildings. Cicero presents the system as follows:

> But these forms and bodies, like all the things that come under our view require an abode [*sede* = seat], inasmuch as a material object without a locality [*loco*] is inconceivable. Consequently (in order that I may not be prolix and tedious on a subject that is well known and familiar) one must employ a large number of localities [*loci*] which must be clear and defined and at moderate intervals apart, and images that are effective, and sharply outlined and distinctive, with the

capacity of encountering and speedily penetrating the mind; (*De Oratore*, 2.87.358).[65]

A similar corporeality and physicality is considered necessary by other Romans as well (see e.g. Lucretius, 1.471-474; Quintilian, 11.2.17).

In *Rhetorica ad Herennium* (written in the 80s BCE) this physicality gets more concrete and becomes associated with the architectural space of the Roman house: 'By backgrounds I mean such scenes as are naturally or artificially set off on a small scale, ... for example, a house, an intercolumnar space, a recess, an arch, or the like' (3.16.29). A century later Quintilian presents a brief but explicit account of the system:

> Some place is chosen of the largest possible extent and characterised by the utmost possible variety, such as a spacious house divided into a number of rooms. Everything of note therein is carefully committed to the memory, in order that the thought may be enabled to run through all the details without let or hindrance . ... However, let us suppose that the symbol is drawn from navigation, as, for instance, an anchor; or from warfare, as, for example, some weapon. Those symbols are then arranged as follows. The first thought is placed, as it were, in the forecourt (*vestibulo*); the second, let us say, in the living-room (*atrio*); the remainder are placed in due order all round the *impluvium* and entrusted not merely to bedrooms (*cubiculis*) and bays (*exedris*), but even to the care of statues and the like. This done, as soon as the memory of the facts requires to be revived, all these places are visited in turn and the various deposits are demanded from their custodians, as the sight of each recalls the respective details. ... What I have spoken of as being done in a house, can equally well be done in connexion with public buildings, a long journey, the ramparts of a city or even pictures. Or we may even imagine such places to ourselves. (*Institutio Oratoria*, 11.2.18-21).[66]

In other words, the architectural layout of a Roman house could, and did, serve as a means for ordering and memorizing speeches, as well as for structuring thought (Elsner, 1995: 77). The Roman used the visual and architectural environment (in the broader sense to include all the *loci* that Quintilian lists in his last sentence) to think and remember, in a three-dimensional way. Then, the notion of order (series > *ordo*) becomes of primary importance for the house: the various *loci* (*vestibulum, atrium, impluvium, exedrae* is what Quintilian suggests) should be memorized in an order, and this helps as one moves through the house to remember a speech (Cicero, *De Oratore*, 2.86.354). This is a crucial characteristic (*Ad Herennium*, 3.17.30), because once the arrangement has been achieved, the orator can 'move' around freely and reconstruct what he has to remember in any order (3.18.30). The significance of this *ars memoriae* has not been sufficiently exploited by art historians and social historians. It undoubtedly bears witness to an elaborate relationship between the rhetorical and the visual capacity of the Romans, or in other words, to an extremely sophisticated culture of viewing (see Elsner, 1995: 77ff). But the most important points for our argument here remain the following: the interrelationship between objects and symbolic meanings set on them without direct relation to the original object; the realization of the importance of *loci* (places) for structuring thought; and the notion of *loci* and objects serving to evoke symbolisms attributed to them at a previous time. The built frame thus was crucial for the Romans as organiser of space, thoughts, and experiences. On the other hand, ancient memory systems were material and spatial. In *Rhetorica ad Herennium*, for instance, the unknown author refers to memory as a 'treasure-house' *(thesaurum)* (3.16.28). So time, space and material culture are connected into an ineradicable association.

We have seen in the previous section that Romans used artefacts to evoke a sense of different places and times. On the other hand, we know that for Cicero (as for Aristotle) beauty meant 'order on a large, often cosmic, or smaller agricultural scale ... fulfilling a function; and ... a certain easily recognized organic unity or identity' (quoted in Small, 1997: 231). When Cicero (and for that matter any other Roman patron) decided to decorate his villa, his sense of beauty, his belief in the evocative power of objects, and his ideas about how memory works together determined the collection of sculpture.

The Roman house as a physical and symbolic structure was identified with both the individual and the collective memory. A characteristic example of the former is the *damnatio memoriae* which included the destruction of the house, so as to erase a person's existence.[67] And the Roman house, with the typical organisation and decoration we have seen (*atrium*, decoration with *imagines*, and so on), invited a set of memories, furnished anchoring points for them and 'places' where they could safely lie. On the other hand, the commonly shared beliefs which determined the decoration experienced the house as a vehicle through which tradition was transmitted from one generation to the other. In this sense, the Roman house with all its objects, inherited or bought, and the memories they carried or which were attributed to them, operated like a dialectic theatre of rituals through which memory and knowledge were constructed (Bergmann, 1994: 226).

Conclusions

To conclude, starting from the basic assumption that collections are a selecting process *par excellence*, and the collector uses them to facilitate or mark the passage of time, and accommodate himself in space, we attempted to show how temporal and spatial notions of the classical world influenced the nature of classical collecting.

The discussion started with the presentation of the philosophical thought developed by ancient Greek and Roman philosophers belonging in the four major philosophical schools, namely the Academics, the Peripatetics, the Stoics, and the Epicureans. Their views about time and space, although developed in association with physical, cosmological, and metaphysical concerns, provided a wealth of general ideas about these qualities, which from their position at the background of classical thought influenced the development of views on other issues. Therefore, time was understood as having the capacity to order and arrange events in a prior/posterior basis, as related to movement and rest, being numerable and measurable. Space, on the other hand, was the container of the body, and essential for the existence and conception of everything in the world. Space arranged things (bodies), just like time arranged events. It was related to the natural place of all elements in the world, and corresponded with biological ideas about order and sequence. Together, space and time guaranteed the cosmic order, and they helped the construction of notions of knowledge and human life at large.

Having these broad ideas in mind about the role and operation of time and space, ancient collectors had the necessary framework and thinking tools to develop ideas about the role of objects and material culture in the arrangement of the world, as well as to develop elaborate techniques of display and patterns of assemblage that would reveal the ideas of order, development, natural positioning, and so on.

Then, an anthropological and mythological discussion of Roman notions of time and space was attempted. Within the philosophical framework that we discussed in the previous section, but also independently, temporal parameters found expression in spatial arrangement, and mythical equivalencies. As linguistic evidence suggests, there have been a number of common arrangements of time to be understood as space, and this was related to ideas about order and cultural concepts. Consequently, cultural constructs, like the pre-eminence of the antique, or of past over future (at different circumstances), or of ancestors instead of descendants, relates to perceptions of order in temporal and spatial terms, and has been endowed with cultural significance and signification power. This of course, influences not only the values attributed to material culture, but also the very way of thinking about life, knowledge, and so on. It also determines ideas about the setting of collections, the organisation of space to reveal world order, and finally, it is an important and explicit way of associating with time. Modern museums still struggle to find alternative ways of structuring their collections other than the chronological, developmental one, where the past (the earliest specimens, previous historical periods) come first, and the more recent ones come afterwards, or the hierarchical one where the most important objects are isolated in cases on high *podia*, in the centre of the gallery.

Next, our attention was focused on the Roman collecting practices. Instead of a comprehensive account of all information on Roman collections held in domestic context, this meant to be a broad discussion of how all the notions we considered in the previous sections found expression in the Roman world. The domestic context in particular, but the public areas too, were defined by a strict set of social and ritual principles. According to this, spaces, objects, and people interacted and structured mutual relationships, to define each other and collaborate so that they constructed a comprehensive and reasonable environment in which to live. Collections were part of this process.

Objects were considered active participants in a two-way process: on the one hand, they defined the place and time they belonged to, while on the other they could carry this dimension with them, and evoke a different temporal and spatial dimension when placed elsewhere. This, being one of the main principles of collecting, has been particularly important. Examples from literary sources, and archaeological evidence indicate that the Romans were very keen to use material culture to recreate and evoke the sense of a different time and place in their private villas, and also in public settings. This aspect of the Roman mind set has been discussed within the context of luxury and social significance so far, but it seems that this has not been understood as a capacity that material culture carries *par excellence*. Therefore, the elaborate architectural settings that a Roman patron/collector had created on his estate were not by themselves sufficient; they needed to be filled with statuary, paintings, and other works of art. These would communicate actively the message of him having recreated an environment from a distant time and place, whether this was a *gymnasium*, a *palaestra*, or a *library*, and consequently, would emphasise that he had appropriated all the cultural values that were associated with them (often these were temporal and spatial as well, for instance, being before they were more important than what came after, and so on).

To evoke a distant time and place, though, means that memory has to be activated. This is another characteristic that the Roman society developed in relation to temporal and spatial terms. The Roman house had a social and ritual role, which was actually fulfilled through collections. This was to evoke a certain feeling (respect, awe), and to facilitate social communication and interrelation, as well as to signal personal and family power. All these messages were transmitted through objects, which were meant to bring past and distant accomplishments in front of the eyes of visitors to the house and its inhabitants. In other words, objects as well as architectural space were meant to bring people in touch with their memory.

The Romans developed a very elaborate mnemotechnic system, where they associated objects and buildings with memories. Again, the influence of philosophical thought as discussed in the earlier part of this chapter comes to mind. Aristotle's elaborate discussion about places found a more practical use in the Roman thought, and was soon developed to become a system of mnemonics based on material culture. The mythological thought that memory (Mnemosyne was the Greek name of the goddess) and her daughters (Muses) could bring someone in contact with other times and places, here found its best expression. The Roman house, and also public buildings, were recognised as a *locus*, where different objects and architectural settings in an orderly arrangement could serve to reconstruct a memory, to transfer the viewer or the visitor to a different place and time, to bring alive in front of him ideas and subjects that would otherwise be lost in λήθη (forgetfulness) - the opposite of αλήθεια (truth), but also of memory. In this sense, we find many similarities between the Roman house and the modern museum. Both are venues of social and ritual practices, and both rely on material culture to achieve a virtual transference to another world (in temporal and spatial meaning). Both transmit cultural and social messages, and aim to facilitate communication between visitors and the social order of things, but also to bring visitors in front of their memory, in front of their past. This can be revealed through the evocative power of objects, as well as through their selective arrangement in time and space, which corresponds to cultural valuations while also defining these valuations.

We are now going to see how the parameters of collecting, as we have presented them in the four previous chapters, relate to classical collecting as this is witnessed in our case-studies, about the four authors.

Notes

1   Translation in Loeb CL, *Ovid, Heroides and Amores*, translated by Grant Showerman, 1957: 351.

2   Translation by Pusey, cited in Yates, 1966: 46.

3   There has been extended discussion of the view that time and space are pre-existent, and not at all sociologically defined notions. For arguments against this view and further bibliography, see Gell, 1992.

4   For collection as a classification process see Pearce, 1995; Baudrillard, 1968.

5   'εἴκω ... κινητόν ... αἰῶνος' (*Timaeus*, 37d).

6   Ὡς δέ κίνηθεν αὐτό καί ζῶν ἐνενόησεν τῶν αἰδίων θεῶν γεγονός ἄγαλμα ὁ γεννήσας πατήρ, ἡγάστη καί εὐφρανθείς ἔτι δή μᾶλλον ὅμοιον πρός τό παράδειγμα ἐπενόησεν ἀπεργάσασθαι' : it is interesting to note here the play with the words (agalma) ἄγαλμα (thing of joy, statue) and ἡγάστη (rejoiced), Loeb CL: 75.

7   Translated in Loeb CL, *Plato (Timaeus, Critias, Cleitophon, Menexenus, Epistles)*, with an English translation by R. G. Bury, London and Cambridge Mass., 1952.

8   Translated by Apostle, 1969.

9   The distinction of prior and posterior in motion arises from spatial difference (Callahan, 1948: 193-194).

10   *Cael.* 2.3, 285a15f; b3ff; *Inc.* 4.750a28-b18; 706a13ff; *Part. an.* 10,656a13; 4.7, 683b19-25; 4.8, 683b35; *Phys.* IV.1, 208b15.

11   'A place, then, is this, namely, the primary motionless boundary of that which contains' (translated by Apostle, 1969).

12   Of the terms *chora* and *topos* the former appears earliest in the sources. It means 'land / region / ground' and when applied to smaller pieces of ground 'stretch / field / ground / place' (Homer, *Od.*, IX.573; XXII.366). The terms could be used interchangeably both in common parlance, and in the first philosophical uses of them:

topos usually to denote relative location, *chora* to denote a larger extension than *topos*. Plato seems to have considered the terms identical and uses them almost interchangeably (only *chora* sometimes is used for larger extensions); he also uses the term *hedra*, another word which could be used as a synonym (Aeschylus, *Eu.*, 11). Aristotle uses the term *topos* exclusively in his *Physics* when he defines his views concerning place, but he uses both terms interchangeably in passages of a dialectical nature. Until the Hellenistic period there was no term used exclusively to denote space. The Stoics and the Epicureans turned these words into technical terms: for the Stoics the term *topos* roughly may be thought to give the notion of 'place', whereas '*chora*' seems to have had different technical and non-technical meanings, and cannot be translated simply as 'space'. Epicurus, as we will see further in this chapter, turned the terms '*topos*' and '*chora*' into technical terms which refer to space in different contexts (Algra, 1995: 31-38).

13   For arguments supporting a developmental approach to Aristotle's views on space see Mendell, 1987; for these and contra arguments see full discussion and bibliography in Algra, 1995.

14   The translations from the Epicurean and Stoic writers that follow are from the first volume of Long and Sedley, 1987, unless otherwise stated.

15   Epicureanism also discusses time in relation to pleasure and death. It is argued that time has no bearing on the quantity of pleasure, and that finite time and infinite time can be equally pleasant as long as one has lived a full life. 'Infinite time and finite time contain equal pleasure, if one measures the limits of pleasure by reason' (Epicurus, *Key doctrines*, 19).

16   'ἀναφής φύσις' is the term that Epicurus used (Sextus Empiricus, *M.* 10.2).

17   The fourth incorporeal in the Stoic ontology is *lekton* (sayable).

18   Major discussion of Stoic theories on time in Goldschmidt, 1979, Sorabji, 1983: 17-32; Lloyd, 1970 and Rist, 1969: chapter 15.

19   This is the definition of Zeno. Another definition of time that the same source has rescued for us is the one by Chrysippus: 'the dimension of the world's motion' (Simplicius, *On Aristotle's Categories* 340, 15-16 - *SVF* 2.510).

20   Plato, without having himself developed a theory of endless recurrence, has provided the myths that many of the subsequent theories employed: for instance, the idea of the Great Year (when all circles - of all the bodies - have resumed their original motion and have returned to their original alignment, that Heraclitus had added (Aetius, 2.32.3) was developed in *Timaeus* (39d; 22b-23c); also see *Phaedrus*, 246a-249c, and *Statesman*, 269b-274e. See also for discussion and bibliography, Sorabji, 1983: 182ff.

21   For a discussion of the distinction between human and divine time as this is perceived by the ancient Greeks see Vidal-Naquet, 1986.

22   Discussion of circular versus linear time in ancient philosophy in Sorabji, 1988: 182ff, where also bibliography.

23   See also Aristotle's views in the previous section.

24   Right and left are not among the categories that represent time (for discussion about this pair see below).

25   Translations in this section are by Bettini (1991), unless otherwise stated.

26   Bettini (1991) discusses at length the terms used to denote anteriority/posteriority in Latin; he reaches the same conclusion for all the pairs of course. In addition, he remarks that the terms denoting 'before' are numerically more (and more elaborate) than those for 'behind'; he uses this remark in his arguments about the superiority of before' in chapter 12; see also pp. 118-120.

27   For another similar example, see Seneca, *De brev. vit.*, 10.5.

28   Seneca reverses this order in a phrase that reveals his existential reflections: 'For in this we are deceived, that we look ahead to death: ... whatever is behind in age, it holds death' (*Ad Lucil.* 1.1-3).

29   For a discussion of the relation between movement (motion), time and space in philosophical terms, see the discussion above.

30   For a discussion of the passive and active role of the individual in time's passing, see Toohey, 1997; also Wallace-Hadrill, 1987, and Beard, 1987.

31   Although Bettini does not emphasise the difference in ideology that these two imply.

32   It is worth mentioning the whole paragraph of Seneca's epistle:

> *Respice celeritatem rapidissimi temporis, cogita brevitatem huius spatii, per quod citatissimi currimus, observa hunc comitatum generis humani eodem tendentis minimis intervallis distinctum, etiam ubi maxima videntur; quem putas perisse, praemissus est. Quid autem dementius quam, cum idem tibi iter emetiendum sit, flere eum, qui antecessit? Flet aliquis factum, quod non ignoravit futurum? ... Intervallis distinguimur, exitu aequamur.*

> Note the rapidity of Time - that swiftest of things; consider the shortness of the course along which we hasten at top speed; mark this throng of humanity, all straining toward the same point with briefest intervals between them - even when they seem longest; he whom you count as passed away has simply posted on ahead. And what is more irrational than to bewail your predecessor, when you yourself must travel on the same journey? Does a man bewail an event which he knew would take place? ... Periods of time separate us, but death levels us.

> Text and translation from Loeb CL.

33   See also Publilius Syrus, *App. sent.* 33R. An example of this kind of perceiving time can be seen in the Roman funerals, where the masks of the ancestors were placed at the front of the procession and in this order. See Bettini, 1991, and Flower, 1996.

34   Cicero in his *De Natura Deorum* says that 'From "going" [*eundo*] the name Janus is drawn, from which open passageways are called "*iani*", and doorways over the thresholds of profane dwellings are named "*ianuae*"'(2.67).

35   The fact that the same god bears both temporal and spatial connections is indicative of the relation between time and space as this was understood by the ancients.

36   Translated in Bettini, 1991: 154.

37   This is addressed to Carmentis, a prophetic deity (Bettini, 1991: 155).

38   Translated in Loeb CL, *Ovid* (in six volumes), volume V, *Fasti*, with an English translation by Sir James G. Frazer (second edition revised by G. P. Goold), Cambridge Mass. and London, 1989.

39   For a thorough discussion of the impact of kinship notions in collecting, see Pearce, 1995.

40   For full discussion of the implications and importance of this custom, see Flower, 1996.

41   We could also add here the funeral procession where the portraits of the ancestors were going first and the portraits of the descendants followed (see Flower, 1996 and Bettini, 1991: 176-183).

42   For a discussion of the body as the generator of ordering principles see also Tuan, 1977: 36 (especially his diagram) and Pearson and Richards, 1994: 10 (the same diagram as in Tuan).

43   See Lloyd's article (1962) about ancient Greek views on right and left; and Konstan (1972) on Epicurus' views on 'up' and 'down'.

44   We are going from now on to focus the discussion on space for two reasons: firstly, because as we have seen time is represented as space more often than not, and

secondly, because space offers a more explicit case for our discussion, since eventually we are going to focus on the domestic context of the Roman world.

45   See also Pearce, 1995: 265.

46   Vitruvius' text has been read from a variety of perspectives, and for a number of reasons: it was usually meant to explain and describe the usual domestic arrangements of ancient Romans, and the main emphasis has been placed on social hierachies as these are revealed through the text, and not as indications of spatial correspondence. Nevertheless, I feel that this has been an area that should have been included in the discussion because it is very much part of social structure and understanding.

47   It is interesting that the formal and thematic arrangement corresponds to rhetorical principles, like *similitudo*, *vicinitas*, *contrarium*, because according to their relative position, things maybe similar, near, or antithetical, they provoke certain lines of thought (see Bergmann, 1994: 246ff for a discussion of the issue in relation to mural paintings).

48   'Or, again with couches in dining rooms: on the one hand you distinguish your *triclinia* using ivory-inlaid couches here, tortoise-shell there; on the other, you create matching sets by ensuring the couches in one setting are matched in height and material and shape, and using the same fabric for cushions, napkins, and so on' (*L.L.* 9.47) (Wallace-Hadrill, 1994).

49   For the same relationship argued in archaeological context for sculptural collections, see Bartman, 1988.

50   For *cubicula* where art collections were kept see Pliny, *HN*, 34.62; 35.3; 35.5; 35.70; Suetonius, *Tiberius*, 43.2; 44.2; *Caligula*, 7.1; *Nero*, 25.2.

51   Greek domestic architecture has been the subject of some very interesting publications, see, mainly, Hoepfner and Schwandner, 1986 and Walter-Karydis, 1994; also Jameson, 1990a and 1990b.

52   For a discussion of other types of Roman housing see McKay, 1977; Boethius, 1960; Wallace-Hadrill, 1994; Zanker, 1979a; Lafon, 1981. Dwyer (1994) discusses in detail and refutes the idea that there is a decline in the atrium type house at the end of the first century BCE onwards.

53   On the hearth as a central part of the Greek home, as well as on the mythological associations of the hearth, Hestia, the goddess-protrectress of the hearth, and notions of space in Greek mythology, see Vernant, 1983a.

54   For a discussion of the atrium, see Vitruvius, 6.5.2; Suetonius, *Vita Iuvenalis*, 12; Seneca, *Dialogues*, 6.10.1; Velleius Paterculus 2.14.1; Ovid, *Metamorphoses*, 5.3; Lucan 10.119; Apuleius, *Metamorphoses*, 6.10; Suetonius, *Gaius*, 41.2; Valerius Maximus 5.8.3; Ovid, *Amores*, 1.8.65; and *Fasti*, 1.159; Elder Pliny, *HN*, 35.5; Seneca, *Dialogues*, 11.14.3.

55   As attested by Curtius 8.12; Sallust, *Histories* frg. 2.86.1.

56   See Horace, *Satires* 2.6.11, *Epistles* 1.5.1; Livy, 39.6.7; Martial, 3.81.6.

57   Note the difference with Greek houses where privacy was meant to be protected (Graham, 1966; Jameson, 1990a).

58   As opposed to the Greek house, see previous note. For a detailed consideration of allocation of space in gender terms in the Roman house, see Wallace-Hadrill, 1996: 104-115.

59   See Wallace-Hadrill, 1994: 10ff.

60   Different views exist about this message: Pandermalis (1971) in a seminal article argues that the sculpture was collected and displayed to express the dichotomy between public and private life, *otium* and *negotium*; Sauron (1980), argues for the evocation and promulgation of Elysian imagery; Wojcik (1986) suggests that the sculpture groups meant to reveal aristocratic values of the Late Republic, and allowed for contradictory and complementray associations to exist among the different groups;

Neudecker (1988) offers yet different allusions and messages to the different groups. Warden and Romano (1994) argue for a carefully planned didactic arrangement of figures: the display of virtue.

61   Lyric poet, much admired in ancient Greece; circa 556-468 BCE.

62   *De Anima*, 427b.18-22; 432a.17; 431b.2 etc.; *De memoria et reminiscentia*, 449b.31.

63   For a discussion of Aristotle and memory see Sorabji, 1972, and Annas, 1984.

64   Aristotle's application of the word 'topos' to patterns of argument gave its name to the treatise 'Topics'; this is where the English words 'topic' and 'commonplace', as well as the expression 'in the first place' originate from. See Sorabji, 1972.

65   Translated in Cicero, *De Oratore*, Loeb CL, by E. W. Sutton, 1948, pp. 469-470.

66   Translated in Loeb CL, *The Institutio Oratoria of Quintilian*, translated by H. E. Butler, 1922, pp. 221-223.

67   The violent death of people was usually accompanied by a complete destruction of their living quarters; see, for instance, Cicero, *De Officiis*, 1.138; *dom.*, 102; Valerius Maximus, VI.3.1c.

PART II

Classical Collectors and Collections

Chapter 6

Visiting Pliny's Collection: reading a 'museum'

It is impossible adequately to describe the multitude of those
spectacles and their magnificence under every conceivable aspect,
whether in works of art or in diversity of riches or natural rarities; for
almost all the objects which men who have ever been blessed by
fortune have acquired one by one - the wonderful and precious
productions of various nations - by their collective exhibition on that
day displayed the majesty of the Roman Empire.

(Josephus, *Jewish War*, VII.132-133)[1]

To collect is to launch individual desire across the intertext of
environment and history.

(Cardinal, 1994: 68).

Introduction

The synthesis of *Historia Naturalis* can be ascribed to the prominent attempt,
in the early Empire, to systematize knowledge and provide an accessible and
comprehensive guide to it. Following the needs of the rapidly expanding
technical and professional classes of Rome, for practical and popularised
knowledge, and as a result of the establishment of scientific curiosity as a form
of cultural consumption, handbooks and encyclopedias of various sorts had
begun to appear in Rome as early as the time of Cato the Censor and M.
Terentius Varro.[2] Balancing between early scientific culture and pure
dilettantism, Pliny's oeuvre points toward the most prolific attempt to provide a
work destined for consultation and imitation (Conte, 1994b: 499-502).

Yet *Historia Naturalis* (hereafter *HN*) is more than just an example of a
literary genre, however exceptional and complete. While it partly shares
characteristics and attributes of the paradoxographic tradition, initiated by

Greek writers in the retinue of Alexander the Great, and rigorously promoted to become a genuinely new literary genre in Rome,[3] it provides a summary and conclusion, an epitome of the culture of the first century CE, the end-product of developments in life, education, literature and philosophy over the previous two hundred years. In the words of Conte (1994a: 90), *HN* should be considered as 'a monumental "culture text"', providing insights not only to the cultural practices, but also to the cultural discourses and paradigms of its era. The second part of this chapter will concentrate therefore on outlining the principles that shape *HN* and the features that differentiate it from other similar texts.

After this, we will focus on a particular category of cultural activity, which plays a prominent role in *HN*, that of collecting. The risks that such an attempt encompasses have been already highlighted by Rouveret (1987: 116):

> Mais il faut au préalable s'interroger sur les sens même des termes "collection", "exposition", "musée". Ne risque-t-on pas de plaquer sur une réalité antique, très differente, des notions modernes, elles-même progressivement constituées et modifiés au fil du temps?

Due to a similar concern, Isager's monograph (1991) has been criticised for assimilating ancient cultural practices with their modern counterparts (Tanner 1995: 184). Sharing these concerns, the present enquiry does not aspire to recover in Pliny's pages 'lost' museums and art galleries in the contemporary sense. On the other hand, it does not share the view that these should be cast out from the discussion of the ancient world, since they are modern and, therefore, irrelevant to past realities. Rather, it claims that 'collecting' and 'collection' can and should be used consciously to introduce new stances in the process of understanding the past, and to consider the interrelation of facts and notions that until now have been kept separate. It also claims that the models which ancient writers, in particular Pliny, provided are largely responsible for the shape that collections and museums have taken in subsequent periods. It is not that there has been a linear development from a 'primitive' stage to a 'mature' one: the emphasis here lies on the cultural categories that led to collecting, but also on the cultural categories in which collecting resulted. *HN* is a product of a two-way process and as such can be an invaluable tool for illuminating both directions.

Pliny's role as a model, and as a source of information about collectors and collecting for Renaissance and subsequent generations, is widely acknowledged and efficiently documented as far as those influenced by him are concerned (see e.g. Findlen, 1989, 1994; Jenkins, 1996; Vickers, 1997). The discussion of Pliny's own work in this light has been scarce and fragmentary. Although words like 'museum', 'collection', and 'art gallery' make their appearance quite often when discussing *HN*, they usually are not meant in a museological sense, and refer only to books 33-37, commonly also known as the 'art history' chapters of *HN*. This section has been at the centre of enquiries which see Pliny mainly as a source of information on the setting up of collections, and occasionally, on their political role too (see for example Rouveret, 1987; Gualandi, 1982; Becatti, 1951, 1956, 1973-1974; Beaujeu, 1982; Isager, 1991). Pliny's attitudes toward art are considered separately from his attitudes toward science, his aesthetics kept separate from his natural philosophy, and his moralism distinct from his curiosity. Here we aim to redress this shortcoming and to advocate an approach that takes into account all these aspects. In particular, we will argue that *HN* corresponds to two of the stages described in Figure 1.2. It is a systematic collection itself, of a kind that will flourish centuries afterwards, and in this sense it corresponds to the second stage of Figure 6.1. It is a meta-language of the phenomenal, factual world. But *HN* also corresponds to the third stage of the Figure, since it is a meta-metalanguage, a 'reading' of other collecting practices and discourses (Figure 6.2). By tracing the formation, taxonomy and aim in both cases, it will be possible to comprehend first, the way the classical world is related to its material culture, and second, how much the categories of art and culture which we have inherited are indebted to the past.

The third part of this chapter will be devoted to Pliny as a source of information on collections and collecting in his era (stage 3), subdivided into the 'museographic' and the collecting discourse parts. Next, Pliny as a collector and as a model for imitation will be considered (stage 2). Finally, all the threads will be drawn together in the conclusions, where Pliny's role in shaping the nature and influence of classical collecting will be considered.

Principles that Shape *HN* and Features that Differentiate it from Other Texts

HN was dedicated in 77 or 78 CE to the heir of the imperial throne, Titus. It consists of thirty seven books[4] which adopt the following scheme: *epistula praefatoria*, indices and lists of sources (Book I), cosmology (II), geography (III-VI), anthropology (VII), zoology (divided according to the elements - earth, water, air, fire) (VIII-XI), botany (mainly trees, but also agriculture and horticulture) (XII-XIX), botany and zoology in medicine (XX-XXXII), and finally, mineralogy and metallurgy (XXXIII-XXXVII) (see della Corte, 1982: 37). The style, which has been often criticised,[5] is very unequal. Pliny[6] has not drawn a clear line between report and comment, and his discussion varies from a lively narrative enriched with historical references and elaborate descriptions, to a body of notes and a dry inventory (Goodyear, 1982: 670). Unlike apparently similar works, like Varro's *Disciplinae* and Celsus' *Artes*, that have their material arranged in books according to the subjects (*artes*) they cover,[7] and technical treatises that confine themselves to a single topic (agriculture, medicine, architecture), *HN* adopts a more holistic approach to knowledge:

instead of a selective coverage of topics that interest the author, it is a unified, comprehensive entreprise.[8] Pliny gives to his book the title *Historia Naturalis*, 'enquiries into the natural world', and claims that *rerum natura, hoc est vita, narratur* (Praef. 13), 'my subject is ... the world of nature, in other words life'.[9] It is this broad subject-matter that differentiates *HN* from the classical tradition of encyclopedic literature (Beagon, 1992).

HN's broad perspective had been determined by the way Pliny perceived nature and the universe. Pliny's view was shaped largely by Stoicism, but we can also find in his work influences from the other three major philosophical schools, Platonism, Peripatetics, and Epicureanism (Beaujeu, 1948; André, 1978a; Gigon, 1982; della Corte, 1982; Sallmannn, 1987; Beagon, 1992). His ideas on cosmology are introduced in Book II, but also appear quite regularly in the introductions to almost every book (Kroll, 1930). Although not consistent throughout, he adopts the stance that the universe (*mundus*) is *numen*, meaning divine.[10]

> The world is sacred, eternal, boundless, self-contained, or, one should say, complete in itself, finite yet resembling the infinite, of all things certain yet resembling the uncertain, embracing in all its grasp all things without and within. (2.2).[11]

The sun is the soul (*animus*) or the mind (*mentem*) of the whole world (2.13). Nature is the world's governing principle. Its power is diffused throughout the universe and its laws not only provide the proper precepts to follow, but also ensure and furnish constancy and inevitableness of things (2.1-27; French, 1994: 197-199; Isager, 1991: 32-33). But what exactly is 'nature'? According to traditional Stoicism, *logos* (reason) and *physis* (nature) are the two key-notions of the natural world. *Physis* meant the 'nature of a thing',[12] and in Greek philosophy it had a rather wider meaning than in Rome.[13] In *HN* in particular, the term is used to denote *rerum natura*, which means 'the expression of some innate force that determines the shape and behaviour of *individual* things' (French, 1994: 199, emphasis in the text); in other words, it is the power that makes things individual. But the term *natura* can be also used collectively to denote the nature of *all* things. In this case nature is a wider principle. Pliny's views on the dual character of nature are summarised in his phrase: *idemque rerum naturae opus and rerum ipsa natura* (at once the work of the nature of things and nature itself)[14] (2.1), where both notions appear simultaneously. The same phrase is translated by Healy (1991: 10): 'The world is the work of Nature, and at the same time, the embodiment of Nature herself'. In other words, Nature is passive and active at the same time, a creator and a creation (also Sallmann, 1987: 258-259).

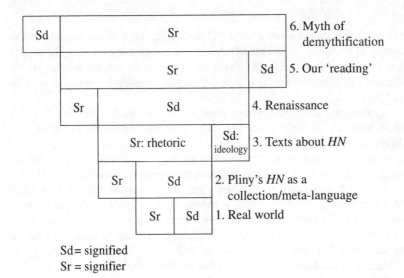

Sd = signified
Sr = signifier

Figure 6.1:   Model of analysis applied to Pliny's *HN* as a collection/meta-language
              (level 2).

Analyzing Pliny's notion of nature and natural history thus can be quite misleading, since often he uses *rerum natura* to denote the variety and number of the natures of individual things, and not a personified, allegorical figure (a collective entity) as we are used to understand nature in our western tradition (French, 1994: 201). The fact that for Pliny nature, besides being the creator, is also embodied in individual things, elucidates his attempt to collect, or assemble the nature of the world in his book. By assembling the units of the world, he brings together the embodiments of nature, and therefore he 'reaches' Nature (divinity) itself by creating a microcosm. In order for man to appreciate *naturae vis atque maiestas*, the greatness and majesty of Nature, he has to grasp the whole picture, and not just specific details (7.7). Nevertheless, every single contribution, however small and humble, does have a value in grasping of this grand overall picture (Beagon, 1992: 47).

A fundamental aspect of the Greek outlook on life was the central place man had in the universe. The link between man and cosmic deity was enhanced by the Stoic identification of the all pervading spirit of the universe with man's highest attribute, mind or reason (*logos*) (Beagon, 1992: 36-37). The centrality of man in Pliny's universe is expressed in the recurring theme of Nature's providence toward the human race. Pliny believes that the world was built with a purpose. His whole theory is underpinned by the notion that Nature provides everything a man needs, but that people, blinded by avarice and luxury, abuse Nature. Pliny attributes man's ingratitude to Nature to ignorance and, thus he hopes to redress that ignorance through his writing. By taking a leading part in the growth of knowledge, he visualizes his role as providential, too. He aims to achieve something that nobody else has: to assemble the knowledge of the world, set the example for people, and thus save mankind from its own folly (Praef. 14).

Pliny does not have an abstract view of man in mind. For him 'man' is Roman man, of his own class and education; the world, as much as it is anthropocentric, is mainly Roman-centred. *HN* is about the development of Roman society. Pliny was aware of the growth of the Roman Empire and the consequent growth in knowledge that such an expansion had brought. He was also aware that man depends on nature's gifts and that many aspects of political history were founded on the desire to obtain more. Pliny's work was a survey of what was available for Roman man. He wanted to cover all fields that earlier texts had not and to avoid theory by reporting only facts, to acquaint Romans with what was theirs in the universe and to preserve them for the future. He could see the possibility of instructing his readers morally as one of the prime benefits of his work (Citroni-Marchetti, 1982; 1991), but he did not aim to follow the Greek philosophical tradition of solving problems that go beyond appearances; instead his work involved the encyclopedic collecting of the phenomenal world (*indicare* 'to point out' - and not *indagare* 'to search', Conte, 1994a: 85).

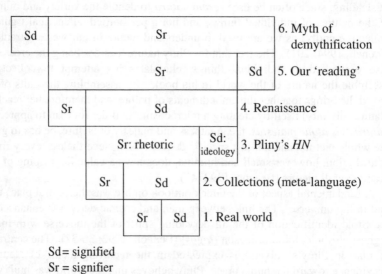

Sd = signified
Sr = signifier

Figure 6.2:   Model of analysis applied to Pliny's *HN* as a source of information on collections (level 3).

Equally central to nature's providence in *HN*, is the idea of man's *luxuria*.[15] Pliny undertakes the role of defining exactly what elements fall into this category, and justifying this by illustrating clearly the reasons why they are included. But Pliny is not particularly innovative in his criticism. Rather, he adopts the monotonous moralistic attitude of all Romans, from Cato to Juvenal. As Wallace-Hadrill (1990: 90) claims, what Pliny did was to follow this traditional Roman approach and to attempt to legitimate the loss of what the Romans rejected on moral grounds. Following the Stoic definition, luxury is failure to live according to Nature. It is a perversion of mind, and therefore, not the correct way for man to live. Luxury goods are not evil in themselves, but they can lead to degeneracy if exaggerated, and false values are attributed to them.[16] Pliny's criticism is not merely philosophical; it is also influenced by practical concerns regarding material value (Beagon, 1992: 76-77). This becomes very clear when he insists on providing the prices of the objects he discusses. His disapproval, although justified in philosophical terms, is mainly directed towards, and founded upon, the untraditional way of using luxurious objects as a means of structuring social hierarchy. This offers new symbols to define social dominance.

Pliny's criticism of luxury, therefore, aims to legitimate through a 'scientific' (in the sense of compliance with moral rationality) approach the traditional social ethics, and, thus the relations of power and control endangered by the misuse of such objects - symbols, as Gordon suggested, of 'kept knowledge' (1979: 12; Wallace-Hadrill, 1990: 92). Furthermore, Wallace-Hadrill (1990: 94-96) claims that Pliny uses the antithesis of nature vs. luxury as a strategy to introduce scientific thought (traditionally associated with the Greeks) to the Roman world by indicating its relevance to it (and thus establishing a bridge between Greek and Roman discourse) (also André, 1978a: 7).

Pliny's natural history is genuinely historical. The notion of history in its original Greek meaning of 'enquiry' and with its strong chronological component had directed his collection and writing of facts (see Fornara, 1983; also Chapter 2 on antiquarianism).[17] Pliny treats history as a search for the remarkable, and wishes to record all things worthy of *historia*. Some things are considered remarkable because of what he already knows about the powers of nature, as he understands the term; some others because of the 'history' of people. A historic view of the world does not mean that the author confines himself to the historical accounts of famous deeds. Pliny's vision of life is much wider. The humble plants and animals, he claims, can be more often of use to man than an individual act of bravery; therefore, they deserve more attention (7.104ff; Beagon, 1992: 55-56). Pliny seeks to depict life in all its aspects, activities, inventions and discoveries that allow man to help both contemporaries and descendants. It is this notion of history in Pliny that accounts for many of the characteristics of his work (French, 1994: 206ff; Healy, 1991: xvii-xviii).

First, the notion of *historia* accounts for the *mirabilia* included so abundantly in *HN*. His interest in the remarkable urges Pliny to collect *mirabilia*, present them to his contemporaries and render them *memorabilia*. In this respect, Pliny owns a lot to a popular form of entertainment, *paradoxography* (from the Greek word *paradoxon*, 'oddity, unexpected thing'); the *thaumasia* had always been a strong attraction for the Greeks, and already in the Hellenistic period there were large collections of this genre (Gigon, 1982: 43). From his indexes, we learn that Pliny relied on several of these miscellaneous collections of *mirabilia* and *paradoxa*.[18] The most famous Roman author of this tradition was Licinius Mucianus[19] (almost a contemporary of Pliny - he died before 77 CE), who is often cited as a source. As a real dilettante, Mucianus recorded new data and experiences, but inscribed them in the traditional models, and lacked that systematic spirit that would render his work scientific (Conte, 1994b: 500). Pliny records many wonders and oddities of nature - but he is quite sceptical, at least by the ancient standards, of many marvelous stories (Beagon, 1992: 11). His recording thus of *mirabilia* seems to relate to, and have been dictated by, his aim to include in his work not only the general and constant but also the unique. He, therefore, assigns a large part of *HN* to *admiranda* and *mirabilia*, and thus his discourse quite often resembles an archive of wonders.[20]

Second, the notion of history accounts for the inclusion in *HN* of aspects, or stories, not obviously relevant to nature. A classic example of that are the so-called 'art history' chapters. Arts and crafts form part of the metallurgy and mineralogy discussion. The modern clear cut division between art and science makes a unified treatment such as this rather puzzling. A very 'convenient' approach in the past has resulted in discussions which look to isolate the art history from the rest of the work (e.g. Jex-Blake and Sellers, 1896). These attempts at division range from positivistic cross checking of Pliny's sources (e.g. Kalkmann, 1898; Münzer, 1897; Schweitzer, 1932) and evaluative reports of the author's credibility, to questions regarding Pliny's personal connoisseurship and aestheticism (e.g. Moorhouse, 1940; Daneau-Lattanzi, 1982; Michel, 1987; Heuzé, 1987). Other scholars, determined to tackle Pliny's inclusiveness, have enumerated three reasons for it: the education of the Roman upper classes, which included the Greek ἐγκύκλιος παιδεία; Pliny's moralistic views on art (he sees the art of his time as *ars moriens);* and his personal connoisseurship (Isager, 1971: 49-50). From another perspective, Gordon argues that primary materials, such as gold, silver, marble, bronze, and so on, and works of art made of them, operated in a more or less similar way as symbols (aniconic and iconic respectively). In this sense, they all invoked elements from the 'encyclopedia of kept knowledge' (1979: 12). The culmination of his argument suggests that it was the refusal of aestheticism in the ancient world that led to the inscription of art into the nature of things (1979: 27). Levidis (1994: 8), in his introduction to the translation of Book 35, attributes the inclusion of art history in *HN* to Pliny's aim to examine the natural sciences in relation to their practical applications. Tanner in a recent discussion (1995), claims the autonomy of art history as a discipline, despite the fact that it is preserved for us as part of an encyclopedia, and contextualises the art history of Pliny in the Greek rationalistic cosmology, which considered the perfect adaptation of a work of art to natural reason a proof of the excellence of human rationality.

However, if we consider *HN* as a whole, it becomes evident that the inclusion of both natural and cultural history are consistent with the views presented throughout the work. *HN* is a story about man's encounter with nature, man's progress in the natural world, and about how man and nature have influenced each other. Arts and crafts are included because of the providential role of nature and the rational adaptation of man. *Artes* imitate nature. The Stoics denied a divine origin for the arts and crafts, and Pliny's approach supports this idea. Inclusive in nature's providence as they are, they belong to Pliny's project to explain and demonstrate the power of nature. Being part of the 'history' of human activity is one more reason for them to belong to Pliny's project to present the progress and culmination of Roman society. The art discussion, therefore, is part of the Stoic purpose to argue that it was not God but Nature - and man through the guidance of nature - that developed human art (André, 1978a; Isager, 1991; Beagon, 1992).

Pliny intended to write not only a natural history, but also a history of civilization and techniques. Although he rejects rhetoric, he employs this method quite extensively on the theme of *luxuria*, which had been a *leitmotiv* for all texts concerned with the evolution of Roman society. From this point of view, the love of works of art was part of the corruption of morals. Roman writers were at pains to prove their ignorance of and indifference to art, even when this was not true (for example, Cicero). Among the other arguments, therefore, Pliny finds one more reason for including art in his *HN*. It was a 'dead art', and therefore, it was a historian's task to preserve whatever possible from something that did not exist anymore (Rouveret, 1981; 1987).

Pliny's view of the world and his project, therefore, seem to be very well described by the title of his work, where he explicitly states his 'territory'. He approaches the natural world as a theatre of Roman power and, consequently, of history. Pliny deals with Roman expansion in a historical way and he understands Roman man accordingly. The acquaintance of the two prime elements (nature and Roman people) is explicitly underlined by the obviously historical way he treats the novelties in every field by the date of their first appearance in Rome. Returning emperors and generals would often stage a triumph in which a display of strange things, flora and fauna as well as art, from distant territories, emphasized their success and the military prowess of Rome.

Pliny as a Source of Information on Collections and Collecting: 'museography'

'Museographic' indexes supplement all standard discussions of Pliny's books 33-37 (e.g. Loeb, book X: 337, André, Bloch and Rouveret, 1981: 25-29, Jex-Blake and Sellers, 1896: 247-252). They assume, and largely shape, a general acknowledgment of the assimilation of Roman temples with 'veritable art museums' (Isager, 1991: 158; Gros, 1976: 157; van Buren, 1938; Lehmann, 1945; Gualandi, 1982: 276-277),[21] and are intended as detailed accounts of the locality of works of art, as mentioned by Pliny, mainly in Rome, but also elsewhere in the Roman world. The emphasis then is transferred from the actual assemblage of works of art to Pliny's sources for such an account, as well as his accuracy, often tested against the actual archaeological finds. It has been suggested that Pliny, in addition to written sources, must have had access to some kind of register of *objets d' art* in public buildings in Rome. Alternatively, he may have relied on catalogues from the Augustan era, since it is with Augustan edifices and collections that he primarily deals. Occasionally the attempts to reach the original source of Pliny's information[22] go as far as to suggest that Pliny himself was appointed *curator operum publicorum*, or that he aided in the compilation of official catalogues (about these and contra arguments see Detlefsen, 1901, 1905 and Hauser, 1905; very detailed review of those in Le Bonniec and Gallet de Santerre, 1953: 66-69 and 81).

Undoubtedly elaborate and thoroughly scholarly as they are, these accounts tend to leave unquestioned both the vocabulary ('museographic') and the particular character of those 'ancient museums', under the assumption that they probably share – or should share – similar values with contemporary museums. Having said that, these attempts are indispensable aids to the study of Pliny and will be used here, although in order to focus on, and possibly redress, their assumptions. This discussion does not aim to be an exhaustive account of all collections held in the Roman world. It will be a quick 'tour' around the main sites of collections mentioned in *HN*, which will leave us with a clear picture first, of models of collecting behaviour, to imitate or criticize, and second, of reasons to do so.

Pliny recounts assemblages of works of art and natural curiosities, deposited by celebrated personalities of the Roman world in public buildings, mainly but not exclusively temples. The definition of the work of art itself is quite broad, since it includes sculpture in bronze or marble and paintings, and also products of fine craftsmanship, like bowls and cups - what we would call decorative arts. The reasons why they are appreciated are diverse and are revealed eventually in the course of the discussion. For a while we are going to 'forget' the dual character of *HN*, as an account of collections and a collection itself, and to concentrate on the former, that is on the collections described by Pliny.

Unlike Gualandi (1982: 262-263) and Serbat (1986: 2164), who claim that Pliny's views on collections are not explicit, I argue that they are as explicit as they could possibly be for a social phenomenon so recent in Pliny's day that it had not as yet acquired a 'name'. We have the privilege today of debating these issues with the confidence gained by having the methodological tools and cultural categories to frame our discussions. Contemporary discussion is able to use the terms 'collection', 'art gallery' and 'museum', with a full set of connotations implied; in the case of Pliny and his contemporaries who stand at the beginning of this intellectual tradition, these terms are still in the process of acquiring their meaning. It is possible therefore to record in Pliny's work this process, which consists of defining and redefining sacred and secular space, textuality and actuality, temple, treasury and text. Consequently, we are going to focus immediately on the 'museographic' concerns, illustrated in the passages from *HN* that have been 'collected' in the process of this research, so that then we can turn to questions such as, what meaning were these objects and collections given in social tradition, how individuals have worked their way within and through these to make meaning for themselves, why and how collected objects were subject to valuations, how judgement of material of collections changed and according to what criteria, and the importance this had. In the following parts, similar questions will be asked for Pliny's own 'collection' and comparisons of models will be drawn in the conclusion.

Gualandi has published the most detailed and up-to-date index, together with a brief discussion of Pliny and art collecting (1982). The appendices of his article in particular are very helpful, since they relate every work of art mentioned in *HN* with the name of its artist, his place of origin, the subject of the work, its date, its display location and the exact reference in Pliny. This list will form the starting point of our discussion and will be enriched with additions of a category largely ignored, that is natural curiosities, in order to give a more complete picture of collections.

The discussion of collections places them directly in the social and historical circumstances that has led to their creation. As is readily observable in many passages throughout *HN*, Pliny distinguishes between luxury and collection. He holds the East and the Greeks (both in a rather abstract sense) responsible for the existence of both in the Roman world, as well as the generals who imported all these objects during their triumphs. Marcellus was the first: after the conquest of Syracuse in 212 BCE, he brought to Rome works of art - after that the Romans became addicted to it. The religious dedication of spoils in temples, and the complete subjugation of the foreign nations that the plundering of their gods meant (*evocatio*) (Pape, 1975), soon gave way to a cultural practice of dedicating works of art. All the great generals, and subsequently the emperors, zealously promoted this tradition, which by Pliny's day had resulted in a series of public collections, and, most disturbingly for him, in a profound change of values.

The Capitolium was the home of a large collection of miscellaneous objects, offered mainly by the military leaders of the Republic. The majority of artefacts are recorded in association with the Temple of Jupiter Capitolinus.

They were pictures by Parrhasios (*Theseus*,[23] 35.69), and Nicomachos (a *Victory with horses*, and a *Rape of Persephone*, 35.108) dedicated by Sylla and L. Munatius Plancus respectively, a gold 'clupeus', that is a shield decorated with embossed likeness (see also Levidis, 1994: 170), dedicated by L. Marcius Septimus (35.14), goblets by Mentor (7.127; 33.154), and a collection of gems, which had belonged to King Mithridates, offered by Pompey along with murrhine cups and bowls from the spoils of his triumph (37.11; 37.18). In the Temple of Jupiter Tonans are recorded bronze statues by Hegias (*Dioskouroi*, 34.78) and Leochares (the cult statue of the god, 34.10; 34.79). In the Temple of Faith (*Templum Fidelitas*) a picture by Aristeides with an old man and a boy (35.100). With no indication of their exact location on the Capitoline Hill are also mentioned bronze statues by Kalamis (4.92; 34.39), Lysippos (34.40), Chares (34.44), Euphranor (34.77), and unknown artists (34.43-44), a marble statue by Praxiteles (36.23), and two natural curiosities: a mass of rock-crystal dedicated by Augustus' wife Livia (37.27) and a cinnamon chaplet embossed with gold offered by Vespasian (12.94) (on the *Capitolinus Mons* see Richardson, 1992: 68-70 and his fig. 19; Platner and Ashby, 1929: 95-98; also Jacobi, 1884: 74-102).

In the Forum Romanum, the largest collection was held in the *Aedes Concordiae*, the temple dedicated by Tiberius in 10 CE, after he had it rebuilt with the spoils from his Germanic campaigns. The design of the new temple had been rather exceptional. Possibly because of its location below the Capitol, the temple's width was greater than its length. A Tiberian coin shows that the central entrance was flanked by two windows that would have lighted the room, and this has been considered the most appropriate for the exhibition of bronze statuary (Becatti, 1973-74, tables XV, XVII). Indeed, this temple has been considered by scholars to have been built with a specific cultural, rather than religious intention in mind (Gros, 1976: 159ff). Becatti (1973-74) suggests that probably Tiberius himself was responsible for the purchases of the bronze statues assembled in it, and that from the beginning the statuary and the temple were thought of as a unity. Therefore, *Aedes Concordiae* was built as an 'exhibition room'. The bronze sculptures included a *Group of Latona, Apollo and Diana* made by Euphranor (34.77), a *Group of Jupiter, Minerva and Ceres* made by Sthenis (34.90), *Mars and Mercury* made by Piston (34.89), an *Apollo and Juno* (34.73) by Baton, and an *Aesculapius and Salus* by Niceratus (34.80). Becatti (1973-74) has also emphasized the stylistic harmony of the series of statuary, since they were all made by artists of the fourth and third centuries BCE, with a late classical or Hellenistic classicizing formal idiom. In addition, the temple housed three paintings, a *Bound Marsyas* by Zeuxis (35.66), a *Dionysus* by Nikias (35.131), and a *Cassandra* by Theorus (35.144), along with two natural curiosities, four elephants made of obsidian dedicated by Augustus (35.196), and a sardonyx from the ring of Polycrates, the tyrant of Samos, dedicated by Livia (37.4), which was part of a gems collection. From other sources we also learn about a statue of *Hestia* (Cas. Dio

55.9). According to Becatti (1973-73: 42), this temple would have been a *monumentum* for Tiberius' victories and an expression of his personal artistic taste (see also Isager, 1991: 159-160; Jacobi, 1884: 40-42).

In the same area (the Forum Romanum), there were also collections held in the temples of *Divus Julius* and *Divus Augustus*. The construction of the former was begun by the triumphirs in 42 BCE, and was dedicated by Augustus in 29 BCE. In its cella it housed a colossal statue of Julius Caesar with a star on his head (2.93-94). But more importantly, it housed paintings, one without indication of artist or subject, but recommended by the fact that it was dedicated there by Augustus (35.27), and another painted by Apelles, *Venus Anadyomene* (35.91), also dedicated by Augustus. When this one deteriorated, it was replaced by Nero with a copy made by Dorotheus (35.91) (Richardson, 1992: 213-214; Jacobi, 1884: 30-32). The Temple of Divus Augustus was built by Tiberius (Cass. Dio 57.10.2), and dedicated by Caligula (Suetonius, *Calig.* 21). It contained two paintings by Nikias, one of *Hyacinthus* and one of *Danaë* (36.28; 36.131). Both were brought from Egypt by Tiberius, and the former was a favourite of Augustus. In the same temple was also a cinnamon-root in a golden bowl (12.94), a gift of Livia (Richardson, 1992: 45-46).

Forum Julii and the Temple of *Venus Genetrix* were dedicated by Caesar in 46 BCE. The temple housed a collection of works of art also dedicated by Caesar. They were two paintings of *Ajax* and *Medea,* the art of Timomachus (7.126; 35.26; 35.136); also, six collections of engraved gems (*dactyliothecae*) (37.11), and a corselet made of British pearls (9.116) (Caesar's love for pearls is attested also by Suetonius). The marble cult statue was left unfinished by Arcesilaos (36.156). From other sources we are informed about a golden statue of Cleopatra (Cass. Dio 51.22.3; Appian *BellCiv* 2.102). Finally, according to Pliny, Caesar permitted the dedication of a statue of himself in the forum (34.18) (Richardson, 1992: 165-167; Jacobi, 1884: 66-69).

Another interesting collection was held in the Temple of Peace (*Templum Pacis*). It was dedicated by Vespasian in 75 CE. The prime reason for its construction was to house the spoils from the capture of Jerusalem (Josephus, *BellJud* 7.5.7) and the many bronze statues that Vespasian removed from Nero's *Domus Aurea* (34.84). Pliny does not discuss these in detail, possibly, it has been argued, because there was no official catalogue listing them yet (Isager, 1991: 168). The works that he actually singles out are three paintings and two stone sculptures. They are a picture of *Eros* by Timanthes (35.74), one of *Skylla* by Nicomachus (35.109), and one of *Ialysus* by Protogenes (35.102). There were also a marble statue of *Venus* (36.27), and a statue of *Nilo* made of basalt and brought from Egypt (36.48). Finally, a cinnamon chaplet embossed with gold (12.94) completes the list of objects that Pliny choses to single out of the collection dedicated in one of the finest buildings of Rome (*HN,* 35.102-103; 35.109; 36.58, Pausanias, 6.9.3; Juvenal, 9.23; Richardson, 1992: 286-287).

In the Campus Martius there were many collections housed in porticoes, temples and other public buildings. The temple of Apollo Sosianus (*in circo*) housed a painting of a tragic actor and a boy by Aristeides (13.53; 35.99-100), a wooden statue of Apollo brought by C. Sosius from Seleukeia (13.53), five marble sculptures by Philiscus of Rhodes (a *Diana*, an *Apollo*, a *nude Apollo*, a *Latona* and *nine Muses*, 36.34), an *Apollo with a lyre* by Timarchides (36.35), and a *group of Niobids* made by either Scopas or Praxiteles (36.38) (also Isager, 1991: 162-163, note 576 with bibliography; André, Bloch and Rouveret, 1981: 26, note 2). In the temple of Neptune, there was a marble group of sea deities by Scopas (36.26). The Temple of Mars had an *Ares and Aphrodite* by Scopas (36.26); the Porticus Philippi paintings by Zeuxis (*Helena*, 35.64), Antiphilos (*Alexander and Hippolytus*, 35.114), and Theorus (*Capture of Troy*, 35.114). In the temple of Fortune were bronze statuary by Pheidias and Pythagoras (36.54; 36.40). In the *Theatrum Scauri*, erected by Aemilius Scaurus in 58 BCE, 3,000 statues were used as decoration (35.114-115). Similarly, the *Theatrum Pompeii*, the first marble theatre in Rome, was dedicated in 55 BCE, and was remarkable for its decoration, which included paintings of marvels, like Eutychis from Tralles, who had 30 children, and Alcippe, who gave birth to an elephant (7.34). The *Porticus Pompeii*, dedicated in 52 BCE, contained a collection of paintings by Polygnotus (35.59), Pausias (*Sacrifice of an Oxen*, 35.126), Nikias (*Alexander*, 35.132) and Antiphilos (*Cadmos and Europe*, 35.114), as well as fourteen figures by Coponius representing the *Fourteen Nations* (36.41). The *Thermae Agrippae* contained bronze and marble statuary; the famous *Apoxyomenos* of Lysippus (before it was transferred to the *cubiculum* of Tiberius) (34.62) and *Caryatids* by Diogenes (36.38), along with paintings (35.26). The *Pantheon of Agrippa* was erected as part of a complex consisting of the Baths, the Temple of Neptune and Saepta Julia. The exact relationship between them is not clear, since their functions seem to have been very different, but they were all major monuments. An inscription on the façade dates the Pantheon to 27 BCE.[24] It is considered an example of the 'new' architecture that was taking into account the 'museographic' significance of the temples (Gros, 1976: 160ff). Pliny mentions the earrings of the statue of Venus which were the two halves of the famous pearl of Cleopatra (9.121), and the noteworthy sculptures of the pediment, the works of Diogenes of Athens (36.38).[25]

The largest and most important collection of the Campus Martius, however, was the one assembled in the *Porticus Octaviae*. It was built by Octavia, Augustus' sister, to complete work undertaken by her son Marcellus. According to Velleius (1.1.3), it replaced the *Porticus Metelli* (itself possibly home of the famous *Group of Alexander's Friends*, by Lysippus, 34.64), but did not change its form substantially. The complex included two temples, of *Juno Regina* and of *Jupiter Stator*, built by the architects Sauras and Batrachos (36.42), a library, a *curia* and a *scholae*. Pliny calls the complex *Octaviae opera* (34.31; 35.139; 36.15). Their construction started in 33 BCE and was completed in about 23 BCE. The whole complex was the home of another superb collection of works of art. In the Temple of Jupiter Stator there were marble sculptures: an *Aphrodite in the Bath* by Doidalsas (36.35), a *Standing Venus* by Polycharmos (36.35), and a group of *Pan and Olympus* by Heliodorus (36.35), as well as a *Jupiter* by Pasiteles (offered by Metellus) (36.40). In the Temple of Juno Regina there were located an *Artemis* and an *Asclepius* by Kephisodotus (36.24), a *nude Venus* by Philiscus (36.35), a *Juno* by Timarchides (36.35), a *Juno* by Dionysius and Polycles (36.35), and works by Praxiteles without further indication (36.35). In the porticus the collection consisted of an *Aphrodite* by Pheidias (36.15), and the famous *Eros of Thespies* by Praxiteles, brought to Rome by Nero (36.22); there were also two paintings by Artemon (a *Laomedon, Heracles and Poseidon*, and the *Apotheosis of Hercules*) (35.139). In the *curia* there were marble statues by unknown artists (two *Aurae, Eros* and *four Satyrs*) (36.28-29). Finally, in the *schola* two paintings by Antiphilos (*Alexander, Philip and Athena*, and another of *Hesione*) are mentioned (35.114).

The collections of Campus Martius have been seen to reflect a certain attitude towards works of art and their value. Mostly dedicated by generals of the Republic, or people from the immediate environment of Augustus, they seem to concentrate consciously on the area of Rome associated mostly with war and victory (it is the campus of Mars after all). Within the zone of Hellenisation, which started taking place after the second century BCE, but at the same time was situated at a convenient distance from the centre of Rome, the Greek works of art transferred there were captives of war, no less than slaves. A renaissance of the tradition during Augustus comes only as a conscious attempt to revive and continue the republican theme of 'triumphs' for mere political reasons (André, Bloch and Rouveret 1981: 26ff; Rouveret, 1987).

Horti Serviliani (Gardens of Servilius) were another type of locality used for displaying Greek art. These were privately owned parks placed at the disposal of the public. Roman literature tells us of a number of extensive parks, and archaeological evidence has shown that these gardens were richly ornamented with Greek art, originals or copies (see e.g. MacDougal and Jashemski, 1981; MacDougal, 1987; also 19.49-51). Pliny singles out *Horti Serviliani* (their exact location is uncertain; it is thought that it was at the south side of the Aventine - see Richardson, 1992: 204), where there were several marble statues: an *Apollo* by Calamis, boxers by Dercylides, a portrait statue of the historian Callisthenes by Amphistratus (36.36), a *Flora (Kore), Triptolemus, and Ceres* by Praxiteles (36.23), and a seated *Vesta* by Scopas (36.25) (Isager, 1991: 167-168; Becatti, 1956).

Although the preeminence of Rome in Pliny's world view is undeniable, occasionally he refers in brief to remarkable objects (either in terms of artistic accomplishment or of natural merit) held in sanctuaries or cities of the East (see also Gualandi, 1982, and his appendix B).   The city of Cnidus is more than once mentioned as the home of the celebrated statue of Aphrodite, the work of Praxiteles (36.20-21; 7.126-127).   The marble statue is used as an example of people's folly and dependence on material culture, since the story of King Nicomedes, who was willing to repay the debt of Cnidus to Rome in exchange for the statue and was rejected by the people of the city, and of the young man who was enamoured with the statue and stayed by it overnight, are mentioned at least twice each (7.126-127; 36.20-25).[26] Cnidus, not specifically the Monopteros, was also the home of a *Dionysus* by Bryaxis, and of a *Dionysus and Athena* by Scopas (36.22).

The temple of Artemis at Ephesus is also associated with remarkable works of art.   A bronze *Apollo* by Myron of Eleutherai (34.58), goblets by Mentor (33.154), a marble *Heracles and Hecate* by Menestratos (36.32), and paintings, like the *Alexander holding a Thunderbolt* by Apelles (35.92) were housed in the Artemision. Three more paintings are also recorded without a specific attribution of locality, but housed in Ephesus: the *Procession of a Megabyzos* (Priest of Artemis) by Apelles (35.93), *Odysseus and Palamedes* by Euphranor (36.129) and an *Artemis* by Timarete (35.147).

The third sanctuary which appears quite often in Pliny's discussion is that of Athena at Lindos, Rhodes.   A work by Boëthus (33.155) and a painting of *Heracles* by Parrhassios (35.71) are recorded there. In the same temple was the breastplate of the former King of Egypt, Amasis (19.12), and a goblet of electrum dedicated by Helen and cast in the shape of her breast (32.81).[27]

Between the private and the public domain rests the collection of Asinius Pollio.[28] Unlike the collections we have discussed so far (except of the *Horti Servilliani*), this one is treated by Pliny as a unity and as evidence of Pollio's interest both in art and in the public benefit.

> Asinius Pollio, being an ardent enthusiast, was accordingly anxious for his collection to attract sightseers. In it are Centaurs Carrying Nymphs by Arcesilas, the Muses of Helicon by Cleomenes, the Oceanus and Jupiter by Heniochus, the Nymphs of the Appian Water by Stephanus, the double busts of Hermes and Eros by Tauriscus (not the well-known worker in metal and ivory, but a native of Tralles), the Jupiter Patron of Strangers by Papylus, the pupil of Praxiteles, and a composition by Apollonius and Tauriscus which was brought from Rhodes, namely Zethus and Amphion, and then Dirke and the bull with its rope, all carved from the same block of stone. These two artists caused a dispute as to their parentage declaring that their putative father was Menecrates and their real father Artemidorus. In the same galleries there is a Father Liber by Eutychides, which is warmly praised ... (36.33-34).[29]

Previously Pliny has also mentioned as belonging to the same collection four sculptures by Praxiteles, *Caryatids, Maenads, Sileni, and Thyiads* (36.23-24), a

Venus by Kephisodotus (36.24) and a *Canephoros* (basket-bearer) by Scopas (36.25).[30] There were also there a large assemblage of portrait busts (probably following the tradition of its models, the libraries of Pergamum and Alexandria), among which it was the portrait of M. Terentius Varro (7.115; 35.9-10).

The collection was held in the edifice that Asinius Pollio had built *ex manubiis* after his triumph against the Parthians in 39 BCE. He was the first Roman to establish a library and most probably it was joined to this edifice. The building was part of the complex called *Atrium Libertatis*, which, according to Livy (34.44.5), was restored and enlarged in 194 BCE. Augustus had given Pollio permission to restore the old edifice in commemoration of his victory and thus to honour his own memory. Consequently, Pliny uses the appellation *monumenta Asini Pollionis*. Subsequently, it gave way to the Trajan Forum (Richardson, 1992: 41; Isager, 1991: 164-165; Pellegrini, 1867; André, Bloch and Rouveret, 1981:145ff).

The selection and setting of the works of art have been subject to rigorous discussion. Becatti (1956: 208) imagines an antithetical grouping of the statues of the collection: Jupiter against Jupiter *Hospitalis*, Thespiads against Appiads, Centaurs against Sileni, Oceanus against Dionysus, and Venus surrounded by Cupids. The Punishment of Dirke was perhaps, according to that arrangement, placed in the centre to enable viewing from all angles. Gros (1976: 164) argues that Pliny's account of the setting of the works of art very much resembles that of somebody who walks in front of the objects, and describes them as one succeeds the other. Besides their setting, the choice of the works themselves present great interest. The 'old masters', Praxiteles, Kephisodotus and Scopas, are present, but the emphasis seems to be on a more recent generation of artists, those of the first century BCE. In the words of Becatti (1956: 207-208): 'Tutta la collezione è importanta ad una concezione artistica basata sulla *charis* dei postprassitelici, sul *genus floridum* microasiatico, sull' *eleganza decorativa* dei neo-attici' (emphasis in text). This led to the conclusion that what differentiates the collection of Asinius Pollio is the fact that unlike other military leaders, instead of plundering works of art for his *monumenta*, he had chosen to commission them from Greek artists active in Rome during this period. His intention therefore, was to create an architectonic and artistic whole and to exhibit it in a specially constructed 'museum'. Furthermore, his taste is considered to be in absolute accordance with Augustus' political aims, which discouraged private collections in order to benefit the public ones, as well as with plundering as a practice (see also Becatti, 1956: 270ff; Isager, 1991: 167). Zanker (1987: 77-78) on the contrary, ventured the idea that the choice of Dirke group might indicate an anti-Augustan attitude from Asinius Pollio, as such a choice of subject is indicative of 'Asiatic sympathies'. However, this suggestion is based on mere stylistic grounds, and seems rather far fetched. Isager (1991: 166-167) strongly questions its validity on the grounds that no direct evidence survives actually to prove first, that the statue imparted such connotations and, second, that this made the collection more 'provocative' than others held in different localities. Another issue that the collection of Asinius Pollio initiates is the preference for marble instead of bronze statuary; this is attributed also to a change in taste through the years (Isager, 1991: 174-178).

Other private collections also are discussed by Pliny. He refers frequently to individual owners of famous works of art, or to the fate of collections after their owners perished. In the latter, we may include his discussion of Nero and Tiberius. Among the collectors he considers is included M. Aemilius Scaurus, who besides using thousands of statues to decorate his public buildings, and being owner of a superbly decorated villa (36.115), is also mentioned as the owner of a collection of gems (37.11), and as the organiser of temporary exhibitions of natural curiosities, like a hippopotamus and five crocodiles (8.96), or the skeleton of the monster of Andromeda (9.11). L. Crassus, the orator, owned engraved *skyphoi* by Mentor (33.147; 34.14). M. Junius Brutus owned an *Ephebus* by Strongylion (34.82).[31]   Q. Hortensius, the orator who defended Verres, owned a sphinx made of Corinthian bronze, which was once part of the Verres' collection (34.48), as well as a picture of the *Argonauts* by Parrhasios, for which he had paid an outrageous amount of money (35.130). Marcus Terentius Varro, surprisingly, was also a collector: he owned a *signum* by Mentor (33.155), and a marble *Winged Cupids Playing with a Lioness* by Arcesilaos (36.41). Even Gaius Gracchus was the owner of silver figurines of dolphins (33.147). Cicero, the wise orator and public defender of Syracuse against Verres, was also accountable for *mensarum insaniae* (13.91-95).[32]

Nero confiscated a *Amazon Euknemon* by Strongylion from the collection of C. Cestius Gallus (34.48; 34.82). Other extraordinary acquisitions of Nero include a Babylonian coverlet he bought for 4,000,000 sesterces (8.196-197), as well as the bronze statues of the *Aurea Domus* that Vespasian finally deposited at the *Templum Pacis* (other 'follies' of Nero in 34.84; 37.20; 37.29). Tiberius is associated with almost as many 'acts of folly' as Nero, as far as works of art are concerned. Twice he transferred works of art from the public domain to his *cubiculum* (private quarters), much to the amazement and disapproval of Pliny for the irrationality of such an act. These were the famous *Apoxyomenos* by Lysippus, formerly at the Baths of Agrippa, and the painting of *Archigallus* by Parrhassios (35.28; 36.28; 36.131, 34.43, 34.62, 35.70, 36.25). The emperor Claudius bought stone sculpture from Egypt through his agent Vitrasius Pollio (36.57). Even Caesar was not innocent of such folly, since in his house in the Palatine he held a picture made by Apelles and Protogenes during a competition for the finest line possible (35.83; 9.116). Augustus is frequently referred to as donor of works of art to public buildings (35.127;131, 35.27-28, 36.196, 35.91, 34.48, 35.93-94, 36.32, 36.13, 36.36, 36.39, 36.28). He also restored to cities of the East works of art that had been taken away as spoils of war (34.58; also *Res Gestae Divi Augusti,* 24.1; Strabo, XIII.1.30; XIV.1.14).[33] Nevertheless, he also removed works of art (for instance, see Pausanias

VIII.46.1.4) and in the *Domus Augustana* (or *Domus Caesariana*) are recorded marble statues by Aphrodisios, Artemon, Hermolaos, Krateros, Polydeukes and Pythodoros (36.38). J. Caesar Germanicus owned two silver cups by Calamis (34.47). Finally, in the *Domus Titi* there were the bronze *Astragalizontes* by Polycleitos (34.55), and the famous *Laocoon* by Hagesandros, Polydoros and Athanadoros (36.37).[34] Another incident of Verres' career, where Antonius proscribed him because of his refusal to submit his murrhine cups (34.6), is also indicative of the folly of two people for objects.

Non-Roman collectors are also briefly mentioned: King Philip of Macedonia, who used to sleep with a golden goblet by his side (33.50), Alexander the Great, who carried with him statues as holders of his tent (34.48), King Attalus of Pergamum (7.126-127; 33.147-150; 35.24-26; 35.130), King Candaules (7.126-127; 35.55) and King Demetrius (7.126-127; 35.104-105). All these shared a special appreciation for material culture.

Pliny as a Source of Information on Collections and Collecting: collecting discourse

The aim of this section is to reveal the collecting discourse that underlies *HN*. There will be an attempt to trace the process of object valuation and its change through time, along with the criteria for these and their importance for the meaning which collections and objects were given in the social tradition. Thus, we will be able to suggest how individuals have worked their way within and through collections and objects to make meaning for themselves.

According to Pliny, objects are 'evidence' (7.210). Deposited in temples or other public buildings, they can testify to a city's, nation's, or individual's prosperity and power (3.120). They can be products of human ingenuity, like paintings, or inscribed tablets of bronze (8.56, 3.210), as well as natural rarities, like monsters' bones, skins of exotic people, or exceptional specimens of flora and fauna. Among the curiosities Pliny records are included the skeleton of the monster of Andromeda (9.11), the skins of the female inhabitants of the Gorgades islands (6.200), a snake 120 ft. long (8.37), a huge octopus (9.93), and a fish (32.5). When the objects are natural rarities, they have a dual role to play. They serve to 'evidence' man's achievements in terms of acquiring the necessary knowledge to reach these objects, but also, and for Pliny most importantly, to be tangible proof of nature's grandeur and wealth.

The need for the preservation of natural specimens, in particular, is recorded often by Pliny. Most of them are 'marvels' that deserve to be catalogued and handed down to posterity as tokens of accumulated knowledge. In other cases, there are marvelous qualities involved in the appreciation of materials, as for instance in the case of electrum and its alleged power to help the detection of poison (33.81). Often Pliny refers to natural specimens, whose reasons for preservation have a cultural ancestry. When, for example, he discusses trees, he insists on those with mythic or historical associations, like the olive-tree of Minerva on the Athenian Acropolis, the oak-trees planted by Hercules, the tree from which Marsyas was hanged, and so on (16.239-240).

The recording of Nature which should be handed down to posterity is opposed to sacrilegious acts of luxury. The satisfaction and fulfillment a man feels in this respect is much grander than whatever artificiality and luxury can procure (12.9). There is a strong association throughout *HN* between luxury and objects that can be collected, in the sense that the same items appear to belong to both categories.[35] Ivory and citrus-wood, two of the materials most commonly associated with the collector's lust for objects, are also two of the most frequently sought-after indications of luxury - which in order to be obtained result in destruction of Nature (5.12; 8.31). Although gold, silver, pearls and tortoise-shell are admired by other nations as well, Romans, according to Pliny, exceed all others in extravagance (6.89).[36]

There seem to be two main lines of thought in *HN* regarding luxury. The first relates to the natural world, from whence the primary materials for luxurious objects originate. Exploiting these for personal reasons therefore, is impious and as such unworthy of the Romans. The second is the notion of luxury in terms of facilities and beauties originating in objects, or through them, which is encountered firstly in the East, in the Epicurean philosophy of ease and degeneracy, which relates to irrationality and extravagance. This conduct is not appropriate for Romans, Pliny argues, who have such an honourable past to protect and from which to receive their paradigms.

The discussion of objects of luxury and their accumulation is structured around one or the other of these two arguments. The passage at 9.117-121, for instance, belongs to the latter. Lollia Paulina and Cleopatra are both representatives of anti-value, in terms of Pliny's system of valuation, or of popular value, in terms of the Roman social practice in the Plinian era. They are women collectors (along with slaves, for example Spartacus, 33.48-50, they are used as examples to be avoided by Roman readers), vain and given to outrageous behaviour and extravagance beyond a man's imagination. The vanity of Lollia Paulina is evidenced by her carrying a fortune in jewellery to an ordinary banquet, that is by her way of relating to her objects. The fact that she can prove them to be 'ancestral possessions', a claim usually much appreciated and respected, does not justify her conduct, Pliny claims, since it merely reminds people that they are the products of her family's disgrace: they are 'evidence' that her grandfather's wealth originated in bribes from the Kings of the East. Cleopatra also came from the East, and in addition to her extravagance, she was prepared even to destroy the creations of nature, her pearls, merely for her own caprice. The earrings of Venus in the Pantheon were token of that story, and simultaneously a natural curiosity (because they demonstrated the size a pearl could reach) (see description of the collection before).

Women collectors are invariably modeled on this stereotype. Always interested in the possession of gems and jewellery, unlike men who have more serious and intellectual concerns (33.40), they relate to their objects through their material value, or sexual connotations (34.11-12), and not artistic appreciation, or intellectual rationale (37.29). Hence, their purchases, along with their conduct, are irrational and unworthy (37.29). Their assemblages of material culture fall into the domain of luxury and misbehaviour, or of the unnatural way of living, that this implies.

'*Tablemania*' is criticised in 13.91-95. Clearly a sign of effeminate behaviour, since it is compared with the practices of women collectors, *mensarum insaniae* had affected even well-known and well-respected personalities of the Roman world. Cicero, Gallus Asinius, King Juba, King Ptolemy of Mauretania, emperor Tiberius, and even freedmen like Nomius, all appreciated and amassed tables made of citrus-wood. To pursue his point about nature and culture, Pliny adds that what is actually so handsomely paid for by the collectors is a disease of the tree (and excrescence of the tree). Therefore, no matter how remarkable some tables were, mainly due to craftsmanship, the valuation of the material does not follow the order of nature: it is man-made and, ultimately, wrong.

The natural and the man-made systems of valuation compete quite often in the pages of *HN*. Pliny supports a natural hierarchy of values, which sets him apart from his contemporaries. He feels that men interfere with nature's valuations, and thus they violate the natural order. Paragraph 16.233 provides an example: tortoise-shell painted to look like wood is priced more highly than real wood. This notion is taken further in 33.4-5 and 6-7, where in a self-reflective monologue Pliny attributes *luxuria*, and consequently misery, to human inventiveness, which is responsible for raising the prices of objects, for they become worthy only because men decide so. 'Man has learned to challenge nature in competition!'[37] exclaims Pliny, with obvious embarrassment.[38] Among the examples of such behaviour, Pliny includes the engravings on goblets, intended to increase the value of the material with the addition of that of craftsmanship.

Nature's providence, which is a key issue in *HN* (see for example 33.1-3), makes one of the strongest arguments in favour of the natural hierarchy of values. Nature has offered to man everything that he needs, and this should be appreciated. But man has been ungrateful. First, he challenged Nature by pricing highly his decorated earthenware;[39] then he replaced it with objects of gold and silver. Eventually, these became unsatisfactory, and man dug from the earth murrhine, crystal and precious stones. Man's luxury and lust for such things is held responsible for all the vices associated with materials (33.139-140). People get crazy (*insaniae*) for objects and thus they reach for materials that were not meant to be taken away from nature, materials whose place is at the bottom of the sea, or in the heart of the earth. Lust for luxurious possessions encourages man to suffer dangers and exaggerate - as if the value of these was inherent and pre-determined. It is not, Pliny protests: if nature, whose providential role could not be more obvious, has not offered them to man, then these are not worthy of man's attention and the value they are given. They are vain acquisitions, violations of the natural will. Their value is bestowed on them by man, it is a product of arbitrariness and avarice. They are not necessary, the pleasure that derives from them ends at night (when people cannot see the objects and feel guilt about their acquisitions) and, consequently, for half of people's lives.

Value is a central notion in Plinian discourse. It refers to both a monetary price and an ethical/moral notion. Works of art or craftsmanship in particular are recorded for two main reasons: as objects for which extraordinary prices have been paid, or as works created by certain artists/craftsmen. Their presence in Rome usually serves as a testimony of either the 'folly' of man, or the genius of an artist (or, quite often, of both) (7.126-127). Monetary value is a measure of evaluating an object's worth in terms of man's desire for it. When Pliny mentions, for example, that King Candaules of Lydia bought a painting for an amount in gold equal to his weight (which we expect to have been large) (35.55), he means to prove first how much the King wanted the object and then how greatly valued and perfected the art was considered to be, since its products were so desirable. In other words, monetary value is considered a medium of appreciation and of establishing 'real' merit.

Pliny's approach to the subject of monetary value seems rather contradictory. Whereas in paragraphs like 35.55 and 35.88 he claims that price has a prominent role in the attribution of value - for instance, people appreciated an artist when his work was highly priced - he disapproves of it as a medium of valuation. In a number of paragraphs, Pliny criticizes his contemporaries for precisely this kind of attribution of value. In 36.1-3, 34.5, 35.4-13, for example, he refers to monetary value as predominant in his society to the disadvantage of 'real' value, placed on their role in the life of people, in craftsmanship, and in honour and tradition respectively. In the last (long) paragraph in particular, Pliny complains that the art of painting portraits had ceased to be practiced in his era; the decoration of houses with ancestral wax-portraits had given way to picture-galleries, whereas the notion of honourable had become synonymous to that of expensive. The same people, Pliny continues his condemnation, bequeath to their heirs not their likenesses and honour, but representations of their money. He describes 'these people' as admirers of Epicurus, who carry around with them his portrait and decorate their bedrooms with it. Pliny refers to his morality resources and his rhetoric (as well as to current ideas about the art of physiognomy - see 11.273-276) to argue that if the facial resemblance is neglected, it is because there is nothing behind it that deserves to be saved for posterity.

The dependence of value on human decisions is the subject of paragraph 8.31. Materials, Pliny argues, acquire their value according to the rarity, or frequency, with which they are encountered in nature. This remark serves as a lesson for his contemporaries, a reminder of the divine force behind everything, and a warning against the arbitrariness that people exercise without thought. The same point is also made in paragraph 33.6-7, where the value of murrhine cups and crystal is attributed to their fragility, and in 37.29, where the impossibility of mending glass is underlined, along with its resemblance to rock-crystal. It is made again in 37.195, where again rarity is offered as a valuation parameter.

Other qualities contributing to the shaping of the hierarchy of values are the creation by famous artists (7.126-127 and all 'museographic' references), the beauty of objects (an aesthetic point made in relation to a natural specimen, and not a product of craftsmanship or art - 32.23), and religious power (32.23), where the objects are appreciated as amulets (also 19.49-51). To their qualities are added antiquity (e.g. 33.154-157; 34.1; 34.5; 35.17-18), intimacy with famous personages and participation (again a notion of 'evidence') in historical and mythic events (34.55-56; 35.88; 36.33), or extraordinary artistry (for instance, marble statues made of a single block of marble) (36.25).

In relation to issues of value, we may also refer to a few anecdotes mentioned by Pliny. They are all meant to criticise collectors, as people whose sound judgment has been destroyed through their irrational dependence on objects. In 36.195 Pliny records a story familiar from Petronius' *Satyrica*. Non-breakable glassware was constructed during Tiberius' reign, but the inventor was executed and his workshop destroyed, because such an invention would result in the lowering of the value of metals. The story naturally is questioned by Pliny, who also records that during Nero's dominance a special technique of glass-making was invented; two tiny cups that were produced in this technique fetched the sum of 6,000 sesterces. Another story is about an ex-praetor who gnawed the rim of his already extremely expensive cup, only to see its value enhanced by those who favoured prestigious associations and passionate relationships with objects (37.18-20). A similar process of enhanced value due to interaction with an object is recorded in 34.62-64. Nero had asked for a statue by Lysippus to be gilded; but that diminished its artistic value, so it was decided to remove the gilding, which unfortunately left traces on the statue. Remarkably, this incident increased its monetary worth.

Quite often, when expressing his views on values, Pliny seeks confirmation in the past. Theophrastus and Homer justify his point that citrus-trees used for tables is a recent phenomenon (and, thus, not honourable enough) (13.100-102). Elsewhere it is Cornelius Nepos and Fenestella who are summoned in aid of Pliny's argument - this time on silver (33.145-146). Homer is sought after again as a legitimating source in 33.6-7, as well as when he refers to barter as a more decent and wiser tradition of exchange for mankind (33.81).

The discussion of Corinthian bronze in book 34 is very illuminating as far as Pliny's and his contemporaries' ideas on value are concerned. He records that Corinthian bronze was appreciated more than silver (34.1), and he criticises the fact that artistry has come in his era to hold a secondary role compared to material. Pliny holds not only the East responsible for such a reversal in the hierarchy of values, but also the generals who tempted Romans to degeneracy through their triumphs. L. Scipio initiated the evil practice by carrying in his processions silverware and gold vessels, Pliny claims. Then came Attalus' bequest to Rome, and luxurious items could be purchased at the auctions of the King's property. In the 57 years that separate these two events, Romans learned to admire and covet foreign opulence. Pliny admits that previous generations were not completely innocent of indulging in luxury: for instance Gaius Manlius drank from a bacchic tankard, like Dionysus, after his victory. However, it was acquaintance with the Greeks and their customs that led to the popularisation and expansion of vice. Anti-Hellenism is another common motif in *HN* (see for example the books on medicine; also 33.48-50; 37.31; 37.40-41), and is always associated with a disregard for nature, disrespect and evil intentions. The 'lust for possessions' and the disgrace this carries are also included in the same argument, as well as the 'lust for gold' and the extremes people may find themselves led into, as for instance M. Antony, who used gold vessels for all his needs, something that even Spartacus could understand as wrong (33.48-50).

Corinthian bronze offers the best opportunity to tackle these issues. The story of its creation during the capture of Corinth is presented in 34.6-8. Then, the 'wonderful mania'[40] for possessing this metal is highlighted, and for its illustration Verres and Mark Antony are employed. The former, whose name was enough to denote passion for objects (see Cicero) is paired with the latter in order, firstly for Pliny to make a political statement (M. Antony is one of the men that Pliny constantly refers to as an example of degeneracy), and secondly, to underline the dangers involved in the passion for artefacts: it could lead to proscriptions, death, eternal disgrace.

It is in relation to Corinthian bronze that Pliny takes the opportunity to distinguish between real connoisseurship and a pretentious one. He explains that the latter is employed by those who wish to differentiate themselves from the uneducated mass, without having any real insight into the matter. To prove his point, he unveils the 'truth' about Corinthian bronze.[41] He argues that Corinth was conquered when metalworking had already ceased to be so prominent a craft, and when famous workers in this medium had long perished. Still the pseudo-connoisseurs appreciated the 'artistry of their Corinthian bronzes'. Pliny corrects this fallacy on the grounds that genuine Corinthian vessels were the ones that the pretend-to-be connoisseurs did not respect much, and converted into dishes, lamps, or wash basins (34.11-12).[42] Real and pseudo-connoisseurs are also the subject in paragraph 34.71, where Pliny ironically refers to their claim to discern the author's feeling when confronting a work of art, and in 36.19, where the '*periti*'[43] (the experienced) are defined as the men who can appreciate artistic taste.

Just a step further from that appreciation lies 'folly' about objects. This means that people are willing to overcome the distance between man and inanimate object, and to associate with them in a passionate way. Pliny records a number of instances, where, in his terms, desire for artefacts reaches the edges of rationality, or, in contemporary terms, objects take the cultural character of 'fetish'. Cultural studies research has identified four underlying cognitive processes that generate what has been termed 'fetish'. These are all present in the three main scholarly traditions that employ a concept of 'fetishism' (that is anthropology, Marxism, psychology). These four principles are the following:

> 1. a concrete existence or the concretisation of abstractions;
> 2. the attribution of qualities of living organisms, often (although not exclusively) human;
> 3. conflation of signifier and signified;
> 4. an ambiguous relationship between control of object by people and of people by object. (Ellen, 1988: 219).

In Pliny's collecting discourse all four of these parameters are present, and help individuals (mainly) to create meaning for themselves. In 15.38 there is a brief comment on the 'statues that share our nights with us'.[44] This refers to the practice of keeping statues in *cubicula* (private quarters), quite popular with some personages of the Roman world (but also in the Hellenistic world, see Philip of Macedonia, 33.50, and Alexander, 34.48). Tiberius' conduct regarding *Apoxyomenos* is the classic example, although by no means the only one, of such behaviour. Pliny explicitly disapproves of what he considers irrational and inconsiderate conduct - a disapproval obviously shared by the Roman people, who compelled the emperor to restore the statue to its public setting. Whether the claim was dictated by artistic appreciation, or it was merely a political praxis of revolt against tyrannical imposition of power, we cannot tell. In any case the emperor had 'fallen in love' with the statue. This motif, far from uncommon in Pliny's discourse, (see for example, 7.126-127; 36.20-25 and note 25), clearly implies a kind of fetishism (34.62-64). The same phenomenon is the subject of paragraph 35.70, where another passion of Tiberius is unveiled. This time he loved, *amavit*, a picture of a *High Priest of Cybele* made by Parrhasios; after he had purchased it for 6,000 sesterces, he carried it to his bedroom.[45] Similar behaviour is credited to Caligula, who developed a 'lust' for paintings - once again a point with strong sexual connotations (35.17-18).

During the discussion about murrhine cups (37.18-20), Pliny refers to a collection of murrhine artefacts that Nero had taken away from the children of the collector after his death, and exhibited for a short time in a private theatre. Pliny was very surprised to see the fragments of a broken cup included in the exhibition:

> It was at this time that I saw the pieces of a single broken cup included in the exhibition. It was decided that these, like the body of

Alexander, should be preserved in a kind of catafalque for display,
presumably as a sign of the sorrows of the age and the ill-will of
Fortune.[46]

The equation between the body of the king, and the fragments of the object
is indicative of the fetishisation of the artefact (and of Alexander). In the
following paragraph another similar incident is recorded. It is the well-known
one of Petronius smashing his cup in order to prevent it decorating Nero's table
after his death. Petronius thought of the object as a symbol of himself, standing
for his perishable body, and therefore he wished to destroy it, exactly like
himself (he committed suicide), rather than surrender it to his enemies (see
Chapter 8). A similar pattern of thought is detected in Nero's behaviour, when
decided to punish his contemporaries, and take vengeance for his death by
making it impossible for another man to drink from his vessels; thus he broke
his crystal cups in a final outburst of rage.

Other acts of 'folly' regarding objects include the proscription of men in
order to appropriate their possessions (33.145-146). M. Antony proscribed the
senator Novius (as he had done with Verres) in order to obtain his famous and
extremely valuable ring. The senator, though, decided to go into voluntary
exile taking with him just that ring out of all his possessions. Pliny wonders
about the savagery of destroying people for the sake of artefacts, but he is even
more amazed that a man could risk his life for an object, when it is well-known
that even animals leave everything behind to save their lives.

The crazy addiction (*furor*) for artefacts is also discussed in 37.29, in
33.147-150, where among the owners of silverware are included G. Gracchus
and L. Crassus, 33.154-157. Once again, celebrated artists and
owners/collectors of silverware are recorded (along with Pliny's belief that the
art of chasing silver had already declined in his era, and, consequently, only
antique specimens and worn engravings deserved to be, and were actually,
sought after). In 34.47-48 there is another account of incidents indicating a
'passion for objects'. The owners of bronze figurines could be led to
exaggeration, because of their dependence on their possessions, such as
carrying them along to the battlefield. Is this a case of passion? Do the
artefacts acquire the status of an amulet? Do they provide indications of a
familiar environment? Do they provide psychological support? Most probably
they do all of these, simultaneously.

The references in *HN* to the methods of ensuring the safety of works of art
are relevant to issues of valuation. Besides the well-known incident of
Mummius' ignorance of the value of objects and their irreplaceability as unique
works of art (Velleius Paterculus, I.13.4), it is mentioned more than once that
the guardians of temples were held responsible for the safety of the works
entrusted to their guardianship, with their lives (36.35, 36.32, 36.29, 36.38).
This can be included also in the fetishisation process, and is indicative of the
work's value. *Objets d' art* were considered more valuable than any sum of

money. This is an interesting thought, relevant to notions of irreplaceability and of the 'value that exceeds any price' in contemporary museums (34.36-38).

Paragraph 37.2-4 is a reflection on the origins of the use and possession of gemstones (admiration/*exarserit*). The myth of Polycrates of Samos is used as an example of the antiquity of the phenomenon, but also of the strength of the relationship between owner and possession. Polycrates felt so strongly for his ring that the loss of it could be considered an atonement sufficient to counter-balance the luck which had given him his prosperity. The use of rings is also discussed in relation to precious metals (33.20-23). Their presence is recorded in association with various incidents of the early history of Rome. But in the past, when, according to the rhetorical motif that Pliny follows, everything was better and people wiser, rings were not necessary, and even women (those vain creatures!) were not owners of rings. But gradually they became symbols of status (see also Trimalchio in Petronius, Chapter 8). In his contemporary world, Pliny argues, the honour and value of the symbol has been replaced by the material and craftsmanship value, whereas luxury had led to gold being associated with objects that traditionally it had not and should not have been.

Pliny's discussion of values is a comprehensive treatment of tendencies existing in parallel, but not quite shared by all. On the one hand, it is a discussion of the values that Pliny's contemporaries attributed to objects, and on the other, it is a glance at the merits that Pliny himself appreciated and advocated. Naturally, Pliny was a Roman with a practical mind. Thus, he appreciated material value as an indication of man's desire to acquire an artefact and, therefore, as an indication of the art's perfection. Elsewhere, he makes clear that objects are appreciated also for the practical role they serve - for example in 36.44-46 on paintings. Finally, in 37.49, he lists the objects that are valued, and reflects on the reasons this is so. A human figurine in amber is more expensive than a human being. Corinthian bronzes are attractive because of the appearance of bronze; chased metalwork because of artistry and inventiveness; pearls and gems because they can be carried away. Therefore, Pliny concludes, all objects of admiration and desirability please because they can be displayed (*ostentatio*) or used (*uso*): except for amber which is an item of private indulgence in luxury. In paragraph 37.204-205, Pliny enumerates the most costly (*pretium*) item of every aspect of nature: it is the source of all, and Pliny ends his work with a request to Mother Nature, the mother of all creatures, to be gracious to him, the only person who has praised her majesty and power.

We can summarise the hierarchy of values that Pliny defends in the following formulae:

Recording of Nature to hand down to posterity	:	Sacrilegious acts of luxury
Sacred	:	Profane (impious)

The West	:	The East
Men	:	Women
Pliny's values	:	Popular values
Divine/natural valuation	:	Man-made valuation
Ethical/moral value	:	Monetary value
'Real' value	:	Monetary value
Tradition	:	Innovation
Reasoned/Justified	:	Arbitrary
Unchangeable	:	Changeable (dependant on
fragility/rarity/new		inventions)
Knowledge	:	Ignorance
'Periti' (experienced,	:	Pseudo-connoisseurs
like Pliny himself)		
Rationality	:	'Folly'
Logic/Rationality	:	Fetish
Honour/symbolic value	:	Material value
'Acquisition' value	:	Display/use value
Recording of items	:	Collecting of items
Textual collections	:	Actual collections

Pliny as a Source of Information on Collections and Collecting: collecting discourse - the notion of collection

In this second part of the analysis of the Plinian collecting discourse, we are going to focus on the notion of collection as this appears in Pliny. Following consideration of the hierarchy of values in the previous section, we are going to examine the meaning of the assemblages of artefacts, and investigate what these were and why they were amassed. In the preceding part the emphasis was placed on the poetics of collecting. Here, we will concentrate on the politics of the process. To achieve our aim, we are going to discuss the setting of the collections, in terms of public and private, sacred and profane, textual and actual. Thus, we are going to proceed further than the 'micro-politics' employed to justify collecting in Pliny (Isager, 1991), and to combine them with a 'macro-political' approach, that exceeds the limits of book 36 (Rouveret, 1981; 1987; 1989), and covers the whole of *HN*, which is understood as a collection in itself.

The dichotomy between the private and public domains seems quite sharp in *HN*. Pliny contrasts the public context for setting works of art in the Greek tradition, with the private context of Imperial Rome. He even associates the decline of the art of painting in the Empire with the impossibility that noble art should thrive in the domestic context (35.118) (Wallace-Hadrill, 1994: 30). In paragraph 36.5, he argues that ivory, gold and precious stones have come to private life through the official, public route, and accuses the previous (unworthy) emperors of weakness in this matter, which allowed degeneracy to intrude and corrupt Roman society. Mummius, for instance, introduced the public possession of paintings, but it was not until Caesar that attribution of value to paintings started to be so widespread (35.24-26). Agrippa was to propose transferring all such works in private hands to public collections (35.24-26). In this sense, Pliny attributes to political figures the power to influence and provide an example - but he also implies a political power inherent in art.

Much has been written on the political powers of art, and its role as propaganda for the official political views of a regime (see for instance the exhibition 'Art and Power in Europe' held in the Hayward Gallery in 1996). This relates to the cultural and moral value attributed to craftsmanship, as a highest level of technical expertise, which besides the inherent skills is also linked with a long-standing personal commitment. Art, therefore, is ennobling, and art collections convey moral prestige upon their owners (Pearce, 1995: 297, 303). It is upon this line of thought that the notion of 'symbolic capital' has been built, in the sense of the capital that allows individuals and groups to participate in the distribution and allocation of power (see for instance Gordon, 1979; Tanner, 1995 - as well as bibliography on the sociology of art and especially on the term 'cultural capital': Bourdieu, 1974; 1984; 1987). In terms of the antique world, Pliny's reference to art has been read as an 'art history with a political message' (Isager, 1991; also Tanner, 1995). Throughout *HN*, political terminology is used when referring to art and particular attention is paid to the use of works of art in political contexts, as a medium of propaganda in favour of the person who has donated, or owns, the artefacts. The deliberate re-employment in Rome of famous Greek works of art seen in a new symbolic context is emphasized (1991: 222). Even the discussion of marble after that of bronze is seen as indicative of a change in taste through time.

The main emphasis, though, is placed on the political propagandistic message of *HN*. Isager (1991) discerns two main groups of figures, each standing for a different set of values: Nero and Caligula (or M. Antony) are on the one side, Vespasian and Augustus on the other. The first two did not show moderation in their relation to art, and their palaces as art galleries display vain, individualistic ostentation. Their villas occupied large spaces, and, thus, give no sign of restraint and appropriateness (36.111). The latter were moderate in their private consumption and were interested in the public benefit, which they promoted through public displays of art (see for example M. Antony: condemn for Nature - 33.50, lack of self-control in a material sense, 37.29, Nero, *insania, luxuria*).

Isager continues his argument by showing how Pliny used art as a departure point for his criticism, whose ultimate goal was to assimilate and identify Vespasian with Augustus. He, therefore, presents his reading of the political message of *HN* in the following set of binary pairs:

Luxuria	:	*Parsimonia*	
Luxuria	:	*Liberalitas*	
Art for private	:	Art for public	
Mark Antony	:	Augustus	
Nero	:	Vespasian	
The East	:	The West	
Greece	:	Rome	
Otium	:	*Negotium*	(Isager 1991: 225).

Consequently, the dichotomy between private and public takes a political turn and seems to work as part of the Flavian propaganda - which Pliny aims to serve, if we judge from the dedication of *HN*. It is true that throughout the book, as well as in the dedication epistle, Pliny employs constant allusions to signal his favourite view of the new imperial family - and the comparison between Nero's selfishness and Vespasian's generosity (*liberalitas*) is constant (for example see 2.18). As a result, Isager concludes as far as the role of *HN* is concerned:

> In his Natural History Pliny has not only rendered an account of the social and political role of art in Roman society. By virtue of the fact that he often in unexpected contexts on the one hand expresses the attitude of his contemporary world to Nero's times and on the other extols the Flavian dynasty and accords Titus and Vespasian moral excellence, which helped to make up the cosmological picture he had presented in his Natural History, his art history and his work as a whole have been made to incorporate a current political message. The usefulness of the work, its *utilitas*, thus operates on two levels, and thus Pliny fulfilled his intentions as declared in his Letter of Dedication. (1991: 229).

In other words, to serve the political order of Rome that the Flavian dynasty ensured (see Praefatio).

Isager believes that what holds the collections of art that Pliny describes together - along with the whole of *HN* - is a current political message regarding the benevolence of the ruling family of the Flavians. Thus, collection becomes a vehicle of propaganda and comparison between the morally accomplished and the degenerates. The criteria for categorising someone as a member of one or the other group involve access to collections and *liberalitas* (generosity), in terms of sharing the inherent moral value of art with people at large.

This collecting model, though, leaves unaddressed a number of issues, as for example criteria for selecting certain works of art instead of others, the message the collection itself can address, and centrally, how a collection can do this, and from whence has this power stemmed? Rouveret, in a series of contributions (1981; 1987; 1989), discusses the collecting model that Pliny provides in a more complete manner, that tackles the above issues and responds to the shortcomings of the previous theory. A collection for Pliny, she argues, is an assemblage of artworks (this is the first limitation of her approach) which are part of military booty and consequently symbolise Roman victory and superiority (1981: 25). The holding power of the units of a collection is, therefore, their political and ideological message (1987: 124), not their aesthetic value (1987: 125) (so copies are accommodated, too). In other words, a collection by itself has inherent meaning - the selection of artefacts that it consists of provide this. This power of the collection stems from the notion of 'memory'. This is an intellectual activity, very prominent especially in ancient rhetoric. A collection becomes a space of artificial memory, or of 'creating' memory. A central part of an orator's education consisted of cultivating his technique of associating the notions that he had to develop in public within a space; then he could recall his line of thought by simply wandering around his imaginary room. It was a firm belief that by bringing the image of somebody or something in front of the eyes, one could bring the thing itself alive (see also Yates, 1966; Rouveret, 1982; Vasaly, 1993; Edwards, 1996: 28-30; for ancient testimonies on the subject see Cicero, *De Finibus*, 5.2; *De Oratore*, 2.351-354; *ad Herennium*, 3.29-40; Quintilien, *Inst. Orat.* 11.2.17-22; for further discussion see Chapter 4). Therefore, by looking at a collection, people can bring in front of them first the deeds of the general (or emperor) who procured the objects - and, therefore, the collection operates as the man's *monumenta* - and second, the glorious past of Rome (1987: 125).

Rouveret's argument, therefore, attributes to Pliny, and the classical world, a rhetorical understanding of collections. In the case of *HN* in particular, Rouveret claims that the collections described by Pliny, along with the collection assembled by Pliny himself (*HN*), aimed to promote the ideal of Roman pre-eminence and establish Rome as a *musée par excellence* (1981: 25). The key-paragraph for such a claim becomes 36.101, where Pliny introduces the discussion of the architectural marvels of the city of Rome:

> But this is indeed the moment for us to pass on to the wonders of our own city, to review the resources derived from the experiences of 800 years, and to show that here too in our buildings we have vanquished the world; and the frequency of this occurrence will be proved to match within a little the number of marvels that we shall describe. If we imagine the whole agglomeration of our buildings massed together and placed on one great heap, we shall see such grandeur towering above us as to make us think that some other world were being described, all concentrated in one single place.

Rouveret argues (1981: 23-24) that these views have an equally important application in the discussion of sculpture, too. The works of art held in Rome - mainly in the Campus Martius - were symbols of the power of Rome:

... les merveilles de Rome sont entasées comme un trophée (*aceruata, cumulum*), leur masse imaginaire transforme Rome en un univers qui a absorbé tous les autres. Cet univers est de l'ordre de l'extrapolation et du récit et il s'agit d'un récit qui s'attache à un lieu: *si mundus alius quidam in uno loco narretur*. Rome est le lieu de mémoire du monde qui sanctionne ainsi sa domination universelle. (1987: 126).

The aim of Pliny then becomes to assemble in one place (in one book) all the marvels of the world - exactly as Rome has assembled all the marvels of the world in tangible terms.[47]

The setting of collections, thus, acquires its own importance. The temples, where traditionally sanctification is achieved, are the natural *locus* for the assemblage of artefacts. Even though some temples seem to have been deprived of almost any religious value and have acquired a mere cultural role (as is usually considered to be the case with the temple of Concordia, or with the temples of the Portico of Octavia), they retain the basic pre-requisites for 'proper enjoyment of the arts'. This has been defined by Pliny as follows:

> At Rome, indeed, the great number of works of art and again their consequent effacement from our memory, and, even more, the multitude of official functions and business activities must, after all, deter anyone from serious study, since the appreciation involved needs leisure and deep silence in our surroundings. (36.27).

This description corresponds to that of a typically understood art museum: silence, leisure, serious study are some of the key-words in our perceptions of museums today.

Private involvement of collectors, though, can upset the 'natural order', according to Pliny - and in the view of many museums today. In the case of Pliny, the question could take the form of how and why cultural places, like the library or the gymnasium came to find a place in the private sphere - and how this changed the cultural patterns involved, namely collecting. The answer lies in the difference between public and private space in Rome, compared to that of Greece, in terms of the client system which was such a prominent characteristic of the Roman social life. This led to a theatralisation and sacralisation of the house (typical in the painting of the second style) (1987: 130-132; Wallace-Hadrill, 1994: 30). Phenomena like the decoration of private space with *pinacothecae*, therefore, or Hortensius placing the painting of the Argonauts by Cydias that he had bought in an *aedes* (shrine) in his villa (35.130-132), or even the freedman who worshipped the lamp that had led him to his freedom and fortune (through a sexual relationship with his mistress) (34.11-12) come therefore to upset and unsettle the notion of sacred and profane, private and public, and to distribute power in a manner that disturbs the 'natural order' and, consequently, the political order. As Wallace-Hadrill has asserted, the *locus* of political decisions has been transferred to the private realm (1994: 29).

If we present schematically the discussion of collections in terms of private-public and sacred-profane, we can reach a diagram like that in Figure 6.3. In the four quarters we can see the perception of collections as these are described in *HN*. The two upper quarters hold the 'justified' collections, whereas the two lower ones the irrational, contemptible ones. Public and sacred is the ideal setting that allows a highly moral and sacralising enjoyment, as that described in 36.27. Public and profane is also 'correct' in terms of compliance with the political order and notions of public morality, benevolence, *liberalitas*. Profane and private is simply an act of extravagance, where all the criticism related to luxury comes. Sacred and private is the ultimate immorality quarter - which dares to appropriate sanctity. It is sacrilegious, irrational, 'fetishistic'.

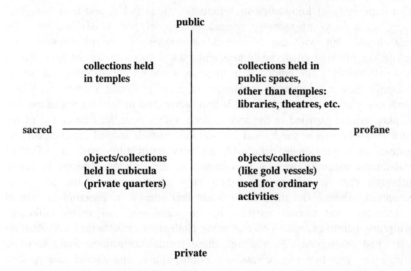

Figure 6.3:   Perception of collections as described in *HN*, and structured on the axes of private: public and sacred: profane.

Where does this leaves Pliny's own collection? Early antiquarianism is recorded in 13.84-86. A chance find recovered the body of king Numa and with him books, which remarkably had survived because of the conditions of burial. The books were later destroyed, because they were products of Greek philosophy, and not even their antiquity could save them. Similar antiquarian spirit is evidenced in paragraphs 35.10-11. Pliny records the tradition of decorating libraries with bronze portraits, in honour of famous men of education and culture. Where likenesses had not survived, the portraits were cast through the guidance of the person's spirit, as for example in the case of Homer. The libraries of Alexandria and Pergamum, as well as those modeled on them like the library of Asinius Pollio, were similarly decorated. Two collections assembled by M. Terentius Varro and Atticus (Cicero's friend) are considered by Pliny equivalent to this decoration. Both collected in a volume the portraits of famous men, in an attempt to offer them immortality. In addition, they aimed to contribute to the expansion of these men's fame all over the world. This is, according to Pliny, a very noble service - and has to be seen in the light of his own collecting attempts, as well as of the equation of the notion of actual with that of textual collections. The first public display of ancestral portraits was provided by Appius Claudius, and it met the approval of Pliny, who found it also honourable and pleasurable.

The term 'textual collection' refers to assemblages held in books, and defined rhetorically. They share all the characteristics of an actual collection, as a depository of knowledge in systematic, quantifiable, and thus 'tangible' form, as a *locus* of memory created to support and satisfy the need for *monumenta*, but with the additional advantages of the non-sinister, non-fetishistic relation to material culture, and a wider spectrum for the appreciation of 'real' values. The emphasis in these falls not on the material, but on the symbolic power of objects, as carriers of more profound knowledge, which finds completion in the act of acquisition rather than in the vain act of use and display, and is justified in the appreciation, rather than the destruction of the natural world, and in the logical and rational attitude toward material culture, instead of a passionate, irrational, arbitrary association with it. Textual collections naturally were not unknown in the previous literary tradition, although very few fragments (often only titles) are available for us to reconstruct them. But there is no doubt that interest in asssembling 'virtual collections' was already existent in the 'catalogues' of votive offerings, sculpture, paintings, and so on that many Hellenistic antiquarians, and Romans later, had assembled. In addition, these textual collections could serve to bridge the gap between private and public space, and sacred and profane domains, by reassuring public accessibility, without actually crossing the boundaries with the sacred world. Being 'virtual' meant that they could complement actual collections (so it is not surprising to find that Varro, for instance, kept an actual collection while he indulged in the creation of textual ones), so that they could mediate between the two domains of sanctity and profanity without resulting in ungratefulness and *hybris*.

Taking into account Figure 6.3, we can argue that Pliny wished his work to be considered as profane, but public (like the collections in the public libraries). But he also wished his work to cross the boundaries between profane and sacred; he hoped to achieve that by transferring the emphasis in his work from the individual deities to the eternal, divine force of nature. This renders knowledge (of nature and facts) sacred, as well, and his work a collection that deserves to be held in posterity. On the basis of the ideas discussed so far, we are going now to turn our attention to the model of collecting *HN* itself offers. But before this, we shall mention in brief a few collecting practices as recorded by Pliny.

Pliny as a Source of Information on Collections and Collecting: practical aspects of collecting

Pliny provides an insight into the practical issues involved in collecting, arranging, and preserving a collection. Paragraph 37.12-17, for example, can be 'read' interestingly in terms of a 'temporary exhibition'. The triumphs of the victorious generals in Rome quite often had the character of a 'temporary' exhibition; all the items that could serve as 'evidence' of the victory and the expansion of the Roman people were exhibited in a kind of a long parade, in a 'Great Exhibition'.[48] In this particular passage, after enumerating the objects presented during Pompey's triumph, Pliny argues that it was more than anything else a triumph of extravagance. He then continues to 'read' the message of it: all these objects were means of ennobling Pompey and adding value to him, but simultaneously they were a bad omen for the man. Pliny continues arguing that such a triumph and behaviour deprived people of the possibility of criticizing extravagance from then onwards, because even Claudius' slippers with pearls, or Nero's masks, or even household equipment inlaid with gems, were modest, when compared to Pompey's triumph.

Here and there in Pliny's accounts occur references to conservation techniques, such as in 15.32, where he mentions that old olive-oil was used for the preservation of the statue of Saturn at Rome (made of ivory). We know that this technique had been used by the ancients in classical Athens (where it was employed for the protection of the statue of Athena on the Acropolis). Conservation techniques are also recorded in 16.213-219, where thought is paid to techniques of nourishing the wood and keeping the joints together. Another indicative of connoisseurship technique is presented in 37.195: gems are boiled in honey to have their colour improved.

Pliny as a Collector

In this section we are going to resume the arguments regarding textual collections, and in particular, *HN* as a collection of facts and artefacts. We have established that in the Plinian hierarchy of values, the recording of artefacts corresponds to the textual collection and is opposed to the pair sacrilegious acts of luxury : actual collections. On the other hand, we have noticed that the notion of public as opposed to private is of prevailing importance. Textual collections undoubtedly serve their public role, since they allow more individuals to access them, while they also permit the appropriate

conditions of thorough enjoyment of them to be reached. A textual tradition of
this kind already had been established during Pliny's era. It is actually the
tradition created by antiquarians (see Chapter 2), and was taken over in the
Roman world by Varro and Atticus, who assembled their collections of
portraits, which as we have seen, were praised by Pliny so much. In this and
the following parts therefore, Pliny as a collector and his influence on the
Renaissance collections will be considered. We will examine the preceding
textual tradition and the collecting model to which it led, the classification and
taxonomy employed in Pliny's collection and how it influenced the subsequent
generations of collectors. But, first, we will question what Pliny himself
thought of his work (and how this fits with the definition of collecting - so that
we expand on the work of Rouveret).

Pliny's view on his *HN* is outlined in the preface of his monumental work.
He recalls an incident with one of his friends, and refers to it in his dedicatory
epistle to emperor Titus: '*quoniam, ut, ait Domitius Piso, thesauros oportet
esse, non libros*' (Praef. 17), 'as Domitius Piso says, it is not books but store-
houses that are needed'.[49] The tone is complacent, as if Pliny congratulates
himself on having succeeded in covering the need identified by his friend. It is
quite clear that Pliny conceives his book as a store-house, a *thesaurus*, like
those holding the holy treasures in the sanctuaries. There he safeguards an
ordered and complete inventory of things - a library of knowledge if we prefer
to think in terms of facts (Conte, 1994a: 72-73). The value of the work is also
guaranteed by the fact that it is dedicated to the emperor, just like those objects
that are regarded very valuable because they have been dedicated to a temple
(Praef. 19). Further down in paragraph 18 he boasts of having collected 20,000
noteworthy 'facts' - for which he uses the word '*res (rerum)*', that is 'thing',
'item'. This is how Pliny himself therefore views his work: an assemblage of
noteworthy 'things'.

Pliny has a long tradition of textual collections to follow. His ideal *vir
bonus*, M. Terentius Varro, had assembled along with an actual collection
(33.155; 36.41), a textual one of portraits. Other antiquarians were also
devoted to such projects. Even artists like Pasiteles (first century) had
assembled in five volumes the '*opera nobilia in toto orbe*', all the noble works
of art in the city - and Pliny uses him as a source in books 34 to 36 (Rouveret
1989: 459). Just the title of Pasiteles' work is indicative: it is an appreciation
of all the works of art produced until then, in a wide geographical and
chronological spectrum, expressed in an assemblage, and a reclassification of a
sort that reminds one of an imaginary museum. Rouveret (1989: 460) attributes
to Pliny a similar wish achieved in the 'art history' chapters, especially in book
36, where Pliny most explicitly adopts a wider stance and views the world with
the eyes of a critic (as Rouveret argues). I would suggest that this is
undoubtedly true in *HN*, but the scope is much wider that has been indicated, so
that it includes the whole of *HN* and not just the art history chapters. Pliny
aimed to assemble, to hoard, a *musée imaginaire* - that is the universe. The

sanctity of the subject reifies the outcome as well. Words, images, and texts are incorporated into a universal encyclopedia of knowledge (Findlen, 1994: 64).

This can be supported not only by the encyclopedic inclusiveness of *HN*; it is also the arrangement, the classification of *HN* that accounts for it. *HN* in collecting terms can and has been read with more than one organisational line in mind. The first is the one that we have been following so far, that is the one that results in 'museographic' lists like those we presented above. But this was not one intended by the author of the work - a fact which leads to the thought that it is not an organising principle *per se*, but a conception that corresponds to subsequent creations and ideas regarding collections and museums. In this sense, the word 'museographic' acquires its inverted commas. Even the art chapters of *HN,* though, are organised in terms of material (precious stones, marble, bronze and so on), and then, creators/artists. Conte (1994a: 100) identifies at least two organisational lines which structure *HN*: one (implicit) articulates according to 'mental' connections, like teleology, or the symbolic anthropocentric thought, whereas the other (explicit) relates to the external order of materials. The latter criterion does not correspond to a single notion structuring classification; there is a ramified scheme: from the central notion, *mundus*, all the beings of the natural world originate. They are divided in kingdoms, groupable in species, but not a single morphological or anatomico-physiological criterion is employed. All divisions are practical and utilitarian. In such a loose criterion, the pressures of the discourse's immediate requirements can be quite powerful. Consequently, analogy with other creatures, phenomena, cultural practices, synonymic contiguity, or even assonance, not to mention juxtaposition,. can lead to a completely different subject or area. This gives to the work the character of a lexicon, or 'a set of notecards', as Conte (1994a: 101) calls it. Despite the scattered structure of the text, though, the requirement of systematicity is not lacking completely. Creatures are presented from biggest to the smallest, whereas the presentation of nature follows a line from animals to plants, and then to minerals (Conte, 1994a: 101-102). Conte has also argued that in this sense Pliny follows the organising principles of natural history that Aristotle had shaped.[50]

Pliny has been criticised: his work is not scientific, not only in terms of the 'science' it contains, but mainly for the lack of organically structured and unified epistemological principle. Consequently, the criticism continues, the particular and individual prevails throughout *HN*, and obscures a possible theoretical centre that we would expect to hold together the description of the world (Conte, 1994a: 103-104). But this criticism largely is unfair, since it ignores the fact that *HN* is not a scientific book in the contemporary sense. The text is unified by the underlying rationale of a collector, who aims to assemble fragments of the universe in an attempt to reach and 'entrap' it, so that it is easily accessible and intelligible even by those who now ignore the truth about it. In other words, he aims to create a 'microcosm', and his ideas on the nature of the world and of things allows him to believe that he can do so.

Philological criticism underlines the encyclopedic character of *HN*, and attributes to the excellent timing of its synthesis, a period when the world was ready for such a self-reflecting enterprise, the fact that the work survived throughout the years (Conte, 1994a: 75). Such an approach privileges Pliny as an individual, and seems to ignore previous attempts that have not survived (at least not in their entirety). Although survival is also a medium of appreciating value in terms of the influence a work exercises over its contemporaries and subsequent generations, it is not the only criterion that we can employ. In the case of *HN*, its survival signals its being the most mature product of a long line of attempts rather than its uniqueness. Both the philosophical purpose along with the formal structure had already been provided; Pliny led the tradition to a culmination.

The pre-eminence given to the textual form of collecting is also justified in a couple of paragraphs from *HN*, which also respond to a criticism of Pliny by Renaissance collectors: the lack of illustrations, especially in the sections on plants and animals. Pliny responds to these future criticisms:

> Besides these the subject has been treated by Greek writers, whom we
> have mentioned in their proper places; of these, Crateuas, Dionysius
> and Metrodorus adopted a most attractive method, though one which
> makes clear little else except the difficulty of employing it. For they
> painted likenesses of the plants and then wrote under them their
> properties. But not only is a picture misleading when the colours are
> so many, particularly as the aim is to copy Nature, but besides this,
> much imperfection arises from the manifold hazards in the accuracy
> of copyists. In addition, it is not enough for each plant to be painted
> at one period only of its life, since it alters its appearance with the
> fourfold changes of the year. (25.8).[51]

And he continues his discourse:

> For this reason the other writers have given verbal accounts only;
> some have not even given the shape of the plants, and for the most
> part have been content with bare names, since they thought it
> sufficient to point out the properties and nature of a plant to those
> willing to look for it. To gain this knowledge is no difficult matter; I
> at least have enjoyed the good fortune to examine all but a very few
> plants through the devotion to science of Antonius Castor, the highest
> botanical authority of our time; I used to visit his special garden, in
> which he would rear a great number of specimens even when he
> passed his hundredth year, having suffered no bodily ailment and, in
> spite of his age, no loss of memory or physical vigour. Nothing else
> will be found that aroused greater wonder among the ancients than
> botany. (25.9-10).[52]

Not only do Pliny's own views on collections become explicit in the above, but we can also recognise the inspiration that it gave to subsequent generations of naturalists. They had to examine the objects themselves, and then discuss them and their properties, as Pliny has done.

Furthermore, many paragraphs in different parts of *HN* read like the standard list of wonders in any respectable museum. For example, we can see paragraphs 32.144-145, where marine animals are listed:

> To begin with large beasts, there are 'sea-trees', blower-whales, other whales, saw-fish, Tritons, Nereids, walruses, so called 'men of the sea', and others having the shape of fishes, dolphins, and seals well known to Homer, tortoises on the other hand well known to luxury, beavers to medical people (of the class of beavers we have never found record, speaking as we are of marine animals, that otters anywhere frequent the sea); also sharks, 'drinones', horned rays (?), sword-fish, saw-fish; hippopotamuses and crocodiles common to land, sea, and river; and, common to river and sea only, tunnies, other tunnies, 'siluri', 'coracini', and perches.[53]

The views of Pliny on the role and value of his collection are also summarised in paragraph 25.1-3, where he discusses the importance that dissemination of knowledge has for the world, and he defines as the supreme task of a great mind the ability to keep within memory the success of the ancients.

Pliny as a Model for Imitation for Renaissance Collectors

Renaissance museums owe to the past more than their name. There is a profound association between ancient models and subsequent practices; this contributed to the philosophical programmes underlying their collecting mode. Museums of natural history are usually associated with the reformulation of the history of nature in the eighteenth and nineteenth centuries (Linnaeus and Darwin); but although undoubtedly this is true, it is the fact that they originated within a predominately Aristotelian and Plinian framework. Naturalists of the Renaissance had the natural philosophers of antiquity as guidance during their researches. Aristotle, for instance, offered philosophical purpose for the collecting of nature, or the method by which one can arrive at a proper name for a previously unidentified phenomenon (Findlen, 1994: 57). Pliny's contribution is even more profound, however.

His encyclopedic spirit, his classification principle, his aims to assemble the world for people, his notions of commemoration, memory and so on, have influenced (and in many senses continue to do so) the collecting process from the Renaissance onwards. In this section, we are going to trace patterns of influence. We are not going to provide a complete list of all naturalists and collections that have been influenced by Pliny, and certainly it is not individual responses to *HN* for which we are searching. Here we are merely going to illuminate, quite eclectically, views on collecting that have dominated the phenomenon since the Renaissance and which we can immediately associate with, and attribute to Plinian influence.

The encyclopedic notion is responsible for a wide range of influences. It inspired naturalists to extend their curiosity to the farthest ends of the known world, and catalogue its wonders. The format of *HN* reminded collectors that all details of nature deserve to be assembled. It offered the compilation of a comprehensive encyclopedia as a model for imitation, and the pursuit of knowledge as the ultimate desire of man (Findlen, 1994: 63-64). Aldrovaldi or Gesner, for instance, perceived the encyclopedia of Nature as dependent on the encyclopedia of knowledge. For example, they hoarded bibliographies, as if the assemblage of the books' titles alone could symbolically convey the possession of the contents as well (Findlen, 1994: 59-60). Consumed by their pursuit of knowledge, they committed themselves to a life organised around collecting, and the organisation of the objects and information they possessed. Following the model of Pliny, Renaissance collectors relied heavily for the creation of their 'natural histories' on numerous other books. As Findlen argues, Aldrovaldi, for example, incorporated worlds, images and texts in his universal encyclopedia, in his '*cimilarchion* and *pandechion*' (1994: 64) (meaning 'the archive of keimelia' and 'the repository of everything', respectively).

The conscious imitation of Pliny is evidenced in direct references to him that we find in Renaissance writings. Federico Borromeo wrote at the beginning of his *Musaeum* (1625): 'To begin this work, I think first of Pliny, above all others, not for the desire that I have to emulate him, which would be excessively foolish and audacious, but, in spite of myself, for the excellence of his example'.[54] Elsewhere Aldrovaldi, referring to the lessons naturalists could receive from *HN,* asserts: 'There is nothing under the sun that cannot be reduced to one of the three genus, that is, inanimate things and fossils, extracted from the bowels of the earth, plants, or animals. Even artificial things may be included in one of these three genus according to the materials [of their composition].'[55] Having the expansive and wide character of *HN* in mind, Renaissance collectors of nature included in their *Wunderkammern* works of art, antiquities and scientific instruments, too. Mercati, for instance, included descriptions of some of the Belvedere statues as examples of marble in his *Metallotheca* (Findlen, 1994: 61-63; Bredekamp, 1995). In Italy, in particular, by the end of the sixteenth century works of art and *naturalia*, that is artistically arranged natural specimens, were introduced into collections (Schulz, 1990: 4).

HN's preface was read by naturalists as a challenge to their ingenuity and perspicacity. In particular, it encouraged a noble antagonism, worthy of humanists: to surpass Pliny in the number of facts and artefacts that they could amass, and thus surpass antiquity in the face of its most distinguished practitioner of naturalism. Numbers seemed extremely important to collectors. Aldrovaldi, for example, was obsessed with the size of his collection, and used to count his 'facts' very often. The number 20,000 that Pliny mentions in his preface (paragraph 17) became quite seminal, and the aim of all collectors was to exceed it. Associated with this tendency, although not exclusively, was the production of literary works which could in length and quantity surpass *HN*. A great compliment that a seventeenth century visitor could bestow on the museum he had just visited was an immediate comparison with Pliny. Lassels who toured the *Studio Aldrovaldi* in the mid seventeenth century remarked, 'in this *Pallace* I saw the rare *Cabinet and Study of Aldrovaldus*, to whom *Pliny the Second* if he were now alive would but be *Pliny the Sixt[h]*; for he hath printed six great volumes of the natures of all things in nature, each volume being as big as all *Plinyes* workes' (Findlen, 1994: 64).[56]

The textuality of the collections relates to more than one notion. Of course, *HN* emerges as a connecting thread between actual collections and textual ones. Renaissance naturalists perceived nature as a text. 'Reading' the book of nature was the prime activity, while collecting contributed to the reactivation and redefinition of the metaphor of the book. Possessing nature was a process that paralleled the possession of the ancient wisdom (Findlen, 1994: 55-56). Furthermore, the collection was not located in the text, nor in the objects alone, but was a dialectic between *res* and *verba* that fully defined the universality of this project. Museums were textual structures both in a literal and a figurative sense. They were created as reference points for the reading that the humanistic educational program required; in order to understand the rationale behind the acquisition of certain objects by collectors one needed to participate in the textual strategy of encyclopedism. Borromeo in his *Musaeum* (1625) laments: 'Moreover how much light would we glean from interpreting the passages of writers, principally Pliny, if we had in sight those things which he told only with words.'[57] The museum, therefore, was a copy of 'originals' long since vanished, since it was shaped according to the texts that had survived, both in terms of contents, and of notion. It was a copy of the notion of collection as an assemblage meant to commemorate and carry forward to posterity knowledge, values, sanctity; but it was also a copy in terms of the contents, because it imitated the 'lost original' by assembling exactly the kind of artefacts that the original contained. (In other words, it was a copy of the books, both in the sense that it copied the idea of collection that books contained, and in that it 'illustrated' the books, it reproduced in tangible objects what the books merely described.). It is worth quoting Aldrovaldi once again, when he says about his rare desiccated plants 'which I conserve pasted in fifteen volumes of my *Pandechion* of nature for the utility of posterity'. Here once again Aldrovaldi reiterates the textual character of artefacts, which became 'books' organised according to his taxonomy of nature. In the words of Cicero (*De Oratore*, III.xxi.125), 'for a full supply of facts (*copia rerum*) begets a full supply of words'.

Quiccheberg also defines a 'museum' as a place or text where extraordinary things are arranged as if in a chamber (Schulz, 1990: 208). His 'theatrum' evolved into a model of the universe in the sense of both a collection of real objects and of an encyclopedic text. Quiccheberg believed that the first collections were described in the Old Testament (Book 2 Kings 20, 12-21 and Book 1 Kings 5 and 6 - of King Hezeki'ah and the Temple of Solomon respectively) (Schulz, 1990: 209). He takes up the idea of the encyclopedic text from *HN*, and preoccupies himself with the need for a catalogue, as complete as possible with all the things in the universe. Furthermore, Quiccheberg wanted to provide instructions of what was to be collected in order to create a complete 'theatrum', serving both the glorification of God and serious study (Schulz, 1990: 208). In this he also imitates Pliny, since instructions concerning what was to be collected were also available in *HN*. Pliny presented in detail the three realms of nature that embrace everything, from elephants to insects, and from plants to sculpture. Even the notion of the three realms (Book VIIIff) was adopted by collectors, who followed it in order to construct their own Natural Histories (Schulz, 1990: 205, 212).

Schulz (1990) argues that there has been an evolving process as far as the relation between actual and textual collections is concerned. Pliny's encyclopedia gave way to an actual collection as comprehensive as possible, which in its turn gave way to encyclopedias, whose ultimate goal was to praise the ordered universe of godly creation. Quiccheberg is a characteristic example of this perception (1990: 205-206). Consequently, she argues that the name of the 'museum' became the title of a literary genre before it become the name of the public collection. It was the literary genre that was comprised of 'all objects that were regarded as being unalterably components of a collection that could justly bear the name "museum"' (Schulz, 1990: 212). This is a completely justified assertion, only it goes back a bit earlier than Renaissance. It is a fair argument to make in regard to Pliny's collection, Pliny's textual 'museum'.

Conclusions

The genuinely historical character of *HN* ascribes the work to the tradition of antiquarianism. Pliny, in a search for the remarkable and the noteworthy, expands the horizon of the traditional historical account, and provides a *Natural History*, in which all the aspects of natural and cultural are included. In our discussion of antiquarianism, we defined the antiquarian as a student of the past, who unlike the historian writes in a systematic order (instead of a chronological one), collects all the items that are connected with a certain theme, whether they can be of any assistance in solving a problem or not, and deals with subjects that are considered more suitable for systematic description than for a chronological account (Momigliano, 1950: 286). Pliny's work fits remarkably well into this description: influenced by Stoic conceptions of nature and the world, he undertakes the role of a systematic recorder of all the *thaumasia* that the city of Rome and the Roman world have amassed, in order to save for the future, but also provide for his contemporaries, a treasury of knowledge about the history of civilisation, and in particular, about the history of Roman power.

Pliny creates the most complete textual collection that survives from the ancient world. He also gives a unique account of other, actual, collections that decorated the city of Rome and other parts of the Roman realm, and were amassed by collectors, whose motives and discourse Pliny saves and interprets for us. For that reason, Pliny's *HN* is important in any discussion regarding classical collecting: he shows us as clearly as we will ever see a collection created during the first century. Attention is usually paid to *HN* as a source of information about collections, rather than to its own character as a collection and as a paradigm of collecting that drew enthusiastic followers many centuries after its formation. In this chapter, we have tried to redress this shortcoming, and to deal with both aspects of *HN*.

At the beginning we reflected on the specific characteristics of *HN* as an example of a literary genre, and the features that differentiate it from other similar texts, as well as on the underlying principles that shape its character and provide its special intellectual background that is of assistance in understanding its dual role. We argued that *HN* has a very broad subject-matter that exceeds the limits usually set for encyclopedic works. Its broad perspective had been shaped by Pliny's perception of the world, which in turn had been defined by Stoic naturalism. Nature is a passive and an active element in life, and as such it is contained even in the humblest little thing. In this sense, Pliny's belief that he can assemble the world in his books seems absolutely rational and justifiable. Furthermore, *HN* is an historical work, in the sense that it presents an attempt to record for posterity the accomplishments of Roman people and the power of the Roman state. This accounts for many of the decisions taken by Pliny, as for instance the inclusion of the 'art history chapters' in his book, as well as his attempt to write a history of civilisation and techniques, along with a natural history.

In the following part, and after having established the intellectual background of the work, we focused on its role as a source of information for collecting in the Roman world. We listed the collections and collectors that Pliny records (although the listing is not comprehensive), so that we systematise and acquire a more complete picture of the public collections held in Rome during that period, as well as of their reception. Then we concentrated on the collecting discourse of that period as this was recorded and interpreted by Pliny. We concluded that the writer defends a hierarchy of values that he defines as distinct from those of his contemporaries, and he exemplifies this in his own work and in his own collection, as opposed to the actual collections that others had assembled. Collections in the public domain, which are the product of beneficient interference of emperors and generals, as well as collections that have resulted from spoils of victorious wars against the enemies of Rome, are very explicitly valued and appreciated. On the contrary, private collections are discouraged, at least as long as they express a sinister relation with material culture, ignorance, or neglect, of the natural values, and lack of rationality.

Pliny does not deny the existence or the necessity for collections; on the contrary, he offers a definition of the notion of collection in the classical world. A collection becomes a set of works of art, artefacts, and natural curiosities set aside as a vehicle of propaganda and comparison between the morally accomplished and the degenerates, as well as symbols of military prowess and Roman superiority. The holding power of the units of a collection therefore are the political and ideological messages and not the aesthetic value of the works. This is so because of the role of the collection as a space of artificial memory. Therefore, collections operate as *monumenta* of illustrious men, and as 'evidence' of human achievements and Nature's grandeur. Furthermore, *HN* presents a rhetorical understanding of the collections.

Based on these remarks, we reached the conclusion that Pliny puts his own views in practice when he writes *HN*, and that the latter is his own collection. Naturally, this development relates to a more general understanding of collections in the classical world, and Pliny offers simply the culmination of a long lasting tradition, where collecting of facts and information has been as important as the collection of tangible materials was, if not even more. Already in the classical Greek world, antiquarians had introduced the tradition of assembling in one book 'objects' of their interest, whether votive offerings in Greek sanctuaries, *heuremata*, or intangible information about practices, beliefs, institutions, or even people. This antiquarian tradition was taken over by Varro and Atticus in the Roman world, not to mention the paradoxographers, and the writers of *mirabilia*. Their collections were textual, of course, limited within the pages of books, but serving the same purpose that the tangible ones were called to serve. They were assemblages of facts, set aside for future generations as well as contemporaries, as sources of knowledge, admiration, political and national pride, that would testify the grandeur of their own society.[58]

Pliny's work was part of this tradition, and in many ways summarised it for future generations. It was not only his collection *per se* that was important for his followers, but also his collecting mode. Pliny's encyclopedic spirit, his classification principle, his understanding of collections as methods of commemoration and *locus* of memory influenced the Renaissance collectors directly or indirectly. The textual character of Pliny's collection influenced their view about the dialectic relation between *res* and *verba*. Their 'museums', 'cabinets' or 'theatres' were the tangible illustrations of their 'museums on paper', which aimed to serve the same purpose and reassured accessibility and popularity. In other words, the early museum catalogues, instead of being a result of the collecting activities, have to be seen as a cause, a reason for them. *Historia Naturalis* undoubtedly is the inspiring flame behind them, and a unique monument whose importance goes far beyond the limits of its era.

Notes

1   Loeb CL, translated by H. St. J. Thackerey, 1957.

2   234-149 BCE and 116-27 BCE respectively; for a discussion of Cato as the first exponent of the Roman encyclopedic tradition, as well as the philosophical origin of encyclopedism in Greek philosophy see Grimal (1965).

3   More about this literary genre in the following part.

4   Or thirty-six, if we do not count, as Pliny does not, the first book which consists of the index and the 'bibliography' of the work.

5   Pliny has received heavy criticism about the purity of his Latin prose; that which he receives from Goodyear (1982b: 670) is not unique, although extremely harsh. Norden in his *Die Antike Kunstprosa* (1898-1918) is also very negative as far as Pliny's style is concerned. Different is the approach of Healy (1987: 3-24); see also Serbat (1986: 2085-2086) with summary of the debate and further bibliography.

6   Gaius Plinius Secundus - usually called Pliny the Elder to be distinguished from his nephew Gaius Plinius Caecilius Secundus (Pliny the Younger) - was born in 22/23 CE in Novum Comum of Transpadane Gaul (northern Italy), and died on 24 August, 79 CE at Misenum, trying to get a clearer view of the eruption of Vesuvius. We do not know much about his family, but it must have been one of standing and wealth. His patron was Pomponius Secundus, whose biography Pliny wrote (*De Vita Pomponii Secundi*) (Pliny the Younger, *Epist.* 3.5.1). He served his military term in Germany (in 47, in 50 and in 57-58), where he met the future emperor Titus, to whom he dedicated *HN*. It was from his experiences in Germany that his first literary work (*De iaculatione Equestri* - On throwing the javelin from the horseback) and his larger German Wars (*Bella Germaniae*) originated. There is not much evidence about his career during Nero's reign. He was possibly officially active (perhaps as a procurator in Africa); but his condemnation of Nero is unquestionable. In the final years of Nero's reign he produced a six-volume work on the education of an orator (it was possibly called *Studiosus*) and an eight-volume grammatical treatise (*Dubius Sermo*). When Vespasian became emperor, Pliny entered upon an intensive career and held many important posts. But he also wrote a Roman history, *A Fine Aufidi Bassi*, and *HN*, his single work that survives. When he died he was holding the post of the prefect of the imperial fleet. His nephew's letters, *Epistulae* 3.5 and 6.16, 6.20 remain the best account of biographical information on Pliny. Also information is offered by Suetonius, (*De Viris illustribus. De historicis*, VI), and a fragmented inscription from Syria, published by Mommsen 1884). (Among the secondary sources see e.g. Conte, 1994b: 497-499; Goodyear, 1982: 670; Serbat, 1986: 2073-2077 with further bibliography; Reynolds, 1986: 1-2; Beagon, 1992: 2-3; Syme, 1979; 1987; Healy, 1991: ix-xi; Levidis, 1994: 7-8).

7   For a discussion of these works see Grimal, 1965: 469ff.

8   For a comprehensive bibliography of Pliny and *HN*, see Hanslik, 1955 and 1964; Sallmann, 1975; Römer, 1978; Serbat, 1986.
9   Loeb CL, translated by H. Rackham, vol. I, 1949.
10   Pliny's main argument, as far as the gods are concerned is that human vices or virtues (e.g. *Concordia, Pudicitia* etc.) can not be considered gods.   He conceives no distinction between God and Nature, following the Stoic beliefs.   But he confuses things a bit, when he includes in the definition of the deity the imperial house (2.18). About Pliny's cosmology and the God see Gigon (1982) with several models.
11   Translated by Healy (1991: 10).
12   For a discussion of Stoicism and its ideas on φύσις, λόγος, *virtus*, see also Watson (1971: 222-229).
13   For the differences between Greek and Roman Stoicism see French, 1994: 149-195; also Arnold, 1958.
14   This translation is by Rackham in Loeb CL, 1949.
15   The word luxury alone occurs in more than sixty passages, see Wallace-Hadrill (1990: 86).
16   About exaggerrated values see for example Seneca, *De brev. vit.*, 12.2; Corinthian bronze which the 'furor' of few makes '*pretiosa*' (see Beagon, 1992: 76, nt. 42).
17   Healy (1991: xvii-xviii) makes an interesting comparison between Pliny and Herodotus: their approach to history seems suprisingly similar at points.
18   Many of the authors who had been distinguished for their collections of *mirabilia* figure in the source-lists of Pliny, as for instance Callimachus and his pupil Philostephanus of Cyrene.   Also in several instances Pliny acknowledges as his sources Isigonus of Nicaea and Alexander Polyhistor.   *HN* is a valuable source for the study of similar writers (Beagon, 1992: 8-9, also nt. 25).
19   For Mucianus see Jex-Blake and Sellers, 1896: lxxxv-xci; Bardon, 1956: 179-182; Le Bonniec, 1953: 38-39 and 78-80.
20   About Pliny and *mirabilia* see Isager (1991: 44-47), where also further references; especially note the computer search of Mayhoff's Pliny edition that provided 831 examples of the root *mir and 83 variants of *mirabilis, admirabilis* (ibid: 46, nt. 149). Also see Shelton (1994: 179) on the word 'mirror' and 'mirari'.
21   Tanner (1995: 212) argues that the resemblance the scholars mention is misleading and is 'rooted in the architectural iconography of modern museums as temples of the Muses rather than in ancient realities'.
22   The search for Pliny's sources has been a very popular subject, especially of German scholarship during the 19th and the beginning of the 20th centuries. Münzer (1897), Sellers (1896), Kalkmann (1898), Schweitzer (1932), Jahn (1850), Ferri (1946) are examples of such an approach.
23   The picture was originally in Athens (Plut., *Thes*. iv) whence it may have been brought from Sulla. Destroyed in fire in 70 BCE (Jex-Blake and Sellers, 1896: 113).
24   But Cass. Dio (53.27.2) implies that it was finished in 25 BCE and was called Pantheon because of the number of statues it contained. See discussion in Richardson, 1992: 283-286, where also bibliography.
25   For a discussion of the bronze capitals of the columns, see 34.13.
26   The motif of the 'ultimate folly' of falling in love with a celebrated statue appears quite frequently in Pliny. For instance, in 36.20-25 a young man is mentioned who fell in love with the reknowned work by Praxiteles, Eros of Parium; he remained with the statue overnight and left a mark of his passion on it. A Roman knight, J. Pisciculus, had fallen in love with one of the Nine Muses formerly in front of the Temple of Prosperity (36.29).
27   For a discussion of Licinius Mucianus as a source on the sanctuaries of the East see Jex-Blake and Sellers, 1896: introduction.

28	For his biography see André, 1949.
29	Papylus was most probably a student of Pasiteles, and not Praxiteles (see Isager, 1991: 165, nt. 584). The paragraph follows the translation of Eichholz, in Loeb CL, 1971.
30	In the same paragraph are also mentioned two pendants of Vesta by Scopas, which was in the Horti Serviliani; scholars do not agree what exactly these were - *lampteras*, as Becatti suggests (1956: 199-201), *camiteras*, or *campteras* (see André, Bloch and Rouveret, 1981: 147-148). Facsimiles of them were kept in the *monumenta Asini Pollionis* (see Loeb CL).
31	For 'Brutus' boy' see also Martial, XIV.171.
32	For a presentation of the 'first generation' of collectors, that is the ones which were responsible for the introduction in Rome of works of art, see discussion in Pape (1975): M. Fulvius Nobilior (p. 12), Q. Caecilius Metellus (p. 15), L. Mummius (p. 16), L. Licinius Lucullus (p. 22), Cn. Pompeius (p. 24), and Augustus (p. 25).
33	See also Gros, 1976: 157.
34	See also Isager, 1991: 168-174, where further bibliography.
35	An interesting article exploring collecting and luxury in Pliny's work was published after the manuscript was sent to the publisher and therefore not in time for consideration in this book (Carey, 2000).
36	Here we may detect what Rouveret argued about Pliny claiming the primary role of Rome, even in consumption of luxury (6.89).
37	Translated by Rackham, Loeb CL, vol. IX, 1952.
38	The same issue of art 'challenging' nature, by producing artefacts so naturalistic that they actually resemble nature is the subject of paragraph 35.94; challenging nature in terms of naturalism is a major issue concerning the art history ideas of Pliny (see Tanner, 1995).
39	A list of luxurious possessions in 35.162-164 includes earthenware dishes sold at an auction by the heirs of Aristotle, a dish that cost a tragic actor 100,000 sesterces, and Vitellius the emperor who had an eartheware worthy of 1,000,000.
40	Translated by Rackham, in Loeb CL, 1952.
41	For Corinthian bronze, see Emanuele, 1989.
42	For a discussion of this see Gros, 1976 and Rouveret, 1989: 454; Rouveret, 1989 also connects this with the notion of '*cessavit...revixit ars*' (34.52), see esp. pp. 454ff.
43	*Peritus, a, um* is an adjective meaning the 'experienced person'.
44	Translated by Rackham in Loeb CL, vol. IV, 1945.
45	For Tiberius called 'ungracious' see 35.27-28. He is criticised as being 'ungracious' (*minime comis imperator*) – as opposed to Augustus who went beyond all others and presented pictures for public display.
46	The paragraph is translated by D. E. Eichholz in Loeb CL, vol. X, 1971. The Latin text reads: '*vidi tunc adnumeri unius scyphi fracti membra, quae in dolorem, credo, saeculi, invidiamque Fortunae tamquam Alexandri Magni corpus in conditorio servari, ut ostentarentur, placebat*' (37.19).
47	For a similar argument about Rome, although with a much broader time horizon, see Edwards, 1996.
48	See Pollitt, 1983 and the descriptions of triumphs he provides; Koch, 1967 (esp. 12-30) discusses the subject in great detail; also see Greenhalgh, 1988; 1989; Bennett, 1995 about the 'Great Exhibition'.
49	Translated by Rackham, Loeb CL, 1949.
50	That there is a gradual transition from one class of organisms to another and not a clear distinction between groups of organisms.
51	Translated in Loeb CL by Jones, 1980 (2nd edn).
52	As above.
53	Translated in Loeb CL by Jones, in 1963.

54   Translated by Luigi Grasselli, in *Il Museo del Cardinale Federico Borromeo*, Milan
        1909, p. 44.
55   Quoted in Findlen, 1994: 62; from BAV, *Vat. Lat.* 6192, Vol. II, f. 656v.
56   It is from Richard Lassels, *The Voyage of Italy, or a Compleat Journey Through Italy.
        In Two Parts* (London 1670), vol. I, pp. 147-148.
57   The translation follows that of Findlen (1994: 69), which is based on Arlene Quint,
        *Cardinal Federico Borromeo as a Patron and Critic of the Arts and His Musaeum of
        1625*, New York, 1986.
58   This is an issue that forms the subject of another research, that the author is planning
        to undertake, i.e. a detailed recording of all the information available on ancient Greek
        works on *heuremata* and material culture in general, in order to discuss their character,
        compare it with textual collections of the Renaissance and reach further conclusions
        about textual museums and collections in the ancient, and the Renaissance world.

Chapter 7

Poet's Gifts, Collector's Words: the epigrams of Martial

Introduction

Martial's *oeuvre* rendered the literary genre of epigram the vehicle of a successful integration of a long established poetic tradition, with critical reflection on Flavian historical and cultural circumstances. Although from a strictly historicising approach Martial's credibility is considerably at risk, since the derisive character of his poetry does not allow it to be taken at face value as a direct reflection of Roman life, an alternative reading allows for some interesting insight into his cultural ambience. It is a presumption of the present enquiry that the validity of the 'answers' provided by the ancient authors depends largely on the validity of the questions, expectations and assumptions set originally. When these are determined by positivism and historicism, inevitably their results are highly disputable. Similarly, the construction of the historical narrative as merely the Same or the Other leads to a monolithic, and thus incomplete comprehension of the past. Consequently, and in compliance with the methodological tools presented and discussed in Chapter 1 (see Figure 7.1), this reading of Martial's epigrams will attempt, by taking into account the characteristics of the genre which defined what both the author and his audience expected, to propose a possible 'reading' of Martial's 'reading' of his society's relation to material culture.

Martial did not contribute to art history or criticism, in the formal sense. Nevertheless, his personal and social relation to material culture and art is more than evident throughout his literary production. The literary genre through which he chose to express himself also becomes indicative, especially when we consider its historical development. As the Greek etymology of the word denotes, επιγραμμα (epigramma) was any word or mark inscribed on a grave, a monument, a building, or an artefact, representing the donor, the maker, the owner, or the dedicatee. In the early Alexandrian period, and due to the extension of the use of the term during the classical period to describe sepulchral, dedicatory or commemorative inscriptions in verse, the word came to cover a whole genre of brief poems. These were reminiscent of, and analogous to, such inscriptions, but they now dealt with almost any subject, sentiment, event, occasion, or person. Earlier models of those epigrams have been written or ascribed to archaic and classical authors,[1] like Sappho, Alcaeus, Simoneides, Anacreon, Pindar and Plato (Sullivan, 1991: 78). The standard subdivisions of epigram, which were established by Cephalas[2] in the tenth century CE, read as follows: 1) votive inscriptions and dedications (αναθηματικα) (AP vi); 2) epitaphs to tomb inscriptions (επιτυμβια) (AP vii and viii); 3) amatory and pederastic epigrams (ερωτικα και παιδικα) (AP v and xii); 4) 'epideictic' (επιδεικτικα), which were a broad group dealing with curious incidents, praising or blaming famous personages or places; within this category we may group the 'ecphrastic' epigrams, describing works of art, monuments and buildings (εκφρασεις) (AP ii, iii, ix); 5) reflectory and advice on life and morality (protreptika) (προτρεπτικα) (AP x); 6) convivial pieces (συμποτικα) (AP xi); and 7) abusive and satirical epigrams (σκωπτικα) (AP xi). Martial worked on all of these subgenres and he particularly developed the αποφορετα (apophoreta) and ξενια (xenia), which were descriptions of gifts, very similar to the descriptions of offerings (εκφρασεις) (Sullivan, 1991: 81-82).

Although Martial clearly distinguishes his epigrams from satire (Coffey, 1989), he shares with it the professed aim of *'pacere personis, dicere de vitiis'* (X.33.10). Without aiming to address or denigrate specific persons, his aim was to castigate vice, ridicule wickedness and inanity, to satirize the social vices of Rome - extravagance, social climbing, legacy-hunting, pretentiousness, greed, stupidity, and other human frailties - but also to entertain. On the other hand, Martial was part of the same society. He himself led the life of a needy client dependant on wealthy patrons; this definitely influenced his poetry and his beliefs. He was part of a society where conspicuous consumption was a fundamental characteristic of social life. Rich possessions and extravagance needed to be conspicuous to serve their purpose in that status-conscious society. Martial, therefore, is fully aware of this when he makes his pleas for money and gifts. Hence also the hyperbolic compliments on grandiose artistic acquisitions and lavish villas (Sullivan, 1991: 124).

These two contradictory approaches will be considered in the epigrams that we are going to discuss. In the first part, in reverse order to that of publication, the poems which have been selected from books I to XII will be briefly presented and discussed. Then we will focus on one of Martial's first books, Book XIV. Finally, all points will be brought together in an attempt to 'read' Martial's attitude toward collecting in a comprehensive mode.

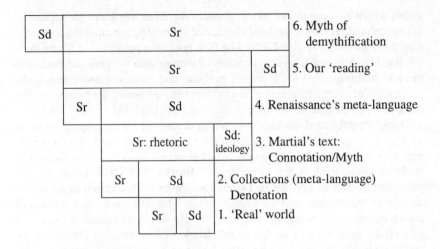

Sd		Sr		6. Myth of demythification
		Sr	Sd	5. Our 'reading'
Sr		Sd		4. Renaissance's meta-language
	Sr: rhetoric	Sd: ideology		3. Martial's text: Connotation/Myth
	Sr	Sd		2. Collections (meta-language) Denotation
		Sr	Sd	1. 'Real' world

Sd = signified
Sr = signifier

Figure 7.1:   Model of analysis applied to Martial's *Epigrams*.

Martial's Views on Collectors and Collecting

Martial published his first book in 80 CE, under the title *Liber de Spectaculis*, to celebrate the opening of the Colosseum by Titus. The book, probably published with the encouragement and support of the emperor to glorify his father and his dynasty, offered the equestrian status to Martial. Books *Xenia* and *Apophoreta* (XIII and XIV respectively in modern editions) appeared in 84-85 CE.[3] From then on he used to publish regularly until 101, when the last book was sent to Rome from Spain.[4]

Books I and II were published around 86 CE, when Martial was an already established, well-known Flavian poet with a circle of influential friends: a man of distinction. Presenting the books to the public was an attempt to develop or acknowledge a wider readership. The next book (III) appeared late in 87 CE; it was sent from Forum Cornelii (in Gallia Togata, the modern Lombardy). As the last epigram of the book suggests, it was offered to a friend of Martial's, a certain Rufus.[5] In this book there are five 'epideictic' poems, among which are introduced for the first time two descriptions of works of art: on a bowl with very realistic fishes supposedly by the hands of Phidias (III.35), and on a cup by Mentor decorated with an equally realistic and threatening lizard (III.40). This genre, which was prominent in the *Apophoreta*, from this point on appears in his miscellaneous books, perhaps stimulated by *ex tempore* challenges or even commissions (Sullivan, 1991:32). The IVth book was published in Rome in 89 CE (IV.11). It presents a greater variety of themes than the previous ones, and there is a strong sense of a greater political and historical awareness. The percentage of satiric epigrams is lower (less than a third of the book). In this book new private patrons are added[6] (Sullivan, 1991: 33-34).

Book V, published perhaps for the Saturnalia in 90 CE, opens with an address to emperor Domitian, honouring him as a guardian and saviour, *rerum felix tutela salusque* (V.1.8). He is asked to accept the volume as the sort of book he could read in the presence of Minerva (V.2.7-8). Book VI was published in 91 CE, perhaps in December. Apart from a dozen or so poems relating to the emperor and his triumphs (e.g. VI.4; 10), there are a number of poems devoted to new patrons and friends.[7] Book VII, published in December 92 (VII.8), again focuses on the court. Book VIII appeared in December 94, and is explicitly dedicated to Domitian: *Imperatori Domitiano Caesari Augusto Germanico Dacico* (Sullivan, 1991: 40). Book IX appeared perhaps in the spring of 95 CE. The brief preface is addressed to Martial's dear friend Toranius (*frater carissime*), known to the reader from V.78 (a dinner invitation). Martial indulges in a little self-congratulation, since senator L. Stertinius Avitus, himself a poet, had decided to honour Martial by placing a portrait or a bust of him in his library along with those of other distinguished writers (Sullivan, 1991: 43). Book X is one of the best of Martial's books, but it presents a number of problems. Posterity has the second edition, published in mid-98, when the poet was preparing to return to Spain. The earlier edition had been put out in December 95, but Martial informs his audience (X.2.3) that many of the poems of the first edition had been revised, and more importantly, that over half of them were new (Sullivan, 1991: 40). Book XII the nucleus of which was perhaps put together for December 101, was given to the public after a silence of about three and a half years (Sullivan, 1991: 52) and was the last one to be published.[8]

Epigrams II.43, II.53, IV.85, VIII.51 belong to the large group of those referring to patronage and patrons. The tradition of patronage was deeply embedded in Roman social and political life.[9] It involved a protective non-commercial relationship between unequal individuals, or social and national groups, in which one, the patron, used resources to help and protect his less powerful friends and dependents. The clients,[10] in return, were expected to provide various tangible or intangible services or gratifications (Sullivan, 1991: 116). For Martial the relationship between patron and his friends was personal and reciprocal. Although an unequal relationship, at least in conventional terms, Martial regarded his services as of special value, since he was in a position to offer to his patrons the gifts of immortality and fame, by the inclusion of their names in his poetry. The patrons, on the other hand, had to provide money, services, legacies, gifts, as well as honour as a poet and respect as an individual. Martial was disappointed with the system of private patronage as he encountered it, and his general criticism is included in an epigram to Domitian (V.19). Although his main addressee is the emperor,[11] private patrons are also often addressed.

The importance of patronage for Martial's poetry is reflected in many ways. The most common motif in his poetry is his plea for tangible proof of friendship and support. He also reflects on the proper relations between client and patron, on the nature of gratitude, avarice, humiliation; he complains about the burdensome *officia* or excuses himself for not presenting for a duty. On the other hand he offers thanks and compliments with his verses.

The strong interest of Martial (and other poets) in money and the obsession with gifts have been discussed extensively by scholars.[12] Whether the poet was dependent on them to support himself though, has been doubted. More importantly, it seems, rich possessions and extravagant gifts were the tokens of friendship, the proof of support; they were 'read' as bearers of esteem and their value was extended to their owners and *vice versa.*[13]

Consequently, stingy patrons and wretched clients figure quite often in his poetry. In II.43, Martial complains to Candidus - the name can be, and probably is, fictitious - for not treating him as equal and real friend. Although Candidus divulges his belief in the Greek proverb 'Κοινα φιλων' (friends must share), he does not practice it. He, therefore, leads a luxurious life, proof of which are - among other more trivial things like clothes and food - 'Libyan tabletops on legs of Indian ivory' (II.43.9) and 'gold-inlaid dishes' (II.43.11) covered with huge mullet.

Similarly, the same gold-inlaid dishes are tokens of dependence and lack of freedom in II.53. This epigram belongs to the category of προτρεπτικα (protreptika), and it may be interpreted as revealing Martial's 'real' feelings about patronage; he encourages Maximus, the person the poem is addressed to, to liberate himself from the enjoyment of material culture, provided by patrons, if he really wants to acquire freedom. This view echoes Cynic ideas that material culture is a kind of slavery, which instead of enjoyment it offers trouble and worries (see also Juvenal, *Sat.* 14.303-308). But not *all* material culture is like this: just the inlaid dishes, the luxurious goods. Interestingly Cinna - another fictitious character - is called 'wretched' (*miseri*), although he possesses these objects of desire. Maximus has to laugh at him, to ridicule his dependance on objects, if he wants to be free. Freedom involves poverty, or at least, self-denial (Sullivan, 1991: 127).

The same motif of the stingy patron is employed again in IV.85 (as above in II.43). Ponticus (another personage of Martial's gallery of fictitious, but probably easily recognizable, personages/stereotypes) uses his luxurious objects, in this case murrhine cups, to disclose his stinginess.[14] The inequality between patron and client is once again brought to the forefront. A rather mocking mood and a clear exaggeration characterize epigram VI.94. The instigator of satire is again the gold-enameled plate. This time the emphasis has shifted from the stingy patron to the mean-spiritedness of the client. Calpentianus is a wretched creature, so dependent on the external signs of wealth that he deserves to be criticised and laughed at through a satiric epigram.

Epigram VIII.50 (51 in 1919 Loeb edition) refers to an autobiographical incident in Martial's life as a client.[15] He describes a cup offered to him by his friend Istantius Rufus. The wrought silver[16] cup decorated with mythological scenes is admired by Martial who wonders who might have been its maker: Mys, Myron, Mentor or Polyclitus. Whether this is an 'eponymous' piece or not is not of prime interest. The compelling point of this epigram is that the attribution of an *objet d'art* to a famous artist from the past could enhance its value. Furthermore, the object acquired its importance not only from the intrinsic quality of its material, but, most importantly, from its associations. Along with this we cannot fail to notice that this appreciation has an art historical aspect as well. Although it is difficult to distinguish where art historical appreciation ends and where compliance with specific requirements of the Greek literary *topos* of ekphrasis starts, it is quite obvious that the writer actually appreciates the artistic merits of the object. Finally, another dimension of the object's value is that it is a token of personal esteem and friendship.

Another group of epigrams includes those which refer to extravagance in the way of living. A characteristic epigram of this category is III.62. It is an aggressive poem, quite rude in its directness, which addresses Quintus, a passionate 'collector', 'accumulator' of luxurious goods. Quintus acquires all the external signs of wealth, among which furniture and silver plate hold a prominent place. Martial's 'objection' to this kind of behaviour concerns the fact that, in his view, precious accumulations cannot 'transform' the person - no matter what Quintus reckons - since it is not his great mind which is projected through acquisitions; rather they are indications of his pathetic disposition. This epigram is of interest for two reasons: first, it provides insight into Martial's thinking, even if we consider it to be only the public façade, as in the case of Cicero for example.[17] Second, it makes clear - even if this is exaggerated - that, at least, some of the Romans considered objects able to transmit their values and their prestige. This is the point upon which Martial organises his criticism.

Objets d'art are also described in many epigrams.[18] The names of Greek artists of the past are what dominate there and indicate parameters of value and artistic appreciation. Although some of these epigrams might have been commissions, or descriptions of works owned by patrons whom Martial wanted to emulate, their inclusion in the books is indicative of a certain state of mind. Two of these epigrams present special interest, IX.43 and IX.44, both referring to Hercules Epitrapezius. This was, according to the literary tradition, a bronze statuette Alexander the Great had commissioned from Lysippus, of Hercules reclining on a rock, where he had spread his lionskin, holding his club and a wine cup.[19] Statius (*Silvae* 4.6) wrote a poem on the same subject. In IX.43

the 'genealogy' of the statue is presented: it belonged to Hannibal, Sylla and, finally, Novius Vindex, a contemporary of both Martial and Statius. Plausible chronologically and historically though this appears,[20] the statue's provenance seems a patent fabrication, at least to Martial. Although in the first epigram Martial intends to ennoble Vindex by aggrandizing the worth of his statuette by exaggerating its genealogy,[21] and Vindex is called learned (*docti*) in antithesis to other, pretentious, connoisseurs, IX.44 reveals a certain facetiousness on Martial's part. Was Vindex a real connoisseur, we may wonder, or was he simply a patron of Martial's? The discussion between 'ignorant' Martial and '*docti*' Vindex, during which is revealed that Vindex trusts that the maker of the statuette is the person whose name appears on its base, makes this difficult to answer. According to Henry (1948: 94), the second epigram is written because Martial did not believe that it was the original statue which was once given to Alexander by its creator. Henry suggests that Martial 'relieves his artistic conscience' by suggesting with his fine irony that this statue was a very good fake. But then, this would make the adjective '*docti*' of the previous one possibly more ironic than the omission of it would be. It does nevertheless concur with Martial's personal disapproval of collectors who bragged of the pedigrees of their possessions (see discussion of epigram VIII.6 below).

Women's relation to material culture is also discussed by Martial. Epigram VIII.81 is about Gellia's passionate relationship to her pearls. She appreciates them more than anything, and they are above any sacred or familial relationship in her hierarchy. Thus Martial wishes for Annaeus Serenus to have been employed; we do not know who he was, whether a thief, as Shackleton-Bailey (1993) suggests, or some notorious wearer of pearls (Ker, 1919). In any case, Martial's wish is for him to remove Gellia's pearls so that 'she would not live an hour' (VIII.81.9), away from her ridiculous - according to Martial - passion.

The same misogynous attitude is exemplified in epigram VII.13. Although the emphasis in this one is on the vain and futile attempts of an old woman, Lycoris, to retain her beauty and remain desirable - a subject which attracts Martial's fierce criticism and disgust - more interesting for the present research is the comparison of Lycoris' beauty practices with those followed for the protection of the 'ivory of an old tusk'. The sulphurous exhalations of the springs at Tibur were supposed to have the property of whitening ivory. Although Martial's aim is not to discuss connoisseurship practices, this information is indeed indicative of them. Lycoris is mentioned again in another epigram (I.102) as owner of a bad quality painting of Minerva. It is doubted that Lycoris was a 'collector' - the painting of Minerva must have been a possession related to Lycoris' profession (Minerva was the goddess of arts and Lycoris was probably a prostitute - see Howell, 1980: 317-8). But even this is indicative: Martial's argument is that women cannot possess good or precious things.

Another very important group of epigrams refers to fakes. Martial discusses fakes explicitly twice (he makes implicit references in other epigrams as well -

see below). Firstly, in epigram VIII.34, he addresses possibly a silversmith who was in the habit of faking his antiques. 'You may not have faked this' says Martial 'but that does not prove it genuine'. Just as in the previous ones, where Martial in order to make his point uses well known examples and practices easily recognisable by his audience as common in everyday life, in this case, he discusses the possession of antiques made by eponymous Greek artists. Not only is possession of antiques desirable, but the demand is higher than the supply, a fact which gives rise to practices like faking. He takes that for granted and builds his point upon it. Similarly, XII.69, addressing Paullus, uses the motif of antique possessions to compare Paullus' friends with: although Paullus considers them authentic, they are as genuine as his antiques; in other words, they are fakes. Once again the collection of antiquities is taken for granted and upon it the point about genuine friendship is built. The vocabulary used in these two epigrams is structured around two words: *archetypos*[22] and the verb *habere*.[23]

The most engaging group of epigrams (for this research), though, is that directly referring to collectors and connoisseurs. These are epigrams IV.39, VIII.6, IX.59, X.80 and X.87. In the last one, X.87, there is a brief mention of the 'aged admirer of our antique forefathers (who) present(s) embossed works of Phidias' chisel' (trans. Shackleton-Bailey, 1993); this periphrasis is used to describe the 'collector of antiquities'. Martial ranks his gift, poetry, among other precious gifts: genuine sardonyxes, embossed works of Phidias' chisel, slaves, and so on.

Epigram IV.39 refers to Charinus, an ardent collector of antique works of art. Undoubtedly the name is fictitious and Charinus probably a stereotype. The emphasis of the epigram is not on collecting *per se*; Charinus is 'attacked' mainly on the grounds of his private life. He has collected (*comparasti*[24]) all (*omne*[25]) silver plate, he *alone* (*solus*[26]) possesses antique works of art by Myron, Praxiteles, Scopas, Phidias and Mentor. He *owns* (*habes*) *genuine* (*vera*[27]) works of Grattius, gold-inlaid dishes and *ancestral* tables. Martial is feigning surprise, that a rich connoisseur of wrought *objets d'art* and tableware has no *argentum purum* in his collection. Sullivan (1991: 246-7) argues that this point has direct sexual connotations (for the use of '*purum*' in this context he provides a series of references). The epigram projects the picture of a passionate relationship between the collector and his objects. The use of the words '*omne*', '*solus*' (repeated four times), '*desunt*' (lack), '*comparasti*' and '*habes*' are used by Martial consciously to make a point about both Charinus and his collecting activities. They sketch the picture of a man who strives towards his completion and his purification through collecting a 'complete' as well as 'unique' set of the much admired tokens of the antique, with all their connotations. Very much in the spirit of the theory of contemporary collecting research, Martial suggests that collecting is for Charinus a mechanism of compensation for his lost purity, along with a powerful symbol of his personal inadequacies. The objects selected and collected participate, in other words, in a process of narcissistic projection on behalf of Charinus: he extends himself to the very limits of his collection and he collects his ideal self, which, as Martial ruthlessly unveils far exceeds the actual personal quality of the collector.

Martial gets to the heart of collecting with this epigram, since he questions the basic assumption behind the process: it is invariably the ideal self that a person collects, and the collection is undoubtedly the bearer of that connotation. But Martial disappoints collectors by arguing that no matter what mechanisms of concealment they employ, their personal inadequacies cannot be disguised behind objects, and they cannot become 'better' or something they are not because of their association with them. This point appears in other epigrams as well, e.g. in III.62. However, there are other instances when the same argument is contradicted, and Martial seems to appreciate objects simply because of their associative value (e.g. XIV.98, VIII.50 and so on). This probably relates to the double capacity of Martial, as a client, who needs to emulate, and as a poet with personal beliefs. As a result, when his poems aim to satisfy patrons, he praises their acquisitions, and celebrates their ownership; when he expresses freely his personal opinion, he is ready to unveil the fallacy in which collectors live. Nevertheless, the personal and circumstantial views of the poet himself aside, it has to be acknowledged fully that Martial's world believes in the connotative capacities of objects. Martial's pains to disprove it cannot but be taken as evidence of its existence, or of Martial's 'reading' of its existence. The inconsistency of his rhetoric is not enough to disprove its presence.

The same inconsistency is evident in VIII.6. Martial rejects Euctus' antiques collection on the grounds of it being 'despicable' (*odiosus*). Based upon the now common motif of enhancing an object's value by attributing prestigious associations to it, Euctus is presented as proud of the prestigious pedigrees of his objects; their defects are proofs of their glorious past, and, therefore reasons for extra appreciation and valuation in actual financial worth. They have 'participated' in famous mythological incidents and well-known Greek and Roman mythological personages have been associated with them. Nevertheless, Martial is sceptical: the collector is not able to distinguish between old and new wine, so how can he appreciate antiques? We have come across a stereotype again - although whether this is the stereotype of connoisseur or of the uneducated person who pretends to be erudite can be disputed. The objects have become the vehicles of pretension - or so Martial believes them to be. If we compare this approach with his own personal appreciation presented elsewhere of 'eponymous' artistic pieces, as well as his plea for gifts, Martial's personal stance on collecting becomes incomprehensible. Is this approach part of a stereotype (following the tradition established earlier in the Roman past of rejecting extravagance), or is it genuine?

Similar considerations emerge in epigram IX.59. Although it was categorized also among those which criticise pretentiousness and social climbing (Sullivan, 1991: 43), the epigram presents interest for this research since it is a unique and vivid picture of the antique market in Rome and of a connoisseur's practices.   Mamurra is a poor man pretending to be a connoisseur.   He wanders in the Saepta Julia (for details of this place as one for the public display of works of art, see II.14), where he behaves in a manner similar to that of all (pretentious) wealthy connoisseurs: he inspects objects, he measures them, he smells (!) them, he values them, he binds and, finally he purchases... two cheap cups that he carries home without the aid of a slave (whom he cannot afford).   Once again collection, connoisseurship and related practices are 'read' as signs of pretension and inanity.   Although Martial recognises that Mentor's handiwork made the cups precious (IX.59.16), Mamurra's craving for them seems to his eyes ridiculous.   Mamurra is most probably a stereotype; nevertheless, his attitude could not have been foreign to Martial's contemporaries.   On the contrary, the choice of this personage by Martial and the assumption that this is a stereotype, are evidence of the routine (for the Romans) that this epigram describes.

Finally, X.80 is a short presentation of another collector, Eros. He weeps and groans whenever he spots objects he desires, objects finer than usual that he cannot acquire. He wishes he could carry home the whole Saepta. Eros is another stereotype, who would normally attract people's laughter, argues Martial. But he is not just that: as a personage, he is a caricature of a large number of Romans who although laughing at the exterior, in their hearts share the feelings of Eros! Martial is shocked and embarrassed to recognize and record that. The description of the collector makes a couple of interesting points. The name Eros itself, chosen for the collector, refers to the point made before about sexual undertones. Furthermore, Martial criticises not collecting as such, but avarice in terms of the acquisition of material culture. This is the point where Martial's contradictory attitudes to material culture is finally resolved.

The last epigram of the discussion is VII.19. Martial aims to improve awareness of, and attract attention to, a piece of wood, part of a vessel, possibly the vessel of the Argonauts. He asserts that despite its old age and fragmentary condition, it is probably more sacred than the unscathed boat.   The contradiction here is between the intrinsically precious objects that other connoisseurs and pseudo-connoisseurs appreciate, and the objects of *real* value that Martial does.   There is also a contradiction between objects of use and objects of admiration, which again might be indicative of Martial's own beliefs.   Intrinsically precious objects are sought after because they advertise the owner's importance when they are used - the objects we should admire though are of a different, internal and associative value.

Collecting seems to be a common practice for his contemporaries, and Martial, a man of his age, certainly shares the cultural pursuits and aspirations of his era.   What estranges him though, and attracts his criticism is the hyperbole related to it. All collectors mentioned, by name or not, share the same assumptions about objects and collections. They all project themselves on them, they all collect these for their intrinsic financial merit, but also for their associative values, in the hope that material culture will ennoble them. The objects are highly desirable as they represent and convey a glorious past, whose virtues and prestige collectors wish to share. The art historical dimension deserves a special reference too, since art appreciation seems quite widespread to people of certain culture and wealth - so much that *nouveaux riches* wish to embrace it as a proof of their newly acquired status. Martial does not disagree with these values in principle. What he criticises is the passion involved in the act of collecting. He appreciates precious and expensive gifts, but he cannot see the point of being enslaved by the appreciation and assemblage of them.

Martial's *Xenia* and *Apophoreta*: their relation to collecting

Book XIV appeared (together with Book XIII) in December 85.[28] It is entitled *Apophoreta*[29] - it contains 223 distichs and describes miscellaneous gifts. The epigrams read like witty descriptive labels, eminently suitable for gifts given at the Saturnalia (Sullivan, 1991: 12). According to Martial's introductory poem of book XIV, the arrangement of the epigrams was intended to present alternately a rich and a poor gift: 'accept those lots, alternately for the rich man and the poor man' (XIV.1.5, trans. by Shackleton-Bailey, 1993). It is alleged, therefore, that the epigrams should be paired with that criterion in mind, and thus scholars, like Birt (1882), Friendländer (1886), and recently Leary (1996), assume textual corrections wherever a textual ordering problem arises. Following this assumption, a gift's value is indicated by its position, or *vice versa*. Other principles of pairing are mentioned by Leary (1996:13): that objects made in identical material, but of different value, are matched; that different gifts with some common element are matched or alternated (e.g. XIV.197-198 where both gifts are animals); and that a poor gift sometimes complements a rich gift (e.g. a ring is complemented by a ring case, XIV.122-123). Epigrams are also grouped according to subjects: e.g. writing materials (XIV.3-11; 20-1; 37-8), household equipment and tools, books and so on. The important description of artistic productions and literary works are kept together (XIV.170-182; 183-196). In some cases, when the above pattern does not seem to apply, a textual corruption is assumed, and the case is similar when a pair finds itself among other items. Difficulties of interpretation (e.g. XIV.183-196; Leary, 1996: 20) are similarly dealt with. Not all scholars agree with this type of arrangement though. Shackleton-Bailey, for instance, thinks that as the couplets now stand, 'they show only residual traces of Martial's intended arrangement' (1993: 2).[30]

Before we discuss *Apophoreta*, we should consider the social phenomenon, which, together with patronage, give the character and tone in Martial's poetry and provide a tool for its understanding: it is the Roman's passion for gift exchange. Martial fully shares this passion, whose complex sociological roots must be taken into account. Rome, like other ancient and some modern societies - the world of Homeric epics and our Christmas gift exchange, for instance (see also Chapter 3) - saw the exchange of goods not just as an economic system, but as a moral transaction, generating and maintaining personal relationships between individuals, divinities and groups. The gift in primitive custom is to be followed by a gift in return. Gifts appear voluntarily, but in fact they are given and repaid under an implicit obligation. The giver, even of something intangible, and the receiver are bound in a sort of contract. Nowhere is this more manifest than in Martial's own epigrams expressing his disappointment at not being rewarded when he has mentioned someone in his work (V.36). Gift-giving is then tied into patronage. By a neat paradox, Martial argues that true return and the safe possession of one's own goods is guaranteed only through generous gift-giving to friends (V.42), somewhat in the spirit of the potlatch (XII.53).

Martial's obsession with gifts, large or small, suitable or unsuitable, generous or stingy, an obsession nowhere more manifest than in *Xenia* and *Apophoreta*, is to be explained then by the moral underpinnings of the exchange of gifts. The greater the estimation that Martial places on his own unique gift, the poetry that bestows contemporary reputation and ultimate immortality, the louder is his insistence on the return due to his friendship and talent, and the greater his demands for the proper observance of the occasions of gift-giving, the Saturnalia, birthdays, anniversaries and so on.[31] Wealth confers honour and power; honour is upheld only by the distribution of wealth for generous purposes, whereas avarice destroys it. Giving is a moral duty, part of a social contract, hence the praise Martial bestows on the emperor for his gifts to the people, to Rome and to individuals in fulfillment of his sacred duty (Sullivan, 1991: 13-14). What you give away is what you most truly own (V.42), according to Martial (Sullivan, 1991: 121-2).

Among these poems, there is special interest for our research in the inclusion as gifts of items of citrus-wood (XIV.3; XIV.89), of maple tables (XIV.90), of a Corinthian candelabrum (XIV.42), of antique cups (XIV.93) and chased gold bowls made by well known artists like Mys (XIV.95), of crystal cups (XIV.111), murrhine items (XIV.113), ivory tusks (XIV.101) and gemmed chalices (XIV.109).

Apophoreta undoubtedly are related to gift-exchange and thus belong to a long established social tradition. Besides the group of the works of art - which will be discussed later on - other distichs provide information mainly on the rhetoric and vocabulary of value. Hence, exotic and difficult to find material is much appreciated, as for instance in epigrams XIV.3 (writing tablets of citrus-wood[32]), XIV.89, XIV.101. Intrinsically worthy material is also appreciated; prominent among this is Corinthian bronze[33] (e.g. XIV.43), silver (e.g. XIV.93), *chrysendetae lances*[34] (e.g. XIV.79), and gemmed chalices (e.g.

XIV.109). But these are not the only values appreciated. The adjectives *antiquus*[35] (XIV.43) and *archetypa* (XIV.93 - see also previous section) which are used to denote 'genuiness' and antiquity - both bear further value related connotations. *Antiquus* can be used to denote origins in the past, but it also has connotations of past simplicity, goodness and thrift. Similarly *archetypa* implies authenticity. This is evidenced also by the reference to ancient Greek masters, like Mentor (XIV.93), or Mys (XIV.95). The objects' authenticity is further confirmed by defects on them made by their use by the artist before finishing them (IV.39 - also before VIII.6). Artistic merit and craftsmanship is also appreciated (IX.59; XIV.93). Similarly, value by association is quite common. Even when the material is not luxurious or intrinsically worthy, previous ownership of an object aggrandizes its value (e.g. XIV.98; XIV.171). Likewise, objects acquire value by association with past glory, as in the case of Arretine ware, which relates to Etruscan ancestry - a source of pride to those who could claim it (Rawson, 1985). Similarly, Martial, when he discusses 'poor' gifts, often implies (with his choice of vocabulary) value relating to old time virtues - e.g. the use of the words *fictilis* (clay) indicates old world frugality, old world poverty and accompanying values (XIV.98.2, XIV.171).

Naturally, the series of objects in the epigrams XIV.170-182 attracted major attention. There has been an interesting discussion about them. Lehmann (1945) suggested that they actually present a collection held in the temple of Divus Augustus, offered by Tiberius. This 'collection', whether actual or not, included: a golden statue or statuette of Victory,[36] a clay image of Brutus' boy,[37] the lizard slayer in Corinthian bronze,[38] a picture of Hyacinthus,[39] a marble Hermaphroditus,[40] a picture of Danae,[41] a German mask,[42] a Hercules in Corinthian bronze,[43] a Hercules in clay,[44] a Minerva in silver,[45] a picture of Europe,[46] a marble Leander[47] and, finally, a clay statuette of a hunchback.[48]

Lehmann (1945) justifies his thesis with the following arguments. Firstly, his is the first attempt to reconstruct the objects in their comprehensive significance. Although for some of the dictichs, commentators and archaeologists have established some relation with the literary tradition or extant monuments, no one ever before had discussed them in their comprehensive significance. Secondly, this literary assemblage of the works of art cannot but reveal some essential trends about the taste of the period. In order to overcome the limitations imposed by the assumption that the distichs are organised according to their value, so that cheap and expensive ones alternate, Lehmann argues that Martial was a poet, so he did not feel obliged to follow that arrangement throughout; thus he chose to change the order as he was taken over by the subjects. To support this argument, Lehmann refers to the alterations in the order of the epigrams that previous scholars had felt necessary, in order to comply with the alternated arrangement; for instance, because of the changes of Birt (1882) and Friendländer (1886) the whole book collapses, he argues, especially if one considers the last two sections, 170-182 on the works of art and 183-196 on books. Furthermore, Lehmann continues, hypothetical and unfounded assumptions need to be made about the value of the objects. He criticises Birt and Friendländer particularly for a reason similar to the one for which we could criticise Leary (1996), i.e. the fact that she assumes that pictures are cheaper than sculpture - a fact which is not absolutely justified by the sources of antiquity (Lehmann, 1945: 260).

The third and most powerful argument refers to the authenticity of each of the *objets d'art* that Lehmann assumes. After a detailed discussion of each of the works, during which the authenticity of each of the pieces is 'proved' or 'not disproved', Lehmann concludes that this was an *actual* collection, on the grounds that at least two of the artefacts were originals (Brutus' boy and Hercules in clay); as far as the others are concerned, there are no arguments against the fact that they were (the) well known originals on display somewhere in Rome. As far as the pieces that are left out of the 'cycle of the originals' (i.e. pictorial relief panels of Hermaphroditus and Leander, as well as the mask) are concerned, Lehmann argues that these are indications of the architectural setting of the collection. Therefore, from the objects of the collection stems the attribution to an original setting: Lehmann suggests that the works of art were displayed in the temple of Divus Augustus, for which we have no actual site and plan; what we know is that the paintings of Hyacinthus and Danae by Nicias were exhibited there (Pliny, *HN* 36.28; 36.131; see also Chapter 6). By assuming that both the original pictures are mentioned in Martial's epigrams, Lehmann 'traces' and reconstructs the setting of the collection as well (Figure 7.2). The existence of a library, attached to the temple futher supports this thesis, so that Lehmann offers an explanation for the following part as well. Hence, Lehmann's reading works to banish textual corruption completely.

The discussion in its entirety relies on the assumptions made on the originality of the works of art described by Martial. There is no doubt that Lehmann wrote this article in a spirit similar to that of his article on Philostratus *Imagines* (1941); he visualised the text, and offered a hyper-realistic image of a gallery envisioned in detail. In order to do that of course, he had to hypothesize on the value of the objects, to prove them originals. According to the archaeological and museological discourse of his era, a clear distinction should be set between 'valuable' originals as opposed to copies. The latter's deposition in a temple (in a museum) was simply incomprehensible. Lehmann thus used archaeological evidence in order to justify the assumptions he made about the value of these objects. In his article, art history emerged in one of its heroising guises, to 'restore' the fallen works of art. Then they were placed in the only space appropriate for high art, the temple (the museum), where they could be admired by a poet and could offer him inspiration. In a setting wholly designed by an art historical approach, the objects were grouped according to their subjects, and the most prominent position was held by the most prominent (in art historical terms) of the works of art. In other words, Lehmann's reading of the epigrams of Martial aimed to associate literary tradition with historical positivism. Furthermore, as Bryson suggested in the case of the article on Philostratus, Lehmann seemed to underestimate the reader in the sense that he could not see him as a reader 'who can see bizarre connections, who can understand hidden mythic narratives within imagery, who can exercise the visual equivalent of the elaborate verbal dexterity that characterises Hellenistic poetry' (1994: 282).   Furthermore, Lehmann's rationality seemed to render its text unaware of its own dimension as text. 'Opening on to other investments and other scenes than that simply of archaeology and reconstruction, Lehmann's text speaks its own unconscious' (Bryson, 1994: 282-3).

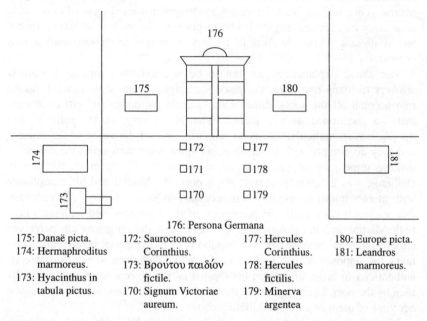

176: Persona Germana

175: Danaë picta.
174: Hermaphroditus marmoreus.
173: Hyacinthus in tabula pictus.

172: Sauroctonos Corinthius.
173: Βρούτου παιδίον fictile.
170: Signum Victoriae aureum.

177: Hercules Corinthius.
178: Hercules fictilis.
179: Minerva argentea

180: Europe picta.
181: Leandros marmoreus.

Figure 7.2:   Possible arrangement of a collection in the Temple of Divus Augustus (after Lehmann, 1945: 269).

At the other end of the same axis lies Leary's (1996) approach. Sharing the same objective with Lehmann, i.e. to be 'neutral' and objective, Leary uses the same German positivist scholarship which influenced Lehmann, but in a different way. Interestingly, Leary does not mention Lehmann neither in her commentary nor in her introduction - possibly because she sees the role of her book as limited to being a commentary and not an interpretation. Basically, she appreciates the role of gift exchange and provides interesting suggestions, although she does not cross the boundaries which the text imposes on her. She therefore discusses the epigrams on the basis that they are a directory of gifts offered at the Saturnalia, and a literary exercise for Martial. She follows Citroni (1989: 207) in the suggestion that *Xenia* and *Apophoreta* belong to the

Saturnalian poetic tradition, but identifies this tradition not with the didactic/mock-didactic verse (as did Citroni), but with the 'catalogue' of gifts, listing presents, as for instance Statius' *Silvae* 4.9. These, usually set in the context of *amicitia*, often would focus on the value of Saturnalian gifts and the extent to which people exchanging them profited or lost. Book XIV therefore reflects the concern of these poems with material value. Furthermore, Leary argues that writing a book of this sort was an intellectual and artistic challenge for Martial, since he would have to strive for variety and interest in order to hold attention to what otherwise would be a boring poem or collection of poems. Last, but not least, Leary acknowledges that the origins of epigram in dedicatory inscriptions might also be responsible for such an attempt, since it would present literary interest to employ received conventions into a new context.

The above explanations are not to be rejected; they provide legitimate answers to many questions and place the epigrams into their context, taking into account all the social dimensions (namely patronage and gift exchange) that we mentioned above. Indeed, Martial's poetry, in its entirety, and *Apophoreta* in particular, focus on *amicitia*, and on the value of the objects, and they do comply with the Saturnalian spirit since they are in the course of making some joke or humorous social comment. Furthermore, the literary challenge was a powerful motive for a poet like Martial and his compliance with literary tradition certainly was necessary in Roman poetry. Nevertheless, this approach does limit our perception of the epigrams, and underestimates both Martial and his audience in the sense that the epigrams are perceived either as literary exercises, or as a handbook of proper social behaviour. Leary takes the opposite stance to Lehmann. While Lehmann argues for objects' authenticity in order to support his thesis that the objects were 'real', actually seen by the poet, Leary argues for them being reproductions, in order to support her view of them as social and literary conventions.

Martial's professed aim was to describe '*apophoreta*'. It is worth quoting in full the two introductory epigrams of Book XIV, which set the parameters of our discussion:

> While the knight and my lord senator rejoice in dinner suits and the wearing of the cup of liberty befits our Jupiter, while the slave as he shakes the dice box does not fear to look at the aedile, though he sees the cold pools so close: *accept these lots, alternately for the rich man and the poor man; let each one give his guest the appropriate prize.* 'They are trash and rubbish and anything worth less than that, if possible.' Who but knows it? Or who denies anything so obvious? But what better have I do in your tipsy days, Saturn, which your son himself gave you in return for the sky? Do you want me to write of Thebes or Troy or wicked Mycenae? 'Play with nuts', you say. But I don't want to lose my nuts. (XIV.1) (emphasis added).

You can finish this book at any place you choose. Every performance
is completed in two lines. If you ask why headings are added, I'll tell
you: so that, if you prefer, *you may read the headings only*. (XIV.2).
(emphasis added) (translated by D.R. Shackleton-Bailey, 1993).

Martial does not state explicitly whether these were real objects,
'*apophoreta*' distributed at an actual dinner, or suggestions for gifts or gift-
labels accompanying actual gifts. Both approaches discussed above have
employed a historicing and positivist stance, in the sense that the objects are
categorised as either genuine or reproductions, either an actual collection or
figments of imagination, either a poetic creation or the echo of an (actual)
social event. It does not take into consideration the fact that they are all of
these at the same time. Far from being either actual or literary, this 'collection'
was a mixture of reality and imagination with witty aspirations. In Martial's
epigrams words and objects melt together. Similarly, ancient traditions of
patronage and gift exchange 'meet' in the appreciation of the status-embodied-
in-the-object, i.e. the gift. So epigram and gift become interchangeable in
Martial's poetry - see also his introduction to Book XIII ('you can send these
couplets to your guests instead of a gift...' XIII.3). This area of inter-
changeability is the area where Martial creates his own 'collection'.

Figure 7.3 is a schematic presentation of Martial's poetic collection, which
stands as a bridge between the literary tradition and the social circumstances for
which it was produced. The epigram thus resides in the common ground
between words and objects as these are accommodated in the literary tradition,
and it corresponds to the gift, which in its turn defines the relationship between
patron and client. In this regard, Martial's poetry bridges the two realms, and is
offered as both a gift and an example of literature. His 'collection' is
formulated in the sphere where the real and imaginary, actual and textual,
literary and social meet, so that in an ideal context these are interchangeable
and equally valuable. An epigram is good enough as a gift in social
circumstances, and a gift can become the area where words and objects meet.
In addition, this is a sphere that transcends the limits of natural destruction,
since literature is an exercise in immortality; a collection of gifts-in-words,
therefore, is the ideal arrangement, that would eternalise the social
circumstances, the poet and the patron.

Thus we can assume that Pliny describes objects he sees around him, maybe
actual collections, maybe not, while he looks for inspiration, expressing at the
same time his wishes about how an actual gift exchange should ideally be.
Consequently, 'the collection' is neither real, nor fictitious, and as such it
belongs to another sphere. Martial 'assembles' his own collection, selecting
from among the objects he can afford (the literary ones), and he formulates it
the way he desires it to be: with objects important for some reason, even
intrinsically cheap ones, but with associative values, that bring the real and the
ideal together.

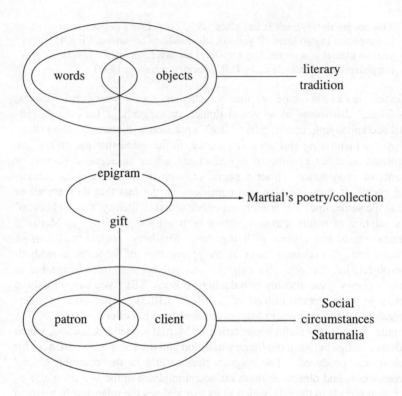

Figure 7.3:   A schematic presentation of Martial's poetic collection

Conclusions

In all epigrams Martial uses stereotypes. This, by the definition of 'stereotype', favours the assumption that he refers to practices and beliefs widespread in the Rome of his era. Martial's personal agreement with these practices is not obligatory and does not alter their actuality. There is a contradiction in Martial's approach. On the one hand, he appeals for gifts, explicitly recognises the enhanced value of objects for their artistic quality (this may be a literary convention up to a point, but the choice of this particular genre cannot be absolutely coincidental and might reveal something about Martial's own interests), and recognizes that objects can be bearers of valuation, personal appreciation, esteem and recognition.

On the other hand, he seems to discourage *nouveaux riches* from believing that objects could transform their ignorance, pretentiousness and vulgarity to refinement, 'purity' and, ultimately, could usher in the ideal self. All the collectors he discusses are unworthy and frivolous. Among their vices he includes ignorance, pretentiousness, inability to behave properly, avarice and the passion for collecting. Consequently, and although he seems to share the belief in the objects/collections' capacity to convey the values of their owners, he cynically and relentlessly denies that this could happen the other way round. The objects then are passive bearers of virtues, but not active transmitters of them.

His contradictory approach can be interpreted in two ways (not necessarily mutually exclusive): it may be that Martial follows the tradition of the early Roman world, when actual appreciation of art and 'dependence' on it was something to be blamed for and no boast of, a sign of contemptible effeminacy and extravagance. Cicero is a good example of such a two-sided approach. On the other hand, it should be taken into account that Romans reserved a special appreciation for what was considered 'appropriate' (*prepon*). In this sense, although it was appropriate for a cultivated man - and a man of means - to own precious works of art and luxurious items, it was not appropriate for him to 'depend' on them, to exaggerate, to be passionately involved in their appreciation. This motif occurs quite often in the epigrams presented above.

On the other hand, and mainly through *Apophoreta*, Martial seems very much concerned with gifts and objects. All those he mentions have some intrinsic or other quality. In the *Apophoreta*, more than anywhere else in his work, though, the social aspect of material culture acquires predominance. No matter whether *Apophoreta* were actually 'apophoreta', labels or gifts exchanged, no matter if they were constructions of the imagination or a handbook of proper social practice, it makes two very interesting points, relating to two practices constantly at the forefront of collecting: the social practice of patronage, and the practice of gift exchange. Martial explicitly asserts that giving is the only way of having, revealing the confirmation of a tradition very much in the spirit of the potlatch with all its connotations. Martial also seems to adumbrate collecting 'proper', as this is defined in the following paragraph by Baudrillard (1994):

> Collecting proper emerges at first with an orientation to the cultural: it aspires to discriminate between objects, privileging those which have some exchange value or which are also 'objects' of conservation, of commerce, *of social ritual, of display* - possibly which are even a source of profit. *Such objects are always associated with human projects.* While ceaselessly referring to one another, they admit within their orbit the external dimension of social and human intercourse. (1994: 22) (emphasis added).

Martial's poetry is an indirect rephrasing of the above paragraph and provides not only an insight into similar practices and beliefs, but also forms the ideology projected. If we add to that the extraordinary and, indeed, unique appeal of Martial's poetry to the men of the Renaissance and onwards,[49] his influence in the shaping of collecting becomes more obvious.

Notes

1   For the history of literary epigram see e.g. Dihle (1994: 121-126); according to Dihle, literary epigram goes back to the eighth century BCE, when it became a habit for the Greeks to use verse inscriptions on graves and on buildings consecrated to gods, and also on those marking the origin or destination of diverse kinds of man-made objects; the next step was taken in the fourth century BCE, when fictitious funeral or consecrational inscriptions were written for a reading public. The Hellenistic age brought *epigramma* at the first rate of literary expression; we have epigrams from nearly all the major poets of Hellenism. For Martial's role in the development of the literary genre of epigram, see Laurens (1980).

2   No other literary genre ever had such a long and unbroken tradition as that of the epigram; on the Greek side, that tradition included the entire Byzantine era. As early as 70 BCE, the epigrammatic poet Meleager from Gadara in Syria put together a large collection of older and contemporary epigrams in alphabetical order, including of course his own works. Around 40 CE the poet Philippus of Thessalonica adopted this collection, adding some more recent specimens. The collection edited by Agathias around 50 CE had a similar genesis but it grouped the epigrams according to the subject matter; that collection was in turn adopted and enlarged around 900 CE by Constantius Cephalas. The latter collection, complemented by an anthology of non-epigrammatic poetry from the late classical and the early Byzantine ages, is presumably what we have in the famous *Anthologia Palatina (AP)*, a codex from the tenth century, one half of which is kept in Heidelberg and the other half in Paris. One later compilation, though largely identical in content, was written by Maximus Planudes around 1300 CE; in his collection features an appendix with four hundred poems which are missing in the *AP* (Dihle, 1994: 123).

3   For the dates of *Xenia* and *Apophoreta* see discussion and notes below.

4   Marcus Valerius Martialis was born in March 38 CE to 41 in the ancient Celtiberian town of Bilbilis, in Hispania Tarraconensis. Although not the offspring of a wealthy family, he received a good education. About 63-4 CE (i.e. the last days of Nero) he came to Rome and attached himself to his countrymen Quintillien, Lucan and Senecas, who were influential poets (although not on very good terms with Nero). Martial was established in imperial favour with the Flavians, and he became an honorary military tribune, which gave him equestrian status, to which accrued the minimum property qualification of an equestrian, 400,000 sesterces (Pliny, *HN*, 33.32). He had been practising the vocation of poet as well as client. He never married (see Sullivan, 1991: 25-26). Martial retired and died in Bilbilis; his attitude to his birthplace changed from idealization to disappointment. Nevertheless, his nostalgic pride in his native town and indeed in his whole Celtiberian ancestry is a recurrent theme in his epigrams (Ker, 1919: vii; Sullivan, 1991:1). For Martial's life see also Bramble (1982), and for an detailed bibliography, see Szelest (1986).

5   Probably Canonius Rufus of Bononia (III.82; III.94) (Sullivan, 1991: 30).

6   Among them the writer Silius Italicus; their relationship was to be continued even after Silius' retirement in Campania (see IV.14).

7   An interesting commentary of that book was published a few years ago; see Grewing, 1997.

8   On Martial's relation to the emperor Domitian as well as a detailed analysis of his literary production in the socio-cultural circumstances see Sullivan (1991: 1-52).

9   See Sullivan (1991:116-129); Saller (1983); Wallace-Hadrill (1989); Gold (1982); White (1978).

10   On the vocabulary of the institution of patronage, see note 9.

11	Martial did not have any illusions about the restoration of the Republic. He was satisfied with the imperial regime as long as the ruler corresponded with the general Stoic idea of kingship: a ruler with mercy, foresight and other kingly virtues, who took good care of his subjects and his clients. It was through this system that Martial had risen to the equestrian status and enjoyed the imperial favour that this secured (Sullivan, 1991: 129).
12	See, for instance, Saller (1982) and White (1978).
13	Similar ideas about the value of objects see XIV.98 and others; also discussion below.
14	This is quite a common subject for Roman literature (cf. IV.68; X.80; Pliny, *HN*, 37.8).
15	Shackleton-Bailey suggests in his comments accompanying his translation in Loeb (1993) that there is a problem with this poem, since although the cup must have been a gift after a banquet at Istantius' house, Martial is in his house as vv. 23-26 seem to suggest and he is the 'master' of v.18, though that verse better suits a wealthy patron. No matter what the circumstances are, his relation to the object remains the same.
16	'The cup was not made of gold and silver like genuine electrum, but of silver and some sort of bronze' (Shackleton-Bailey, 1993).
17	See also discussion about Cicero; it had to do first with what they considered appropriate, or not - collecting was reasonable, passion was not - and second with the relation to Greek works of art and current political circumstances.
18	Paintings: I.102; I.109.18-23; IV.47; V.40; VII.84; IX.74; IX.76; X.32; XI.9; V.55; Sculpture: VI.13; VII.15; IX.23; 24; 64; 65. cf. VII.44 and 45 (death mask) - for antiques see II.77; III.35; 40; IV.39; VI.92; VIII.6; 34; 50; IX.43; 44; X.87.15-16; 89. cf. IV.47; VII.11; XII.69. This complies with the Hellenistic tradition of *ekphrasis*, which is descriptions of works of art (for *ekphrasis*, see Chapter 8).
19	The term '*epitrapezius*' (on the table) probably refers to the small scale of the statue, 'it was made to be put on the table' (see Bartman, 1984).
20	The chain of owners included generals who plundered many famous works of art from the artistic capitals of Greece and the East (see Pape, 1975).
21	Objects that once belonged to a famous person were highly desirable and their previous owners are often mentioned. Friendländer (1886) and Wissowa (*RE*, II 331-332) cite several examples, including Caracalla's claim to having drinking vessels and weapons that once belonged to Alexander the Great (Cassius Dio, 72.7.1).
22	*archetypus, -a, -um* (adjective): means taken from life, original, genuine. OLD (I) 163.
23	*habeo, -ui, -itum, -ere* (verb): means to possess, to own, see OLD (I) 780-782.
24	OLD 1968 (1), 373: 'to collect, secure, merchandise, to purchase, buy; (of a connoisseur) to 'collect'.
25	OLD (II) 1248-9: *omnus, -a, -um:* means every single thing, all things.
26	*solus, -a, -um:* means sole, exclusive, with no equal, unique; see OLD (II) 1789.
27	*verus, -a, -um:* means real, genuine, authentic; see OLD (II) 2046-2047
28	Whether the traditional date for both books in 84/5, which became standard after Friendländer (1886), is correct or not, see the discussion in Leary (1996: 9-12), where the arguments of other scholars are summarised.
29	MS evidence cited by Friendländer (1886: 17) makes it plain that the title '*Apophoreta*' was Martial's intended title. Initially employed for food given to guests to take home after dinner, 'apophoreta' came to apply by extension to non-edible gifts associated with dinners, an adherence to gifts of all kinds, whether given at meal times or not (Leary, 1996: 9).
30	Leary (1996:13) finds this too extreme.
31	He may also joke about it, cf. XII.6.
32	Citrus-wood tablets were exceptionally valued since the tree it comes from seldom grew large enough for its wood to make a table-top. The base of a citrus-wood table

invariably was ivory. The writing tablets of the epigram derive their value from the fact that the wood from which they were made was originally suitable for table-tops, but instead had been cut, extravagantly, into small thin leaves (Leary, 1996: 58-59).

33   Corinthian bronze was famous in antiquity and was nearly as costly as gold (Pliny, *HN*, 34.1; Petronius, 50.2, Cicero, *ad Att.*, 2.1.11; Martial IX.59; XIV.172; 177). Pliny identifies three varieties (*HN*, 34.8) that in which the main ingredient was silver, that in which the main ingredient was gold, and that containing a blend of metals in equal proportions. He tells of how (*HN*, 34.6) it was first produced by accident when Corinth was sacked by Rome; for further discussion, see Emanuele, 1989, where there is also a list of all ancient references to Corinthian bronze.

34   *Chrysendetae* (XIV.97) seem to have been silver dishes with gold inlay. Whenever Martial mentions them, it is in the context of wealth and ostentation. The *lanx* was a serving dish, usually fine and of precious metal (those at Martial IV.15.4 are very valuable) but sometimes also of clay or glass. *Lances* appear to have been common Saturnalian gifts (Leary, 1996: 158-159).)

35   cf. OLD s.v. *antiquus* paragraph 6a.

36   Martial relates this to the victories of Domitian in Germany. Leary believes that this was a *sigilla* and she argues that extant examples of golden Victory *sigilla* are scarce. (Leary, 1996: 231). Lehmann, on the other hand, believes that it could be a Roman or earlier Greek work (Lehmann, 1945: 261).

37   'Brutus' boy' was a clay statuette; it has been recognised that the figure is identical to a work which Pliny mentions and which was greatly admired by Brutus. It was made by Strongylion in the 4th century BCE (Pliny *HN*, 34.82, Martial II.77.4; IX.50.5-6). No copies of Strongylion's statue survive today. The statue mentioned here was taken to be the original one by Lehmann (1945: 261), whereas Leary (1996: 232) suggests that it would have been a copy replica.   Her argument relies on the assertion *'gloria...non est obscura'* which, together with the pentameter, she believes to indicate that its value was not intrinsic but derived from Brutus' association (about value by association, see also XIV.98).

38   *Sauroctonos Corinthius* was a work by Praxiteles, in bronze, representing the young Apollo, arrow in hand, about to stab a lizard. Also described by Pliny, *HN*, 34.70 (Leary, 1996: 233). The statue Martial describes has been widely accepted to be a copy, see Lehmann, 1945: 262, and previous bibliography in note 16.

39   Hyacinthus was represented dying after having been hit by the discuss thrown by Apollo. A connection might exist between this picture (or relief) here and a famous picture of Nicias (see Pliny, *HN*, 35.130). This was taken to Rome by Augustus after the fall of Alexandria (Leary, 1996: 235) and held in the Temple of Divus Augustus (Pausanias, III.19.4).   According to Lehmann, Martial here refers to the original (1945: 262).

40   Hermaphroditus is in marble - possibly a relief. It refers to the metamorphosis of Hermaphroditus that resulted from his love with the nymph of the fountain Salmakis (Ovid, *Metamorphoses*, IV. 285-389).

41   Since *'in tabula'* is not specified (as in XIV.173) it is possible that we have here not a painting but a coloured statue (for such *sigillaria*, see Leary, 1996: introd.). If a painting, the work could well be associated with Artemon's famous picture, as Ker (1919) argues (Pliny *HN*, 35.139) or a picture by Nicias, as Lehmann believes, also mentioned by Pliny (*HN*, 35.131). Whether statue or painting, the gift appears cheap after the expensive Hermaphroditus, according to Leary (1996:237).   Lehmann believes this to be the original, removed from Alexandria by Augustus, and corresponding to the other famous painting by Nicias, held in the same temple (1945: 263).

42   Birt (1882) has argued that an epigram describing an expensive gift has fallen out
      between XIV.175-176. This view is also adopted by Leary (1996: 237). Lehmann
      (1945: 263) solves the problem by taking it as having a decorative function.

43   There are various Hellenistic and Roman works of this kind. Lehmann argues that this
      epigram could refer to either a bronze copy of any of those or to an original held in
      Temple of Divus Augustus (1945: 263-264).

44   Possibly a replica of Hercules *fictilis* made by Vulca in the time of Tarquinius Priscus.
      Fragilis does not necessarily indicate absence of value, but does so here given that it
      describes pottery. Again, value by association with an important figure is claimed for
      another earthenware gift (XIV.98). If the great Hercules is not ashamed to be called
      fictilis and to be a cheap *sigillum*, the recipient of such a gift should also be happy
      (Leary, 1996: 240-241). Lehmann (1945: 264), on the other hand, suggests that this
      was the original, on the grounds of it coming in the same idiomatic form used for the
      Brutus' παιδιον, and on the lack of any serious argument against that.

45   This epigram is part of a poetic tradition of dialogue exchanges between artwork and
      viewer; see Lausberg (1982: 206-207) for discussion.

46   This 'poor' epigram describes either a statue (Leary), or a picture (Lehmann 1945:
      264). It relates to XIV.175, both questioning Zeus/Jupiter's course of action when
      dealing with mortal women. Europa featured frequently in art. For instance, there was
      a famous picture by Antiphilus in the porticus Pompei (*HN,* 35.114). From Martial we
      learn of another representation, be it picture or statue, which seems to have been near
      the Saepta Julia in the Campus Martius (see Martial II.14; III.20.12; XI.1.11) (Leary,
      1996: 243).

47   *Marmoreus* identifies this Leander as a rich man's gift. Lausberg (1982: 204) thinks
      in terms of a marble relief, which would allow for easier depiction of a drawing
      swimmer than would a statue and would accord with the painted tablet of XIV.173
      (Leary, 1996: 244).

48   Hunchbacks were considered ugly and in consequence had the same appeal as dwarfs
      to Romans, most of whom delighted in grotesqueness. Statues of monstrosities were
      no doubt commonly given as Saturnalian gifts - although Mohler (1927/1928) suggests
      that this gift might have been suitable for a child (Leary, 1996: 245).

49   For a discussion of Martial's influence on Winkelmann, for instance, see Closa Farres,
      1987.

Chapter 8

'Luxury is Not for Everybody': collecting as a means of sharing cultural and social identity

When the ex-consul Titus Petronius was facing death, he broke, to spite Nero, a murrhine dipper that had cost him 300,000 sesterces, thereby depriving the Emperor's dining-room table of this legacy.
(Pliny, *HN*, 37.vii.20)[1]

Introduction

Satyrica is an ironic, sarcastic and self-reflective response to the cultural ambience of the reign of Nero. Through the distorting mirror of irony and satire, Petronius reflects not only on the culture of his era, but also on the standard responses toward this culture. Having an insight in the life of the court, but without being an indispensable member of it,[2] Petronius addresses his work to an intellectual elite, who would share his sense of humor and cultural refinement, evident throughout *Satyrica*. Whether his stance was critical, didactic, and ultimately moralising, or merely self-indulgent cannot be safely concluded. Alternative readings have favoured different interpretations of both the author's intentions and his success in accomplishing them.[3] Discussions usually involve the scale of the book, its structure and plot, along with its genre and style, while even the author's name and date of the book's composition have been subject to dispute.[4]

If we can name the author with relative certainty, it is due to a growing consensus among scholars who identify the author Petronius Arbiter with T. Petronius Niger,[5] Nero's '*elegantiae arbiter*', whom Tacitus[6] (*Annals*, 16.18) describes as a connoisseur, 'the finished artist of extravagance' (Jackson, 1951). The references to contemporary figures, allusions to court events, features of daily life, the economic and social indications offered by the book, the legal arguments and the literary connections with the younger Seneca and Lucan make this Neronian date highly probable (Walsh, 1996: xiii). Therefore, the work's composition dates to Nero's reign, between 66 CE to 65 CE,[7] and its dramatic setting, possibly, slightly earlier.[8]

The rewards for including this work in our enquiry are evident immediately. Besides its difficulties, briefly outlined above and pursued in greater detail in the second part of this chapter, *Satyrica* maybe more than any other work, offers an indispensable insight into Neronian society and its relation to material culture and collecting. At a primary level, it makes practicalities concerning collecting and material culture evident: the extent to which these phenomena are common is exemplified by the portrait of a collector, Trimalchio, and inclusion of the picture-gallery among the central institutions of the Roman world, where action takes place. At a secondary level, interpretations of how Petronius' contemporaries viewed their relation to material culture and art, and of how they constructed their identity in relation to it, are also available to the scholar. At a tertiary level, finally, the narrator's and Petronius' personal appreciation and 'reading' of these attitudes, along with the interaction of these with social reality can also be deduced.

Before we proceed to the analysis of Petronius' and his contemporaries' views on collecting, we will explore briefly some of the issues we may encounter during our attempt. In particular, we will consider the genre to which *Satyrica* belongs, how it reflects the author's stance, how distanced the work is from social reality and, finally, what are the conditions for our 'recovery' of it.

Having set the framework which relies on hermeneutical discourses developed so far, we are going to discuss Petronius' and his society's relation to material culture, as this is illustrated in ten central and several other minor passages from *Satyrica*.[9] Instead of attempting to understand or put Petronius' ideas about art in an art historical context (for example, Slater, 1987; Elsner, 1993), the present discussion takes a rather different perspective and considers the material aspect of it. Trimalchio, the central figure of the extant work, is surrounded by objects: lavish, expensive, vulgar, they follow the latest trends, but also his personal obsessions. The questions that arise then are: what exactly is Trimalchio's relation with his objects, how do they shape his connection to the world, what sort of identity does he hope to acquire through them, where does this expectation stems from, what are the symbolic dimensions of it, and whether we can talk about structuring his life through the collection, or not?.

The incident in *pinacotheca* (paragraph 83ff) needs to be studied in a similar light. Although the existence of *pinacothecae* is well attested in the Roman world (see discussion below) there has been little, if any, consideration of the reasons it was considered necessary to build and hold collections of *pinakes*, whether they were actually collections of objects or images (and what is the difference), what changes between the sacred and the secular this meant for the objects, what was the difference between collections held in temples and public *pinacothecae* and those held in houses, and finally, what conclusions, if any, concerning issues of display and taxonomy we can extract from their study.

The Literary Character of *Satyrica*

The title *Satyrica*, commonly also known as *Satyricon*,[10] corresponds to titles such as *Milesiaca* (Milesian tales) and *Poimenica* (shepherd's stories) and thus suggests affinities with the Greek romantic novel, a genre already established in Petronius' times. It means 'satyr stories' or 'a recital of lecherous happenings' - as more freely translated by Walsh (1996: xv).[11] Naturally, the work has nothing to do with the satyrs of Greek mythology, but the title is quite appropriate for a tale about lecherous rogues. The word *Satyrica* is ambivalent: it may have recalled the word *satura* (a medley), similar in sound but not in meaning, and in this sense it could have been a pun suggesting a satirical purpose.[12] At one time it was generally conceded that the *Satyrica* was an example of Menippean satire, mainly because of the formal feature of this alternative convention of satire, that is *prosimetrum* (the mixture of prose and verse in the same genre). Recently published papyrus fragments (Parsons, 1974; Henrichs, 1982) have complicated the issue, since they demonstrated that a mixture of prose and verse was also possible in the Greek novel.[13]

There is no need to go into the connection between *Satyrica* and satire: the satiric element is evident throughout the work, not only in the subject matter - the various ordeals that a couple of aged pederasts go through - but also in characterisation and in the employment of parody. On the other hand, though, *Satyrica* is something less than a full satire, since Petronius does not follow the full path of satirists, in other words, he does not attempt the stance of protest, denunciation and preaching. Nevertheless, the work is fully dominated by parody and irony (Conte, 1994b: 463). Unlike the satiric conventions, the tale is told not by Petronius himself, or his rhetoric *persona*, who thus would grasp the opportunity to express his own views on the subjects he discusses; on the contrary, the tale is told by Encolpius, a man who besides being the narrator is also an active participant in roguery. Although, in some cases it is quite probable that Encolpius expresses Petronius' own disdain at the events (for example at Trimalchio's dinner party he is appalled and amazed), at other times his behaviour and attitudes are equally contemptuous.[14] In other words, Petronius' personal opinion, filtered through an actively involved narrator, is granted or withheld, but overall it remains enigmatic (Coffey, 1989: 186-187; Horsfall, 1989: 75; Conte, 1996).[15]

The 'quest for the genre'[16] approach to *Satyrica* is not dictated merely by a philological interest; it also relates to its interpretation. The author's intentions (if we agree to pursue this line of thought) along with the work's realism, largely depend on (or can be facilitated by) a clear attribution of the work to one literary genre. Unfortunately though, such an attribution seems impossible.

Audience-oriented criticism (Slater, 1990: 18) maintains that *Satyrica* was a puzzle even to its contemporary Roman reader, who would not have been able to say whether *Satyrica* was a Menippean satire, a comic novel, or something else. There is no point in trying to argue in favour of one genre or the other. *Satyrica* is very much indebted to both the novel and the satire, yet in its complexity and richness of effects it transcends both traditions (Conte, 1994b: 462; 1996). It is a long narrative, enriched with ironic and self-reflective contrasts, evident in both the style and tone of the prose as well as in the verse parts. Consequently, it provides the reader with a response toward contemporary culture, a way of looking at things (material and immaterial); it responds not only to the culture itself, but also to other possible responses to this culture. The irony is directed toward life and its delusions, but it is also directed toward literature, the models it proposes, and the work itself.[17]

There seems to be no doubt that Petronius selects his satirical targets among features of his contemporary society.[18] He pays close attention to realistic details. He ridicules, exaggerates, frowns, inflates, but does not fundamentally misrepresent that part of the Roman cultural life he had decided to explore (Horsfall, 1989: 76; Walsh, 1996: xxvii). In *Cena Trimalchionis* in particular - but also during the description of other characteristic places and characters of the Roman realm - we are allowed to explore the world as representing a novelist's construction, which actually *did* exist. The cultural world of *Satyrica* must, therefore, rest on realistically conceived detail and cannot be mere fantasy (Horsfall, 1989: 76). Trimalchio - who is at the centre of the extant work and for this reason offers the most detailed picture of the author's intentions - is a clear combination of the two kinds of experience succesfully combined by Petronius' creative imagination: the observation of the real world and literary reminiscence. Petronius' characters are recognisable from other sources types of their era and their portraits incorporate the attitudes and mannerisms of living figures. Besides the *nouveaux riches* and the other Roman types Petronius had encountered in the flesh, we find parallels too with the main and subordinate characters of the plot in Seneca (for example, portrait of Calvisius Sabinus in *Epist.* 27.6), Horace's host Nasidienus (*Sat.* 2.8), or Theophrastus' *Characters.* These melt together with descriptions matched by archaeological evidence (for example, parallels of the picture of the dog described in paragraph 29 discussed below have been found in Pompeii) and evidence provided by other contemporary writers (for instance certain characteristics of Trimalchio correspond to Suetonius' Nero). In this sense, therefore, it has been argued that the work of Petronius has

> collected, reinterpreted and parodied all the literary genres and
> cultural myths of his day (Homer and Virgil, tragedy, elegy, history
> and philosophy), as well as popular literature (sentimental novels,
> short stories, mimes, declamations, and sensational tales of witches,
> magic and werewolves). Petronius may be studied as a shrewd

depicter of customs and also as the author of a kind of literary encyclopedia of Imperial Rome. (Conte, 1994b: 464; also see Griffin, 1984: 152-153; Walsh, 1996: xxivff).

Those who favour the satiric aspect of *Satyrica* are mainly those willing to argue for a moralizing intent behind its writing. Epicurean credentials have been established for Petronius (e.g. Raith, 1963). Among the most elaborate attempts to justify such an approach we find Highet (1941), Bacon (1958) and Arrowsmith (1966) - although they do not agree on the model of moral attitudes they advocate for Petronius. In his paper, Highet (1941) argued that Petronius was an Epicurean, but not the debased Roman type of Epicurean; he did not regard philosophy of the garden as justification for tasteful self-indulgence and the pursuit of such pleasures as one felt appropriate. He believed that violent pleasures were to be avoided, like politics, in the interest of *ataraxia* (the freedom from violent passions), the contentment that Epicurus himself and true Epicureans are thought to have advocated and found (also Sullivan, 1985a: 1671). Bacon accepted that Petronius' conscious criticism of his corrupt society has a fundamental gaiety; however, she argued that behind that gaiety lies a 'deep, searching analysis of the death-throes of Classical Romanitas' (1958: 276), for Petronius is the last classical author where a firm moral ethos underlies the prose. Arrowsmith (1966), on the other hand, takes the stance that *Satyrica* is a sophisticated Epicurean satire against the vision of satiety and *luxuria* as a description of an entire culture.

> Petronius believes that perversion and also impotence are typical symptoms of a luxurious and unnatural society ... As constipation stands to food, so impotence stands to sexuality; both are products of *luxuria* in a society which has forgotten its cultural modalities and which cannot recover life, except by Epicurean *askesis* – by rediscovering the sense of true need, of necessary economy, in pleasure ... (Arrowsmith, 1966: 127).

On the other hand, the novel-approach seems to favour the 'entertainment version', which argues that *Satyrica* was an intellectual game, written for the amusement of the Neronian literary circle; 'it pandered to the tastes and snobbisms of that group; and relied on its literary sophistication for appreciation. When morality lifts is head, in the *Satyrica* it turns out to be a parody of moralizing, whose implications are properly "placed" by contextual irony' (Sullivan, 1985a: 1686). Central among the counter arguments[19] against the moralistic view is that the plot of *Satyrica* is disorganised and arranged so as to depict the author's sense of the world as irrational, confused and illusory (see also Zeitlin, 1971: 676ff). Although this seems quite an accurate analysis of Petronius' outlook on the world, it still remains to consider whether this attempt was seriously undertaken, or it was simply *un jeu d' esprit*. Internal evidence regarding the tone in which the book is written, along with the brief biography by Tacitus, strongly support the latter (Walsh, 1970: 79-80; also 1974).

Cena Trimalchionis: dinner at the house of a (not-very-original) collector

Cena Trimalchionis is a critical description of a pretentious dinner party and thus belongs unmistakably to the tradition of Roman satire. But it is also indebted to Greek descriptions of feasting and the symposium (for instance Plato's and Xenophon's Symposia were the setting for philosophical discussion) (Coffey, 1989: 187-188). In the Roman satiric tradition, which Petronius selects to follow, the host characteristically appears as a boorish figure condescending to his intellectually superior guests and humiliating his freedmen by serving them with inferior food and wine (e.g. Juvenal Sat. 5, Martial, III.60). Trimalchio, then, is described deliberately to evoke the themes recognizable from the Roman satire. But he is also more than that. Trimalchio is a rich creation in whom Petronius achieves a synthesis of the traditional portrayal of the unrefined, arrogant master and the contemporary freedman of substantial wealth - that is between the vulgar man in Theophrastus and Horace, and the vulgar man of Petronius' own observation; in short, Trimalchio is a combination of the literary and the observed (Walsh, 1970).[20] From this synthesis, Petronius created a portrait underlining three features that particularly offended him in his contemporary society: the vulgar abuse of wealth, evident in both the boorish behaviour at the dinner and the contemptuous treatment of the slaves, the pretentious claims to learning, and the superstition that dominates his thought. These criticisms make it possible to see that Petronius proclaims the opposites of the above, in other words: social refinement, literary taste and a rational attitude toward life and death (Walsh, 1974: 187; also in Walsh, 1996: xxvii-xxxiii).

These values (or anti-values) are evident immediately as Encolpius enters Trimalchio's house. In paragraph 29, the hero-narrator comes across the first symbols of Trimalchio's vulgarity: the depiction of a dog on a chain, with the subscription 'Cave canem', probably quite popular during Petronius' time (cf. the House of the Tragic Poet, and the House of Paquio Proculo, Pompeii),[21] but hardly the essence of elegance. Interestingly, Encolpius is deceived by the dog-mural. The colonnade inside the front door is decorated with more frescoes, or picture-panels, depicting scenes from Trimalchio's own life (as was evident from the inscriptions identifying the participants), as well as from the Odyssey, the Iliad and Laenas Gladiatorial Games; these are explained by one of Trimalchio's slaves. The scenes were indebted to the mythological tradition, and Trimalchio was shown accompanied by his gods-protectors, Mercury, Minerva and Fortune. In the corner, Encolpius also notices a large cupboard-lararium, where Trimalchio kept silver house-gods (Lares) and a marble image of Venus, along with a golden casket containing his first beard. The *depositio barbae*, marking the transition to manhood, was a solemn occasion for Romans, but not for an ex-slave from Asia. Some scholars (for instance Walsh, 1996: 163) have supposed that Petronius is drawing a parallel here with Nero, whose first shaving-hair was likewise enclosed in a golden casket (Suetonius, *Nero* 12).

This interesting assemblage of artefacts is used by Petronius as a clever refinement of his techniques of characterisation (Walsh, 1970: 118). More thorough and effective than a simple descriptive characterisation, this 'leaves the facts, rather the objects, to speak for themselves' - and their owner. Objects usually found in public, sacred places are in this case deposited in a private, self-indulgent environment - to shape the owners' self-indulgent identity. They are curiosities - the beard especially of a sort that could very easily be called fetishistic in other contexts - with a symbolic and sentimental value: relics from the past, a status-symbol for the future, and so stand for their vulgar owner.

Paragraph 31 is an example of the objects that Trimalchio held dear. The statue of a donkey (Corinthian bronze, of course), is used to serve olives for the *hors d'oeuvre* to the diners, and there are two silver dishes that bear Trimalchio's name and their weight[22] inscribed on them! The fact that Trimalchio appreciates Corinthian artefacts does not come as a surprise: collecting these was far from being uncommon during the period. Trimalchio uses the objects he praises to display his wealth and refinement. But he does not consider the mere existence of them prominent enough and thus he adds to their intrinsic value two more indications: the inscription of their weight and of his name.

Paragraphs 32-33 also discuss personal - although not strictly speaking collected - objects and their use as status symbols. Not only is Trimalchio the owner of important and precious artefacts, but he uses them to display his wealth and social position on every possible occasion. In a way, he uses them to 'forge' his social status. He wears a gilded ring (only equestrians of free birth were allowed to wear gold rings), whereas his other, gold, ring is hidden by iron stars (which make it an amulet, that is a mark of his superstition). His golden bracelet is another feature shared with Nero (Suetonius, *Nero* 6). It is a further mark of a man of low taste to have no regard for the value of his possessions (Walsh, 1970: 119). The most trivial and mean of utensils - here a quill, in other paragraphs a chamber pot (27.3), a dish for foot-ointment (70.8), a bird-cage (29.1) - are made of precious metals. Similarly, in paragraph 34, when a silver dish accidentally dropped on the floor and is swept away with the debris, the slave who tried to save it, is punished.[23] The motif is the same throughout. Silver objects with intrinsic financial value are not important to Trimalchio because he is sensationally wealthy. Hence, Petronius satirizes the *nouveau riches* of his era, who appreciates only financial value and lacks those qualities, like refinement and education, to appreciate and share other values as well.

Trimalchio owns two libraries - one Greek, one Latin (paragraph 48). Such an assertion from a man whose ignorance has been so carefully illustrated throughout the scene[24] is quite hilarious. This is made even more hilarious by the fact that in many MSS there is the number (III), instead of (II), and only two libraries are mentioned.[25] The point here may be simply that Trimalchio boasts of possessing something that a bettter educated person would take for granted. The reading *tres* and the subsequent failure to describe the third library would produce a bizarre effect (Smith, 1975: 130). Literary appreciation has not been among the qualities of the man described. This is just another comic reference to the lack of education on behalf of the *nouveaux riches*, who acquire the external signs of culture without the ability to appreciate them, and believe that in this way they can counterfeit it.[26]

Paragraphs 50-52 are the most explicit both in terms of Trimalchio's collecting habits and of Petronius' response to it. Trimalchio claims that he is the sole owner of real Corinthian bronzeware. Encolpius thinks this is just another boast of wealth, but it turns out to be a pun: Trimalchio's dishes are made by a man named Corinthius. Trimalchio is very concerned not to be thought 'ignorant' (*nesapium*[27]), so he caps this with a hilariously scrambled account of the origin of Corinthian ware. In his attempt he mixes the cities of Ilium and Corinth, the sack of Corinth with the seizure of Spain by Hannibal, Hannibal with Mummius.

Clearly, to collect Corinthian ware was no longer by Trimalchio's age a sign of luxury or vulgarity.[28] The fashion of Corinthian bronze is frequently attested to by most authors. Cicero recurrently refers to it (see Chapter 9), and Augustus was notorious from his youth for being *'pretiosae supellectilis Corinthiorumque praecupidus'* (Suetonius, *Aug.* 70). However, it was thought that the fad had become a mania and a menace. Velleius Paterculus (1.13.4) deplored the popularity of Corinthian ware in 30 CE, and blamed it on the *rudis* Mummius for his sack of Corinth in 146 BCE. This connection was stressed by the elder Pliny, who thought that most devotees of Corinthian artefacts were ignorant chasers-after-fashion who could easily be fooled by counterfeit items (*HN*, 34.6-7). By contrast, the younger Pliny found these objects on the table of the respectable Vestricius Spurinna, and thought it acceptable since Vestricius followed the fashion with restraint (*Epist.* 3.1.9). Elsewhere, the younger Pliny mentions his own purchase of a *Corinthium signum*, bought *'ex hereditate quae mihi obvenit'* and destined for the temple of Jupiter at Comum. Pliny states that he will not retain the item for private delectation: *'emi autem non ut haberem domi (neque enim ullum adhuc Corinthium domi habeo)'*. Trimalchio's private story of the original Corinthian ware created by Hannibal at Troy is more than a confused version of Mummius and Corinth. He is mocking both the myth and the fashion. This becomes clear a few lines below; while presenting the reasons for his personal preference of glass, he maintains that 'at least it does not smell', referring indirectly to the pretentious practice, attested to by Martial (IX.59) and the younger Pliny (*Epist.* 3.6), of connoisseurs and collectors who used to smell Corinthian bronzes to detect their authenticity! Awareness of the myth is subtly indicated also by his later mention of Mummius' bequest of one thousand cups to his patron, who in turn left them to Trimalchio (*Sat.* 52) - if we allow for this reading of the text (Baldwin, 1973: 46-47).

Trimalchio continues in the same line with his confession that he prefers glass, but he does not collect it because it is very cheap! The assertion is complemented by a cautionary tale of the danger of too much knowledge - a man who knows how to make malleable glass dies because of this knowledge. Various versions of this anecdote were current in antiquity.[29] In this case, the tale along with Trimalchio's confession serve to emphasize the interdependency of Trimalchio's setting of values with intrinsic merit. Material which is cheap in financial terms is not appreciated, the only value is gold. Petronius' personal point about the existence of other values besides the ones Trimalchio can discern seems present once again.

Paragraph 52 is Trimalchio's clear admittance that he has a 'great passion for silver' (*studiosus sum*). He admits the ownership of cups engraved with mythological scenes, like that of Cassandra killing her sons (*sic*).

> I have something like a hundred three-gallon bumpers ... with the motif of Cassandra killing her sons; the boys are lying there so vividly dead that you'd think they were alive! I have a bowl which King Minos bequeathed to my patron; on it Daedalus is enclosing Niobe in the Trojan horse. I've also got in relief on goblets all of solid silver the fights of Hermeros and Petraites. I wouldn't sell these evidences of my learning at any price. (*Sat.* 52).[30]

Bactrian imitations of such Greek silver cups in fact survive (see Horsfall, 1989 with references; also Ville, 1964). Trimalchio's clearly did not have labeled figures, as many of the surviving mould-made imitations of such lost silver originals in fact do. Naturally, it was not Cassandra who killed her sons (52.1) but Medea. As for the bowl that Minos - or Mummius (the reading depends on the MSS[31]) left to his patron and he bequeathed to Trimalchio, it also bears engravings that again confuse incidents of Greek mythology. The error here concerns three unrelated events of the Greek mythology, Daedalus, Niobe and the Trojan horse, which are brought together in Trimalchio's mind - the man who owns two libraries. However, more than his mythology is confused.[32] His praise for the realism of the 'Cassandra cups' fits in with a disturbing sense of naive realism. There is here a fundamental 'confusion of the modalities of life and death' (Arrowsmith, 1966: 311), mediated through realistic art - which is in turn satirized (Slater, 1990: 67-68). Trimalchio also owns silver goblets decorated with the fights of Hermeros and Petraites.[33] The bizarre combination of these gladiators with the preceding mythological motifs recalls the wall-paintings at paragraph 29.

The concluding remark summarizes both the literal and metaphorical notions of the paragraph. All the above collector's items are beyond anything else 'evidence of learning', and as such cannot be sold at any price. The hilarious mixture described above, though, undermines the importance of such a statement. Trimalchio thinks that these are evidence of his learning, but in fact they are quite the opposite.[34] He possesses neither the literary-mythological, nor the art-critical knowledge to understand, and thus Trimalchio represents the antitype of the true connoisseur. In other words, he is in the position that Bourdieu (1984: 323ff) calls 'cultural allodoxia', that is 'the mistaken identification and false recognition which betray the gap between acknowledgement and knowledge', and which means that although there is good will, the lack of 'real' knowledge, guidelines and principles do not allow him to find his way in the cultural world, and reach the cultural fulfilment of connoisseurship (also Tanner, 1995: 197-198).

Petronius' irony lies exactly in this naiveté, or ignorance of ignorance, which purports to know, and *does* know, the symbol and the symbolism, but ignores the meaning of the latter. In Trimalchio's case, obviously, what collecting stands for - knowledge, culture, education - are clear; and so is the medium for such a symbolism: objects (lavish, expensive, engraved ...). But the true meaning of the symbolism escapes him.

Trimalchio has an obsessive relationship with his objects. Petronius uses the medium of art and artefacts to underline that obsessive character of some of Trimalchio's tastes and interests, repeating them (gladiators, his own career, dogs) in different forms (Horsfall, 1989: 198). He prizes them for their costliness, which depends on the intrinsically valuable material; he also appreciates their 'meaning': that is their mythological scenes. They are bearers of prestige and knowledge: they bring alive the possibility of having their owner included in a social and intellectual, cultural élite. Undoubtedly, Petronius recognizes the fact that Trimalchio and his like can and do recognise the possibilities offered to them by the objects. But exactly because this is so, while not being *all*, Petronius criticises him. The author of *Satyrica* could not have been the man who would distance himself from the futilities of life. The accounts by both Tacitus and Pliny argue for quite the contrary. In Pliny's account (*HN*, 37.20), Petronius breaks his favourite murrhine cup to 'spite Nero', not to let him have it on his table. In Tacitus' version he breaks his signet ring, so that his personal validity dies with him. A man so immediately and passionately associated with material culture, could not have considered it disreputable for somebody else to relate to it as well. The emphasis is placed elsewhere. Trimalchio follows a road well lit by his predecessors. Collecting Corinthian ware was by then a common practice. Similarly common were the 'qualities' that such a collection carried with it: distinction, wealth, worthiness, knowledge, education. This is the identity that he hopes to shape for himself and share. But where do all these values stem from?

Petronius offers a clue.   They probably stem from their patterns of acquisition. If we examine the text closely, especially paragraph 52, we come along the following pattern:

Sacred	:	Profane
Inherited	:	Bought
(Gift) given	:	Bought
Priceless	:	Expensive
Authentic	:	(False) counterfeit

Petronius seems to operate within the above schema. Although Trimalchio is obsessively proud of his career (paragraph 29) and personal advancement, when it comes to his collection of jugs he admits inheritance! This is also a witticism from Petronius. The man who so abruptly admits and exhibits his low descent, has the lack of subtlety to suggest that he has inherited his collection! He is so bereft of culture that he inscribes the weight on the objects, as if their value was measurable; he even inscribes his name on them, as if this is necessary for the noble inheritance tradition. The 'real' (?) connoisseur would by this point be appalled. The confusion of the mythology serves to emphasise the same point. Trimalchio confuses the most basic erudition; he confuses knowledge in both the 'measurable' sense (know your myths) and the immeasurable (know about your objects).

Paragraph 73.20-24, finally, is a description of the 'collection' of Fortunata, Trimalchio's wife. She owns statuettes of bronze fishermen, tables of solid silver and pottery with gold settings, in other words the collection that one would expect from a female: objects of intrinsic value related to the household (see Pearce, 1995).

A Visit to the *Pinacotheca*

The next two paragraphs are from a different setting: the action is now taking place in a picture gallery, where Encolpius seeks temporary solace from the problems of his personal life. Paragraph 83 describes Encolpius' entrance in the art gallery where an astonishing (*mirabilem*) collection of paintings was hung. He lists the works he sees - definitely betraying the taste of his era as we know it from other literary sources, mainly the elder Pliny - paintings by Zeuxis, rough drawings by Protogenes, the work of Apelles.[35]   Encolpius praises what he sees in art historical/critical terms: he recognises the names of the painters,[36] uses the formal aesthetic vocabulary of art criticism (realism, naturalism), and succeeds where Trimalchio had failed earlier, that is in recognising the codes and stories of Greek mythology. He concentrates on specific paintings - whose artist(s) we do not know - to 'read' their subjects: one is the picture of Jupiter and Ganymede, another of Hylas and Naiad, the third of Apollo and Hyacinthus. The pictures remind Encolpius of his own affairs and he regrets his choice of companion. His personal concentration is interrupted by the entrance in the gallery of an aged, shabby-looking man, Eumolpus.[37]

The second paragraph (88) describes a further stage of the two heroes' acquaintance. After the men have met, and Eumolpus has introduced himself as a poet and also as a pedagogue of satire (his credentials are his self-attested talents in seducing young boys, paragraphs 84-88), 'stimulated by this conversation' he is about to draw on his interlocutor's superior (?) knowledge about art. He is interested in the works' antiquity and themes. He is also eager to discuss the decadence of the arts during his lifetime! Eumolpus very eloquently attributes the latter to the increasing importance money had gained in their generation, which had transformed their culture from a superior to one 'obsessed with wine and women of the street' (trans. Walsh, 1996). He concludes his speech with an *ekphrasis* (?) of the painting that had attracted Encolpius' attention, the Fall of Troy - an *ekphrasis* not much related to what he actually sees, but rather a free poetic composition (paragraph 89).

Following the tradition of the Greek sanctuaries, where the rooms for the display of picture-panels had been an almost standard feature (for example the Propylaea on the Athenian Acropolis, the Stoa Poikile in the Athenian Agora, the Lesche of the Cnidians in Delphi), private art collections were formed in Rome. Testimonies about picture-galleries in private or public settings are available from many sources (see, for instance, the debate about the actual existence of the gallery of Philostratus' *Imagines* in Lehmann-Hartleben, 1941 and Bryson, 1994; Ebert, 1950 with references; van Buren, 1938; Leach, 1982b; 1988). They were held in public or private spaces, and their presence was taken for granted (Vitruvius, *De Archit.* VI.iv.2; VI.v.2). They formed a characteristic element in the luxurious mansions of the period, and were a manifestation of the aesthetic tendencies of the age - collection and appreciation (van Buren, 1938). *Pinacothecae* are described from the time of Lucullus (Varro, *R. R.* I. 2. 10) and Varro (*R. R.* I. 59. 2). The elder Pliny (*HN*, 35.4; 148) was not very favourable towards those who collected *pinakes*, although it was a widespread practice in his era. Imperial *pinacothecae* are also mentioned in an inscription dated in 153 CE (*CIL* VI. 10234 = Dessau *ILS*, 7213, line 2ff) (van Buren, 1938: 76).

The picture of art collections that our literary and inscriptional sources construct is that of a practice motivated chiefly by the craving for ostentation; the collections consisted of works from earlier periods, many forgeries, copies of famous originals or panels attributed to Old Masters, whereas a special place was reserved for works of art that had belonged to distinguished personages. The pretensions of collectors to expertise and their lack of true feeling for art have been recounted (Friendländer, 1921). The common motif during the account of these collections has been the one created by Roman writers themselves, of a decadent materialistic civilization. Obviously there has been more to it than simply that, and Petronius can contribute to its unveiling.

The incident in the *pinacotheca* of *Satyrica* can easily be placed in the context of the novel tradition. Similar incidents occur more that once: the romantic pattern of lovers as viewers of art is found also in Longus' *Daphnis and Chloe*, and Achilles Tatius' *Adventures of Leucippe and Clitophon* (Zeitlin, 1994: 151). Non-erotic, but similar patterns also occur in works like Cebes' *Pinax*, the Philostrati's (Elder and Younger) *Imagines* and Lucian's *De domo*. At a first level, therefore, the incident in the *pinacotheca* is a satiric adaptation of a popular motif that contributes to the denseness of the literary texture of *Satyrica* (Slater, 1987: 170). At another level, it can be interpreted as an example of a highly elaborate literary game, which aims to question the views of the world that Petronius and his contemporaries share. It questions the act of interpretation itself and laughs ironically at all attempts, even his own, to interpret the world (Slater, 1987: 167; Elsner, 1993). The thrust of his irony rests on Stoicism and the notion of *phantasia*.

To follow and comprehend Petronius' highly sophisticated irony we need to see what are the interpretative qualities that novels attribute to works of art and how these operate, and then to compare this with Petronius' 'reading' of that interpretation, as well as with practices known from other sources. Thus we will be enabled to reach conclusions about the role of painting collections and their settings, in the pattern of the questions outlined at the introduction.

Within the tradition of romance, the work of art possesses instructive or interpretative functions (for example, Longus' painting instructs and consoles). The work of art can transfer – usually through an *exegetes* – a moralistic and redemptive message. The medium through which the instructive message can reach the viewer is *ekphrasis*. This, in turn, relates to Stoicism and the notion of *phantasia* ('visualisation' or 'presentation'), central to this philosophical system.[38] Unlike the Platonic theory of the moral influence a work of art can have on the viewer, Stoicism embraces a rather different view of art and its functions. It argues that Truth can be derived from a sensual perception of reality, and art - like all objects - can assist the mind in building up a *kataleptike phantasia*, a comprehensive representation of reality, which is something more than simply a *mimesis* of appearance. '*Phantasia* can teach the viewer something which he cannot, or cannot as easily, learn without the work of art. The merit of the work of art then is not measurable by its approximation to reality, but by its power of invention and suggestion' (Slater, 1987: 173).

However, *phantasia* does not exist in isolation, but can be communicated in its entirety by language/*ekphrasis*: 'language makes *phantasia* explicit, and *phantasia* brings language into existence' (Imbert, 1980: 182). In the novel tradition, a picture, or assemblage of pictures, arouses wonder (*thauma* - the Greek word for *mirabilis*) and demands an interpreter (*exegetes*) who comes to encompass the literary transformation of the painting. The movement is

Socratic, Imbert (1980: 205) maintains: first comes wonder, then interpretation by a master, then *ekphrasis* which brings out the truth. Alternatively, the viewer/speaker attempts to become part of the beauty he confronts by actually performing it. To go away speechless after merely looking at the splendour of a place would not be appropriate contact for a connoisseur (*philokalos*), nor of one in love with the most beautiful things. A man of culture (*pepaideumenos*), as opposed to an ordinary man, cannot be mute in front of beautiful things. He needs to pay homage to their beauty through speech (Zeitlin, 1994: 151-152). In other words, the work of art excites in the mind a vision (*phantasia*), which in turn gives rise to an utterance (*ekphrasis*). *Phantasia* is also the initial vision that an artist has in order to create an art object; the viewer/speaker (*rhetor*, *exegetes*) receives the same vision when he looks at the picture, and transmits it to the viewer/listener through an *ekphrasis*.[39] So, *ekphrasis* through *phantasia* tells the truth and offers access to epistemological reality (Elsner, 1995: 23-28).

Petronius addresses interpretation on two levels: first as a process to understand art, and then as a process to reach the truth through art. His heroes, Encolpius, Eumolpus and Trimalchio, in their attempt employ in varying extents, the fourth of the categories of ancient art criticism that Pollitt (1974: 11-12) has distinguished.[40] This is the 'popular' tradition, which emphasises three standards of value: realism, magical (marvelous) properties and costliness. There is no doubt that these three values persist throughout *Satyrica*, to record appreciation of the arts and use of them to interpret the world that Petronius does not share and, what is more, of which he disapproves. Naturally, costliness as a value that Petronius could share is easily dismissed (Slater, 1987: 167). Although at points (especially at *Cena*) he clearly expects his narrative audience to appreciate it, Petronius himself could not have shared such an appreciation, and he could not have expected his authorial audience to do so either.[41] Nevertheless, this value persists throughout the book, and records a fact. It is used by Petronius to dismiss Trimalchio as embodiment of all those who lack the necessary refinement to understand otherwise. In this sense, we are dealing with two values: one, the financial merit and the other, the cultural alternative that Petronius maintains in silence.

Realism, on the other hand, is also questioned. Right from the start (paragraph 29), but also in Trimalchio's discussion of 'Cassandra's sons', and later during Encolpius wandering in the gallery, it has become apparent that realism for Petronius' heroes means deception and confusion (Slater, 1987: 167). In the gallery incident, in particular, realism and marvelous qualities (*mirabilis*) in a sense interact. The works are marvelous because they are amazingly realistic but also because they arouse emotional and intellectual reactions to the viewer - although these are melodramatic and overacting as usually with Encolpius (Panayotakis, 1995: 119). But even these are questioned by Petronius. Encolpius is unsure where he stands as a viewer in the gallery in relation to the paintings, so at first (and despite the seemingly appropriateness of vocabulary, Plinian taste, and so on), the pictures are just puns on the artists' names. Later they become projections of his own self. Eventually, and despite the 'heroic' attempt of Eumolpus to introduce an *ekphrasis* and consequently, *phantasia*, that is to reach the truth, he manages only to be thrown out of the gallery pursued by a hail of stones. Naturalistic/realistic art is used to illustrate how deceptive appearances are and, therefore, is used to dismiss the function of *mimesis* in Platonic theory.[42] Both the 'popular' way of appreciating art, along with the equally ill-fated attempt to reach the moral values inherent in realistic works have failed. Similar failure results from the *Troiae Halosis ekphrasis* and its use to reach *phantasia*. The poem that Eumolpus cites is a long narrative that ignores any relation to the painting and fails to make any contact with it. In other words, the viewer in the Petronian *pinacotheca* fails to confront the paintings meaningfully, and all attempts, initiated from whatever philosophical perspective fall 'into the empty air'. Petronius' heroes have not been able to reach the truth, whereas the initiation in the symbolic meaning, which would be expected in other circumstances to be the result of such a meeting (of a viewer, an *exegetes* and a painting), becomes initiation of a sexual kind (Elsner, 1993: 41).

Where does this discussion leave us as far as the collecting of art is concerned? Through the failures and shortcomings of Petronius' characters, we can reach some interesting conclusions about what a collection of paintings was supposed to be. More than merely a collection of objects, an assemblage of paintings is a repository of knowledge and a medium to interpret the world, through the appropriate philosophical concerns. This is stated explicitly in the elder Philostratus' *Imagines* (I.4.26-30), where the phrase 'οὕς ἐμοί δοκεῖ οὐκ ἀμαθῶς συνελέξατο', besides containing the key-word 'συνελέξατο' (sinelexato - the verb 'to collect', in its past tense), it also includes the phrase 'οὐκ ἀμαθῶς',[43] which means 'not without knowledge'. It is clear, therefore, that collecting pictures implied a certain sort of knowledge or appreciation on behalf of the collector, knowledge that did not exhaust itself in the mere assemblage of pictures made by famous artists, or in the appreciation of qualities like realism (which equals deception). Petronius' caricature of the motif of the novel tradition clarifies and underlines the true nature of collecting behind the widespread practice.

In the novels, the paintings are placed either in temples/sanctuaries, following the Hellenic tradition, or in private spaces. Longus' picture in the preface of *Daphnis and Chloe* and Cebes' *Pinax*, for instance, are kept in shrines, while Philostratus' *Imagines* and Lucian's objects of admiration are in private settings. Although there seems to be unanimous agreement as far as their capacity to communicate the truth is concerned, there seems to be a difference in the kind of truth that is advocated in each case. Elsner (1995: 21-48), for instance, compared Philostratus and Cebes to conclude that their stance toward 'reality' (truth) differs radically. Cebes' truth is symbolic; the paintings resemble a door to a reality that is outside known cultural and psychological expectations, and which involves a detour into things divine (Elsner, 1995: 22). In Philostratus the viewer is encouraged to think that 'reality' is within his reach, within ordinary physical and psychological expectations, and, therefore, the 'Other' is, or can be, under control. I would like to take this point further and argue that although collections of paintings are collections of the truth, the setting of the works of art has implications for the 'type' of truth which *objets d'art* reveal.

Relatively recently the discussion of *pinacothecae* in the ancient Roman world was extended to include the interior decoration that turned parts of the Roman house into picture galleries. With the growth of private art collections in Rome, rooms depicting the same motif in painting came to be incorporated in the luxurious villas of late Republican nobles. In the mid Second Style,[44] imitation *pinakes* already were represented standing on picture mouldings, much as they might have done in a theme on mural decoration. By the end of the Fourth Style well-off householders were collecting reproductions or adaptations of Greek Old Masters in much the same way that more recent generations have collected copies of the Mona Lisa (Ling, 1991: 135). This development from the actual repositories of works of art brought into Italy before the mid-first century, to the *pinacotheca* theme of wall-painting, was attributed to the political initiative attested by Pliny (*HN*, 35.9) of Asinius Pollio and Augustus, who in their propagandistic building programme encouraged the deposition of pictures and other objects into public 'museums', e.g. the theatre of Pompey, or the Public Library of Asinius Pollio (Leach, 1982b: 162-164). To attract attention to this initiative Asinius Pollio delivered his famous oratory recommending that collectors should not retain their objects for private delectation, but should place them on public display (*HN*, 35.26-28; see also Chapter 6). In addition, this trend of the painted galleries was attributed to the personal taste of the middle-class house-owners/patrons who had realized that through the imitation of the public displays of works of art, they had an opportunity to participate in and share notions of culture and wealth. Picture-gallery decoration, therefore, was taken to attest the refinement and comfortable well-being of the private man. Furthermore, it was argued that the theme offered to artists an easily adaptable format, and to house-owners opportunities for individualism.[45] In addition, the mythological orientation of Pompeian *pinacothecae* was taken to indicate the placement of emphasis upon the display of acquired learning rather than anything else. In this sense, the painted picture-galleries were considered to be of vital help to the understanding of the owner's level of culture. Consequently, Trimalchio's case has been interpreted as an example of a man who chose in his house to connect art, literature and life in the most intimate way (29) (Leach, 1982b: 166-167).

We will argue that all these issues had made an appearance in Petronius' work, which thus offers a valuable insight into the trends and the ideology accompanying them. Petronius' gallery is a public *pinacotheca*, set in a temple (90.1). Obviously, it belongs to the canonical tradition, and forms a model of what has been suggested as proper and even patriotic. The political reasons, behind the encouragement of public collections as opposed to private ones, relate to the role of the collections as sources of knowledge and therefore, power. They aimed to discourage the strong men of the Republic from advertising themselves as possessors of such power through their collections. Clearly, collecting artefacts had become something more that actual, financial wealth by the time of the late Republic, due to the rapid changes in political, economic and social fields related to the Roman expansion. It had become 'cultural capital', in other words able to mark élite status, culture and power. Petronius' penetrating eye satirises what was considered to be a standard motif (in critical terms of romance) and a politically correct behaviour. The pretense that galleries were public so that all people could use them to find 'consolation from the ordeals of life' and share this capital is not valid, according to Petronius. The remedies for the decadence of society/arts - a decadence that Petronius illustrates and lives - are not found in making cultural goods available to the mass, as the argument might have run. The role and essence of these collections is read thus as being assemblages of knowledge (moral and epistemological more than anything else); but Petronius argues that it takes more than their public display for them to disseminate this knowledge. It takes cultural refinement, education, ability to 'read' literally, mythologically and critically, in other words, it takes participation in the real and philosophical knowledge, more than in the accumulated practices and trends.

By satirising the motif of the novel, Petronius also provides his 'reading' of the transfer of *pinakes* from the sacred to the secular. Although the *pinacotheca* in question is in a temple, the assemblage of works of art does not transmit the same message of unity that it used to in the sanctuaries of the Hellenic tradition. There, the works of art carried sacred messages; now, he argues, they have lost their sacred meaning, the *exegetes* is not necessary (because he may be somebody like Eumolpus!), and the experience of art is 'pure'. The institution of the gallery, as described by Petronius, is an abstraction from the original setting, (in the manner of the modern museum, we could add). In this sense, paintings instead of being organic parts of a sacred whole, become profane, units brought together to illustrate artificial - and false - stories. In this case, it is the story of the personal life of Encolpius, a little later it becomes the self-deceptive story of Eumolpus as a heroic Trojan. In this sense, Trimalchio's collection (29) and the public collection were equally deceptive and similarly misunderstood. They became a sort of repository of knowledge, albeit illusory, self-centred and ultimately wrong. Although the sacred role of objects superficially was still there, this role was not delivered organically any more, but was artificially retained and imposed.

Furthermore, the setting of the collection implies a certain attitude toward the source of knowledge. By assembling collections, private patrons transfer the source of knowledge, 'collect' in their hands the power to consecrate and initiate. Truth does not stem anymore from the sacred domain. The wealthy patron considers himself, falsely and arrogantly Petronius insists by the example of Trimalchio, in a position to be actively involved in the process of consecration and initiation; but he also uses the objects/paintings to consecrate and initiate himself by placing these in his house (Bourdieu, 1987: 203). In other words, collections originate a dual evolution: personal distinction for the patron as an individual, through his participation in the cultural élite community.

Petronius does not offer any information on the display of the works of art and their arrangement in the gallery - although from Encolpius' monologue we may assume that the works were not organised chronologically or according to their painter. They seem to be arranged in subjects - although this, of course, may be just part of the satiric point. In so far as the collections of paintings are programmatic, the interest in their arrangement may lie in the underlying theme - in this case the amorous adventures of the lovers. Petronius' criticism of his heroes, that they can see only the subject in the paintings, may lead to the suggestion that the relationships between the paintings in the galleries were those of rhetorical articulation (Tanner, 1995).

A few Words on Objects from the *Bellum Civile*

The last passage of interest (119.1-32) is part of the long poem Eumolpus recites while the heroes are on their way to Croton. After criticizing the historic poems (118) for violating the epic tradition in two ways, first because they recount the adventures and feelings of men in verse, and second because they lack the divine activities of deities, the ambitious albeit outcast poet exemplifies his disapproval by composing verses on the *Bellum Civile*. The poem starts with a general introduction on Rome's abuse of world dominance that made civil war inevitable (lines 1-84), continues with the evil forces conspiring in Hades to cause war (85-171), and Julius Caesar's arrival in Italy (172-301), and reaches its peak with the involvement of the gods and the commencement of battle (302-363). The poem evokes Virgil and echoes Lucan, together with a few phrases derived from Seneca, Horace and Ovid (Walsh, 1996: 191).

Whether Petronius aims with this poem to criticise Lucan's homonymous verse composition[46] or not, has been the subject of dispute. Undoubtedly, Petronius knew part of Lucan's poem - he must have read or heard in a recitation the first three books that Lucan had ready in 61 CE. Nevertheless, the poem itself does not turn against merely Lucan. It is a semi-serious critique, which might be connected with other poetic attempts as well (for instance Seneca or Nero's *Troica* have been two of the alternative suggestions) (Coffey, 1989: 190; Heseltine, 1919: introduction).

In any case, the poem is a satiric self-reflection of the type we have already noticed in Petronius. In the first 20 lines, Eumolpus criticises Rome's plundering of the resources of the world, as has been the *topos* in other literary sources as well (see Virgil, *Georgics*, 2.463ff; 503 ff; Pliny, *HN*, 12.1.2 and so on). He insists on all those materials used to promote *luxuria* and, consequently, vice and effeminacy. Among them we note Numidian marble, Chinese silk, Arabian perfumes, beasts for public shows, and so on. In the following lines, 21-44, Encolpius reflects on how these imports had led to the moral degeneration of Rome. From the collecting point of view, we may notice that among the objects related to that moral decadence were Corinthian bronzes[47] and tables made of citrus-wood (which fetched high prices in Rome, cf. Pliny, *HN*, 13.29ff).

Of course, a speech following the traditional Catonian example of criticising decadence from the mouth of Eumolpus, who is far from being the model of virtue himself, produces only laughter (Conte, 1994a: 463). Like the incident in the *pinacotheca*, decadence (moral and artistic - here mentioned in relation to poetry) becomes a vehicle of self-reflection and irony on the part of Petronius, who questions even his own assertions. The immorality of the imported luxuries has been also criticised in verse in paragraph 55.5. In that case, the lines were put in the mouth of Trimalchio, another character that could not have had claims to morality and restraint. Not surprisingly, material goods stand once again for moral, ethical and artistic judgements.

Conclusions

To conclude, *Satyrica* is a full account of all the implicit and explicit codes regulating collecting in the Roman context of the first century CE. Besides recording current practices, it documents accepted beliefs and responds to them, questioning their validity and debating their legitimacy. With the portrait of Trimalchio,[48] a rather standard collector, similar (for reasons of literary composition, if not of realism) to other portraits of collectors delivered through other contemporary texts, eponymous or not, we have the opportunity to see in greater detail than usual the mechanisms (social and psychological) behind the formation of a collection. In addition, Petronius' negation of such a model records a far deeper and substantial role for collections. Trimalchio is the anti-type of the true connoisseur: he does not share even the most basic qualities necessary to participate in the status he claims to have gained through his material assemblages. With no *paideia*, no literary-mythological and art-critical knowledge, exemplified by his mixture of mythological events and his preoccupations with the futility of life, Trimalchio's claims to have joined the élite with the power of his possessions are proved inadequate and ultimately hilarious.

But there is more to it than that. Trimalchio does not share the essence of collecting, the code that connects objects and their possessors in that intimate sacred and consecrating link. He claims inheritance, while his actions and words prove that this is not true, and although he may consider objects able to make his life transcend the limits imposed by physiological constraints, that is death, he does not really recognise the path in this direction. Petronius' criticism could not have been the same if he did not share some of these aspirations, or at least, if he did not know that there are some who did.

In the incident in the picture gallery, we are taken a step further into the discussion of the nature of collecting. Although here the heroes share at least the external signs of culture - they recognise the creators of the paintings, they use the appropriate terminology, they identify the mythological themes - they still do not fully participate in the power that potentially the assemblage of pictures bears. Apparently, there needs to be an initiation process that will enable the individual to redeem the real worth of collections, that is have access to the truth. By questioning and taking an ironic stance to all the standard features of such a procedure, i.e. the setting of the collection, the presence of the mediator, the philosophical concerns that lead to that end, and have shaped such a view of it, Petronius questions not only the practices of his era, but even himself. He ends by dismissing all these codes and secret/sacred meanings. In the process though, we have the opportunity to record what was there for his contemporaries to see and choose from. Trimalchio, Encolpius and Eumolpus' attempts share an ill-destined end, as far as Petronius' approval is concerned, no matter what procedures they follow. But although this is so, Petronius provides examples of two ways of appropriating art and objects - each with its shortcomings. In the latter, Petronius overcomes the limits of *paideia*, and concentrates on the philosophical and political dimensions to indicate that there is an undeniable connection between appreciation of material culture and concepts of power and control.

Notes

1   Translated by D. E. Eichholz in Loeb CL, *Pliny Natural HIstory*, 1962.
2   Petronius was in the inner circle of Nero's friends and was the 'arbiter of *elegantiae*', in other words a judge of the pleasures of life at court. It seems safe though to conclude that he did not receive literary patronage from the court. The fact that he was forced to commit suicide is indicative of his dispensability (Morford, 1986: 2013).
3   See discussion below.
4   For a bibliography of Petronius see Smith, 1985, Holzberg, 1995a and the one compiled by Panayotakis in Walsh, 1996: xlv ff.
5   Elder Pliny (*HN*, 37.20) and Plutarch (*Moralia*, 60 D) refer to Petronius as Titus. A single MS of Tacitus refers to him as Gaius; at Petronian MSS there is no *praenomen*, just the title Arbiter, which must have been an attempt to associate the author with the bearer of the imperial title.
6   From Loeb CL, Tacitus, *Annals*, vol IV, (translated by John Jackson, 1951).

XVI.xviii. Petronius calls for a brief retrospect. He was a man whose day was passed in sleep, his nights in the social duties and amenities of life: others' industry may raise to greatness - Petronius had idled into fame. Nor was he regarded, like the common crowd of spendthrifts, as a debauchés and wastrel, but as the finished artist of extravagance. His words and actions had a freedom and a stamp of self-abandonment which rendered them doubly acceptable by an air of native simplicity. Yet as proconsul of Bithynia, and later as consul, he showed himself a man of energy and competent in affairs. Then lapsing into the habit, or copying the features of vice, he was adopted into the narrow circle of Nero's intimates as his Arbiter of Elegance; the jaded emperor finding charm and delicacy in nothing save what Petronius had commended. His success awoke the jealousy of Tigellinus against an apparent rival, more expert in the science of pleasure than himself. He addressed himself, therefore, to the sovereign's cruelty, to which all other passions gave pride of place; arraigning Petronius for friendship with Scaevinus, while suborning one of his slaves to turn informer, withholding all opportunity of defense, and placing the greater part of his household under arrest.

XVI.xix. In those days, as it chanced, Caesar had migrated to Campania; and Petronius after proceeding as far as Cumae, was being there detained in custody. He declined to tolerate further the delays of fear or hope; yet still he did not hurry to take his life, but caused his already severed arteries to be bound up to meet his whim, then opened them once more, and began to converse with his friends, not in a grave strain and with no view to the fame of a stout-hearted ending. He listened to them as they rehearsed, not discourses upon the immortality of the soul or the doctrines of philosophy, but light songs and frivolous verses. Some of his slaves tasted of his bounty, a few of his lash. He took his place at dinner, and drowsed a little, so that death, if compulsory, should at least resemble nature. Not even in his will did he follow the routine of suicide of flattering Nero or Tigellinus or another of the mighty – he detailed the imperial debauches and the novel features of each act of lust, and sent the document under seal to Nero. His signet-ring he broke lest it could render dangerous service later.

7   Tacitus' Petronius died in early 66 CE - Lucan committed suicide in 65 CE; Petronius seems to know and satirise Lucan's unfinished epic, see also section V.

8   About the date of the composition see Rose, 1966 and 1971; for a more sceptical view see Smith, 1975. For a discussion of the economic and social factors see D' Arms, 1981; for literary connections see Sullivan, 1985b.

9   For a complete list of Trimalchio's material possessions as described in *Satyrica* see Horsfall, 1988: 9-10.

10   It has been argued that the title *Satyricon* is incorrect (see, for instance, Goodyear, 1982a: 635; also Coffey, 1989: 181 and Highet, 1941: 176, nt.1). *Satyricon* is the genitive plural with *libri* understood, whereas *Satyrica* is a neutral plural. In this book the latter is preferred.

11   An account of 'lecherous happenings' in Walsh, 1974: 185.

12   The relation between *satura* and *satyroi* (satyrs), as well as with the satyresque drama is pursued by Conte, 1996: 74ff; Holzberg, 1995b: 63-64.

13   Both papyrus fragments date from the second century CE. They are *P. Ox.* 3010 and fragments of Lollianus romance. They are translated by G.A. Sandy in *Collected Ancient Greek Novels*, edited by Reardon (also see Walsh, 1996: xix).

14   On Encolpius as narrator and participant in the *Cena Trimalchionis*, see Beck, 1975.

15   Conte (1996: 22ff) describes the *persona* that Petronius creates as author of his text as 'the hidden author'; in other words, the writer creates a kind of conspiracy between the reader and himself, behind the back of the narrator of his novel, Encolpius. Although the latter is the one who reaches the reader directly, Petronius aims to gain the reader's approval for himself, as an indirect voice in the background of the novel, who believes

in a normality his narrator definitely does not. The reader therefore has to identify not
with the narrator, as would have been expected, but with the 'hidden author'; together
they should feel superior to the narrator, whose faults and shortcomings,
inconsistencies and mistakes, they can discern easily. This literary technique has
implications for our discussion as well. It is expected that the reader share the values,
the criteria and the views about material culture that the 'hidden author' maintains.
For this see also discussion below.

16   This phrase is used too as a title of a chapter discussing the genre of *Satyricon* by
        Conte (1996).

17   There is an extensive discussion about the influence of Menippean satire in the writing
        of *Satyrica*, and the genre to which the work belongs in Conte, 1996: 140-167.

18   Since Auerbach's essay (1953), the banquet of Trimalchio has been the most
        renowned for its representation of reality in ancient text. Although not fully accepted
        any more, Auerbach's declaration that Petronius' ambition was to imitate the
        everyday, contemporary milieu with its sociological background intact, and that he
        reached the ultimate limit of the advance of realism in antiquity, has shaped
        subsequent generations' understanding of realism in Petronius (Auerbach, 1953: 30).
        For similar views see Sullivan, 1968: 98-106 and Arrowsmith, 1966: 304; for different
        views see Jones, 1991 and for another perspective on the subject see Slater, 1987. In
        support of the 'realistic' approach has been the use of a realistic language during the
        Cena, see Boyce, 1991. For a view supporting the belief that *Satyrica* is more
        concerned with the misintepretations of reality, rather than reality itself, see Conte,
        1996: 171-194. About the difficulties of using texts to extract historical conclusion
        see Bowersock, 1994; Bowie, 1971; Bartsch, 1989; Lane Fox, 1996 and more
        bibliography there.

19   Walsh (1974: 184 ff) presents the arguments against the moralistic view: These can be
        summarised briefly as follows: 1. The character of the author as derived from Tacitus,
        2. The title *Satyrica* suggests low comic rather than moralising intent, 3. Absence of a
        moral point of reference in the story, 4. Petronius' constant reference to the world of
        the mime, 5. Almost every scene of *Satyrica* has a literary point of reference.

20   For a discussion of Trimalchio as an example of a social type or category of this
        period, see Veyne, 1961.

21   For the decoration of the House of the Tragic Poet, and examples of this mosaic
        decoration, see Bergmann, 1994: 228-229 and figures 3-4; also previous bibliography.
        For the similarity with the House of Paquio Proculo, see Bagnani, 1954: 23. See, also,
        Mau, 1899.

22   Of the 108 items of the Boscoreale treasure, 30 bear the owner's name, 4 the weight,
        and 8 both; there is a single signed mirror (Horsfall, 1988: 10). See also Strong, 1966.

23   The same attitude occurs when crystal glasses are shattered in a fight between the dogs
        (64.10).

24   There are many examples of Trimalchio's ignorance: for example, *homeristae* (par.
        59), his philological comparison of Cicero with Publilius Syrus, the composer of
        mimes, (par. 55); his confusion of Hercules, and the incident of Ulysses and the
        Cyclops (par. 48), and so on.

25   Müller (edn 1965: p. 92, note 10): *post Mentelium Bücheler*: tres (bibliothecas); Loeb
        CL (1969: p.98, note 4): duas *Mentel*: II *Buecheler*: tres (III).

26   For similar incidents see Seneca, *Tranq. An.* 9.5 on buying books to decorate the
        dining rooms, and Juvenal, *Sat.* 3.203-207.

27   *nesapius, -a, -um*: (*ne-sapio*) adjective which means man without knowledge, not
        wise.

28   See Pliny, *Ep.* 3.1.9, 3.6.1, against Seneca, *De brev. vit.* 12.1 (cf. Smith on 50.1) and Martial, IX.59.11 (though Martial is not consistently condemnatory XIV.43; 172; 177, IX.57.2).

29   See also Pliny, *HN*, 36.195, and Dio Cassius, *Roman History*, 57.21.7. From Dio we learn that the Emperor was Tiberius.

30   Translated by Walsh, 1996: 41.

31   There are various emendations of which '*patronorum unus*' (Goes) and '*patronus meus*' (ed. Patav.) are the simplest (Loeb 1969: 106, note 1). See also Müller (edn 1965: 98, note 5/6). According to Walsh (1996: 173) the reading '*patrono meo rex Minos*' is Müller's ingenious emendation.

32   'Triple confusion by Trimalchio: In Greek mythology Niobe, wife of Amphion, a traditional King of Thebes, had nothing to do with the Trojan war and the wooden horse; nor had Daedalus the Athenian architect and craftsman who built or designed the labyrinth at Cnossos in Crete. He did, however, make a wooden cow for Pasiphaë (wife of King Minos for whom that labyrinth was built) who loved a fine white bull and hid inside the cow so as to be covered by it. She gave birth to the monstrous Minotaur for which the labyrinth at Cnossos was built' (Warmington, 1969: 106-107).

33   These were gladiators. The first name appears on a first-century lamp found in Puteoli, the second on several commemorative cups speculatively dated to the Neronian period (see, Walsh, 1996: 173).

34   Huet (1996: 29ff) argues that the imagery is the crucial factor in this case, and not the objects themselves; she also asserts that these objects were used only for display, and therefore as bearers of 'ekphrasis'. This view seems to rely exclusively on the art-historical approach to art objects, and to neglect the social parameters involved in their appreciation. The materiality of the objects is an indispensable part of their roles as signifiers of wealth, power and distinction.

35   They are all Greek painters of the fourth century BCE.

36   Although at the beginning his appreciation of them does not extent further than their names being puns (see Elsner, 1993: 32).

37   The names of the characters in *Satyrica* denote role-playing: Eumolpus means roughly 'Good singer', Encolpius 'On the bosom', Giton (Encolpius' boyfriend and the source of his worries) 'Neighbour' in the sexual sense, etc. See also Walsh, 1996: xvii-xviii.

38   On *phantasia* see Imbert, 1980; Watson, 1988; 1994; Ioppolo, 1990 and bibliography there.

39   On *ekphrasis* see Friedländer, 1912 and Palm, 1965.

40   Pollitt (1974: 63) summarises these as follows: the professional artist's tradition, a philosophical discussion of moral and epistemological value of artistic experience, a tradition concerned with style, and finally, the 'popular' tradition. In addition, he discusses the Roman in origin *decor* theory of Vitruvius. Also Slater, 1987: 166.

41   For the terms 'authorial' and 'narrative' audience see Rabinowitz, 1986.

42   For a discussion of the role of *mimesis*, see Koller, 1954.

43   In the Loeb edition (1931) it is noted that in Reiske and Thiersch 'ἀμαθῶς' is corrected with 'ἀπαθῶς', in which case 'οὐκ ἀπαθῶς' means 'not without passion' or 'not without suffering'. This correction also has interesting implications for collecting.

44   For the four Pompeian styles that were firstly introduced by Mau (1882) see e.g. Ling, 1991. Roughly the styles correspond to the following: First Style: 3rd century BCE - c. 80 BCE. Second Style: c. 90/80 BCE - 20/10 BCE, Third Style: c. 20/10 BCE - 50/60 CE, Fourth Style: 50/60 CE - 79 CE (also Descoeudres, 1994).

45   For the limitations relating to classical collecting as expression of individualism see Chapter 3; basically such comments are based on an inadequate, or incomplete understanding of the implications of the term 'individualism', and they usually mean

to define much simpler developments than those the term leads to. In this case, I believe that the argument that the pictorial depiction of *pinacothecae* offered to the patrons opportunities for individualism, aims to suggest that it offered them the opportunity to choose an environment, or decoration, that could be made acccording to their choices, rather than their means or availability, or other factors that usually dictate and restrict actual collections of works of art (the wish to own a Van Gogh cannot always be satisfied), and not one that would signify personal importance above communal ideals.

46   Petronius' poem has no title, but we may conclude from chapter 118 that it can be called *Bellum Civile*. Lucan's poem has the title *Bellum Civile* in the best MSS, the title *Pharsalia* (from Pharsalus, scene of the final defeat of Pompeius by Caesar) in others (Heseltine, 1919: 381).

47   Is the fact that he refers to soldiers a cross-literary reference, we may wonder, related to Mummius and his army, or are soldiers mentioned simply to emphasise the size of decadence?

48   Bodel (1994) reads *Satyrica* in the context of the ancient novel and discusses *Cena Trimalcionis* as depicting the *Katavasismotiv*. He argues that the visual decoration of Trimalchio's household decor is added to Petronius' narrative to suggest that this trip to the underworld, besides being modelled on the high culture of Aeneid's underworld, is related inextricably to Trimalchio's status as a freedman. The lack of the essential quality of having been born free is the reason of melancholy in Trimalchio's table and of his constant preoccupation with death, evident throughout (the clock that counts the time he has left to live, the silver skeleton brought to the table, the poem about the vanity of life he cites, his interest in astrology, and so on). His attitude is explained by Bodel as being an attempt to make up for a past which can be neither redeemed, nor effaced (Tatum, 1994: 11-12). Paragraph 29 then is discussed as depicting funerary decoration (similar to tombs and sarcophagi reliefs) which aims to characterise Trimalchio's world as an underworld of ex-slaves. This point of view provides an interesting insight into Trimalchio's objects as well. If Trimalchio's house is the underworld, then the obejcts he possesses are funeral goods! They are sacred, they mediate between the upper- and the under-worlds. Banquet utensils and funerary banquets are well documented in other sources as well. Can Petronius have made such a connection? This is a question that again refers to the stance that we choose to take when we read the work. It is the gap between realism and symbolism, that Bodel argues he wants to cross. For this reason he reads employing a literary and a social historical stance. But such a reading, besides its claims, is based on a rather serious stance toward *Satyrica*. It implies a writer who had a serious intent behind the work (whether we agree to call it moralising or not does not really matter). It seems to me that it takes *Satyrica* too seriously. Another alternative way of 'reading' the events at *Cena Trimalchionis* and the role of objects in them has been offered recently by Toohey (1997) who discusses *Cena* in the light of notions of 'time'.

Chapter 9

'Furnishing' the Collectors' World: Cicero's *Epistulae* and the *Verrine Orations*

> For capitalists and farmers of the revenue, somewhat comfortable and
> showy apartments must be constructed, secure against robbery; for
> advocates and public speakers, handsomer and more roomy, to
> accommodate meetings; for men of rank who, from holding offices
> and magistracies, have social obligations to their fellow citizens, lofty
> entrance courts in regal style, and more spacious atriums and
> peristyles, with plantations and walks of some extent in them,
> appropriate to their dignity. They need also libraries, picture-
> galleries, and basilicas, finished in a style similar to that of great
> public buildings, since public councils as well as private law suits and
> hearings before arbitrators are very often held in the house of such
> men.
>
> Vitruvius, *De Architectura*, VI.v.2[1]

Introduction

A prolific writer and an active participant in the political and intellectual scene
of Rome, Cicero[2] is also one of the best testimonies available for our better
understanding of the frame of mind of Roman amateurs and collectors. *Verrine
Orations* and his *Correspondence*, in particular, but also extracts from other
parts of his work, offer an insight into the collecting practices and discourse of
the late Republic along with individual and communal responses to them. In
fact, there are two collecting paradigms that can be discerned in the Ciceronian
work: that of the passionate connoisseur, which finds its best expression in the
person of Verres, and that of the rational, intellectual collector, like Cicero
himself.

The *Verrines* and Cicero's private *Epistulae*, which illustrate each of the
above respectively, have been discussed extensively by scholars, mainly in an

attempt to account for the leading orator's reluctance to talk about art in the former text, and about aesthetics in the latter. The formal and public character of the *Verrines*, intended to be delivered (or, rather be read) in front of an audience by Cicero as the prosecutor of Verres, as opposed to the private interests expressed in the *Epistulae*, which were not meant to be published (Conte, 1994b: 203) and were addressed to an intimate friend, is usually a strong argument that accounts for the seemingly contradictory views Cicero professes towards collecting.   Nevertheless, his unclear and quite often incoherent ideas on art (Rawson, 1985: 198, nt. 63; Bardon, 1960a: 5) have initiated a debate about his aesthetics and their influence on his collecting discourse and practice (for example Göhling, 1877; Bertrand, 1890; Showerman, 1904; Cayrel, 1933; Carcopino, 1969; Bardon, 1960a and 1960b; Michel, 1966; Desmouliez, 1949; 1976). This was based mainly on the widespread, Romantic, assumption that collecting of art relates merely to individual notions of connoisseurship.

It is only recently that the study of the decorative programmes of the houses and villas excavated in Pompeii and elsewhere shed a new light on Cicero's texts, and suggested a compromise, by arguing for an intellectual rationale and social aspirations behind the decoration of the private dwellings of the late Republican Romans (e.g. see Leach, 1988; Marvin, 1989; Bartman, 1994; Leen, 1991; Pantermalis, 1971; Sauron, 1980; Lafon, 1981; Coarelli, 1972; Neudecker, 1988, to mention only a few). Collecting theory is also a new subject that has allowed for alternative views to be developed in relation to the amateurs' interest in objects of virtue. The aim of this chapter therefore is to take these perspectives further, focus on the collecting issues of Cicero's *oeuvre*, and restore them in their unity within the broad context of the Ciceronian philosophical and cultural system, as well as of the collecting history of the long-term (Pearce, 1995).

As has rightly been observed, Cicero '[I]n semiotic terms was less interested in the signifier - the arrangement and decoration of his house and gardens - than in the signified - the philosophical and political connotations of his property...' (Leen, 1991: 244-245).   This is undoubtedly true, whether he discusses the decoration of his villa, or Verres' collections.   Therefore, there will be an attempt here to discuss the rhetoric of each of the texts, and to define the 'signified', the ideology, Cicero promotes in each case (see also Figures 9.1 and 9.2).   Thus we will be able to reconstruct - as far as possible and within the limitations discussed already in Chapter 1 - the collecting paradigms of the Roman era.   We will argue that Cicero's views on collecting fall within a broader philosophical discourse and his proposal of a cultural model, which although conservative, in the sense that it was still dominated by traditional virtues, aimed to strip them of their rigidity and render them more responsive to a rapidly transforming world (Conte, 1994b: 184). Furthermore, by placing his views within the collecting process of the long term, we will be able to appreciate the phenomenon to its full extent and impact.

The second part of this chapter will focus on the *Verrine Orations* and the rhetorics and ideology of collecting it advocates. Next, we will turn our attention to Cicero and his private views expressed in his *Correspondence*. All the arguments will be brought together and enriched with examples from other Ciceronian texts, so that in the final part, the conclusions, we will able to evaluate collecting and its significance for Cicero and his era.

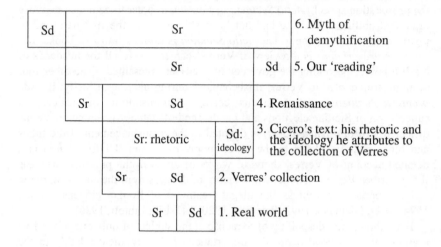

Sd= signified
Sr = signifier

Figure 9.1:   Model of analysis applied to Cicero's *Verrine Orations*.

Verres' Collecting Paradigm

Having won the reputation of an honest and scrupulous governor during his quaestorship in Sicily in 75 BCE, Cicero was asked by the Sicilians to prosecute their case against Verres, the governor of their province for the years 73 to 71 BCE.[3] The representatives of important cities of the island (except Messana and Syracuse) demanded Verres' punishment for the systematic and rapacious looting of their province (*de repetundis*). Cicero managed to overcome the problems Verres' supporters, the old Roman nobility, brought in his way and to collect the necessary evidence in a short time that allowed for the trial to take place before the change of the year, a fact which would have had an immediate impact on the verdict, since the political conditions of the following year were far more favourable to Verres (Q. Hortensius Hortalus, his defense orator was going to be a consul in 69 BCE). In order to speed up the process Cicero chose to deal with the political background of the trial rather than the facts of the case in his opening speech (*Actio Prima*), and to proceed immediately in calling up the witnesses and letting them present the evidence. Overwhelmed by it Verres fled into exile before the second part of the trial, and was sentenced by default.[4] Subsequently, Cicero published the second part of the prosecution speech, *Actio Secunda in Verrem*, in order to demonstrate those oratorical abilities which he had not been able to do in the first part, and to justify Verres' conviction.[5] The *Actio Secunda* is divided into five books: II.1 (*de praetura urbana*) is a review of Verres' career, where all the misdeeds of his life before becoming the governor of Sicily are presented. The other four orations are devoted to Verres' misbehaviour during his rule of Sicily: II.2 (*de praetura Siciliensi*) refers to his corrupt administration of justice, his supervision of Sicilian elections and his demand of statues to commemorate his office; II.3 (*oratio frumentaria*) is devoted to the mismanagement of the tithes and other matters related to the grain supply of Rome; II.4 (*de signis*) is a detailed account of Verres' thefts of works of art from the province, whereas II.5 describes Verres' conduct while facing of dangers from the slaves' uprising and the pirates, as well as the illegal treatment of Roman citizens (Conte, 1994b: 179; Dickison, 1992; Peterson, 1920: 141-170; Lintott, 1986).

Even though the despoiling of Syracuse is the subject of only one of the five orations of the second *actio*, the importance of the argument relating to the works of art is emphasised by its presence in all the parts of Cicero's prosecution procedure. Even in the *divinatio*, the short speech he delivered in order to prevail against a rival prosecutor, Q. Caecilius, a friend of Verres and member of the Roman nobility, Cicero mentioned this important aspect of Verres' misconduct. In the *exordium* of that speech (i-ix), where he justifies his undertaking of the role of prosecutor, the fact that Verres had 'carried off the holy images of the gods and their most sacred shrines' (I.3),[6] and that he had plundered and stolen all the beautiful things of the island (v.19), becomes part of Cicero's own moral responsibility towards the people and their province, as well as his ethical justification for undertaking the case. Paragraph I.v.14 of the first *actio* against Verres is written in a similar spirit. During the presentation of the charge against the ex-governor, Cicero produces a complete list of values attributed to the works of art that had been removed from Sicily: they were famous and ancient (*antiquissima monumenta*), some were gifts of wealthy kings, some of Roman generals who thus commemorated their victories. Others came from the holiest and most venerated sanctuaries (*sanctissimis religionibus*). Whether private or religious, these objects were all of superb workmanship and admirable in terms of antiquity and artistic merit.

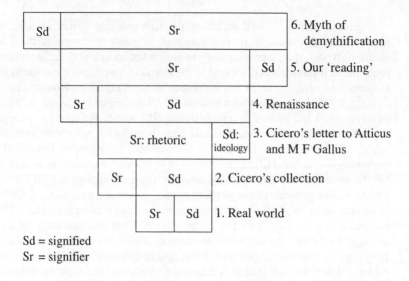

Figure 9.2:   Model of analysis applied to Cicero's *Epistulae*.

The obvious aim of this presentation was to arouse the indignation of the Roman judges towards the man who had the impertinence to remove objects endowed with such a complex and powerful set of associations. Cicero relies largely upon this rhetorical line of argument to support his case against Verres' pillage (Vasaly, 1993: 104). Although the plunder of precious objects was far from uncommon among his contemporaries, Cicero builds a rhetorical strategy in order to differentiate Verres' deeds from other enterprises, similar in spirit, if not practice, to appropriate and justify the past, and thus alienate and ostracise what Verres represents.

Verres' rapacity, cruelty and wickedness had characterised his life even before he went to Sicily, as Cicero argues in the *de praetura urbana* (II.1). A list of his thefts in Achaia and Asia offered to Cicero the opportunity to attack Verres' moral quality, but it also offers to his readers an insight into the collections held in the East and peoples' feelings about them. We learn that Verres stole pictures and statues, which are not specified, from Achaia, he was responsible for a major theft from the Athenian Acropolis, and he participated in the attempted plundering of Delos by Dolabella (II.1.45-46). He forcibly carried off statues from Chios, Erythrae and Halicarnassus and removed the statue of the patron god from the island of Tenedos (1.49-51). He also robbed the sanctuary of Juno (Hera) in Samos and carried away all the statues of the city of Aspendus (ancient city of Pamphylia) (II.1.53-61). The city of Perga and the sanctuary of Diana did not escape his greed either (II.4.71). All looting resulted in the despair and sorrow of the people who suffered the loss.

Cicero of course is well aware of the fact that impressive as it is, mere enumeration of Verres' thefts is not enough to reach the hearts of the Roman nobility. It was, therefore, necessary to enrich his speech with information that could make it immediately relevant to the Romans, show how these thefts relate to them and steadily build his argument about Verres' un-Roman character (Vasaly, 1993: 110). The stolen objects are all described by Cicero as 'ancient' (*antiquissima*) and beautiful, (*pulcherrima*) (II.1.45-46; II.1.49-51). They were not unknown to the Romans, who had seen them during temporary exhibitions organised to celebrate aedilships (as, for instance, the statue of Tenes). It was customary for Romans to ask the owners of celebrated works of art to lend them for the occasion; afterwards, they returned them as appropriate (II.1.49-51).[7] Verres, unlike generals of the past and contemporaries, removed the objects not to display them in public but to keep them for his private enjoyment. Cicero maintains that he had seen the stolen statues from the sanctuary of Samos arranged in Verres' house, when he went to collect the evidence for the trial. They were set by the pillars and in the spaces between them, and also in the garden. When the trial started, Verres tried to mislead the court by transferring the statues to friends' places, but he still kept two of them (II.1.49-51) 'set beside the rainpool' in his hall (II.1.61).

This was quite contrary to the practice of celebrated generals like M. Marcellus, who captured Syracuse, (characterised as a 'treasury of art'), L. Scipio, who prevailed Antiochus in Asia, Flamininus, who conquered King Philip and Macedonia, L. Aemilius Paullus, who overcame King Perseus, L. Mummius, who captured Corinth (a city full of art treasures) and many other cities of Achaia and Boeotia.[8] They offered everything to the gods and the city of Rome, although they had the right to keep their plunder. To the generals of the past, Cicero adds a contemporary of Verres, P. Servilius, who had conquered the city of Olympus. His integrity and virtue is compared to Verres' viciousness. He removed the objects during peacetime, stole them from venerated sanctuaries and stored them in his house, whereas Servilius, after displaying them in his triumphal procession, entered them in the official catalogues of the public Treasury. Cicero, therefore, compares Verres' individualism with the satisfaction the public benefaction entails. In addition, he offers an example of the ideal recording of works of art. This should include the number of statues involved, their size, shape and pose.[9]

On one occasion, we hear, Verres had adorned the Forum and the Comitium (II.1.59-61). Cicero admits remembering it. But he also recalls the ambassadors of Achaia and Asia who were present then in Rome weeping at the sight of their stolen treasures. The fact that Verres displayed some of his spoils in public is not enough to justify his acts. The method of acquisition is also of prime importance. Verres had acquired the objects through robbery and despoiling of friends and allies. The fact that he received encouragement from other 'servants of desire for such things', that is passionate collectors according to the orator, is indicative of a certain disease of their society (a fact that may be interpreted in the light of the nobility versus 'new men' controversy).[10]

In the same paragraph we also learn about an art market available for those who wanted to acquire *objets d'art*. How unbecoming the participation in such activities was for a governor is ironically underlined. So is the fact that Verres' accounts were either falsified or non-existent, and, therefore, could not allow for his claims to have purchased the works to be verified.[11]

Verres' avarice regarding objects of virtue and works of art also finds a place in the presentation of his mismanagement of the province of Sicily (II.2 and II.3). Prominent citizens were deprived of their property (II.2.20, the case of Dio) and legacies (II.2.35-36; II.2.46-47). Heraclius of Syracuse, for instance, a man who had also a 'crazy passion for such things' (*cupiditate ... insanias*) was forced to submit to Verres all the interesting objects, and family heirlooms he had inherited, after the governor conspired with the '*curatores*' of a park to accuse him of not fulfilling his only condition of inheritance, that is to erect statues in the park. Thus, several pairs of goblets, costly silver jugs, a large quantity of fabrics, and some valuable slaves found their way to the house of Verres. The inclusion of slaves in the list of valuables usually is understood to be indicative of the value attributed to human life when enslaved. It would be interesting to reverse this reading though, and consider that it may well be indicative of the value attributed to certain objects (equivalent to that of human beings - see also Chapter 3 about gift exchange).

Cicero offers an extensive list of Verres' thefts from public and sacred buildings (Figure 9.3), and also from individuals.[12] These were all collectors, as Cicero's remarks make clear: for instance, he mentions Malleolus (II.1.91), who had 'a morbid passion' (*morbo et cupiditate*) for silver plate (a union between himself and Verres); Heraclius of Syracuse felt a 'crazy passion' for such things (II.2.35-36). Sthenius of Thermae, whose misfortune is discussed in II.2.83-85, was also a keen collector (*studiosus*) of Delian and Corinthian bronze of 'special elegance', pictures and fine-wrought silver, objects of 'unusual beauty' that Verres naturally desired and did not hesitate to remove. Nevertheless, Sthenius is contrasted with Verres. Instead of criticizing him for sharing Verres' passion, Cicero justifies his collection with the argument that Sthenius acquired the objects in order to receive his guests appropriately. It is emphasized that the collection was 'less with a view to his own enjoyment' (*non tam suae delectationis causa*) and more for a utilitarian purpose. This is a main point of the Ciceronian discourse: works of art should have a reason for their existence, since mere enjoyment is not enough. Although this could well be a point Cicero makes in order to structure his arguments against Verres and present Sthenius as a victim - which could not be achieved if the man was as guilty of cupidity as Verres himself - it is still an important remark, since it is expected to be a valid and appropriate justification.

Verres, on the contrary, displayed his usual 'cupidity' for which he was 'notorious' all over the world, and 'fell in love' with some 'very fine and ancient statues' (*Interea iste cupiditate illa sua nota atque apud omnes pervagata, cum signa quaedam pulcherrima atque antiquissima Thermis in publico possita vidisset, adamavit*) (II.2.85). These were held in public in Thermae (II.2.87-88): they included the bronze statues of Himera, 'of exceptional beauty', of the poet Stesichorus, 'a very fine work of art', and of a she-goat, 'a clever and charming bit of work'. Verres who had a 'frantic craving to acquire' (*ad insaniam concupiverat*) is contrasted with Scipio Africanus, one of the heroes of the Latin tradition. Scipio preferred to return the objects to the people of Thermae, instead of keeping them to decorate his own house. His justification for such a preference is presented by Cicero, and seems valid for contemporary donors of collections as well: if Scipio had kept them, the objects would have been called his own while he was alive. Afterwards, they would have been called his inheritors'. By returning them, he ensured that they would be remembered always as his.

The political implication that Verres' behaviour had for Rome and its relations to alliances and friends is a subject quite frequently mentioned by Cicero (for instance II.2.142; II.2.158-159; II.5.126-127; II.4.60-71). But it is also a question of internal politics: Cicero wonders how could the judges, and in consequence the Roman people, tolerate the private and public spaces of Rome to be filled with objects that were acquired in such a manner. The orator posed a dilemma to his audience: would they forgive Verres and prove that they shared his 'greedy passion', and ignore the country's tradition, history and pride (to which Verres was continually opposed) or punish the man and prove that although they liked fine things, they were rationally predisposed against them? (II.3.9)

This argument finds its intellectual justification in another work by Cicero written many years after the oration against Verres. In passage III.30-32 of the *De Legibus*, a political treatise written by Cicero in 52 BCE, the same idea becomes more concrete. Cicero directly accuses the Roman senatorial order of not providing the correct role model for the rest of the citizens. He refutes the argument of Lucius Lucullus, who in an attempt to justify the criticism of his luxury and abundance of works of art in his villa at Tusculum, had claimed that he had the right to enjoy a quality of life maintained even by his neighbours who were inferior in rank and wealth (an *eques* and a freedman). Cicero argues that 'if you had not indulged in it, it would not have been permitted for them to do so' (*non vides, Luculle, a te id ipsum natum, ut illi cuperent?*), and suggests therefore that it is the behaviour of the prominent men of a country that is imitated and has to offer a role model for all the others to follow. If they approve, or simply allow, the citizens to fill their houses with statues, paintings, and other objects, which were partly public property and partly sacred (*partim publicis, partim etiam sacris et religiosis*), then they are 'guilty of the same passions' (*cupiditatis eiusdem tenerentur*), and share the same 'inordinate' (*eorum libidiness*) desires. A transformation in a country, Cicero argues, needs to start from the way the leading men of it live. Such a power is entrusted to their hands.[13]

In book II.4 of the *Actio Secunda* all the arguments regarding collecting and works of art are resumed and expanded. Verres appropriated everything 'his heart has coveted': vessels of silver, Corinthian and Delian bronze, pearls and jewellery, bronze, marble or ivory statuary, paintings, embroidery. Whether in private dwellings, public buildings, or sanctuaries, it did not make any difference - it was the same, whether the owner was an ally or an enemy, a Sicilian or a Roman (II.4.1-2). In order to present his case, Cicero links the individual accounts thematically and develops them through a number of repeated images and ideas (Vasaly, 1993: 110-111).

The first incident he discusses is the removal of the statues from the *sacrarium* of Heius in Messana (II.4.4-28; also II.2.13).[14] This was an extremely sacred place (*sacrarium ... perantiquuum*) handed down to Heius from his ancestors. Within it, and behind altars, stood four statues of exceptional beauty - a marble Cupid by Praxiteles, placed next to a bronze Hercules by Myron, and two small-scale bronze Canephoroe (maidens carrying baskets). Cicero pays special attention to the Cupid, which was similar to the one by the same artist in Thespiae (a city of Boeotia in Greece); when Mummius captured the city, he respected it and did not carry this away because it was consecrated; but he removed all the other celebrated, profane statues, among which was the 'Ladies of Thespiae' which was then transferred to the Temple of Good Fortune. Heius' Cupid had been borrowed earlier by G. Claudius Pulcher to celebrate his aedilship and was returned to its owner after the end of the celebrations. Cicero contrasts this behaviour with that of Verres. The only object that was left behind was a wooden figure of Good Fortune, an object possibly too primitive to attract Verres' interest. All the previous governors of Sicily had visited the chapel, which was open daily for visitors,[15] but none before him had the impudence to remove the statues. Cicero invests the objects in question with mystery, importance and value for outsiders (*idiotae*, II.4.4-5) and Heius alike. Besides their aesthetic value, that traditionally ordinary Romans would not appreciate, as Cicero constantly reminds his audience, the objects had sacred value for Heius; they were handed down to him from his ancestors, they were worshipped by him and his family, they were part of his patrimonial duties and responsibilities, as well as honour.

In the next part of the narrative (II.4.11-14), Cicero confronts the claim of the defense that Verres had purchased, rather than extorted, the objects from Heius. Cicero refutes the argument by evidence and by probability: the 'purchase' was not allowed, but even if it was, the amount stated in Verres' inadequate accounts is absurdly low – an equivalent of £16! The current practice of the art market of Rome[16] would have put higher prices on works by the Old Masters. Of course, the orator hurries to claim that he does not share these views and places little value on such objects. He contrasts that with the value attributed to them by Verres – although the price he allegedly paid was low enough, the fact that he risked a public scandal and violent censure shows the importance he bestowed on them. Cicero notes that it was not uncommon in his day for a small bronze to fetch (an equivalent of) £400 in the market, and usually people were prepared to pay even more to acquire what they wanted (Cicero himself, according to Pliny's testimony, *HN*, 13.91). He then makes another valid point: the prices of objects depend on people's desire for them.[17] On the other hand, Cicero argues that Heius had no reason, financial or other, to sell the statues at all, much less for such a sum.

VERRES' THEFTS (Public)

Location of works	Nature and author	Circumstances	Reference in *De Signis*
Agrigentum			
• Temple of Aesculapius	statue of Apollo, by Myron	memorials of P. Scipio	II.4.93
• Temple of Hercules	statue of Hercules in bronze		II.4.94
Assore	marble statue of the River Chrysas		II.4.96
• Temple of the River Chrysas	one small statue of bronze		
Catina (Catane)			
sanctuary of Ceres	statue of Ceres	stolen by slaves	II.4.99
Engyion	Corinthian helmets and		
sanctuary of the Grand Mother	breastplates, waterpots, and other artefacts from the same material	they were offered by Scipio and had his name engraved on	II.4.97
Henna			
• Temple	marble statue of Ceres statue of Libera		
• Temple	one more, bronze with torches		II.4.109-110
• in front of the temple of Ceres	statue of Ceres carrying a Victory		
• left in place	statue of Triptoleme		
Segesta	bronze statue of Diana	taken by the Carthaginians and restored by Scipio	II.4.72
Syracuse			
• Temple of Apollo	statue of Apollo Temenite	Verres removed the ivory carvings of	II.4.119
• Temple of Minerva	pictures presenting the cavalry of Agathocles, 27 portraits of the kings and tyrants of Sicily, the ivory ornaments of the doors of the temple	the door which where done with major interest and art; in these were included the very beautiful head of Medusa surrrounded by serpents	II.4.122 II.4.123 II.4.124

Syracuse	a statue of Sappho by	an ancient inscription	
• (prutaneion)	Silanion	on its base that Verres apparently could not read	II.4.126-127
• Temple of Aesculapius	statue of Paean		II.4.127
• Temple of Bacchus	statue of Aristaeus		II.4.128
• Temple of Jupiter	statue of Jupiter Imperator that the Greeks called Urios		II.4.128
• Temple of Libera	a marble bust from Paros		II.4.130
Tyndaris			
• gymnasium	a statue of Mercury		
• various locations	from all the sacred edifices marble tables from Delphe bronze vessels large number of Corinthian vases		II.4.131
Melita (island)			
Temple of Juno	huge ivory tusks, great quantity of other ivory, many objetcs of art including figures of Victory	had been removed from King Masinissa during the Punic War - returned with written apologies	II.4.103

Figure 9.3:   Public thefts of Verres from Sicily and Melita (after Chevallier, 1991: 115-116).

In the final part (II.4.15-28), Heius' feelings towards the objects are once more emphasised: they were sacred (*sacra*, II.4.17), handed down to him from his forefathers (II.4.17, *deos penatis...patrios*). He, therefore, demands that the 'images of the gods' (*deorum simulacra*) be returned to him. The deep piety that motivates Heius is expected to be shared by the Roman senators, if it is not by Cicero himself. There is a clear contrast between Verres, who had no shame, no sense of piety, no fear (II.4.18: *pudor/religio/metus*) and did not hesitate to steal the statues from his host, and Heius (and Cicero and the Roman jurors, in consequence) who appreciated their religious value, and their role as paternal gods and demanded their restitution (II.4.18: *quia religioni suae ... in dis patriis repetendis ... proximus fuit*); Heius' moral quality is further underlined by his compliance with the laws of his city, that had sent him to praise and defend the man who had robbed him of everything dear and sacred (II.4.16).

In this narrative, the statues, and Cupid in particular, constitute the focal visual image used to symbolise ideas and arguments. They are associated with the acts of greed from Verres, of piety from Heius and of rationality from Cicero and his audience. The statue of Cupid and the reference to its similar Cupid of Thespiae is an opportunity to make a comparison between Verres and Marcellus. Cicero distinguishes between the practices of *evocatio* and the plundering of Verres on the sacred versus profane grounds (II.4.122). He indicates that the Romans believed that the sacred objects that became victims of the Roman arms were 'deconsecrated'. Marcellus, after the fall of Syracuse, 'had rendered all things profane' (II.4.122). There is a great distance, therefore, between Verres and the generals' plundering. The former removed the objects when still sacred, and thus his behaviour was utterly disgraceful and sacrilegious (Vasaly, 1993: 107).

The list of Verres' thefts includes more collectors that the ex-governor deprived of their objects: Phylarchus of Centurippa, from whom Verres removed embossed silverware, once the property of king Hiero; Aristus of Panhomus, from whom Verres took another famous set; Cratippus of Tyndaris, who was the owner of a third (II.4.29). The discussion of the theft of the artefacts of Pamphilus from Lilybaeum is preceded by a presentation of Verres' methods of acquiring objects: he had agents chosen to pursue the booty on his behalf. These were two brothers, Tleptolemus and Hiero from Cibyra, both artists, accused of having robbed a temple, who found support and protection in Verres' retinue. When Pamphilus was asked to submit his beautifully decorated cups to the governor, after he had already been robbed of his exquisite jug made by Boethus, he resolved his distress and melancholy by bribing the two men and keeping his objects. This incident is characteristic for a number of reasons. First, it aims to question the moral quality of Verres' accomplices, who did not hesitate to betray for money even the man who had rescued them. Second, it aims to question Verres' capacity as a connoisseur. Cicero argues that Verres was below all human levels and thus not endowed with the humanity necessary for art appreciation. (Of course, this does not answer how the two brothers - who were not much better qualified in moral terms - could perform aesthetic judgments). Cicero, therefore, assumes that Verres tried hard to pose as a connoisseur, although he was not one. As an example of his attempts and evidence not only of the importance he attributed to such a public perception, but also of his incurable relationship and attachment to objects, Cicero mentions the events that took place at the house of L. Sisenna at a dinner party held there, after the trial had already started. Verres, although currently accused of exactly these vices, did not hesitate to inspect closely the silverware, much to the amazement of all those present, who would have expected more restrained behaviour. It was also an act, Cicero argues, dictated by his incredible passion - since no connoisseurship, as Cicero understands it, can be attributed to the man. In any case, the orator uses the incident to argue that since Verres could not control his passion when in danger, he could certainly not do so when the circumstances were different.

Finally, the incident reminds us that Verres' passion was shared by other people as well, Pamphilus being one.

Other thefts include those from Marcus Coelius, Gaius Cacurius, Quintus Lutatius Diodorus (from whom he took a citrus-wood table), Apollonius of Drepanum (who had become a Roman citizen with the name Aulus Clodius - this is the only theft Cicero justifies on the grounds that this person was so disreputable that he deserved it), Lyso of Drepanum (from whom Verres took a statue of Apollo), and Gaius Marcellus (chased goblets). Cicero summarises Verres' activities with this phrase 'reveal you not merely his greed, but the insanity, the madness, that sets him apart from all other men' ('... *rem eius modi ut amentiam singularem et furorem iam, non cupiditatem eius perspicere possitis*') (II.4.38).

The list of people who had suffered from Verres includes Diodorus from Melita, whom the governor attempted to deprive of his embossed silverware, of the Thericlian type, made by Mentor. Verres conceived a passionate desire for them, without actually having seen the objects. While he sent to ask for them, Diodorus left the island and chose to stay in exile rather than lose his exquisite plate. Verres considered himself 'robbed' of the objects he did not succeed in acquiring, and felt an irrational rage about the loss. Cicero compares his feelings with that of Eriphyle, the mythical queen who became responsible for her husband's death because of her greed for an object. Verres was even worse, according to Cicero, since his passion was aroused merely by hearing about the objects' beauty; he did not need to see them (II.4.39). The governor did not hesitate to prosecute Diodorus (a glance at his own fate - see Pliny, *HN*, 34.6-8)[18] because of his covetous desire for his figured silver plate. Diodorus went to Rome and asked for the support of important figures there. But it was only with the intervention of Verres' father that he managed to save his life, although he still could not return to Syracuse.

The narrative of Verres' villainous activity continues with more examples of his thefts. The knight Gnaeus Calidius had also a collection of 'beautiful' silver plate, although, like Sthenius before, he intended them to be used to decorate his house and entertain his guests. But of all the visitors G. Calidius received in his house, it was only Verres, the unscrupulous and impudent 'madman', who had the arrogance to remove these 'famous' and beautiful artefacts. The enumeration of thefts has no end. Lucius Papinius was another victim, from whom Verres took embossed silverware. He returned the vessels, after having removed the decoration. Cicero points out that this was part of Verres' attempt to be thought of as a connoisseur, not interested in precious metals, but in precious artefacts; a claim that Cicero later refutes, when he refers to the removal of the gold knobs from the doors of the temple of Minerva at Syracuse (II.4.124). Aeschylius and Thrasso, both of Tyndaris and Nymphodorus of Agrigentum, were also Verres' victims. He could not resist a beautiful object even when the sacred rules of hospitality did not allow such behaviour. For instance, he did not hesitate to take a plate during a dinner organised for him by his host Gnaeus Pompeius (Philo) of Tyndaris, or two small cups when he was invited to dine with Eupolemus of Calacte (II.4.46). In all cases, Verres returned the objects after he had removed the artwork.

Sicily, Cicero argues, had a tradition of producing such objects of art; it was natural, therefore, for all households to have specimens of these products of ancient artists and of fine craftsmanship. The Sicilians appreciated them as treasures. Verres removed all of them, in order to satisfy not only 'his single appetite, not the lust of his eyes, but the perverted desires of all the most covetous of men' (*Nonne robis id egisse videtur ut non unius libidinem, non suos oculos, sed omnium cupidissimorum insanias, cum Romam revertisset expleret?*) (II.4.45). These thefts, conducted mainly by Verres' agents who, like 'hounds', hunted everything of some value, left the women of the island most distressed. Although they were small things, Cicero continues, women tend to get distressed about them. There is here the now familiar motif of women's relation to material culture: 'poor' women value these objects that they use for their religious ceremonies, that they have in their homes, and have inherited from their kinsmen (II.4.44-52). A sentimental relationship with objects thus is attributed easily to effeminacy.

When Cicero illustrates with his words the situation in every city (for example Catina, Agyrium, Halluntium – see Figure 9.4 for their location), where Verres ordered the inhabitants to bring him their valuables, we get a clear picture of people's feelings about them, as well as about the appreciation and value these enjoyed. The scenes described during the plundering of Halluntium resemble that of Ilium, after the Trojan horse was admitted. Vessels were stripped of their decoration (like women of their clothes), they were torn from women's hands (like children from their mothers), the houses were forced open for the objects to be taken away (just like they would do for people). And everybody was in the deepest distress at loosing their beautiful silver treasures to the hands of a stranger. After the depredation had finished, the people with their stripped vessels in their hands returned home – a description very much resembling that of people returning home after the war.

As soon as Verres had collected (*collegerat*) all these decorations, he set up a workshop and had them attached onto new gold vessels of his own. He used to attend the workshop in a grey tunic and a Greek mantle (II.4.54), another sign of incomprehensible, effeminate behaviour that proved the un-Roman attitude of the ex-governor (see also Desmouliez, 1976: 242-243 with similar views).

The narrative is enriched with other minor events, like Verres dragging off the signet-ring of Lucius Titius, or the description of his 'incredible passion' for furnishings and woven cloth (another traditionally sacred category of artefacts) (II.4.58), until Cicero comes to discuss another major theft, that of the candelabrum that Verres tricked Antiochus, crown prince of Syria, into surrendering (II.4.60-71). The story starts with Verres tricking the prince into surrendering a series of precious objects of unique workmanship, among which

were gold vessels adorned with jewels, a wine vessel with a ladle hollowed out
of a single precious stone and a handle of gold. He borrowed them, never to
return them to their owner's hands. But such an act was really minor compared
with the theft of a magnificent candelabrum the prince intended to dedicate to
the temple of Jupiter Optimus Maximus in the Capitol, as soon as it was
restored, after the fire of 83 BCE. This was not a simple act of theft. The gods
were violated, the reputation and authority of the Romans was impaired, the
duties of hospitality betrayed and the interest of the Roman state harmed. The
symbolism of this behaviour is stereotypical: Verres was greedy, impious, cruel.
Cicero wished at this point to mark the degeneration of Verres into the
archetypal tyrant, a man who resembled the cruel tyrants of the island before the
Romans (II.4.73; II.4.123; II.5.145) (Vasaly, 1993: 118-119).

Figure 9.4:   Map of Sicily (after Dickison, 1992: ii).

Immediately after that, Cicero recounts the story of the theft of the statue of
Diana from Segesta (II.4.72-83), an ancient city related to Rome through their
common founder, Aeneas. Segesta was the host of an ancient statue of Diana, a

work of fine workmanship. The statue had been plundered by the Carthaginians. Many years later, when Carthage fell to Scipio Aemilianus, the statue was returned and reinstalled with an inscription commemorating the Roman general. When Verres, the 'enemy of all that is holy and sacred' (*sacrorum omniumet religionum hostis*) (II.4.75) saw the statue, he became almost mad with desire to acquire it. Cicero leads his audience to see the meaning of the statue in religious terms, but also as a monument to Scipio's victory and a symbol of Roman rule (II.4.75; II.4. 78). Verres' corrupt administration blackened the reputation of the upper classes and endangered the Roman power and hegemony. The statue comes to stand for the virtues of the Roman rule, justice, diligence, self-control, protection of the wretched (II.4.81).

The same issue of the value of objects and their significance recurs in the speech. Already in II.2.88 Cicero had offered the signifieds of the objects in question: they were 'the memorial of our fathers', 'trophies of victory', 'gifts of illustrious benefactors', 'tokens of their alliance and friendship with the Roman nation'. Similarly, in II.4.88 he refers to the removal of the statue of Mercury from Tyndaris as a multiple offence: against monetary issues, since the statue was particularly valuable in the art market; against the Roman people, since it is to them that the statue ultimately belonged: it had been taken from Rome's major enemy and erected by one of its leading generals; a crime of treason, since Verres removed the memorial of Roman triumph, fame and power, as well as of impiety because it was also a holy object; finally, a crime of cruelty because its removal meant the torture of friends and allies of Rome. Similar patterns appear in paragraph II.4.93-96 where Verres' thefts (of a beautiful statue of Apollo by Myron, also a memorial of Scipio) from the temple of Aesculapius at Agrigentum is recorded, along with the removal of a bronze image of Hercules by his sanctuary in the same city. People were devastated of the 'loss of so many things at once: Scipio's benefaction, their own religious peace of mind, their city's art treasures, the record of their victory, the evidence of their alliance with Rome'.

More examples of similar ideas are recorded: the removals of the statue of the River Chrysas from Agrigentum, of the Corinthian breastplates, helmets and vessels from the sanctuary of Great Mother near Engyion. All these were symbolic events depriving the people of objects bestowed with ideological value: spoils, memorials of great commanders, ornaments of the holy place, from then onwards they were destined to be described as Verres' property (II.4.96-99). The dichotomy between private and public comes thus to the forefront, along with questions of aesthetic appreciation. Is it possible for such behaviour to originate from the appreciation of beautiful things? The answer is negative, since it entails qualities Verres lacked: he was uncultivated, illiterate and ludicrous. On the other hand, Scipio, who was quite the opposite and thus could appreciate the aesthetic value of such works, was rational enough to judge them appropriate for adorning cities and temples, and for being memorials for future generations, rather than individual property.

The fourth extended narrative of *De Signis* (II.4.105-115) refers to the removal from the shrine of Ceres at Henna of the most sacred cult image of the goddess - a bronze statue of outstanding workmanship, although of moderate size. He carried off also an extraordinarily beautiful (II.4.110: *pulcherrime factum*) statue of Victory, standing on the right hand of the goddess. As previously (and quite unlike what he had claimed about Verres' motives), the orator denies that consideration of monetary loss was the principal complaint, and attributes the grief, indignation and desperation of the inhabitants to the sacrilegious character of such an act. Verres once again is compared to the ancient tyrants, who were cruel, governed by whims rather than reason, greedy for wealth and power, dissatisfied with everything. The portrait Cicero draws of Verres presents extraordinary similarities with that of Dionysius, the tyrant of Syracuse, whom he describes in his *De Natura Deorum*, one of the philosophical works, written in 45 BCE (Conte, 1994b). In passage III.83-84 Cicero describes the sacrilegious acts of Dionysius: apart from plundering the temple of Proserpina at Locri, he stole from the temple of Zeus at Olympia the god's golden mantle that had been a present of the tyrant Gelo after his victory over the Carthaginians; from Epidaurus, he removed the golden beard of the statue of Aesculapius. From both sanctuaries he appropriated the Victories and the vessels that stood in the open hands of the statues, as well as all the silver tables. When he returned to Syracuse, he sold everything at an auction, only to issue a proclamation soon afterwards whereby he ordered all those who had sacred objects to return them immediately. Dionysius was a man who did not hesitate to do injustice to gods and humans alike; neither fear, nor piety prevented him. It is interesting to note the marked similarities between Verres and this cruel tyrant.

Moreover, there is another characteristic of the tyrant - and the collector - that functions as a kind of emblem for the depravity of his character: it is the sexual *libido*. Verres had this characteristic, as well. It is evidenced not only through his behaviour to women (II.1.63-85), but also in relation to images of women. In II.4.5, for instance, two of the statues removed from Heius had the appearance and clothing of virgins; in II.4.7, the marble Cupid regretted his end in the house of a prostitute; the statue of Diana in Segesta was that of a virgin (II.4.74), that nobody 'could lay hands upon' (II.4.77), except Verres, of course. In Syracuse, Verres also removed beautiful paintings and exquisite doors from the temple of Minerva, thereby 'transferring the embellishments of the virgin Minerva to the house of a prostitute' (II.4.123). The seizure of the image of Ceres, the goddess most sacred to Sicily, could not but be the culmination of his acts. And the symbolism goes further. Since the story starts with the abduction of Proserpina from Pluto, Cicero brings Verres to resemble Orcus (Pluto) (II.4.111: *alter Orcus*); and exactly as Ceres (Demeter) mourned the loss of her daughter to the distress of people, so did this abduction end in the general desolation and the abandonment of the rich Sicilian fields. Cicero wished his audience to 'read' the events as an allegory of Verres' rape of Sicily herself.[19]

The vocabulary Cicero chose in order to discuss Verres' thefts very frequently reveals the disturbed sexuality of the passionate collector: '*cupiditas*' (love) (II.4.41-42; 44-49; 58; 85; 96-99; 101 and so on), '*concupisco*' (to desire) (II.4.87-88; 101), '*libido*' (desire) (II.4.44-49), are the terms Cicero uses to describe the acts of Verres and, by extension, the man himself.

Among the thefts from the public and sacred places are included also those from the island of Melita. There was a temple of Juno there, which held many works of art and rarities. Among them there were ivory tusks of incredible size, which were transferred to king Masinissa, after the Punic army captured the island. However, even he returned them immediately with his written apologies when he realised where the tusks came from. Verres, on the contrary, knowingly removed the tusks from the holy sanctuary along with other ivories and objects of art, ancient and of exquisite workmanship (II.4.103). In addition, he stole the adornments of the door of the temple of Minerva in Syracuse, along with twenty-seven pictures, including portraits of the tyrants and kings of Sicily, that besides their aesthetic value were also of historical importance, since they preserved for the future generations the likenesses of these important public figures (II.4.121-124).[20] This remark evidences another quality - that of evidence - attributed to objects by Cicero; consequently, this means that he expects his audience to understand and appreciate his point (maybe related to the tradition of family wax portraits).

Although quite frequently in his speech Cicero refers to works of art with terms that display admiration (for instance *pulcherrima*), he is very cautious not to be too enthusiastic about them. He continually professes personal ignorance in matters of art.[21] He claims little aesthetic judgment himself - not equal to the number of statues he had seen (II.4.94). He calls himself and his audience '*idiotae*' (II.4.4) and '*rudes*' (II.2.87) in the field of art, and, although well informed about the art market, he denies that he places any value on objects of this sort (II.4.13), a statement easily proved rhetorical by comparison with information from other sources and with passages from other parts of his work.[22] When describing the statues from the shrine of Heius, he pretends not to remember the names of Praxiteles, Myron and Polyclitus (II.4.4-5). On the other hand, he refers with an almost patronising tone to the feelings of the Greeks towards their objects (II.4.132-134; II.4.124). Even statues of their enemies, like Mithridates, were held in honour and protected - except of that of Verres (II.2.157-158). For this reason, generals of the past had allowed the conquered people to retain many of the works that offered - unduly - such delight to them, as a kind of solace for the loss of their independence (II.4.124; 135). It is highly improbable, Cicero reassures the judges, that the Greek cities would agree willingly to sell to Verres any of the works of art in their possession (II.4.132-134). The attachment to objects, therefore, is presented as another un-Roman characteristic that Verres shares with the Greeks.

The procedure against Verres was a character trial (May, 1988). Cicero's rhetoric relied on differentiating between two ways of relating to material culture: one rational, patriotic, religious, the other irrational, insane and profane. Both were well known to his audience. Cicero only had to underline the moral and ideological investment in each of them, sketching a clear model, possibly much more simplified than the one he and the judges shared in real life. For this reason, Cicero's speeches are invaluable for the insight they offer into the collecting of the antique world. The audience had to decide which model they preferred, and on which side of this set of binary pairs they stood, in theory if not in practice:

Verres	:	Cicero
Robbery	:	Purchase
Libido	:	*Logos*
Insania	:	Rationality
Non-religious	:	Religious
Profane	:	Sacred
Treason	:	Patriotic sentiment
Enjoyment	:	Utility
Delectatio	:	*Decor*
Inappropriate	:	Appropriate
House	:	Temple/public building
Private	:	Public
Individual	:	Collective
Monetary interest	:	Connoisseurship
Monetary interest	:	Humanity
tyrant	:	Roman rule

There is no reason to argue that Cicero in the *Verrines* expresses his disapproval of collecting as a notion and a practice already largely present in the Roman world. On the contrary, by introducing an extensive list of individual collectors, along with the public collections, and by using the objects to reveal the character of their owners, he admits a profound understanding of the power and role of material culture in shaping human identity. It is exactly on this point that he founds his prosecution strategy. Verres is the character that Cicero wants to incriminate, and it is the *kind* of collection he kept, the *way* he had acquired it, and the *ideology* it conveyed that are used in order to achieve that. The orator manipulates his audience to feel repelled by the values Verres bestows on his collection, and not by the collection itself.

Other collectors, Cicero argues, endow their collections with different values, and render them respectable and justified. Heius' assemblage, for instance, is cherished and appreciated as an example of a 'good' collection, for expressing piety towards the gods, and compliance to the ancestral tradition, a sentiment with which the Roman audience could certainly empathise. Antiochus of Syria used the objects of his collection to honour his guests, and treated the precious candelabrum described in the narrative as a token of his piety and respect for the chief Roman god and the Roman state. The citizens of Segesta also endowed the statue of Diana with their admiration and respect for Scipio Aemilianus (II.4.82), and they understood it to form a bond between their city and Rome. Similarly, in Henna, the statue of Ceres was seen as a deposition of piety and honour upon the city in particular, and the island in general (Vasaly, 1993: 126). The assemblage of the artefacts, or even the objects themselves are not criticised by Cicero. It is the collecting paradigm of Verres that meets with his disapproval and contempt.

Verres had all the characteristics of a vicious man, and a 'bad' collector. His passion for the material collected reached the point of insanity. His relationships with other people were problematic, and largely formed through donating objects (for example, see the gift of a Sphinx to his lawyer, Hortensius).[23] His love for works of art, as compared to his cruelty towards people, testifies to the disturbed nature of his character, including his sexuality (Forrester, 1994; Edgar, 1997). Greedy (he had too many objects, and he was still unsatisfied), tyrannically cruel, and villainous, Verres represents the 'bad' collector, the dangerous kind, whose relation with material culture resembles that of Eriphyle. His collection, then, can be described as follows:

Collection	:	Collection
Verres	:	Cicero
Orcus	:	Jupiter
Eriphyle	:	Ceres
Profane	:	Sacred/mystified/mysterious
Traitor	:	Patriotic
Woman	:	Man
Useless	:	Useful
Otium	:	*Negotium*
Inappropriate	:	Appropriate
Occupy living space	:	'*Ornamenta*'
Meaningless	:	Meaningful
Without a context	:	In a context
Greek	:	Roman
Bad	:	Good
Abnormal	:	Normal
Non-virtuous	:	Virtuous
Dangerous	:	Safe

Nevertheless, Verres was not a unique example of such a collecting mode. Similar behaviour (or, similar 'readings' of collecting) is recorded in other parts of Cicero's works. In the *Paradoxa Stoicorum*, V.36-38, for instance, the very first of his philosophical works, written in 46 BCE, and dedicated to Marcus Brutus (Conte, 1994b), Cicero openly criticises those who take *excessive* delight in statues and pictures, Corinthian bronzes, and silver plate. His disapproval relies on their belief that the possession of these objects makes them superior to the rest of the world. This is not true, he argues; on the contrary, the people 'who had given themselves up to coveting that sort of thing' occupy the lowest place in the slave-order. He accuses them of not holding a spirit deserving praise when they stand 'spell-bound' in front of a statue or a picture (*stupidum detinet*). Even if the questions of provenance and method of acquisition are ignored, the mere fact of being enchanted by works of art, of 'gazing and marvelling and uttering cries of admiration' (*intuentem te admirantem calmores tollentem cum video*) is enough to denote a slave of material culture. The fact that these objects are delightful, does not justify such behaviour. In this case, Cicero admits that he has 'trained eyes' (*oculos eruditos habemus*) as well. But clearly he draws a line and urges the Roman citizens not to allow appreciation to take them too far. As he did repeatedly in the *Verrines*, he brings to the discussion the celebrated generals of the past, Mummius and Manius Curius, and rhetorically asks how would they have felt if they could see their compatriots handle 'eagerly' and 'covetously' the artefacts (*matellionem Corinthium cupidissime tranctantem*), products and symbols of ideas and people they had fought against (*cum ipse totam Corinthium contempsisset*). The same pattern of 'covetousness' and its result for people occur in other paragraphs of the same work (paragraphs 13, 49). It is evident that Cicero places the emphasis not with the collection *per se*, but with the loss of moderation regarding the collectors' desire for them. Other collectors who had lost their moderation and had succumbed to let their desire lead their life are also mentioned. In *Philippics* II.109, Antonius, for instance, is presented as so irrational that he even removed from the city objects that had been donated to the Roman people by Caesar himself. His irrationality is compared to that of Verres; he was the one who proscribed the ex-governor for not submitting his Corinthian bronze (Pliny, *HN*, 34.6-8). In the *Pro Sexto Roscio Amerino* (XLVI.133), Cicero uses the collection in order to criticise Chrysogonus: the abundance of objects, the man's irrational behaviour displayed in the enormous amount he had paid for a single vessel, his luxury and insatiable appetite for acquisitions, become indicative of his moral unworthiness.

The notion of desire is discussed by Cicero in an interesting passage from the philosophical dialogue *De Finibus Bonorum et Malorum*. This was written in 45 BCE, and was dedicated to M. Brutus, as are many others of Cicero's works (Conte, 1994b); it deals with ethical questions, that is the problem of the highest good and the highest evil, as the title indicates. In books 1 and 2, it is the Epicurean philosophy which is examined. On more than one occasions Cicero refers to works of art as being sources of pleasure (*voluptas* and *delectatio*) (II.207; II. 23-24). Nevertheless, in paragraph II.115 he argues that those who believe that pleasure is the chief good decide that with the lower part of their mind, that is the faculty of desire (*nisi quod is qui voluptatem summum bonum esse decernit non cum ea parte animi in qua inest ratio atque consilium, sed cum cupiditate, id est cum animi levissima partem deliberat?*). This is a central notion in Ciceronian philosophy and in his collecting paradigm alike. When a man admits pleasure as the chief good, it is because he operates outside *Logos*, which should provide his prime guidance. The faculty of desire misleads men, and drives them to misbehaviour and sacrilege. In the case of Verres, this has been amply exemplified. This paragraph is also an example of Cicero's disapproval of the doctrine of 'art for art's sake' and, consequently, of his entirely different way of understanding collecting and art.

Cicero's Collecting Practice and Discourse

To unravel Cicero's character and personality, the clues provided by his *Correspondence* with friends and acquaintances are invaluable. These are real letters, not written in order to be published, and show the unofficial side of Cicero, who reveals and shares his thoughts, doubts, fears, concerns and wishes. The style in which they are written confirms their genuine character, and reflects the everyday language of Rome. Four main sets of letters have been transmitted to us: the first consists of sixteen books of *Epistulae ad Familiares*, friends and relatives, which date from 62 to 43 BCE. The second group includes sixteen books of letters *Ad Atticum*, Cicero's most intimate friend who lived in Athens. They cover the period from 68 to 44. There are also three books *ad Quintum Fratrem*, from 60 to 54, and two books of disputed authenticity *ad Marcum Brutum*, with letters dated from 43 BCE. All were published long after Cicero's death, and were edited most probably by his freedman Tiro (Conte, 1994b: 202-203).

A series of ten letters to Titus Pomponius Atticus,[24] dated between November 68 and the summer of 65 BCE, according to the arrangement of Shackleton Bailey (1965: 65-75; 277), and a much later letter (46 BCE) addressed to another friend, M. Fabius Gallus, are the most revealing evidence regarding the orator's personal collection and the rationale that led to its formation. Atticus and Gallus had undertaken the assignment of finding and purchasing statues for Cicero, and it is to this project that the orator refers in his letters. They are also a unique first-hand testimony, the only direct communication of a Roman collector with his agents/suppliers available down to our days, and as such has often been regarded as representative of its era as a whole, and thus used as a textual support for many discussions of archaeological data.[25]

Cicero endowed his commissioners with complete confidence, justified in the case of Atticus, not quite so in the case of Gallus. This, along with the brevity of his references to the subject (sometimes just a short phrase), and the lack of details regarding his commissions (like style, date, workmanship, beauty, originality, artist, and so on), have been interpreted as personal indifference and/or lack of aesthetic judgement (Vermeule, 1977; Lafon, 1981; Bardon, 1960a; Showerman, 1904). Therefore, the 'collection' was seen as been part of a decorative programme alone, and was deprived of any personal meaning and rationale. In other words, Cicero was not discussed as a collector (but as a commissioner).[26] This seemed to conform quite well with the purported criticism of collecting in the *Verrines*, and overemphasised the role and importance of the decorative programme, that did not allow for personal expression. On the other hand, it tacitly denied the existence of any but the art-historical, taste-oriented approach to the formation of art collections.

The element that such a view had overlooked is that Cicero had a very clear idea of what he wanted to buy, and this is reflected clearly in the consistency and precision of his language in the letters (Leen, 1991: 237). The key-notion is 'suitability'; he constantly urges Atticus, or criticises Gallus, for objects that would bear this characteristic and chief value. The choice of vocabulary he uses is indicative: *convenire* (1.7), *dignum* (5.2), *proprium* (9.3) (all three mean appropriate), *gratum* (9.3) (pleasant), οἰκεῖον (6.3) (πρέπον = appropriate),[27] *esse videtur* (4.2) (δοκεῖ μοι), γυμνασιώδη (2.2; 5.2).

This last term, *ornamenta* γυμνασιώδη, which appears more than once (2.2; 5.2), defines the kind of statuary Cicero commissions by referring to the setting for it. He is interested in objects being 'suitable for a gymnasium';[28] the term refers to the Greek building type originally intended for the training of athletes, but gradually associated with places where young men went to study philosophy. Wealthy Romans followed the tradition of their Hellenistic precedents of internalising and privatising gymnasia by naming parts of their extensive private houses after this Greek public building type (Delorme, 1960; Marvin, 1989; Dickman, 1997). The aristocratic and philosophical associations of gymnasia made them particularly popular. Cicero, who had studied philosophy in Athens (and whose nostalgia for those days is often evident in his dialogues, for instance *De Finibus* V.1.1-2; V.2.4), could not but follow the trend. He therefore defines the destination of his collection: it is going to be the gymnasium and the palaestra (2.2; 4.2; 5.2; 6.3; 10.5), sometimes designated as the Academy (5.2; 7.3; 9.3), a *xystos* or colonnade (4.2), the library (3; 6.4), the *exhedria* (*ad Fam.*, VII.23), and an *atriolum* (6.3). These were all parts of an architectural ensemble including a garden (Shackleton Bailey, 1978: 282-283). The terms gymnasium, palaestra, and Academy are used interchangeably (Grimal, 1969: 246-247). Cicero actually was in the process of constructing two gymnasia at Tusculum, situated on different terraces, one above the other, the higher one called the Lyceum and the lower one the Academy (*Div.* 1.8; *Tusc.* 2.9; Shackleton Bailey, 1965: 282), both named after the two gymnasia of Athens, were Plato and Aristotle had taught respectively. Each consisted of a garden surrounded by a *xystos* and annexed buildings; in the case of the Lyceum this was a library (Grimal, 1969: 249).

The function of space, consequently, is related immediately to the selection of objects for its decoration. The place itself reminds its owner of these needs, as Cicero remarks to Atticus (*ut me locus ipse admoneret*) (2.3-4). Similarly, it is on the grounds of appropriateness and of finding the right space for them in his house that he rejects the purchases made by Gallus. He cannot think of a room in his properties where they could fit appropriately (*ad Fam.* VII.23). It is obvious therefore, that Cicero looks for two primary values when it comes to the objects of his collection: suitability (*decor*) and utility (*utilitas*), the two key-principles of Roman aesthetics.

Decor clearly is the first. It is the aesthetic equivalent of the ethical term of *decorum* (Pollitt, 1974). It can be defined broadly as 'suitability of style to place and purpose, or to tradition' (Rawson, 1985: 187). Cicero himself defines the notion in the *Orator* (xxi.69-xxiii.74): 'propriety is what is fitting and agreeable to an occasion or person', and he develops this in his ethical system presented in *De Officiis* (I.93-98). The notion finds its origins in the Hellenic ethic philosophy of Aristotle and the Peripatetics; they used the word πρέπον (prepon), and more often the phrase πρέπον καί καλόν (prepon kai kalon), to denote a behaviour appropriate to the character of the person and the circumstances. Panaetius gave wider significance to the term to indicate the sense of measure and the harmony of human behaviour which is disciplined by *Logos* (final virtue, moderation). Cicero adopted the Greek doctrine and transformed it to include the social life: 'Le sens du prepon était pour le Grec le sens de sa propre mesure. La vertu du decorum selon Cicéron consiste pour l'homme à s'adapter au milieu humain' (Desmouliez, 1976: 304). Cicero followed the Greek tradition, but he turned the πρέπον from an internal notion to an external one. It is not that moral beauty is reduced by a code of appropriateness; it is that human morality is engaged in the social life. The social orientation of *decorum*, therefore, is its chief characteristic; it is a concept realised in others' approval. Within the dense web of obligations and responsibilities of the Roman social milieu, the measure of success is the reception by others. In the case of collecting, the Roman amateur aims to project through his purchases an appropriate self-image, bearing the correct values and social standing, constantly attending to what others may think. In other words, Cicero's collecting has a clear social orientation and shares the view that the house (the space, the arrangement of it) defines the man (*De Officiis* 1.138-139) (Conte, 1994b: 197-198).

We then come to the second value, *utilitas*. The works of art Cicero assembled were more than appropriate for their setting. They also served the purpose of creating and promoting an identity for their owner, of enhancing his image. Cicero spoke of the utility of art in order to manifest the relation between beauty and function. Again it is a notion originating in Greek ethical philosophical thought. Panaetius, and before him, Socrates and Aristotle, had already connected the beautiful with the useful (Xen., *Mem.* III.8.4ff; Arist., *De part. an.*, I.1, 639b, 19; 5, 645a, 22ff) (Svoboda, 1960: 111). Cicero follows their tradition but transforms it, so that he creates his own rich and complex system of aesthetic ideas, which although neither fixed nor original, does fit into the Roman reality (Desmouliez, 1976, where an extensive discussion on the term).

The list of statues that Atticus had bought for Cicero is indicative of this view. Atticus sent a Hermathena (double bust of Minerva and Hermes, made of Pentelic marble with bronze heads). The object met the most unreserved approval and satisfaction, expressed more than once (10.5; 9.3). Cicero found the object appropriate both for his Academy and for himself: 'Hermes is the common emblem of all such places and Minerva special to me' (*Hermes commune est omnium et Minerva singulare est insigne eius gymnasi*) (9.3). Atticus and Cicero knew that the Athenian Academy had a sanctuary of Minerva in it, one of the tutelary deities of the place. This, along with the philosophical connotations of Minerva as goddess of wisdom, is seen to fit well into Cicero's views about what constitutes an object γυμνασιῶδες and what is appropriate as a personal symbol. Similarly, the promise of Atticus to send him a Heracles herm[29] is accepted with enthusiasm (9.3). In *Brutus* 24, we also learn about a statue of Plato that Cicero possessed, although it is unclear whether this was part of his Tusculan collection, or of another of his villas (see also Valenti, 1936: 265).[30] Gallus' purchases, on the contrary, are rejected exactly on the same grounds: besides their price, which is the polite excuse Cicero uses to refuse the acquisitions, the rejection is based on their inappropriateness: they are statues of Bacchantes and of Mars. The orator finds them totally unbecoming for the environment he wants to create around him, and the image of himself he wants to promote: Bacchantes, which Gallus compared with Mettelus' Muses, had no place in a household devoted to literary pursuits - although the Muses could have been appropriate for the decoration of his library. As for the statue of Mars, Cicero cannot see where such a figure can stand in the house of an author of peace (*auctor paucis*).

The attempt to create evocative spaces in a villa is quite typical, as excavated material and literary evidence came to show. Atticus, for instance, shared his friend's collecting paradigm and created an Amaltheium in his house (I.16). Cicero asked Atticus for a description of the place, as well as for poems and tales about Amaltheia, in order to decide whether it would have been 'appropriate' for his public *persona* to create one at his villa at Arpinum, something which he later did, as we find out in other letters of the series (II.1.11; II.7.8) (Lafon, 1981: 165-167; Neudecker, 1988: 9-11; Grimal, 1969: 302-304). Varro earlier had created a *musaeum* in his villa (Varro, *R.R.*, III.5.9).[31] The term refers to a sanctuary devoted to the Muses, as was already common in the Greek world (for instance, see Pausanias, 9.27ff about the first 'Museum' in Helicon, Boetia).[32] The exact arrangement of these 'museums' is not clear, and the presence of an actual temple in them is highly doubtful. In Plato's Academy there was an altar devoted to the Muses (Pausanias, 1.30.2), and in Aristotle's Lyceum there was a Museum (μουσεῖον), probably a small temple; Theophrastus was concerned about it and left instructions to his successors to finish its rebuilding, and to make sure that a bust of Aristotle was installed in it, together with all the other offerings (ἀναθήματα) that were there before the destruction (Diogenes Laertius, V.51). The Alexandrian Museum was, after all, an intellectual construction of the Peripatetics. It has been argued that since the very first 'museums' were mainly open-air sanctuaries discernable as such only because of the offerings that decorated them, their transition to the Renaissance and modern museums was much facilitated, since the term was used to denote not primarily a temple, but mainly a collection of works of art and relics set aside in a sacred garden or grove consecrated by the presence of the divine Muses (Roux, 1954: 45). In any case, this Greek type influenced the arrangement of the Roman gardens, where intellectuals and upper class Romans used to enjoy their role and importance as successors of their famous Greek predecessors. The objects these amateurs displayed in their gardens assimilated the arrangment in the Greek μουσεῖα, by hosting statues, portraits of famous personages, and so on.[33]

The finds from the villa of the Papyri is another example of a decorative arrangement by the owner (Calpurnius Piso) to exeplify the Epicurean ideals (Sauron, 1980). Sperlonga is also an example of the transformation of a grotto into a landscape of heroic mythology (Marvin, 1989: 33; Stewart, 1977). In the Palatin there was a *Hermaeum* where emperor Claudius sought refuge (Suetonius, *Claudius,* X). Finally, the villa of Hadrian at Tivoli, in the second century CE, also used sculpture in architectural settings to elicit a special world for the visitor. These decorative programmes are centred around the parts of the Roman house that would be accessible to the public, and thus allow for the public image to be created: 'lieux de promenade (portiques-jardins) [et] lieux de travail intellectuel au sens large, comme les *musaeum* connus chez Varron et Cicéron, bibliothèques et éventuellement salles d'exposition de collection, comme les pinacothèques dont l'usage était devenu canonique des Auguste' (Lafon, 1981: 157-158). These were appropriations of Greek building types, very common during the Roman era. The Greek institutions, reworked during the Roman period, were meant to satisfy practical needs, and were associated with a whole set of connotations. They were not simply architectural types, they had become architectural symbols that connoted philosophical and intellectual rationale. In this sense, they formed the context for a lifestyle for the Roman elite, which was elevated in intellectual terms. This process is very similar to the one noted when the first museums were built; they were constructed in the shape and form of their ancient equivalents as these were understood, the Greek and Roman temples.

The dichotomy between private and public makes its appearance quite often when discussing collections and collecting. The most common approach is the one that criticises private collections as inappropriate and individualistic, collections can be, and are, used to benefit the individual rather than the public, considered to be the 'right' thing to do (see discussion in other case-studies). Behind these concerns, of course, lie political considerations, which have to do with the power that the possession and acquisition of works of art entail (see Bourdieu, 1974). Cicero himself, in *Tusculan Disputations*, V.101-102, discusses briefly this part of the idea, with the argument that it is the public collections that benefit everybody, and that they are much more important and valuable than the private ones; the public collections are set to balance the inequality of poor and rich, by providing to the latter access to something continually acknowledged as a source of pleasure.

The notions of private and public are brought to the forefront again when the discussion goes to Cicero's own collection and rationale. Although the country-villa, which was the collection's destination, was the backdrop of the world of *otium*, the very counterpart of the *negotium* which expressed the public duties and responsibilities, no Roman involved in public life could claim complete privacy there.[34] Vitruvius highlighted the social role of the Roman house, when he insisted on the different domestic and architectural needs of each class. Private houses therefore were designed with the public in mind, and Roman domestic architecture was a statement of social status (Leen, 1991: 243-245). Instead of being a strictly private space, as we more or less consider the house today, the Roman dwelling was a microcosm in itself, and contained both private and public spaces. They were arranged in architectural terms so that one space followed the other and thus allowed for a gradual progression from the public to the private domain. Yet the axial arrangement gave a certain public access deep into the house (Stambaugh, 1988: 164).[35] In Elsner's (1995: 60) words: '(the Roman house) was both a vital constituent of the Roman social world (in standing for "private space" and thereby establishing the opposition with "public" space), and at the same time, it was a central cultural mechanism for negotiating the very distinction of "public" and "private" (which it in part was responsible for setting up).'

Cicero in the *De Oratore*, I.161-162, presents a discussion about a visit to a Roman house:

> ... as though I had entered some richly stored mansion, wherein the draperies were not unrolled, nor the plate set forth, nor the pictures and statuary displayed but all these many and splendid things were piled together and hidden away ...

Obviously, visitors expected to see these objects displayed in front of them, for their honour. The dialogue continues with a suggestion:

> ... why not do then, ... , as you would do, if you had come to some mansion or country-house that was full of objects of art? If these were laid aside, as you describe, and you had a strong desire to behold them, you would not hesitate to ask the master of the house to order them to be brought out, especially if you were his familiar friend.[36]

In a home where visitors were expected, or allowed, to scrutinise every detail during their visit, as Cicero suggests, the painted decoration, and the architectonic and statuary embellishment, as well as any other display of artefacts, must have enjoyed an enormous importance (see Leach, 1988; Wallace-Hadrill, 1994). The collection of artefacts within the Roman house, therefore, must have been an act of negotiation between the very distinction of private and public. In other words, choosing what was appropriate for the decoration of someone's house, and placing it in the appropriate setting, was equivalent to setting boundaries and defining the private and the public space in that house. Collections, in other words, together with their painted equivalents,[37] were means of defining space.

No one seemed to understand this better than Cicero. Although all the Romans, as well as the ancient Greeks, could appreciate complex cultural messages of this sort (see for instance, the political exhibitions of art decorating the temples in Greece), Cicero and the other Roman orators seem to have one more reason for developing such a sensitivity to allowing objects to define their space. Their awareness of a topographical sense of flow in architectural space led them to use it in the most remarkable way as a mnemotechnic tool to structure the way they memorised their speeches. According to Quintilian (*Instit. Orat.* II.2.18-20) and Cicero (*De Oratore*, 2.86.351-88.360),[38] the house, the *locus*, and the images created within it, statues and objects included, could be used by the orator to elicit an emotional reaction, but also to make a link with large and complex ideas. The *ars memoriae*, therefore, provides a theoretical link between the attempt to create images in the minds of the listeners and the technique to attach symbolic values to those images (Vasaly, 1993: 101; see also discussion in Chapter 5). This line of thought makes the decoration and arrangement of a house an issue of careful planning and consideration, and indicates a clear relationship between space and men. From this point of view, it is interesting to note the common description of memory as a 'treasure-house'. If we leave aside the obvious connection of memory with a store-room where memories, personal treasures, are kept, the comparison becomes even more important: memory is a treasure-house, in the sense that we can recall any narrative, by simply following around the objects held in our treasure-house; in other words, a treasure-house is, and can be, our memory.

The phenomenon of decorating private space in order to evoke a series of feelings and ideas is not confined merely to the Roman era. Even in the contemporary world, where the idea of privacy seems to enjoy enormous appreciation and is protected by law, people tend to decorate their private spaces, like the public ones, in order to convey messages about their identities, their beliefs, the social, economic or other status they enjoy or have claims to. Visitors form a view about the inhabitants of a house, according to the 'decoration' (*ornamenta*), the artefacts they have chosen to surround themselves. Collections are consciously or unconsciously used to make an impression upon others; in this sense, they are intended to play a public role in a private setting, and thus make a statement towards a wider group of peers, friends, or family. They allow for the domestic space to be defined (and domesticated); and finally, they help to shape the notions of privacy and public access. Viewed from this perspective, collections are grounded, in every sense, in their 'capacity to place objects into significant spatial relationships' (Pearce, 1995: 258, 270).

Although there is no doubt that Cicero's choices about his collection were directed by a consciously and carefully prepared plan, his letters allow for a more personal characteristic to emerge as well; its presence might affect the formality that compliance to a decorative programme can imply. Cicero was prepared to pay 20,400 sesterces for Megarian statues, which Atticus had purchased for him (*signa Megaricis*) (3; 4.2).[39] The term itself, unaccompanied by any further description, has been found rather confusing: Megara was never celebrated particularly for its artistic production, although it is the provenance of a fine quality dark-coloured marble. It has been suggested that the statues were antiques bought at Megara (Marvin, 1989: 31). In any case, Cicero was prepared to pay a high price for them, in contrast to what he was protesting a few years earlier during Verres' trial.

In another letter (5.2), he urges Atticus to spare no expense in order to buy the objects he requires, since his '*voluptas*' (pleasure, satisfaction, desire) (5.2) makes him indifferent to the cost. These views come to confirm, in his own words, the testimony of Pliny[40] (*HN*, 13.91). So do the words '*delectatio*' (*admodum delectant*) (4.2; 7.3; 10.5) and '*studium*' (7.3; 4.2), associated with collections and collectors in the *Verrines* already, although the references had not always meant to be positive there. Similar words accompany Cicero's request to buy Atticus' library: books also bring '*delectatio*' (3), they are a 'stand-by for the old age' (6.4) (*subsidium senectuti*), and provide wealth beyond that of Crassus (9.3) (*supero Crassum divitiis*). The same library is called a treasure house (*thesauris*) in another letter, dated on 44 BCE (XV.27). Finally, in his epistle to F. Gallus, Cicero reveals that 'if anything of that sort gives me any pleasure at all, it is painting' (*etenim, si quid generis istius modi me delectat, pictura delectat*) (VII.23). Consequently, it becomes clear that Cicero was not completely alien to many of the collecting 'flaws' he had attributed to Verres and other collectors. Nevertheless, these seem to lose their disadvantageous character, since now they are put into the service of an intellectual rationale that defined the formation of the collection; so the 'passion' has been put into the service of *logos*, and thus justified.

Cicero is one of the most reliable sources about the art market in Rome.[41] Martial's epigrams inform us of the location of the actual art market of the city of Rome, in the portico of Saepta Julia: there connoisseurs and collectors assembled in order to acquire the objects of their desire (II.14; IX.59). But the supply of art and antiques for an art market presupposes the presence of art dealers who undertake the responsibility of locating, transporting, and selling the artefacts. Information about these people is available also in the ancient literary sources. Atticus offers his services to Cicero on a friendly base. He actually locates and purchases for his friend objects that meet with his own approval, as a man of taste, and with his friend's requirements in mind. Then he arranges for these to be transferred to Rome, to their final destination. So does F. Gallus, another one of Cicero's agents. The most common way of transferring the artefacts would be by sea. Cicero mentions Lentulus as the person who would undertake the transportation (about his identity see Coarelli, 1983: 45-46).

Direct testimony about these transportations and the routes of the art trade are available from the archaeological remains. Ship-wrecks on the seabed of the Mediterranean have been very valuable in determining these routes, as well as aspects of the Roman taste. Among the most well-known wrecks that provide information on the art trade are those of Madhia, that dates from approximately 86 BCE, and Antikythera (c. 80-70 BCE), the first testifying to a trade from Athens, the second to one from Delos.[42] Examples of similar cases are the Riace warriors, found in Sicily (1972), and the discovery at Piraeus in 1959 of a quantity of works possibly part of the booty of Sylla ready to be transferred to Italy. The intermediaries in this art trade, however, were not only friends. They were also specially employed agents, like the ones Verres had hired, or the more decent Damassipus whom both Cicero and Horace mention (Horace, *Satires*, II.3.18). The trade also supported a range of other professionals, among whom were conservators, like C. Avianus Evander mentioned by Cicero (*ad Famil.* XII.2; XIII.23), and fakers, like those named by Martial (IV.88; VIII.34).

The prices of works of art that writers record for us also indicate not only their importance, but also the folly of collectors (this is the context where these are usually presented), as well as the prosperity of the market. Cicero often refers to prices, either to suggest that the ones Verres paid to his victims as compensation were ridiculous, in which case he expects the judges to understand and appreciate this as an argument, or in order to express his desire for his own objects, in which case he urges Atticus to acquire them without sparing any money. Pliny is also an important source for learning about enormous prices, again in order to suggest the false values people of his era, and collectors in particular, appreciate. From Pliny, for instance, we learn that Attalus offered 100,000 denarii for the picture of Father Liber by Aristides, and thus made Mummius interested in the value of works of art (35.24); that Agrippa bought two pictures for the sum of 1,200,000 sesterces (35.26); that Alexander paid Apelles 20 talents of gold for his work (35.92); that Hortensius paid 144,000 sesterces for the *Argonautica* of Cydias, and so on (other examples in 35.98; 100; 107; 125; 131; 136; 156; 163; 24.39; 45; 195 etc.).

Cicero in his private correspondence reveals a collecting paradigm very closely resembling the 'good collecting' described in the *Verrines*, in opposition to Verres' 'bad' collecting. It is a rational attitude toward works of art, whose importance is acknowledged in terms of signifying cultural and intellectual aspirations, as well as social characteristics. In addition, the value of material culture as defining power of human identity is acknowledged. Cicero organises his space so that it evokes a refined individual with intellectual pursuits. His collection's power relies on its capacity to place objects into significant spatial relationships, which define space and shape notions of privacy and public access. Moreover, it has the capacity to define the individual in question and place him within a broader community of peers. Therefore, Cicero's collection remains the same in both texts and there is no 'gap' or contradiction, as it has been usually assumed. The ideal collection Cicero advocates in the *Verrines* is the one he assembles in his *Epistulae*: it is a collection shaped by *decor* (appropriateness) and utility, virtuous and appropriately acquired through purchase. The ethical value of the collector is illustrated through his collection, exactly as the opposite was displayed in the *Verrines* with the ex-governor.

Cicero is representative of a category of collectors, for whom the objects were not important for themselves, as they were in the case of Verres (Desmouliez, 1976, argues that Verres was interested in the 'intrinsic quality' of the objects). This category appreciated collecting for its social and political function, together with its moral (in a philosophical sense) and intellectual significance. Their tastes, as Cicero's, were eclectic, and determined by philosophical ideas and the influence of classical and rhetorical education. Preisshofen (1978) suggests that the aesthetic judgements of Cicero are based on rhetoric schemas and classicistic theories, which had been developed since the second century BCE; these theories rejected the ancient criteria of artistic form *(diligentia* and *symmetria)* and replaced them with moral criteria *(decor, auctoritas, pulchritudo).* This collecting category was not interested in the qualities the 'passionate' collectors appreciated. The main difference between these two collecting modes is neither the objects they were collecting, nor the prices they were prepared to pay, or even the social prestige that collectors were trying to accumulate through their collections. The main difference is the intellectual rationale which exists behind the latter category, and the lack of one behind the former.

Cicero represents the 'intellectual' collectors, who introduced new notions: collecting as *dignitas*, as *humanitas*, as *nobilitas* and as *virtus. Dignitas* is related to the worthiness that collecting added to the collectors; *virtus* is related to the excellence of mind associated with a preoccupation with such activities; *nobilitas* expresses the superior quality which was expected by the collectors; *humanitas,* finally, embodies that Roman amalgam of kindness and culture, width of mind and tact of manner (Chevallier, 1991). Cicero personified this kind of collecting, which belongs to the cultural model he had envisioned for his contemporaries, and which although conservative (in the sense that all the above mentioned values are aristocratic in origin) conforms with the changes taking place in the rapidly changing world of the end of the Republic and the beginning of the Empire; collecting not only is seen as part of this world, but also seems to have been appreciated for its power of defining this world.

Conclusions

Cicero and Verres provide two examples of the collecting paradigms prominent in the late Roman Republic.[43] Although largely exaggerated due to the rhetorical purpose of the *Verrine Orations*, there is no doubt that the two portraits correspond quite well with the growing tendencies of the Roman aristocrats toward material culture. Verres as an example of a 'bad' collector, concentrates in his person characteristics and attitudes that have been traditionally associated with the individualistic, sterile, and largely animistic relation to material culture. It is interesting to note that his collecting motive is described by Cicero as being a passion for works of art. This is based not on rational criteria, such as conforming to the social role expected from a man in his rank, and attempting to promote his personality and culture through art (as was the case with Cicero himself) but on a blind love for everything beautiful and ancient. In addition to him being uncultivated, unorthodox in his methods, and irrationally predisposed against objects, or rather, exactly because of this, Verres is compared to tyrants, and even to perverted philanderers. There is a long tradition that views the personality of collectors of the passionate kind, unfolding within exactly these boundaries: unconsummated passion, leading to inadequate social relations, based upon the objects themselves; the insatiable desire for objects finds an equivalent in an insatiable desire for women, and completes the model of the socially handicapped person. This model extends from the antique world, as our discussion has shown, to contemporary views of collecting in popular fiction and literature (Edgar, 1997; Wilkinson, 1997). It is not that Verres was uninterested in his public image. It was that the public image he wanted to create for himself, that of the connoisseur, was incorrectly perceived; not that his practice was differed greatly from that of his contemporaries (although Cicero tries hard to prove the opposite), but it was endowed with a set of values that were too selfish and individualistic to be appreciated.

Verres behaviour towards material culture resembles very much that of female collectors, as all four writers have described it. Women's relation to material culture is structured around the traditional female stereotypes. According to these, women can be associated with the domestic environment, the female domain, and the adornments of the house, or religious practices and the objects that are used for these. In this case, they conform with the stereotype of the pious and respectful Roman matron, who is interested in the welfare of her household, and thus fulfills the desired model for a woman. In Petronius' *Satyrica*, for instance, Fortunata tries, in vain, to persuade the participants in her husband's banquet, and the readers, that she is a typical noble Roman matron (73.20-24). Similarly, Cicero tries to win the sympathy of his audience by presenting exactly this picture of the good and honourable women of Sicily, who know their position in society, and they develop relations with their material culture based on the objects being parts of religious ceremonies, part of the domestic decoration and inheritance from their relatives (II.4.44-52); these may not make sense to rational Roman judges, but still provide recognisable and respectable models. The second stereotype that associates women with material culture, is the one that refers to objects of personal adornment. Material acquisitions of this category, mainly jewellery, offer the model of the woman as a frivolous, vain, time-wasting person, unconcerned with the civic life, who instead presents a danger to society, since personal adornment of this sort aims at men's seduction, and the making of biased decisions. The women that Pliny presents, Lollia Paulina and Cleopatra, belong to this category (HN, 9.117-121; also 33.40; 34.11-12; 37.29; 13.91-95), and so does Gellia in Martial's epigram (VIII.81). In Martial also we come across a comparison of beauty practices applied by women with connoisseurship (Lycoris follows the same practice for the beauty of her skin that the connoisseurs use for whitening objects of ivory - VII.13).

The use of both these stereotypes implies an unnatural and irrational relation to material culture, and thus aims to alert the male readers of the dangers involved in such behaviour. Firstly, women are expected to be more passionate and irrational when it comes to acquiring personal property (as, for instance, Eriphyle, the mythic queen, was), and therefore, passionate collecting can be related to behaviour appropriate for women. Secondly, just like the wrong sort of attention to his appearance is considered to undermine man's status as a male and exposes him to the charges of effeminacy (Wyke, 1994), so does interest in 'things female'. In this sense, collections that belong to the household, silverware, statuettes, furniture, and so on, along with objects that traditionally belong to the adornment of women, like jewellery, rings, etc., are meant to imply a man's unorthodox behaviour, that exceeds what is appropriately male, and thus puts at risk his male identity. Interest in them therefore can be considered a sign of effeminacy, and therefore degeneracy. Pliny declares this view in his words 'the tablemania which the ladies use as a retort to the men against the charge of extravagance in pearls' (13.91-95). Finally, women's collecting that we have seen so far relates to the private domain rather than the public (although the presence of female public benefactors is attested to in the literary sources - see, for instance, Fischler, 1994; Van Bremen, 1993; Kleiner, 1996), and therefore, 'private' and passionate collecting is expected to bring feminine behaviour to mind.

Cicero, on the contrary, in the *Verrines* as well as in his correspondence and other parts of his work, presents the other end of the collecting spectrum. He conforms to the social role he has adopted for himself, complies with the social and cultural expectations his position entails, and practices collecting as an activity based on a clearly planned rationale, that views material culture as a medium for creating and extending one's self. Interestingly, it is exactly on this belief that he bases his criticisms of Verres when charging him with the thefts of works of art. It is not collecting *per se* that he finds distressing and reprehensible, it is the kind of self that is expressed through that particular practice, that particular collection of which he disapproves. In his view, the way an individual relates to his material culture, that is the poetics of collecting, reveals the personality of the man: his social, personal, and political aspirations. For this reason, his collection is a carefully planned manifestation of his social and other aspirations and beliefs. Collections should be rational, he professes, should respect the religious and patriotic character of Rome, be appropriate and useful, and display a connoisseurship that goes beyond the mere appreciation of appearances, to a profoundly philosophical appreciation of art, to *humanitas*. Objects have to be conceived within a context, a meaningful Roman context, that will empower the viewer, the visitor, and the collector himself to domesticate, to make sense of the values (his) collecting advocated. Collections, therefore, are meant to be used as a medium of allocating use of space, of differentiating between notions of public and private, and of structuring the collector's relationship with his immediate world. In addition, space and its decoration are for the Romans an *aide-memoire*. In this sense, collections are also part of the attempt to structure memory; we have here the basis of the operation of collecting as souvenir (Stewart, 1993; Pearce, 1995).

In the case of Verres and Cicero therefore, we reach an epitome of the nature of classical collecting; collections can be and are used to help their owners structure their identity, memory, past and future, they are indications of power and wealth, they are media of communication with the sacred domain, they are definitions of space use and means of appropriating spatial and temporal distance. But they can also be carriers of negative meaning, when their role is misunderstood and their power unduly used. Unconventional, unlawful, and destructive methods of acquisition, as well as associations that emphasise individuality and egotism above communal ideals and compliance with human-defined valuations, which are nature-oriented, humanistic and carry sacred connotations, are to be condemned. In a surprisingly modern manner, collections acquire their supreme power in the right place, defined as the public, sacred, or semi-sacred realm, where memories of individuals blend to provide identity for communities at a 'national', or 'international' level - a description remarkably equivalent to that of the 'museum'. The dichotomy between collectors and 'museums' thus has been firmly founded in the Graeco-Roman past, and its legacy defines many aspects of museum work and thought today.

Notes

1   Translated by H. Morgan, in *Vitruvius: Ten Books on Architecture*, New York: Dover Publications Inc., 1960.
2   Marcus Tullius Cicero was born at Arpinum in 106 BCE; he was the son of an equestrian family and received a good education in rhetoric and philosophy at Rome.

He had as his teachers L. Licinius Crassus and the two Scaevolas. There he also formed a friendship with Titus Pomponius Atticus that was to last all his life. He made his debut as a pleader in 81. In 80 he defended Sextus Roscius, a case that brought him into conflict with the Sullan regime. Because of these troubles, he had to leave Rome; consequently, he travelled to Greece and Asia, between 79 and 77. There he studied rhetoric under Molon of Rhodes. In 75 he was quaestor of Sicily, and in 70 he undertook the prosecution of Verres, the ex-governor of the province. He was aedile in 69, praetor in 66, and consul in 63, when he suppressed the conspiracy of Catiline. In 58 he was accused of having put to death without trial Catiline's accomplices, and he went into exile. He was recalled in Rome in 57, and during 56 and 51 he attempted to collaborate with the triumphirs, although without much success. During this period he composed the *De Oratore*, the *De Republica* and began working on the *De Legibus*. In 51 he was governor of Cilicia. During the civil war he joined the side of Pompey. After Pompey's defeat he obtained pardon from Caesar. In 46 he wrote the *Brutus* and the *Orator*. In 45 his daughter Tullia died. While Caesar's domination kept him removed from public affairs he composed a long series of philosophical works. He returned to political life in 44 after the death of Caesar, and attempted a fierce confrontation of Antony (the *Philippics*). When Antony joined the second triumphirate, Cicero was proscribed and was slain by Antony's assassins in December 43 (From a vast bibliography devoted on the different aspects of the life of Cicero see: Conte, 1994b: 175; Peterson, 1920; Mitchell, 1991; Rawson, 1994; Shackleton Bailey, 1971; Habicht, 1990; see also *Plutarch's Life of Cicero*, translated by J. L. Moles, 1988).

3   C.Verres was born at the end of the second century BCE (121/2, or 151, or 115 BCE, according to different scholars), when luxury had already invaded Rome and established a new way of life (Bonnafé, 1867: 9-10). He was the son of a senator, and he was soon involved in the overcrowded and highly competitive world of Roman politics himself. He begun his political life as a suppporter of the Cinnan regime. He became a quaestor in 84 and he served under the consul Cn. Papirius Carbo. He joined Sulla in 83, and after the latter's victory he was rewarded with lands in Beneventum. He became a legate to the governor of Cilicia, Cn. Dolabella, in 80 BCE, then urban praetor in 74 BCE, and finally, propraetor in Sicily in 73-70 BCE. Verres also succeeded in gaining the friendship of a number of leading nobles. Foremost among them were the celebrated orator Q. Hortensius and the three brothers of the powerful Metellan clan, Quintus, Marcus and Lucius. Furthermore, Verres accumulated sufficient wealth to allow full exploitation of his expertise in political bribery and machination. Cicero implied more than once that his friends' support was sustained by bribes. Such collaboration with the powerful was typical of Verres' political life, and his opportunism, combined with effective use of his wealth had brought him a place of considerable prominence and influence in Roman politics (Bieber, 1977; Mitchell, 1991: 5-6, and Peterson, 1920; for a detailed biography of Verres see Cowles, 1917).

4   There is a debate about the actual delivery of a defence speech by Hortensius, with some scholars denying it in view of information presented by other writers and Cicero himself, whereas some others believe that Hortensius did defend his client, although not successfully. It is generally agreed though that it is a great misfortune that we have only one side of the story intact. For a detailed review of both sides, and support of the latter, see Alexander, 1976.

5   For a detailed account of Cicero's profits from publishing the second speech see Peterson, 1920: 142, and May, 1988.

6   The translated phrases and words that are quoted throughout this part are from the Loeb edition of the *Verrine Orations*, translated by Greenwood (1948/1953).

7   Similar events are recorded in a number of passages: in II.1.57 Cicero refers to the triumph of P. Servilius, in II.4.6 in the aedilship of C. Claudius Pulcher, in II.4.126 in the statues and ornaments of the Temple of Felicitas, the temple of Fortuna, the Porticus Metelli, the villas of Verres' friends and the shows of *aediles*, in II.4.133 to the aedilships of L. Crassus, Q. Scaevola, G. Claudius.

8   The events are dated in 212 BCE, 194 BCE, 190 BCE, 168 BCE, and 146 BCE, respectively. For the plundering that took place during these events see Pape, 1975.

9   For a discussion of the practices of Roman collecting and methods of documentation, see Strong, 1975.

10   For this see May, 1988.

11   The argument of purchase is often used by Cicero; it has been suggested that it must have been an argument made by Hortensius when he presented his side of the story; it is also used as an argument to support that such a speech was actually delivered by Hortensius, and that he did not desert his client and friend. See note 4 here, and Alexander, 1976.

12   The 'temple treasures' in the works of Cicero are discussed in detail in Griffiths, 1943.

13   Wallace-Hadril (1994) discusses this paragraph in chapter 7 of his book; also see pp. 289-290 here.

14   For the *sacrarium* of Heius, its reconstruction and the statues involved see Zimmer, 1989.

15   When describing the sites and collections Verres stripped of precious artefacts, it is mentioned always that these had been visited by all Romans travelling abroad before. We have come across a practice of cultural tourism here, already known from other sources, Pliny and Pausanias in particular. In paragraph II.4.132 he refers to the 'mystagogues' of the temples, who were available to guide visitors around the sanctuary and display the precious offerings, very much like modern guides in museums. Elsewhere, when describing the *sacrarium* of Heius, he refers to the fact that it was open every day for visitors, and that all governors of the island had at some point visited it. The same assumption is made for other sights worth visiting in the island, as for instance the sanctuary of Ceres at Henna (II.4.109). The famous Cupid of Thespies is mentioned also as the only reason that makes a visit to the city worth undertaking.

16   Cicero provides ample information on the art market in Rome through his books; not only in the *Verrines*, but also when corresponding with Atticus about his commissions, he seems to be well informed and quite familiar with the art market practices of his era. For more information of the subject see Coarelli, 1983; and the articles on the Madhia ship wreck in Hellenkemper Sallies, G. (ed), 1994.

17   Elsewhere too in his private correspondence Cicero argues that no price is expensive if somebody wants something (see Carcopino, 1969).

18   'and there has been a wonderful mania among many people for possessing this metal - in fact it is recorded that Verres, whose conviction Marcus Cicero had procured was, together with Cicero, proscribed by Antony for no other reason than because he had refused to give up to Antony some pieces of Corinthian ware'; Pliny, *HN*, 34.6-8 (translated by Rackham, 1952).

19   For the collector as a philanderer and the sexual connotations of collecting, see Edgar, 1997 and Forrester, 1994.

20   The notion of assembling the likenesses of old rulers, philosophers, and so on, is also exemplified in the 'collections' of Varro and Atticus, who had created a corpus of likenesses; it is the same rationale that led to the creation of the picture and bust galleries from the Renaissance, see also Chapter 2 on antiquarianism.

21   The validity of such a claim has been the subject of the most fierce debate regarding Cicero's aesthetic appreciation. Whichever position we take, there is no doubt that in

the *Verrines* Cicero pretends to be more ignorant than he actually is. He must had had some kind of art education, even if he did not have a profound understanding of Greek art. In other parts of his work some interest and knowledge of art becomes evident: for example, *Brutus*, 70, 75, 228, 257; *Orator*, 5; *De Oratore*, III.195; *De Officiis*, III.15. The fact that in the *Verrines* he pretends to be ignorant for rhetorical reasons becomes even more evident when we compare his assertions with similar ones as for instance in *De Oratore*, II.56, where there is the pretence that the speaker cannot quite understand what is written in Greek.

22   Quite frequently, Cicero leaves for what could be considered as connoisseurship to interfere in his work: small tips, or comparisons, during his speeches and dialogues, betray Cicero's, and his audience's, familiarity with the world of connoisseurship: for instance, in *Brutus*, 261, the right embellishments for the oratorical style are compared with the effect one has when placing a well-painted picture in a good light. Or, in the same book, paragraph 320, Hortensius' development was compared to the slow fading of the colours in an old picture. In *Tusculan Disputations*, IV.32, gifted men are compared to Corinthian bronze which is slow to be attacked by rust, whereas in the *De Oratore*, III.98, the old and the new pictures are compared in terms of attractiveness and the offering of pleasure.

23   There is no agreement in the sources about the material of the sphinx Verres gave to Hortensius; nevertheless, the gift is recorded in many ancient authors: Pliny, *HN*, XXIV.xviii.47-48; Plutarch, *Cicero*, 7.8; Plutarch, *Moralia*, 205b; Quintilien, *Inst. Orat.* 6.3.98; also see Alexander, 1976: 50-51 with discussion.

24   109-32 BCE; for an ancient biography of Atticus, see also Cornelius Nepos, *Atticus*. See also Feger, in *RE*, 1956: 503-547.

25   Together with the text of Petronius on Trimalchio; see, for example, Leach, 1988, Wallace-Hadrill, 1994.

26   Although there are discussions of Cicero as a collector, see Valenti, 1936.

27   The word οἰκεῖον is used as a synonymous for πρέπον by both rhetoricians and literary critics. See for instance, Aristotle *Poet.* 3.7.4, and Demetrius, *Eloc.* 114.

28   Shackleton Bailey (1965) translates the word γυμνασιώδη as appropriate for a 'lecture-hall'; clearly, Cicero does not mean a lecture-hall, but a gymnasium, after the Greek building type.

29   'Herm' is the archaeological term used for this particular type of quadrangular shaft surmounted by a sculptured head (Pollitt, 1974: 76, nt. 138).

30   In the *Orator* 110, there is a reference to a bronze statue of Demosthenes held in a Tusculan villa, most probably that of Cicero's brother Quintus. Also in a letter to Atticus (4.10), Cicero expresses the wish to have been able to be in his friend's house, which is denoted with the phrase 'in that niche of yours under Aristotle's statue', an indication of space decorated with a work of art appropriate for both men. It is interesting that the little corner is a connotation for the whole house.

31   *'Qu<o>i ego, Cum habeam sub oppido Casino flumen, quod per villam fluat, liquidum et altum marginibus lapideis, latum pedes quinquaginta septem, et e villa in villam pontibus transeatur, longum pedes DCCCCL derectum ab insula [ad musaeum], quae est in imo fluvio, ubi confluit altera amnis, ad summum flumen, ubi est mus[a]eum, circum huius ripas ambulatio sub dio pedes lata denos, ab hac [ambulatio] est in argum versus ornithonis locus ex duabus partibus dextra et sinistra maceriis altis conclusus.'* (Varro, *Rerum Rusticarum*, III.5.9 - Teubner edn).

32   For a very detailed presentation of the ancient sources referring to the Greek μουσεῖα, and the genealogy of the museum in the ancient world, see Oberhummer, 1933.

33   A more detailed discussion of the role and form of those early museums, as well as of their influence in the creation of the institution of the museum, will be pursued further by the author in a short article.

34 For *otium* and *negotium*, see Dangel, 1996 and André, 1996.
35 For the ancient sources testifying the axial arrangement of the Roman house, see Stambaugh, 1988: 360, nt. 15: Livy, 6.25.9; Suet. *Augustus*, 45.4; Martial, 1.70.13-14 and so on.
36 Translated by Rackham, 1942, in Loeb CL.
37 I refer to the decoration that resembles *pinacothecae*, which were modelled on them; see also Chapter 8.
38 Also in *Auctor ad Herrenium*, 3.15.27-3.24.40; the work is now considered falsely attributed to Cicero.
39 As a general indication of value we may refer the example cited by Varro (*R.R.*. 3.2.15), who claims that a farm of two hundred iugera (about 130 acres) should produce an annual income of about HS 30,000; see also Marvin, 1989: 44, nt.18 and Pensabene, 1983.
40 '*There still exists a table that belonged to Marcus Cicero for which with his slender resources and, what is more surprising, at that date he paid half-a-million sesterces;*' Pliny, *HN*, XIII.91 (translated by Rackham, 1945, Loeb CL).
41 With the term 'art market' we mean the purchase and sale of works of art and antiques; we include neither the market for primary materials for artists, like marble, bronze, etc, nor the workshops of artists, where patrons could place their orders.
42 For the Madhia wreck, see, for instance, Fuchs, 1963; Hellenkemper Sallies, 1994; about the Antikythera wreck, see Weinberg, *et al.*, 1965; Bol, 1972.
43 For a brief discussion of Cicero and Verres as expressing two different modes of collecting in the antique world, see Zimmer, 1994: unfortunately his article does not deal with the subject in depth.

Conclusions

Illuminating the genesis, meaning, and limitations of ideas in their own time, we might better understand the implications and significance of our own affinities for them in our own time. (Schorske, 1985: xxv).

I suggest that research into the deep origins of this strange and pervasive creature of human societies - the museum - is the most critical museum research today. To undertake this task there must be new perspectives and priorities in museology. (Cameron, 1995: 48).

This book set out to explore the nature of classical collecting as this is revealed through the literary sources that record contemporary perceptions and interpretations of the phenomenon. The limitations posed by the chronological distance between our enquiry and the Latin writers used as data, along with the textual character of the sources, and their use as a form of historical evidence instead of as literary attempts, were recognised and carefully taken into consideration. Thus we aimed to reach an insight into the classical world, which although not devoid of modern misconceptions and prejudices, would allow for a set of valid conclusions to be drawn regarding our subject.

The discussion was structured around four parameters that relate directly to collecting and define its character: the notion of the past and the role of material culture as a mediator between people and their perception of it; the gift-exchange as a social tradition with deep anthropological roots, that structures relations between people, people and God(s), and people and the material world; the notion of identity at a communal and individual level and the capacity of objects to shape and structure it; and, finally, the notions of time and space, whose understanding and appreciation requires the mediation of material culture. The discussion of each of those parameters comes together in the four chapters on the Latin authors, Gaius Plinius Secundus, M. Valerius Martialis, T. Petronius Arbiter and M. Tullius Cicero.

Antiquity appears as a common motif in the discussion of collections. In addition, the phenomenon of antiquarianism is deeply embedded in the creation of modern museums. Therefore, the second chapter of this thesis was structured around an attempt to trace the relation Greeks and Romans developed toward their past and its material remains, and in particular the role objects and monuments held in their efforts to (re-)construct and comprehend that past. These questions are immediately related to antiquarianism, as a strand of historiography, and the shape this took during the classical period. Historiographical traditions incorporate philosophical thought and reflect a society's ideas and feelings toward its past. We distinguished two areas where the interest of ancient historians focused: the recent past, which attracted the attention of the major historians and developed in accordance with the view that only that for which personal testimonies are available deserves to be studied; and the distant past, which formed the area of interest of erudite men and antiquarians: their task was to assemble in a systematic manner all data available (monuments, objects and inscriptions included), in the form of lists and catalogues, in order to shape a coherent picture of the past and save it for the future. This latter approach reflects philosophical concerns that legitimise erudition and support it by denouncing political historiography as interested only in the mundane and the particular instead of in general truths, but also complies with the assumption that material culture as an embodiment of technological progress corresponds to the level of civilisation.

Therefore, material culture acquired the status of a source of information and knowledge, and eventually the power to symbolise, signify, 'stand for' events, personalities, actions, 'the past'. In this sense, material remains were the 'evidence' of 'reality' (true versus false), of the acquisition of knowledge and the power this entails. They signified ideas and notions distant or imminent (in time and space), that could define the self and the 'Other'. These capacities of objects were brought forward in collections assembled in order to construct the narrative the collector wished in order to prove his 'reality', to document his knowledge and power, to appropriate the distant and the exotic. In other words, collections narrated stories about the collector's self, as well as about his perception and appropriation of the 'Other'; they were poetic metaphors of this self and 'Other', and therefore, defining mechanisms for the construction and understanding of identity.

The impact of these views on both the practice and the politics of classical collecting, as well as the poetics of it, were illustrated in the work of writers, mainly Pliny and Petronius, and further discussed in the chapter on the concept of individual and related ideas.

Pliny's *HN* belongs to the antiquarian tradition, although it undoubtedly expands the horizon of the traditional historical account to include all aspects of natural, as well as cultural history. He collects in a systematic manner all items relevant to his aims, all *thaumasia*, that the city of Rome and the Roman world at large had amassed, in order to provide a treasury of knowledge about the history of human civilisation and of Roman power. Thus Pliny can be held responsible for creating the notion that antiquarians of subsequent periods adopted, that Rome was the 'archetypal museum', the 'Ur-collection', that combined in the most complete manner ever achieved natural and cultural excellence. *HN* is based on Pliny's perception of the world as defined by

Stoicism: nature, a simultaneously passive and active element, is inherent in the world as a whole, but also in every little individual creature or thing. Consequently, the assemblage of these creatures or things leads to an assemblage of nature in its full scale. The aim of the work therefore was to amass nature and record it for posterity, so that the Roman people and their accomplishments could be celebrated.

The perception and pursuit of Pliny's aims relies on his understanding of material culture in antiquarian terms; this becomes explicit from his 'definition' of collection as a set of works of art, artefacts, and natural curiosities set aside to symbolise and prove Roman military prowess and superiority. The holding power of the units of the collection were the political and ideological messages, and not the aesthetic value of objects. This was so because of the role of the collection as a space of artificial memory. Therefore, collections operated as *monumenta* of illustrious men, 'evidence' of human achievements and of Nature's grandeur.

HN itself is an example of this kind of collection; it subscribes to the antiquarian tradition of assembling in a book objects of interest, lists of votive offerings in sanctuaries, inscriptions, *heuremata*, along with intangible information on practices, beliefs, institutions, which thus were set aside for the benefit of future generations, sources of knowledge, admiration, symbols of political and national pride, that would bear witness to the grandeur of their society.

In this sense, Pliny bridged the transition from the ancient antiquarian tradition to the Renaissance one: he provided not only the myth of success for the ancient collections and an extensive description of the 'archetypal museum', but with his *HN* he also offered the model of a collecting mode that would be extremely influential. His encyclopedic spirit, his classification principles, his understanding of collections as a holistic phenomenon, as methods of commemoration and *locus* of memory, as well as the dialectic relation between *res* and *verba* that he advocated, provided the model on which Renaissance collectors and antiquarians shaped themselves.

The chapter on the concept of the individual and its influence on classical collecting aimed to focus on the notion of identity, self and 'Other', and follow further the assumption that collections shape identities, define the self, and reconcile individual agents with centres of power. We examined the arguments supporting an alleged 'rise of individualism' during the Hellenistic period, when the first private collections were formed. The argument maintained was that the collections in the classical world signify an advanced role for the individual, but that cannot be associated with the 'rise of individualism'. On the contrary, they were means through which classical collectors aimed to create a niche for themselves in the social sphere, by acquiring access to a community of culture and prestige that the assemblage of Greek works of art and other precious artefacts signified. Far from being an exercise in individualism, classical collections, we argued, were attempts to prove belonging to a tradition of excellence, that would transfer to the owner the prestige and qualities that belonging to such a community implied. In other words, the collections of the Hellenistic and Roman eras aimed to help their owner gain his individuality through the perfect accomplishment of his social role.

To support this argument, we reviewed the philosophical concepts regarding individuals as these were developed in Hellenistic philosophies (Cynicism, Stoicism and Epicureanism), and concluded that despite a phenomenal encouragement of individuality, these philosophies maintained a remarkable faith in the traditional communal organisation, although they redefined it for purposes of the changing world. They advocated alternative communities, where the person would be able to achieve completion and ethical excellency. The social perception of these values is particularly prominent in the Roman world, where the notion of *decorum* propagates this responsibility of the individual to comply with his internal nature, but also with the social circumstances in which he finds himself involved. Collections were part of the social role the individual had to fulfill, and sources of pre-eminence within this social framework.

These views found their most explicit justification in the works of Petronius and Cicero. *Satyrica* records these beliefs, while it questions their validity and debates their legitimacy. Petronius draws the portrait of Trimalchio, a typical anti-connoisseur (very similar to those described by Martial), and provides an account of the social and psychological mechanisms that led to the creation of such a collection. Trimalchio aimed to construct a narrative about himself through his material possessions, that would allow him participation in a cultural élite - to which he did not belong - and the power, actual and symbolic, this entails. His collections therefore were means of constructing a 'self', and appropriating the cultural 'Other'.

Their effectiveness, though, is questioned by Petronius, who extends his doubts to include also the beliefs assigned to public collections. In another part of *Satyrica*, the narrative takes place in the picture-gallery. Although the heroes of this episode share at least the external signs of culture - they are educated enough to recognise the artists, to use appropriate terminology, and to identify the mythological themes, all areas in which Trimalchio had failed - they still cannot participate in the power that the assemblage of pictures potentially carries. Petronius thus goes even further to invalidate current views about how this power, which is equated to truth, can be approached, and how the public assemblage of legitimately acquired collections differs from the private ones in effectiveness. According to these views, echoes of which we have in the other authors, the process of appreciating material culture assemblages consisted of the setting of the collection in a special public space, the presence of a mediator, and the initiation into philosophical concerns, along with sound literary, art-historical and mythological education. By presenting his anti-heroes as fulfilling all these requirements, but still unable to reach the truth, Petronius debates the legitimacy of these views supporting a formal and rational, initiated, relationship to collections and collecting as that presented above.

Martial draws portraits of collectors similar to that of Trimalchio, and records and debates the belief that it is through objects that collectors aim to shape an ideal self, and appropriate qualities that will transform their ignorance, pretentiousness and vulgarity to refinement, knowledge and 'purity'. We come across the same point here again: the widespread belief in the capacity of objects to bring moral and cognitive metamorphosis, as a result of their treasuring.

The difference between private and public collections is a recurrent one in the classical sources. The dichotomy between the false values that individual collectors allot to their possessions, as opposed to the real values represented by the public collections, occupies a central place in the discussion of all four writers. Before we proceed to summarise these, though, we should note the interrelation between this dichotomy and the notions of time and space.

Ancient Greek and Roman philosophical thought was concerned with time and space as physical, cosmological, and metaphysical concepts: time was perceived as having the capacity to order and arrange events on a prior/posterior basis, as related to movement and rest, as being numerable and measurable. Space was understood as the container of the body, and essential for the existence and conception of everything in the world. It arranged bodies, just like time arranged events. It was related to the natural place of all elements in the world, and corresponded to biological ideas about order and sequence. Space and time together guaranteed cosmic order and helped the construction of notions of knowledge and human life at large. With these broad ideas in mind, classical collectors had the necessary framework and thinking tools to develop ideas about the role of objects in the arrangement of the world, as well as to develop elaborate techniques of display, and patterns of assemblage that would reveal ideas of order, development, and natural place.

Furthermore, linguistic evidence suggests that time can be understood as space, and could be related to ideas about order and cultural constructs, like the pre-eminence of the past over the future, of the ancestors over the descendants, of what comes before, first or higher, over what comes after, or lower. These ideas influence values attributed to material culture, but also the very ways of thinking about life, and knowledge, as well as ideas about the setting of collections, the organisation of space to reveal world order, and to associate with time. The impact of these ideas still can be detected in the chronologically arranged collections of modern museums.

In the Roman period, the capacity of objects to define the time and place to which they belonged, and to carry this dimension with them so as to evoke a different temporal and spatial dimension when placed elsewhere, was well recognised. Examples drawn from literary sources, and archaeological finds, suggest that the Romans used material culture to recreate and evoke the sense of a different time and place both in private and in public. Therefore, collections were a vital element of the attempts of Roman patrons and collectors to recreate in their villas the environment they longed for - usually a Greek public building type, now appropriated to the private domain, bearing philosophical or cultural associations - be it a *gymnasium*, a library, or a *musaeum*.   The social and ritual role of the Roman house could thus be fulfilled only through collections that would evoke certain feelings, and would facilitate communication and interrelation by providing well-recognised signifiers for that.   In addition, they were expected to signal personal and family power. All these were accomplished through material objects that were expected to bring past and distant ideas, beliefs and accomplishments to the eyes of their owners and visitors. In other words, objects were meant to bring people in touch with their imagination and previous knowledge, their memory.

The mnemotechnics developed by Romans was largely a system connecting material culture (in the form of artefacts and their setting) with memory and the depths of the human mind. Aristotle's elaborate discussion of places thus was put into practical use in Roman thought, as were the mythical associations of memory (Mnemosyne) with her daughters (Muses) who could bring a man (usually a poet, or a historian) in contact with other times and places, his inner memory and thought. Roman houses and public buildings were the *loci* where orderly arrangement led to the transference of the viewer to another temporal or spatial dimension, to the reconstruction of memories which would bring in front of him the ideas that would otherwise be lost in λήθη (forgetfulness), the opposite of ἀλήθεια (truth), but also of memory. In this sense, ancient and modern venues of collections share many similarities, that go beyond the fact that they accommodate collections: they are both venues of social and ritual practices, and rely on material culture to achieve a virtual transference to another world (in temporal and spatial meaning). Both transmit cultural and social messages, aim to facilitate communication between visitors and the social order of things, but also to bring visitors in front of their memory, in front of their past. This is revealed through the evocative power of objects, but also through their selective arrangement in time and space, that corresponds to, and defines cultural valuations.

The appreciation of exactly these qualities of material culture is expressed by Cicero, who defines 'reasonable collecting' (we will return to this) as a carefully planned manifestation of the social, religious and patriotic character of Rome, which would be 'appropriate' for the social role of the individual, and 'useful', displaying a connoisseurship rooted to a profound philosophical appreciation of art, to *humanitas*. Collections therefore were understood as parts of a meaningful Roman context, meant to allocate domestic or public space, to differentiate between notions of public and private, and to structure the collector's relationship with the world. In other words, they meant to empower the collector, as well as the visitors, to domesticate, to make sense of the values (his) collecting advocated, and to be part of the socialisation of the collector, and of the necessity for him to express and support in every possible way the social *status quo*.

At this point lies the major issue of classical collecting: the dichotomy between the public and the private domains. All four writers are concerned with this dichotomy and their views are remarkably similar (although Petronius chose to differentiate himself, by adopting an ironic stance toward public collections along with his criticism of the private ones): only public collections were acceptable and justified. The idea of public has to be seen through Roman eyes though: in this sense, even collections held in what we would consider a private space, that is a Roman villa, were acceptable when they had an explicitly social character and lacked any hint of personal attachment to the artefacts, or appreciation that went beyond what was considered rational and 'normal'. Here we should bear in mind that the notion of domestic privacy as we understand and appreciate it, was not valid in the Roman world, and that Roman houses were simultaneously private and public spaces. Therefore, collections held in the 'public areas' of the Roman house, and addressed to the fulfillment of the social responsibilities and aspirations of the owner, were still acceptable.

Naturally, the collections held in public buildings attracted much praise, and were associated with honourable motives: Pliny, for instance, approves of the collections in the public domain, since they were products of beneficial interference by emperors and victorious generals, as well as of collections which were the result of the 'rightful' spoliation of the enemies of Rome after their defeat on the field of battle. Similarly, Cicero praises the generals of the past for using the spoils of their victorious military campaigns to adorn the city of Rome, and create *monumenta* of their personal magnificence and Roman glory.

In opposition to this, collections meant for private delectation were discouraged, as suspect for encouraging a sinister association with material culture, ignorance or negligence of natural values, and for a lack of rationality. Cicero condemns Verres for acquiring his collection by plundering cities during peace time, and for keeping the objects of his pillage for himself, instead of offering them to the public. The portrait of the typical collector all four writers drew was that of an ignorant, *nouveau riche* anti-connoisseur, who confused external appearances with profound values, and when not assembling objects for vulgar and contemptible reasons, developed sinister relations to material culture, 'depended' psychologically on material possessions, and was unduly and passionately involved in their appreciation and acquisition. Verres was the epitome of this category of collecting: uncultivated, unorthodox in this method of acquisition, irrational in his relation to objects, and compared with tyrants and philanderers. Collectors of this sort, present also in Martial's descriptions, suffered from unconsummated passion, that led to inadequate social relations, which in turn led to an insatiable desire for objects, used to compensate for social inadequacies.   This found an equivalent in an insatiable desire for women, and thus completed the model of the socially deficient person.

Material culture and women are issues of particular interest in classical collecting. The act of collecting itself was described as 'effeminate' when it did not conform to the rational patterns the authors thought appropriate for men. Being a part of material culture themselves in the very early notion of precious items, women were seen as developing an irrational and passionate relation to objects with intrinsic financial value, but rarely to any other kind. Wherever in our texts discussion was concerned with women collectors, we saw them assembling objects that related to personal vanity or household interest, that is objects that relate to the female stereotypes: the housewife whose intelligence is exhausted in the efficient running of her household, and the *femme fatale* whose vanity is a danger for society at large and men in particular. Feelings about these objects, as well as proper behaviour in terms of setting and displaying the collection cannot be controlled. Grief for the loss of material possessions overcomes women, desire for material acquisitions leads to dangerous associations. In this sense, all women were 'bad' collectors, who lacked the intellectual depth for a 'good' collection, and similarly all 'bad' collections were signs of effeminacy and degeneracy.

At the other end of the spectrum was the rational collector, who practiced collecting as a clearly planned rational activity, who viewed material culture as a medium for creating and extending one's self, but within the limits set by community laws. Interestingly, all four writers juxtapose their own 'true criteria' and 'real value' of objects with the criteria imposed by the collectors, and the values they appreciated. Even Petronius, who seems to adopt a completely ironic stance toward both public and private collections, implies that there is a different, more profound, set of values that ordinary collectors simply miss.

The notion of object valuation is paramount in the discussion of the fourth of the parameters we set out in the introduction, the gift exchange tradition. We examined the presence of the phenomenon in Homeric epic poetry, where we isolated the vocabulary used and the values most commonly associated with precious objects. We located in these the power of objects to mediate between sacred and profane worlds, divine and human realms, their capacity to create relationships between people, to carry moral value, and to transfer it to people. We focused then on the treasuries built in Greek sanctuaries during the sixth century BCE; their presence, name and role suggest that they simply signify another stage in the same tradition. The objects kept in these treasuries, and the buildings themselves, held similar powers: they mediated between men and gods, they developed relations of perpetual dependence, and they carried symbolic meanings. The value of the objects goes beyond their financial worth, derives from their symbolic rather than actual use, and relates to their power to communicate with the Other. The main notion remains the one which has been central in the gift exchange: the objects participating in it are inalienable - although they are given away they never parted from their owner. Here we find the roots of their value as carriers of parts of human psyche, and of the notion of prestigious genealogy. These dimensions are 'mythologised' – in myths we come across objects as mediators of interpersonal relations, but also as seals of the mythic character of facts. Consequently, objects become parameters of stability, reassurance of the social and individual identity, as well as of the social order and hierarchy.

Martial is the writer most explicitly associating the tradition of gift-exchange with object valuation and collections. He asserts that giving is the only way of owning, a long-lasting notion associated with gift-exchange, and relates the 'true' value of objects with their participation in social practice, namely the relation between patron and client. His poetry - even in the choice of the genre - stands at the crossroads between real and imaginary worlds, individual and social order, tradition and innovation. Martial inscribes collecting, through the views expressed in his poetry but also through the poetry itself, into a cultural context that discriminates and privileges objects as parts of social ritual, of display, of social interaction. There collections were propagated as the result of a social phenomenon, deeply committed to the aim of reproducing dialogue between individuals, social order, imagination and the real world.

A similar dichotomy between the 'real' values, that coincide with those defined by the gift-exchange tradition, and the 'false' values appreciated by collectors, appears implicitly or explicitly in all four writers. They formed a vital criterion of the distinction drawn between 'good' and 'bad' collections.

Classical collections, therefore, could and were used to help their owners structure their identity, personal and communal, memory, past and future; they were expressions of power and wealth, and means of appropriating spatial and temporal distance. They were intended to mediate with the sacred domain, and to empower their owners to accomplish their role as participants in cultural pre-eminence and thus power and control. Their method of acquisition was part of their role and meaning, and therefore, unlawful and destructive methods of acquisition were condemned along with the emphasis on individuality, egotism and human-defined (rather than nature-oriented) values. Collections acquired their supreme power when placed in the right context, that is the public, sacred, or semi-sacred realm, where memories and thoughts of individuals blend together to provide identity for communities. This description corresponds well with the one of contemporary museums, and it is in this dichotomy between 'good' and 'bad', public and private collecting that we would find the foundation of the dichotomy between collectors and museums today.

The study of classical collecting, its nature and relevance to collecting traditions of subsequent periods, is very rewarding for the researcher, whether it is approached with the stance of a classicist or that of a museum professional. The aim of this book has been to discuss classical collecting as a phenomenon that deserves special consideration, to focus on the motives behind the interest in collecting that developed in the period under examination, and to provide more elaborate and analytic suggestions about these motives than the usual descriptive ones. In particular we aimed to examine the collecting attitudes in the classical world, and to trace the seeds of this practice and mentality in the shared tradition that runs through European thought. For that purpose, we structured our argument around four parameters that belong at the centre of this tradition. We thus hoped to put the discussion of classical collecting on a broader and deeper foundation than that of the historical circumstances of the short-term, as other attempts have done in the past. The examination of the immediate implications of this classical mentality to Renaissance collecting has been beyond the scope of this work, for practical reasons, length and time, but also because early modern collecting has received some attention already, and therefore we felt that the 'archaic phase' can, and should, be at the centre of this work. In the process of writing the thesis from which this book developed, many issues have emerged, like the role of the women collectors, or the religious and ritual character of the 'museum' before and after the creation of the Museum in Alexandria, or even classical collecting as practiced and experienced before and after the period that I have chosen to confine myself within, which deserve more than the limits of a thesis and a book with a different aim can provide, in other words a full discussion of their own. These will be pursued further in the future. The thrust of the argument of this book, however, has been to bring out classical collecting as a phenomenon in its own right, that deserves to be studied and can contribute immensely to a more profound appreciation of the history of collecting in the long term, of the origins and cultural character of the museum institution, and of the relationship between society, individual and material culture in the Western tradition. And this we hope we have achieved.

Bibliography

Editions, translations and commentaries of texts

Ad C. Herennium, De Ratione Dicendi (Rhetorica ad Herennium), edited and translated by H. Caplan, Loeb Classical Library, London and Cambridge Mass.: William Heinemann Ltd and Harvard University Press, 1954.

Aristotle, Physics, translated with commentary and glossary by H.G. Apostle, Bloomington and London: Indiana University Press, 1969.

Aristotle, The Poetics, edited and translated by W. Hamilton Fyfe, Loeb Classsical Library, London and Cambridge Mass.: William Heinemann Ltd and Harvard University Press, 1946.

Cicero, Academica, edited and translated by H. Rackham, Loeb Classical Library, London and Cambridge Mass.: William Heinemann Ltd and Harvard University Press, 1951.

Cicero, Brutus, edited and translated by G.L. Hendrickson and *Orator*, edited and translated by H. M. Hubbell, Loeb Classical Library, London and Cambridge Mass.: William Heinemann Ltd and Harvard University Press, 1952.

Cicero, De Finibus, edited and translated by H. Rackham, Loeb Classical Library, London and Cambridge Mass.: William Heinemann Ltd and Harvard University Press, 1951.

Cicero, De Inventione. De Optime Genere Oratorum. Topica, edited and translated by H.M. Hubbell, Loeb Classical Library, London and Cambridge Mass.: William Heinemann Ltd and Harvard University Press, 1949.

Cicero, De Natura Deorum - Academica, edited and translated by H. Rackham, Loeb Classical Library, London and Cambridge Mass.: William Heinemann Ltd and Harvard University Press, 1951.

Cicero, De Officiis, edited and translated by W. Miller, Loeb Classical Library, London and Cambridge Mass.: William Heinemann Ltd and Harvard University Press, 1947.

Cicero, De Oratore, Books I and II, edited and translated by E.W. Sutton, and completed with an introduction by H. Rackham, Loeb Classical Library, London and Cambridge Mass.: William Heinemann Ltd and Harvard University Press, 1948.

Cicero, De Oratore together with *De Fato, Paradoxa Stoicorum, De Partitione Oratoria,*edited and translated by H. Rackham, Loeb Classical Library, London and Cambridge Mass.: William Heinemann Ltd and Harvard University Press, 1942.

Cicero, De Oratore, edited and translated by E.W. Sutton, completed with an introduction by H. Rackham, Loeb Classical Library, London and Cambridge Mass.: William Heinemann Ltd and Harvard University Press, 1948.

Cicero, Laws (De Legibus), edited and translated by C. Walker Keyes, Loeb Classical Library, London and Cambridge Mass.: William Heinemann Ltd and Harvard University Press, 1943.

Cicero, On Duties (De Officiis), edited and translated by M.T. Griffin and E.M., Atkins, (Cambridge Texts on Political Thought), Cambridge: Cambridge University Press, 1991.

Cicero, Philippics, edited and translated by W.C.A. Ker, Loeb Classical Library, London and Cambridge Mass.: William Heinemann Ltd and Harvard University Press, 1951.

Cicero, the Speeches (Pro Publio Quinctio - Pro Sexto Roscio Amerino - Pro Quinto Roscio Comoedo - De Lege Agraria I, II, II.), edited and translated by J.H. Freese, Loeb

Classical Library, London and Cambridge Mass.: William Heinemann Ltd and
Harvard University Press, 1945.

Cicero, *Tusculan Disputations*, edited and translated by J.E. King, Loeb Classsical Library,
London and Cambridge Mass.: William Heinemann Ltd and Harvard University
Press, 1945.

Cicero, *The Letters to Atticus*, edited and translated by E.O. Winstedt, Loeb Classical
Library, London and Cambridge Mass.: William Heinemann Ltd and Harvard
University Press, volume 1, 1920.

Cicero, *The Letters to his Friends*, edited and translated by W. Glyn Williams, Loeb Classical
Library, London and Cambridge Mass.: William Heinemann Ltd and Harvard
University Press, in four volumes: volume 1: 1952; volume 2: 1953; volume 3: 1972;
volume 4: 1979.

Cicero, *Verrines Orations*, edited and translated by L.H.G. Greenwood, Loeb Classical
Library, London and Cambridge Mass.: William Heinemann Ltd and Harvard
University Press, volume 1: 1948; volume 2: 1953.

Epictetus, *The Discourses as reported by Arrian, the Manual and Fragments*, edited and
translated by W.A. Oldfather, Loeb Classical Library, London and Cambridge
Mass.: Harvard University Press (in 2 volumes), 1946.

Herodotus, *Histories*, edited and translated by A.D. Godley, volume 1: (Books I-II), Loeb
Classical Library, London and Cambridge Mass.: William Heinemann Ltd and
Harvard University Press, 1946.

Homer, *The Iliad*, edited and translated by A.T. Murray, Loeb Classical Library, London and
Cambridge Mass.: William Heinemann Ltd and Harvard University Press, volume
1: 1954.

Homer, *The Odyssey*, edited and translated by A.T. Murray, Loeb Classical Library, London
and Cambridge Mass.: William Heinemann Ltd and Harvard University Press,
volume 2: 1953.

Josephus, *The Jewish War*, volume 2: (Books I-III), edited and translated by H.St.J.
Thackeray, Loeb Classical Library, London and Cambridge Mass.: William
Heinemann Ltd and Harvard University Press, 1956.

Martial *Epigrams*, edited and translated by D.R. Shackleton Bailey, Loeb Classical Library,
London and Cambridge Mass.: Harvard University Press and William Heinemann
Ltd, (in three volumes), 1993.

Martial *Epigrams*, edited and translated by Walter C.A. Ker, Loeb Classical Library, London
and Cambridge Mass.: William Heinemann Ltd and Harvard University Press, (in
two volumes), 1919.

Ovid, *Fasti*, edited and translated by Sir J.G. Frazer, (second edition revised by G. P. Goold),
Loeb Classical Library, Cambridge Mass. and London: Harvard University Press and
William Heinemann Ltd, volume V (out of VI), 1989.

Ovid, *Heroides and Amores*, edited and translated by Grant Showerman, Loeb Classical
Library, Cambridge Mass. and London: Harvard University Press and William
Heinemann Ltd, 1957.

Petronius, *Satyricon*, edited and translated by M. Heseltine, Loeb Classical Library, New York:
G.P. Putnam's Sons. 1919 (revised by E.H. Warmington, London and Cambridge
Mass.: Harvard University Press, 1969).

Petronius, *The Satyricon*, translated with introduction and notes by P.G. Walsh, World's
Classics, Oxford: Oxford University Press, 1997.

Philostratus, *Imagines-Callistratus Descriptions*, edited and translated by A. Fairbanks, Loeb
Classical Library, London and Cambridge Mass.: William Heinemann Ltd and
Harvard University Press, 1931.

Plato, *Timaeus, Critias, Cleitophon, Menexenus, Epistles*, edited and translated by R. G. Bury,
Loeb Classical Library, London and Cambridge Mass.: William Heinemann Ltd and
Harvard University Press, 1952.

Pline l'Ancien, Histoire Naturelle, Livre XXXIV, introduction, translation and commentary by H. Le Bonniec and H. Gallet de Santerre, 1953; second edition 1983, Paris: Budé, Belles Lettres.

Pline l'Ancien, Histoire Naturelle, Livre XXXVI, introduction, translation and commentary by J. André, R. Bloch and A. Rouveret, 1981, Paris: Budé, Belles Lettres.

Pliny the Elder - Natural History: A Selection, introduction and translation by J. Healy, London: Penguin Books, 1991.

Pliny the Elder, Peri tes Archaias Ellenekes Zografikes (On the Ancient Greek Painting)- *35o Vivlio tes 'Fisikes Istorias* (35th Book of the 'Natural History'), translated by Tassos Roussos and Alekos Levidis, Athens: Agra (in Greek), 1994.

Pliny the Elder, The Natural History, in ten volumes, 1938-1963, edited and translated by H. Rackham, (vols. I to V, 1938-1950), W.H.S. Jones (vols. VI and VII, 1951-1956), W.H.S. Jones (with E.H. Warmington, vol. VIII, 1963), H. Rackham (with E.H. Warmington and T.B.L. Webster, 1952, vol. IX), D.E. Eichholz, (vol. X, 1962), Loeb Classical Library, London and Cambridge Mass.: William Heinemman Ltd and Harvard University Press.

Plutarch's Lifes: Theseus and Romulus, Lycurgus and Numa, Solon and Publicola, edited and translated by B. Perrin, Loeb Classical Library, London and Cambridge Mass.: William Heinemman Ltd and Harvard University Press, volume 1, 1914

Plutarch: The Life of Cicero, edited and translated by J.L. Moles, Waminster, Wiltshire: Aris and Phillips Ltd, 1988.

Quintilian, The Institutio Oratoria, edited and translated by H.E. Butler, Loeb Classical Library, London and Cambridge Mass.: William Heinemann Ltd and Harvard University Press, volume IV (out of IV), 1922.

Seneca, Ad Lucilium Epistulae Morales, edited and translated by R.M. Gummere, Loeb Classical Library, London and Cambridge Mass.: William Heinemann Ltd and Harvard University Press, volume III: 1962.

Strabo, Geography, edited and translated by H.L. Jones, Loeb Classical Library, London   and Cambridge Mass.: William Heinemann Ltd and Harvard University Press, volume IV (out of VIII), 1954.

Tacitus Annals, edited and translated by J. Jackson, Loeb Classical Library, London and Cambridge Mass.: William Heinemann Ltd and Harvard University Press, 1951.

Thucydides, History of the Peloponnesian War, Books I-II, edited and translated by C. Forster Smith, Loeb Classical Library, London and Cambridge Mass.: William Heinemann Ltd and Harvard University Press, volume 1, 1951.

Vitruvius, The Ten Books On Architecture, translated by H. Morgan, New York: Dover Publications, Inc., 1960.

References

Adkins, A.W.H. (1970), *From the Many to the One: A Study of Personality and Views of Human Nature in the Context of Ancient Greek Society, Values and Beliefs*, London: Constable.

Adorno, T.W. (1967), 'Valery Proust museum' in *Prisms*, translated by S. and S. Weber, London: Spearman.

Albore-Livadie, C. and Widemann, F. (eds) (1990), *Volcanology and Archaeology*, PACT 25, Strasbourg: Conseil de l' Europe.

Alcock, S.E. (1993), *Graecia Capta: The Lanscapes of Roman Greece*, Cambridge: Cambridge University Press.

Alexander, E.P. (1979), *Museums in Motion: An Introduction to the History and Function of Museums*, Nashville: American Association for State and Local History/Altamira Press.

Alexander, E.P. (1997), *The Museum in America: Innovators and Pioneers*, London: Altamira Press.

Alexander, M.C. (1976), 'Hortensius' speech in defence of Verres', *Phoenix* 30, 46-53.

Algra, K. (1995), *Concepts of Space in Greek Thought*, Leiden: E. J. Brill.

Alsop, J.W. (1982), *The Rare Art Traditions: The history of art collecting and its linked phenomena wherever these have appeared*, London: Thames and Hudson.

André, J. (1949), *La vie et l' oeuvre d' Asinius Pollion*, Paris: Librairie C. Klincksieck.

André, J.-M. (ed.) (1978b), *Recherches sur les Artes à Rome*, Paris: Publications de l'Université de Dijon.

André, J.-M. (1978a), 'Nature et culture chez Pline l'Ancien', in André, J.-M., (ed.), 1978b, 7-17.

André, J.-M. (1996), 'L' otium romain à l' époque impériale: continuité et ruptures' in André, J.- M., Dangel, J. and Demont, P. (eds) (1996), 240-257.

André, J.-M., Dangel, J. and Demont, P., (eds) (1996), *Les loisirs et l'héritage de la culture classique*, Actes du XIIIe Congrés de l'Association Guillaume Budé (Dijon, 27-31 août 1993), Bruxelles: Latomus.

Annas, J. (1984), 'Aristotle on memory and the self' in *Oxford Studies in Ancient Philosophy*, IV, 99-117.

Annas, J. (1991), 'Epicurus' philosophy of mind' in Everson, S. (ed.) (1991), 84-101.

Annas, J. (1992), *Hellenistic Philosophy of Mind*, Berkeley: University of California Press.

Appadurai, A. (1986), *The Social Life of Things: Commodities in Cultural Perspective*, Cambridge: Cambridge University Press.

Arafat, K.W. (1992), 'Pausanias attitude to antiquities' in *BSA*, 87, 387-409.

Arafat, K.W. (1995), 'Pausanias and the temple of Hera at Olympia' in *BSA*, 90, 461-473.

Archer, L.J., Fischler, S. and Wyke, M. (eds) (1994), *Women in Ancient Societies: An Illusion of the Night*, London: MacMillan.

Ardener, S. (ed.) (1993), *Women and Space: Ground Rules and Social Maps*, Oxford: Berg.

Ardener, S. (1987), '"Remote areas": Some theoretical considerations' in Jackson, A. (ed.) (1987), 22-46.

Arethusa, 7 (1974), *Psychoanalysis and the Classics*.

Arethusa, 8 (1975), *Marxism and the Classics*.

Arethusa, 10 (1977), *Classical Literature and Contemporary Literary Theory*.

Arethusa, 16 (1983), *Semiotics and Classical Studies*.

Arethusa, 19 (1986), *Audience-Oriented Criticism and the Classics*.

Aristides, N. (1988), 'Calm and Uncollected' in *American Scholar*, 57 (3), 327-336.

Arnold, E.V. (1958), *Roman Stoicism*, London: Routledge and Kegan Paul.

Arrowsmith, W. (1966), 'Luxury and death in the *Satyricon*' in *Arion*, 5, 304-331 (also reprinted in *Essays in Classical Literature*, edited by N. Rudd, Cambridge 1972).

Audiat, J. (1933), *Fouilles de Delphes* II, 1, 4: *Le Trésor des Athéniens*, Paris: École Française d' Athénes, E. de Boccard.

Auerbach, E. (1953), *Mimesis: The Representation of Reality in Western Literature*, translated by W.R. Trask, Princeton: Princeton University Press.

Austin, M.M. and Vidal-Naquet, P. (1977), *Economic and Social History of Ancient Greece: An Introduction*, Berkeley: University of California Press.

Austin, M.M. (1981), *The Hellenistic World from Alexander to the Roman Conquest*, Cambridge: Cambridge University Press.

Bacon, H.H. (1958), 'The Sibyl in the bottle' in *Virginia Quarterly Review* 34, 262-276.

Badian, E. (ed.) (1979), *Roman Papers*, vol. II, Oxford: Clarendon Press.

Baekeland, F. (1981), 'Psychological aspects of art collecting' in *Psychiatry*, 44, 45-59.

Bagnani, G. (1954), 'The house of Trimalchio' in *AJPh*, 75, 16-39.

Baker, F. and Thomas, J. (eds) (1990), *Writing the Past in the Present*, Lampeter: St David's University College.

Bal, M. (1994), 'Telling objects: A narrative perspective on collecting' in Elsner, J. and Cardinal, R. (eds) (1994), 97-115.

Baldwin, B. (1973), 'Trimalchio's Corinthian plate' in *Classical Philology* 68, 46-47.

Baran, V.N. (1976), 'L' expression du temps et de la durée en Latin' in Chevallier, R. (ed.) (1976), 1-21.

Bardon, H. (1956), *La littérature latine inconnue*, tome II, Paris: C. Klincksieck.

Bardon, H. (1960a), 'Sur le goût de Cicéron à l' époque des Verrines' in *Ciceroniana*, 1-13.

Bardon, H. (1960b), 'La leçon de Verres' in *Studi di Onore di Luigi Castiglioni*, I, Florence: G.C. Sansoni Editore, 25-40.

Barker, S. (ed.) (1996), *Excavations and Their Objects: Freud's Collection of Antiquity*, New York: State University of New York Press.

Barnes, J., Schofield, M., Sorabji, R. (eds) (1979), *Articles on Aristotle: 3. Metaphysics*, London: Duckworth.

Barthes, R. (1967), *Elements of Semiology*, translated by A. Lavers and C. Smith, London: Jonathan Cape.

Barthes, R. (1972), *Mythologies*, translated by A. Lavers, London: Jonathan Cape.

Barthes, R. (1975), *S/Z*, translated by R. Miller, London: Jonathan Cape.

Barthes, R. (1990), *The Fashion System*, translated by M. Ward and R. Howard, Berkeley: University of California Press.

Bartman, E. (1984), Miniature Copies: Copyist Invention in the Hellenistic and Roman Period, Unpublished Ph.D. thesis, submitted at the University of Columbia.

Bartman, E. (1988), '*Decor et Duplicatio*: Pendants in Roman sculptural display' in *AJA*, 92, 211-225.

Bartman, E. (1994), 'Sculptural collecting and display in the private realm' in Gazda, E. (ed.) (1994), 71-88.

Bartsch, S. (1989), *Decoding the Ancient Novel*, Princeton: Princeton University Press.

Baslez, M-F., Hoffman, P. and Pernot, L. (eds) (1993), *L'invention de l'autobiographie d'Hésiode à St. Augustin*, Paris: Presses de l'École Normale Supérieure.

Baudrillard, J. (1968), *Le Système des objets*, Paris: Gallimard.

Baudrillard, J. (1994), 'The system of collecting' in Elsner, J. and Cardinal, R. (eds) (1994), 7-24.

Bazin, G. (1967), *Museum Age*, translated by J. van Nuis Cahil, Brussels: Desoer.

Beagon, M. (1992), *Roman Nature: The Thought of Pliny the Elder*, Oxford: Clarendon Press.

Beard, M. (1987), 'A complex of times: No more sheep on Romulus' birthday' in *PCPhS*, 33, 1-15.

Beard, M., Bowman, A.K., Corbier, M., Cornell, T., Franklin, J.L., Hanson, A., Hopkins, K. Horsfall, N. (eds) (1991), *Literacy in the Roman World*, Ann Arbor: University of Michigan Press.

Beaujeu, J. (1948), 'La cosmologie de Pline l'Ancien dans ses rapports avec l'histoire des idées', in *REL*, 26, 40-41.

Beaujeu, J.M. (1982), 'A-t-il éxisté une direction des musées dans la Rome impériale?' in *Comptes Rendus de l'Academie des Inscriptions et Belles Lettres*, Nov.-Dec., 671-688.

Becatti, G. (1951), *Arte e gusto negli scrittori latini*, Florence: Sansoni.

Becatti, G. (1956), 'Letture Pliniane: Le opere d' arte nei monumenta Asini Pollionis e negli Horti Serviliani', in *Studi in Onore di Calderini e Paribeni*, vol. 3, Milano: Ceschina, 199-210.

Becatti, G. (1973-1974), 'Opere d' arte greca nella Roma di Tiberio', in *Archeologia Classica*, 25-26, 18-53.

Beck, R. (1975), 'Encolpius at the *Cena*', *Phoenix* 29, 271-283.

Bejor, G. (1979), 'La decorazione sculptorea dei teatri romani nelle province africane' in *Prospettiva*, 17, 37-46.

Belk, R.W. (1988a), 'Collectors and collecting' in *Advances in Consumer Research* 15, 548-553.

Belk, R.W. (1988b), 'Possessions and the extended self' in *Journal of Consumer Research*, 15, 139-168.

Belk, R.W. (1991), 'Possessions and the sense of past' in *Highways and Buyways*, Provo, Utah, Association for Consumer Research, 114-130.

Belk, R.W. (1995), *Collecting in a Consumer Society*, London: Routledge.

Belk, R.W. and Wallendorf, M. (1990), 'The sacred meanings of money' in *Journal of Economic Psychology*, 11 (3), 63-67.

Belk, R.W., Wallendorf, M., Sherry, J. and Holbrook, M. (1990), 'Collecting in a consumer culture' in *Highways and Buyways,* Provo, Utah: Association for Consumer Research, 3-95.

Benjamin, W. (1969), 'Unpacking my library' in Benjamin, W., *Illuminations*, (edited by H. Arendt, translated by H. Zohn), New York: Schocken, 59-67 (initially published in German in 1931).

Benjamin, W. (1979), *One-Way Street and Other Writings*, translated by E. Jephcott and K. Shorter, London: NLB.

Bennett, T. (1995), *The Birth of the Museum*, London and New York: Routledge.

Benton, S. (1934-1935), 'The evolution of the tripod-lebes' in *BSA*, 35, 74-130.

Benveniste, E. (1973), *Indo-European Language and Society*, translated by E. Palmer, London: Faber.

Bergmann, B. (1994), 'The Roman house as memory theater: the House of the Tragic Poet in Pompeii' in *The Art Bulletin*, LXXVI (2), 225-256.

Bergquist, B. (1967), *The Archaic Greek Temenos: A Study of Structure and Function*, Swedish Institut, Athens, ser. 4, vol. 13, Lund: Gleerup.

Berry, J. (1997), 'Household artefacts: toward a re-interpretation of Roman domestic space' in Laurence, R. and Wallace-Hadrill, A. (eds) (1997), 183-195.

Bertrand, E. (1890), 'Cicéron artiste', *Annales de l' Enseignement supérieur*, Grenoble, 95-164.

Bettini, M. (1991), *Anthropology and Roman Culture: Kinship, Time, Images of the Soul*, Baltimore and London: The Johns Hopkins University Press.

Bieber, M. (1977), *Ancient Copies: Contribution to the History of Greek and Roman Art*, New York: New York University Press.

Birt, T. (1882), *Das Antike Buchwesen in seinen Verhdltniss zur Litteratur*, Berlin: W. Hertz.

Blümner, H. (1873), *Dilletanten, Kunstliebhaber und Kenner in Altertum*, Hamburg-Berlin: Lüderitz.

Blundell, S. (1986), *The Origins of Civilization in Greek and Roman Thought*, London: Croom Helm.

Boardman, J., Griffin, J., Murray, O. (eds) (1986), *The Oxford History of the Classical World*, Oxford: Oxford University Press.

Bodel, J. (1994), 'Trimalchio's underworld' in Tatum, J. (ed.) (1994), 237-259.

Boedecker, D. (1993), 'Hero cult and politics in Herodotus: The bones of Orestes' in Dougherty, C. and Kurke, L. (eds) (1993), 164-177.

Boethius, A. (1960), *The Golden House of Nero*, Ann Arbor: University of Michigan Press.

Boisacq, E. (1950), *Dictionnaires étymologique de la langue grecque*, Heidelberg: C. Winter.

Bol, P.C. (1972), *Die Skulpturen des Schiffsfund von Antikythera*, Berlin: Gebr. Mann.

Bommelaer, J.-F. (1991), *Guide de Delphes: Le Site*, Paris: École Française d' Athènes.

Bonnafé, E. (1867), *Les Collectionneurs de l' Ancienne Rome: Notes d' un Amateur*, Paris: Aug. Aubry.

Bourdieu, P. (1974), 'Les fractions de la classe dominante et les modes d' appropriation de l'oeuvre d' art' in *Information sur les Sciences Sociales*, 13 (3), 7-32.

Bourdieu, P. (1984), *Distinction: A Social Critique of the Judgement of Taste*, London: Routledge and Kegan Paul.

Bourdieu, P. (1987), 'The historical genesis of a pure aesthetic' in *Journal of Aesthetics and Art Criticism*, 201-210.

Bowersock, G.W. (1994), *Fiction as History: Nero to Julian*, Berkeley: University of California Press.

Bowie, E.L. (1971), 'The novels and the real world' in Reardon, B. P. (ed.) (1971), 91-96.

Boyce, B. (1991), *The Language of the Freedmen in Petronius' Cena Trimalchionis*, Leiden: Brill.

Bramble, J.C. (1982), 'Martial and Juvenal' in Kenney, E. J. and Clausen, W. V. (eds) (1982), 597-623.

Braudel, F. (1973), *The Mediterranean and the Mediterranean World in the Age of Philip II*, (volumes I and II), 2nd edition, London: Collins.

Breckenridge, J.D. (1973), 'Origins of Roman republican portraiture: relations with the Hellenistic world' in *ANRW*, I.4, 826-854.

Breckenridge, J.D. (1981), 'Imperial portraiture: Augustus to Gallienus' in *ANRW*, II.12.2, 477ff.

Bredekamp, H. (1995), *The Lure of Antiquity and the Cult of the Machine*, Princeton: Marcus Wiener Publishers.

Briggs, A. (1990), *Victorian Things*, London: Penguin.

Briggs, M.S. (1947), *Men of Taste: From Pharaoh to Ruskin*, London: B.T. Batsford.

Brinkmann, V. (1994), *Beobachtungen zum formalen Aufbau und zum Sinngehalt der Friese des Siphnierschatzhauses*, Munich: Biering and Brinkmann.

Brooks, E. (1954), *Sir Hans Sloane*, London: Batchworth Press.

Brunt, P.A. (1973), 'Aspects of the social thoughts of Dio Chrysostomus and of the Stoics' in *PCPhS*, (n.s.) 19, 9-34.

Bryant, J.M. (1996), *Moral Codes and Social Structure in Ancient Greece: A Sociology of Greek Ethics from Homer to the Epicureans and Stoics*, New York: State University of New York Press.

Bryant, J. (1989), 'Stamp and coin collecting' in Inge, T. (ed.) (1989), 1329-1365.

Bryson, N. (1994), 'Philostratus and the imaginary museum' in Goldhill S. and Osborne, R. (eds) (1994), 255-283.

Bulloch, A., Green, E. S., Long, A. A., Stewart, A. (eds) (1993), *Images and Ideologies: Self-Definition in the Hellenistic World*, Berkeley: University of California Press.

Burk, C.F. (1900), 'The collecting Instinct' in *Pedagogical Seminary*, 7, 179-207.

Burkert, W. (1982), 'Craft versus sect: the problem of Orphics and Pythagoreans' in Meyer, B.F. and Sanders, E.P. (eds) (1982), 1-22.

Burkert, W. (1983), *Homo Necans: The Anthropology of Ancient Greek Sacrificial Ritual and Myth*, translated by P. Bing, Berkeley: University of California Press.

Burkert, W. (1987), 'Offerings in perspective: surrender, distribution, exchange' in Linders, T. and Nordquist, G. (eds) (1987), 43-50.

Butsch, R. (1984), 'The commodification of leisure: the case of the model airplane and industry' in *Qualitative Sociology*, 7, 217-235.

Cairns, D.L. (1993), *Aidos: The Psychology and Ethics of Honour and Shame in Ancient Greek Literature*, Oxford: Clarendon Press.

Callahan, J.F. (1948), *Four Views of Time in Ancient Philosophy*, Cambridge Mass.: Harvard University Press.

Cameron, A. and Kuhrt, A. (eds) (1993), *Images of Women in Antiquity*, London: Routledge.

Cameron, D.F. (1995), 'The pilgrim and the shrine, the icon and the oracle: A perspective on museology for tomorrow' in *Museum Management and Curatorship*, 14 (1), 47-55.

Cannon-Brookes, P. (1992), 'The nature of museum collections', in Thompson, J.M.A., Basset, D.A., Duggan, A.J., Lewis, G.D. and Fenton, A. (eds) (1992), 500ff.

Canter, D. (1977), *The Psychology of Place*, New York: St Martin's Press.

Carcopino, J. (1969), *Cicero: The Secrets of his Correspondence*, vol. 1, New York: Greenwoood Press.

Cardinal, R. (1994), 'Collecting and collage-making: The case of Kurt Schwitters' in Elsner, J. and Cardinal, R. (eds) (1994), 68-96.

Carey, S. (2000), 'The problem of totality: collecting Greek art, wonders and luxury in Pliny the Elder's Natural History', *Journal of the History of Collections*, 12 (1), 1-13.

Carr, E.H. (1986), *What is History? The George Macaulay Trevelyan Lectures delivered in the University of Cambridge, January-March 1961*, second edition by R. W. Davies, London: Macmillan.

Carrithers, M., Collins, S., Lukes, S. (eds) (1985), *The Category of the Person: Anthropology, Philosophy, History*, Cambridge: Cambridge University Press.

Cary, M.M. (1951), *A History of the Greek World from 323 BC to 146 BC*, London: Methuen.

Cassiano dal Pozzo (1993), Quaderni Puteani 4, London: Olivetti.

Caygill, M. and Cherry, J. (eds) (1997), *A. W. Franks: Nineteenth-Century Collecting and the British Museum*, London: British Museum Press.

Cayrel, P. (1933), 'Autour du De Signis' in *Melanges de l'École Française de Rome*, 120-133.

Chevallier, R. (1991), *L'artiste, le collectionneur et le faussaire: Pour une sociologie de l'art romain*, Paris: Armand Colin.

Chevallier, R. (ed.) (1976), *AION: Les temps chez les Romains*, Paris: Editions Picard.

Citroni, M. (1989), 'Marziale e la letteratura per I Saturnali', in *Illinois Classical Studies*, 14, 201-26.

Citroni-Marchetti, S. (1982), 'Iuvare mortalem, l' ideale programmatico della Naturalis Historia di Plinio nei rapporti con il moralismo stoico-diatribico' in *Atene e Roma*, 27, 124-148.

Citroni-Marchetti, S. (1991), *Plinio il Vecchio e la tradizione del moralismo romano*, Pisa: Giardini.

Clarke, J.R. (1991), *The Houses of Roman Italy, 100 BC- AD 250: Ritual, Space, and Decoration*, Berkeley: University of California Press.

Clarke, M. and Penny, N. (eds) (1982), *The Arrogant Connoisseur: Richard Payne Knight, 1751-1824*, Manchester: Manchester University Press.

Clifford, J. (1988), 'On collecting art and culture' in *The Predicament of Culture: Twentieth-Century Ethnography, Literature and Art*, Cambridge Mass.: Harvard University Press, 215-251.

Closa Farres, J. (1987), 'Marcial y la escultura antigua' in Costas Rodriquez, J. (ed.) (1987), 95-97.

Coarelli, F. (1972), 'Il complesso Pompeiano del Campo Marzio' in *Rendiconti Della Pontificia Accademia di Archeologia, Roma*, 44, 99-122.

Coarelli, F. (1983), 'Il commercio delle opere d' arte in età tardo-repubblicana' in *Dialogui di Archeologia*, 1 (1), 45-53.

Coffey, M. (1989), *Roman Satire*, Bristol: Bristol Classical Press.

Cole, T. (1967), *Democritus and the Sources of Greek Anthropology*, Cleveland, Ohio: Western Reserve University.

Collingwood, R.G. (1993), *The Idea of History*, Oxford: Clarendon Press.

Connors, C. (1994), 'Famous last words: authorship and death in the *Satyricon* and Neronian Rome' in Elsner, J. and Masters, J. (eds) (1994), 225-236.

Conte, G.B. (1994a), *Genres and Readers: Lucretius, Love Elegy and Pliny's Encylopedia*, Baltimore and London: The Jonhs Hopkins University Press.

Conte, G.B. (1994b), *Latin Literature: A History*, translated by J.B. Solodow, Baltimore: The Johns Hopkins University Press.

Conte, G.B. (1996), *The Hidden Author: An Interpretation of Petronius' Satyricon*, Berkeley: University of California Press.

Cook, R.M. (1955), 'Thucydides as archaeologist' in *BSA*, 50, 266- 270.

Coombes, A. (1988), 'Museums and the formation of national and cultural identities' in *Oxford Art Journal*, 11, 57-68.

Costas Rodriguez, J. (ed.) (1987), *Actas del Simposio sobre Marco Valerio Marcial poeta de Bilbilis y de Roma, vol. I: Cronica de Comunicaciones Conferencias*, Zaragoza: DPZ.

Couch, H.N. (1929), *The Treasuries of the Greeks and Romans*, Wisconsin: George Banta Publishing Company.

Coulson, W. and Kyreleis, H. (eds) (1992), *Proceedings of an International Symposium on the Olympic Games*, Athens: Deutsches Archäologisches Institut.

Courbin, P. (1980), *L' Oikos des Naxiens*, EAD 33, Paris: Diffusion de Boccard.

Cowles, F.H. (1917), *Gaius Verres: An Historical Study*, Ithaca, New York.

Cox, P. (1983), *Biography in Antiquity: A Quest for the Holy Man*, Berkeley: University of California Press.

Crane, G. (1993), 'Politics of consumption and generosity in the Carpet scene of the Agamemnon' in *Classical Philology*, 88 (2), 117-136.

Crimp, D. (1989), 'This is not a museum of art' in Goldwater, M. (ed.) (1989), 71-2.

D' Arms, J.H. (1981), *Commerce and Social Standing in Ancient Rome*, Cambridge Mass.: Harvard University Press.

Danet, B. and Katriel, T. (1989), 'No two alike: Play and aesthetics in collecting' in *Play and Culture*, 2, 253-277.

Danet, B. and Katriel, T. (1994), 'Glorious obsessions, passionate lovers, and hidden treasures: collecting, metaphor, and the Romantic ethic' in Riggins, S. H. (ed.) (1994), 23-61.

Daneu Lattanzi, A. (1982), 'A proposito dei libri sulle arti' in *Plinio il Vecchio sorto il profilo storico e letterario*. Atti del Convegno di Como 5/6/7 Ottobre 1979, Atti della Tavola Rotonda nella Ricorrenza centenaria della morte di Plinio il Vecchio, Bologna, 16 Dicembre 1979, Como: Banca Briantea, 97-107.

Dangel, J. (1996), 'L' otium chez les Latins de l' époque républicaine' in André, J.-M., Dangel, J. and Demont, P. (eds) (1996), 231-239.

Danish National Museum (1993), *Museum Europa: An Exhibition about the European Museum from the Renaissance to our time*, Copenhangen: The Danish National Museum.

Dannefer, D. (1980), 'Rationality and passion in private experience: Modern consciousness and the social world of old-car collectors', in *Social Problems*, 27, 392-412.

Dannefer, D. (1981), 'Neither socialisation nor recruitment: the avocational careers of old car enthusiasts' in *Social Forces*, 60, 395-413.

Daux, G. (1936), *Pausanias à Delphes*, Paris: A. Picard.

Daux, G. and Hansen, E. (1987), *FdD, vol. 2, Le Trésor de Siphnos*, Paris: Diffusion de Boccard.

de Jong, I.J.F. and Sullivan, J.P. (eds) (1994), *Modern Critical Theory and Classical Literature*, Leiden: E.J. Brill.

de Lacy, P.H. (1977), 'The four Stoic *personae*' in *Illinois Classical Studies*, 2, 163-172.

de Ste. Croix, G.E.M. (1975), 'Aristotle on history and poetry (*Poetics* 9, 1451a36-1451b11)' in Levick, B. (ed.) (1975), 45-58.

della Corte, F. (1982), 'Tecnica espositiva e struttura della Naturalis Historia', in *Plinio il Vecchio sorto il profilo storico e letterario*. Atti del Convegno di Como 5/6/7 Ottobre 1979, Atti della Tavola Rotonda nella Ricorrenza centenaria della morte di Plinio il Vecchio, Bologna 16 Dicembre 1979, Como: Banca Briantea, 19-39.

Delorme, J. (1960), *Gymnasion*, Paris: Éditions de Boccard.

Delorme, J. (1975), *Le monde hellénistique 323-133 av. J-C.*, Paris: Société d' édition d'enseignement superieur.

Dennet, D. (1979), *Brainstorms: Philosophical Essays on Mind and Psychology*, Sussex: Hassocks.

Déotte, J.-L. (1995), 'Rome, the archetypal museum, and the Louvre, the negation of division' in Pearce, S.M. (ed.) (1995), 215-232.

Descoeudres, J.-P. (ed.) (1994), *Pompeii Revisited: The Life and Death of a Roman Town*, Sydney: Southwood Press.

Desmouliez, A. (1949), 'Sur l' interpretation du *De Signis*', in *Revue Universitaire*, 155-166.

Desmouliez, A. (1976), *Cicèron et son goût: Essai sur une definition d' une aesthetique romaine à la fin de la République*, Bruxelles: Latomus.

Detienne, M. and Vernant, J.-P. (eds) (1989), *The Cuisine of Sacrifice among the Greeks*, translated by P. Wissing, Chicago: University of Chicago Press (first published in French, as *La cuisine du sacrifice en pays grec*, Paris, 1979).

Detlefsen, D. (1901), 'Die eigenen Leistungen des Plinius für die Geschichte der Künstler' in *JDAI*, 16, 75-107.

Detlefsen, D. (1905), 'Die Benutzung des zensorischen Verzeichinisses des römischen Kunstwerke in der Nat. Hist. des Plinius' in *JDAI*, 20, 113-122.

Dickison, S.K. (1992), *Cicero's Verrine Oration II.4*, with notes and vocabulary, Detroit: Wayne State University Press.

Dickmann, J.-A. (1997), 'The peristyle and the transformation of domestic space in hellenistic Pompeii', in Laurence, R. and Wallace-Hadrill, A. (eds), 1997, 121-136.

Digger, J. (1995), The People's Show at Walsall, Unpublished M.A. dissertation, Department of Museum Studies, University of Leicester.

Dihle, A. (1993), 'Response to part four' in Bulloch, A., Green, E.S., Long, A.A., Stewart, A. (eds) (1993), 287-295.

Dihle, A. (1994), *Greek and Latin Literature of the Roman Empire: From Augustus to Justinian*, London and New York: Routledge.

DiMaggio, P. (1982), 'Cultural entrepreneurship in nineteenth-century Boston: The creation of an organizational base for high-culture in America' in *Media, Culture and Society*, 4, 33-50.

Dinsmoor, W. B. (1947), 'The Hecatompedon on the Athenian Acropolis' in *AJA*, 51, 124ff.

Dittenberger, W. (1905), *Orientis Graeci Inscriptiones selectae II*, 277ff, no. 586, Leipzig: S. Hirzel.

Dittman, H. (1991), 'Meanings of material possessions as reflections of identity' in Rudmin, F.W. (ed.) (1991), 165-187.

Dodds, E.R. (1951), *The Greeks and the Irrational*, Berkeley: University of California Press.

Donley-Reid, L.W. (1990), 'A structuring structure: the Swahili house' in Kent, S., (ed.), 1990, 114-126.

Donohue, A.A. (1988), *Xoana and the Origins of Greek Sculpture*, Atlanta: Scholars Press.

Dougherty, C. and Kurke, L. (eds) (1993), *Cultural Poetics in Archaic Greece: Cult, Performance, Politics*, Cambridge: Cambridge University Press.

Douglas, A.E. (1968), *Cicero*, New Surveys in the Classics: Greece and Rome, Oxford: Clarendon Press.

Douglas, M. and Isherwood, B. (1979), *The World of Goods*, New York: Basic Books.

Doxiades, K.A. (1972), *Architectural Space in Ancient Greece*, Chicago: MIT Press.

Drees, L. (1968), *Olympia, Gods, Artists and Athletes*, London: Pall Mall Press.

Droysen, J.G. (1836-43), *Geshischte des Hellenismus*, 3 vols., Hamburg: Friedrich Perthes.

Duclos, R. (1994), 'Postmodern/postmuseum: New directions in contemporary museological critique', in *Museological Review*, 1 (1), 1-13.

Dumont, J.C. (1990), 'Le décor de Trimalchion' in *MEFRA*, 102, 959-981.

Dumont, L. (1970), *Homo Hierarchicus: The Caste System and its Implications*, translated by M. Sainsbury, London: Weidenfeld and Nicolson (originally published in French in 1966).

Dumont, L. (1982), 'A modified view of our origins: the Christian beginnings of modern individualism', *Religion*, 12, 1-27.

Dumont, L. (1983), *Essais sur l'individualisme: Une perspective anthropologique sur l'ideologie moderne*, Paris: Seuil.

Duncan, C. (1995), *Civilizing Rituals: Inside Public Art Museums*, London: Routledge.

Durkheim, E. (1915), *The Elementary Forms of the Religious Life*, London: Allen and Unwin.

Durost, W. (1932), *Children's Collecting Activity Related to Social Factors*, New York: Bureau of Publications, Teachers' College, Columbia University.

Dwyer, E. (1994), 'The Pompeian atrium house in theory and practice' in Gazda, E. K. (ed.) (1994), 25- 48.

Dyer, L. (1905), 'Olympian treasuries and treasuries in general' in *JHS*, 25, 294-319.

Ebert, F. (1950), 'Pinacotheca' in *RE*, 20, 2, 1389ff.

Economou, G. (1934), 'Genesis kai exelixis tou mouseiou' (Genesis and evolution of museum) in *Vradini* (Evening), 11-12 June, Athens (in Greek).

Edgar, K. (1997), 'Old masters and young mistresses: the collector in popular fiction' in Pearce, S.M. (ed.) (1997), 80-94.

Edwards, C. (1996), *Writing Rome: Textual Approaches to the City*, Cambridge: Cambridge University Press.

Ellen, R. (1988), 'Fetishism' in *Man* (n.s.), 23, 213-235.

Elsner, J. (1993), 'Seductions of art: Encolpius and Eumolpus in a Neronian picture gallery' in *PCPhS*, 39, 30-47.

Elsner, J. (1994a), 'A collector's model of desire: the house and museum of Sir John Soane' in Elsner, J. and Cardinal, R. (eds) (1994), 155-176.

Elsner, J. (1994b), 'From the pyramids to Pausanias and Piglet: monuments, travel and writing' in Goldhill, S. and Osborne, R. (eds) (1994), 224-254.

Elsner, J. (1995), *Art and the Roman Viewer: The Transformation of Art from the Pagan World to Christianity*, Cambridge: Cambridge University Press.

Elsner, J. and Cardinal, R. (eds) (1994), *The Cultures of Collecting*, London: Reaktion Books.

Elsner, J. and Masters, J. (eds) (1994), *Reflections of Nero: Culture, History and Representation*, London: Duckworth.

Elsner, J. (ed.) (1996), *Art and Text in Roman Culture*, Cambridge: Cambridge University Press.

Emanuele, D. (1989), '*Aes Corinthium*: fact, fiction, and fake' in *Phoenix*, 43 (4), 347-358.

Engberg-Pedersen, T. (1990), 'Stoic philosophy and the concept of person' in Gill, C. (ed.) (1990), 109-135.

Erskine, A. (1990), *The Hellenistic Stoa: Political Thought and Action*, London: Duckworth.

Everson, S. (ed.) (1991), *Psychology: Companions to Ancient Thought 2*, Cambridge: Cambridge University Press.

Fabian, J. (1983), *Time and the Other: How anthropology makes its object*, New York: Columbia University Press.

Fanti, S. *et al.* (1982), 'Pulsion de collection' in Hainard, J. and Kaehr, R. (eds) (1982), 181-183.

Farrar, C. (1988), *The Origins of Democratic Thinking: The Invention of Politics in Classical Athens*, Cambridge: Cambridge University Press.

Feger, R. (1956), 'T. Pomponius Atticus' in *RE Suppl.* VIII., 503-547.

Ferri, S. (1946), *Plinio il Vecchio, Storia delle Arti antiche*, Rome: Fratelli Palombi.

Findlen, P. (1989), 'The museum: its classical etymology and Renaissance genealogy' in *Journal of the History of Collections*, 1, 59-78.

Findlen, P. (1994), *Possessing Nature: Museums, collecting, and scientific culture in early modern Italy*, Berkeley: University of California Press.

Finley, I.M. (1979), *The World of Odysseus*, Harmondsworth: Penguin.

Finley, I.M. (1986a), 'Myth, memory and history', in Finley, I. M. (1986b), 11-33.

Finley, I.M. (1986b), *The Use and Abuse of History*, London: Hogarth Press.

Firth, R. (1965), *Primitive Polynesian Economy*, London: Routledge and Kegan Paul.

Fischler, S. (1994), 'Social stereotypes and historical analysis: the case of the Imperial women at Rome' in Archer, L. J., Fischler, S. and Wyke, M. (eds) (1994), 115-133.

Fish, S. (1980), *Is There a Text in This Class?: The Authority of Interpretive Communities*, Cambridge Mass.: Harvard University Press.

Flashar, H. and Gigon, O. (eds) (1988), *Aspects de la philosophie hellénistique*, (Entretiens sur l'antiquité classique), Vandoeuvres: Fondation Hardt.

Flower, H.I. (1996), *Ancestor Masks and Aristocratic Power in Roman Culture*, Oxford: Clarendon Press.

Fornara, C.W. (1983), *The Nature of History in Ancient Greece and Rome*, Berkeley: University of California Press.

Forrester, J. (1994), '"Mille e tre": Freud and collecting', in Elsner, J. and Cardinal, R. (eds) (1994), 224-251.

Foucault, M. (1986), *The Care of the Self, volume 3: The History of Sexuality*, translated by R. Hurley, Allen Lane: The Penguin Press.

Fränkel, M. (1891), 'Gemälde-Sammlungen und Gemälde-Forschung in Pergamon' in *JDAI*, 6, 48-60.

Frazer, J.G. (1898), *Pausanias Description of Greece*, i-vi, London: MacMillan and Co. Ltd

Frazer, O.M. (1972), *Ptolemaic Alexandria*, Oxford: Clarendon Press.

Frege, G. (1970), 'On sense and reference' in Geach, P. and Black, M. (eds) (1970), 56-78.

French, R. (1994), *Ancient Natural History*, London and New York: Routledge.

French, R. and Greenaway, F. (eds) (1986), *Science in the Early Roman Empire: Pliny the Elder, his Sources and Influence*, London and Sydney: Croom Helm.

Friedländer, L. (1865-1871), *Darstellung aus der Sittengeschicte Roms in der Zeit von Augustus bis zum Ausgang der Antonine*, I-IV, Leipzig: S. Hirzel.

Friedländer, L. (1886), *M. Valerii Martialis Epigrammaton Libri*, Leipzig: S. Hirzel.

Friedländer, P. (1912), *Johannes von Gaza und Paulus Silentiarius*, Leipzig and Berlin: B. G. Teubner.

Friedländer, L. (1921), *Darstellungen aus der Sittengeschichte Roms in der Zeit von August bis zum Ausgang der Antonine*, band III, Leipzig: S. Hirzel.

Frischer, B. (1982), *The Sculpted World: Epicureanism and Philosophical Recruitment in Ancient Greece*, Berkeley: University of California Press.

Frisk, H. (1957), *Griechische etymologisches Wörterbuch*, Heidelberg: C. Winter.

Fuchs, M. (1987), *Untersuchungen zur Austattung römischer Theater in Italien und den Westprovinzen des Imperium Romanum*, Mainz am Rhein: P. von Zabern.

Fuchs, W. (1963), *Der Schiffsfund von Mahdia*, Tübingen: W. Wasmuth.

Gabba, E. (1981), 'True history and false history in classical antiquity' in *JRS*, 71, 50-62.

Galinsky, K. (ed.) (1994), *The Interpretation of Roman Poetry: Empiricism or Hermeneutics*, Frankfurt am Main - New York: Peter Lang.

Gamwell, L. (1996), 'A collector analyses collecting: Sigmund Freud on the passion to possess' in Barker, S. (ed.) (1996), 1-12.

Gathercole, P. (1989), 'The fetishism of artefacts', in Pearce, S. M. (ed.) (1989), 73-81.

Gauthier, Ph. (1993), 'Les cités hellénistiques' in Hansen, M. H. (ed.) (1993), 211-231.

Gazda, E.K. (ed.) (1994), *Roman Art in the Private Sphere: New Perspectives on the Architecture and Decor of the Domus, Villa, and Insula*, Ann Arbor: The University of Michigan Press.

Gazda, E.K. (1995), 'Roman copies: the unmasking of a modern myth' in *JRA*, 8, 530-534.

Geach, P. and Black, M. (eds) (1970), *Translations from the Philosophical Writings of Gottlob Frege*, Oxford: Basil Blackwell.

Gelber, S. (1992), 'Free market metaphor: the historical dynamics of stamp collecting' in *Comparative Studies in Society and History*, 34, 742-269.

Gell, A. (1992), *The Anthropology of Time: Cultural constructions of temporal maps and images*, Oxford: Berg.

George, M. (1997), 'Repopulating the Roman house' in Rawson, B. and Weaver, P. (eds) (1997), 299-320.

Gernet, L. (1981), 'The mythical idea of value' in *The Anthropology of Ancient Greece*, translated by J. Hamilton and B. Nagy, Baltimore: The Johns Hopkins University Press, 73-111.

Gigon, O. (1982), 'Pline' in *Plinio il Vecchio sorto il profilo storico e letterario*. Atti della Tavola Rotonda nella Ricorrenza centenaria della morte di Plinio il Vecchio, Bologna 16 Dicembre 1979, Como: Banca Briantea, 41-52.

Gill, C. (1988), 'Personhood and personality: The four-*personae* theory in Cicero, *De Officiis* I' in *Oxford Studies in Ancient Philosophy*, 6, 169-199.

Gill, C. (ed.) (1990), *The Person and the Human Mind*, Oxford: Clarendon Press.

Gill, C. (1991), 'Is there a person in Greek philosophy?' in Everson, S. (ed.) (1991), 166-193.

Gill, C. (1994), 'Peace of mind and being yourself: Panaetius to Plutarch' in *ANRW*, II.36.7, 4599-4640.

Gill, C. (1995), *Greek Thought*, Oxford: Oxford University Press.

Gill, C. (1996), *Personality in Greek Epic, Tragedy, and Philosophy: The Self in Dialogue*, Oxford: Clarendon Press.

Giovannini, A. (1993), 'Greek cities and Greek commonwealth' in Bulloch, A., Green, E.S., Long, A.A., Stewart, A. (eds) (1993), 265-286.

Goffman, E. (1979), *Gender Advertisements*, London: Macmillan.

Göhling, W. (1877), *De Cicerone artis aestimatore*, Halle (Diss.).

Gold, B. (ed.) (1982), *Literary and Artistic Patronage in Ancient Rome*, Austin: University of Texas Press.

Golden, M. and Toohey, P. (eds) (1997), *Inventing Ancient Culture: Historicism, Periodization, and the Ancient World*, London: Routledge.

Goldhill, S. (1994), 'The naive and knowing eye: ecphrasis and the culture of viewing in the Hellenistic world' in Goldhill, S. and Osborne, R. (eds) (1994), 197-223.

Goldhill, S. and Osborne, R. (eds) (1994), *Art and Text in Ancient Greece*, Cambridge: Cambridge University Press.

Goldschmidt, V. (1979), *Le systéme stoicien et l'idée de temps*, Paris: J. Vrén.

Goldwater, M. (ed.) (1989), *Marcel Broodthaers*, Minneapolis and New York: Walker Art Gallery.

Goodyear, F.R.D. (1982a), 'Petronius' in Kenney, E.J. and Clausen, W.V. (eds) (1982), 635-638.

Goodyear, F.R.D. (1982b), 'Technical writing' in Kenney, E.J. and Clausen, W.V. (eds) (1982), 667-673.

Gordon, R.L. (1979), 'The real and the imaginary: production and religion in the Graeco-Roman world' in *Art History*, 2 (1), 5-34.

Graham, W.J. (1966), 'Origins and interrelations of the Greek house and the Roman house' in *Phoenix*, 20, 3-31.

Gray, D.H.F. (1954), 'Metal-working in Homer' in *JHS*, 74, 1-15.

Green, P. (1990), *Alexander to Actium*, Berkeley: University of California Press.

Green, P. (ed.) (1993), *Hellenistic History and Culture*, Berkeley: University of California Press.

Greenhalgh, P. (1988), *Ephemeral Vistas: the Expositions Universelles, Great Exhibitions and Worlds Fairs 1851-1939*, Manchester: Manchester University Press.

Greenhalgh, P. (1989), 'Education, entertainment and politics: lessons from the great international exhibitions' in Vergo, P. (ed.) (1989), 74-98.

Gregory, C.A. (1980), 'Gifts to men and gifts to gods: gift exchange and capital accumulation in contemporary Papua' in *Man* (n.s.), 15 (4), 626-652.

Gregory, C.A. (1982), *Gifts and Commodities*, London: Academic Press.

Gregory, C.A. (1984), 'The economy and kinship: a critical examination of the ideas of Marx and Lévi-Strauss', in Spriggs, M. (ed.) (1984), 32-81.

Grenier, J.-C. (1989), 'Essai de reconstitution et d'interpretation du décor statuaire du Serapeum au Canope de la villa Hadrienne' in *MEFRA*, 101-2, 925-1019.

Grewing, F. (1997), *Martial, Buch VI, (Ein Kommentar)*, Göttingen: Vandenhoeck & Ruprecht.

Griffin, M.T. (1984), *Nero: The End of a Dynasty*, London: B.T. Batsford.

Griffith, G.T. (1968), *The Mercenaries in the Hellenistic World*, Groningen: Bouma's Boekhuis.

Griffiths, A.H. (1943), Temple Treasures. A Study Based in the Works of Cicero and the Fasti of Ovid, A dissertation in Latin, presented for the Degree of Doctor of Philosophy, Philadelphia.

Griffiths, J.G. (1989), 'Hellenistic religions' in Seltzer, R.M. (ed.) (1989), 66-72.

Grimal, P. (1965), 'Encyclopédies antiques' in *Cahiers d' Histoire Mondiale*, 9, 459-482.

Grimal, P. (1969), *Les jardins romains*, Paris: Presses Universitaires de France.

Gros, P. (1976), *Aurea Templa: Recherches sur l'Architecture religieuse de Rome à l'époque d'August*, Rome: École Française de Rome.

Gualandi, G. (1982), 'Plinio e il collezionismo d' arte', *Plinio il Vecchio Sotto il Profilo Storico e Letterario*, Atti del Convegno di Como 5/6/7 Ottobre 1979, Atti della Tavola Rotonda nella Ricorrenza centenaria della morte di Plinio il Vecchio, Bologna 16 Dicembre 1979, Como: Banca Biantea.

Habicht, C. (1985), *Pausanias' Guide to Ancient Greece*, Berkeley: University of California Press.

Habicht, C. (1990), *Cicero the Politician*, London and Baltimore: The Johns Hopkins University Press.

Hainard, J. and Kaehr, R. (eds) (1982), *Collections Passion*, Neuchâtel, Switzerland: Musée d'Ethnographie.

Hall, R.W. (1963), *Plato and the Individual*, The Hague: Martinus Nijhoff.

Hallowell, A.I. (1953), 'Culture, personality and society' in Kroeber, A.L. (ed.) (1953), 597-620.

Hammond, M. (1951), *City-State and World State in Greek and Roman Political Theory until Augustus*, Cambridge Mass.: Harvard University Press.

Hansen, E.V. (1971), *The Attalids of Pergamon*, Ithaca and London: Cornell University Press.

Hansen, M.H. (ed.) (1993), *The Ancient Greek City-State*, Copenhagen: Royal Danish Academy of Sciences and Letters.

Hanslik, R. (1955) 'Forschungsbericht über Plinius d. Ae. I' in *AAHG*, 8, 193-218.

Hanslik, R. (1964), 'Plinius des Aeltere, II. Bericht' in *AAHG*, 17, 65-80.

Hanson, V.D. (ed.) (1991), *Hoplites: the Classical Greek Battle Experience*, London and New York: Routledge.

Harden, D.B. (1954), '*Vasa murrina* again', *JRS*, 44, 53ff.

Harris, D. (1995), *The Treasures of the Parthenon and Erechteion*, Oxford: Oxford University Press.

Harris, G.G. (1989), 'Concepts of individual, self, and person in description and analysis' in *American Anthropologist*, 91, 599-612.

Hartog, F. (1988), *The Mirror of Herodotus: The Representation of the Other in the Writing of History*, Berkeley: University of California Press.

Harvey, D. (1989), *The Condition of Postmodernity*, Oxford: Basil Blackwell.

Haskell, F. (1993), *History and its Images: Art and Interpretation in the Past*, New Haven: Yale University Press.

Hauser, F. (1905), 'Plinius und das censorische Verzeichnis', in *MDAI (R.)*, 20, 206-213.

Healy, J.F. (1987), 'The language and style of Pliny the Elder' in *Filologia e forme letterarie. Studi offerti a Franscesco della Corte*, IV, Urbino: Università degli Studi di Urbino, 3-24.

Healy, J.F. (1991), 'Introduction' in *Pliny the Elder - Natural History: A Selection*, translation, introduction and notes by J.F. Healy, London: Penguin Classics, ix-xxxl.

Heizer, R.F. (ed.) (1969), *Man's Discovery of his Past*, Valo Alko: Been Publications.

Hellenkemper Sallies, G. (ed.) (1994), *Das Wrack. Der antike Schiffsfund von Madhia*, (Kataloge des Rheinischen Lnadsmuseums, 1.1-2, Bonn 1994), Rheinland: Verlag GmbH, Köln.

Henrichs, A. (1982), *Die Phoenikika des Lollianos*, Bonn: R. Habelt.

Henry, M.N. (1948), 'On Martial IX.44' in *Hermathena*, 71, 93-4.

Herklotz, I. (1994), 'Neue Literatur zur Sammlungsgeschichte' in *Kunstchronik*, 47 (3), 117-135.

Hermann, R.J. (1855), *Ueber dern Kunstsinn des Römer und deren Stellung in der Geschichte der alten Kunst*, Göttingen: Universitatis-Buchdruckerei von E. A. Husth.

Herrman, F. (1972), *The English as Collectors*, London: Chatto and Windus.

Herrmann, K. (1992), 'Die Schatzhäuser in Olympia' in Coulson, W. and Kyreleis, H. (eds) (1992), pp. 25-32.

Heseltine, M. (1919), 'Introduction' in *Petronius, Satyricon*, Loeb CL, N. Y.: G. P. Putnam's Sons, i-xix.

Heuzé, Ph. (1987), 'Pline "critique d' art"? Les avis contradictoires de Diderot et Falconet' in *Helmantica*, 38, 29-39.

Hiesinger, U. (1973), 'Portraiture in the Roman Republic, *ANRW*, I.4, 805-825.

Higbie, C. (1997), 'The bones of a hero, the ashes of a politician: Athens, Salamis, and the usable past' in *Classical Antiquity*, 16 (2), 278-307.

Highet, G. (1941), 'Petronius the moralist' in *TAPA*, 72, 176-194.

Hodder, I. (ed.) (1987), *Archaeology as Long-Term History*, Cambridge: Cambridge University Press.

Hodder, I. (1986), *Reading the Past*, Cambridge: Cambridge University Press.

Hoepfner, W. and Schwandner, E.L. (1986), *Haus und Stadt im klassischen Griechenland, Wohnen in der klassischen Polis I*, Munich: Deutschen Kunstverlag.

Hofman, H. (ed.) (1991), *Groningen Colloquia on the Novel*, IV, Groningen: Egbert Forsten.

Hofmann, J.B. (1949), *Etymologisches Wörterbuch des Griechischen*, Munich: R. Oldenbourg.

Holst, N., von (1967), *Creators, Collectors and Connoisseurs: The anatomy of artistic taste from Antiquity to the present day*, New York: Putnam.

Holzberg, N. (1995a), 'Petron 1965-1995' in Müller, K and Ehlers, W. (eds) (1995), 544-560.

Holzberg, N. (1995b), *The Ancient Novel: An Introduction*, translated by C. Jackson-Holzberg, London and New York: Routledge.

Hooker, J.T. (1989), 'Gifts in Homer' in *BICS*, 36, 79-90.

Hooper-Greenhill, E. (1992), *Museums and the Shaping of Knowledge*, London: Routledge.

Hornblower, S. (1987), *Thucydides*, London: Duckworth.

Horsfall, N. (1988), 'Patronage of art in the Roman world' in *Prudentia*, XX (1), 9-29.

Horsfall, N. (1989), '"The uses of literacy" and the *Cena Trimalchionis*' in *Greece and Rome*, 36, I: 74-89, II: 194-209.

Hossenfelder, M. (1986), 'Epicurus-hedonist malgré lui' in Schofield, M. and Striker, G., (eds) (1986), 245-264.

Howard, S. (1986), 'Pergamene art collecting and its aftermath' in *Akten des XXV Internationalen Kongresses Fur Kunstgeschte*, Wien 1983: IV/4. Der Zugang zum Kunstwerk: Schatzkammer, Salon, Ausstellung, 'Museum', Vienna: H. Bühlau, 25-36.

Howell, P. (1980), *A Commentary on Book One of the Epigrams of Martial*, London: The Athlone Press.

Hubbard, W. (1984), 'The meaning of monuments' in *The Public Interest*, 74 (Winter), 17-30.

Hubert, H. and Mauss, M. (1899), 'Essai sur la nature et la fonction du sacrifice' in *Année Sociologique*, 2, 29-138.

Huet, V. (1996), 'Inventing imperium: texts and the propaganda of monuments in Augustan Rome' in Elsner, J. (ed.) (1996), 9-31.

Hunter, M. (1983), *Elias Asmole and his World*, Oxford: Asmolean Museum.

Hunter, V. (1982), *Past and Process in Herodotus and Thucydides*, Princeton: Princeton University Press.

Huys, M. (1995), *The Tale of the Hero who was exposed at Birth in Euripidean Tragedy: A Study of Motifs*, Leuven, Belgium: Leuven University Press.

Huxley, G. (1973), 'Aristotle as antiquary' in *GRBS*, 14, 271-286.

Huxley, G. (1979), 'Bones for Orestes' in *GRBS*, 20, 145-148.

Imbert, C. (1980), 'Stoic logic and Alexandrian poetics' in Schofielf, M., Burnyeat, M., and Barnes, J. (eds) (1980), 182-216.

Impey, O. and MacGregor, A. (eds) (1985), *The Origins of Museums*, Oxford: Clarendon Press.

Inge, T. (ed.) (1989), *Handbook of American Popular Culture*, vol.3, New York and London: Greenwood.

Ioppolo, A.M. (1990), 'Presentation and assent: a physical and cognitive problem in early Stoicism' in *Classical Quarterly*, 40 (2), 433-449.

Isager, J. (1971), 'The composition of Pliny's chapters on the history of art' in *Analecta Romana Instituti Danici*, 6, 49-62.

Isager, J. (1991), *Pliny on Art and Society: The Elder Pliny's Chapters on the History of Art*, London and New York: Routledge.

Jackson, A. (ed.) (1987), *Anthropology at Home*, London: Tavistock.

Jackson, A.D. (1992), 'Arms and armour in the Panhellenic sanctuary of Poseidon at Isthmia' in Coulson, W. and Kyrieleis, H. (eds) (1992), 141-3.

Jackson, A.J. (1991), 'Hoplites and the gods: the dedications of captured arms and armour' in Hanson, V.D. (ed.) (1991), 228-252.

Jacobi, F. (1884), *Grundzüge einer Museographie der Stadt Rome zur Zeit des Kaisers Augustus*, Speier: L. Gilardone'sche Buchdruckerei, vorm Dl. Kranzbühler.

Jahn, O. (1850), 'Über die kunsturteile des Plinius', *Berichte Sächsische Akademie der Wissenschaft*, Leipzig, 105-142.

Jameson, M.H. (1990a), 'Domestic space in the Greek city-state' in Kent, S. (ed.) (1990), 92-113.

Jameson, M.H. (1990b), 'Private space and the Greek city' in Murray, O. and Price, S. (eds) (1990), 171-195.

Jenkins, I. (1992), *Archaeologists and Aesthetes*, London: British Museum Press.

Jenkins, I. (1996), '"Contemporary minds": William Hamilton's affair with antiquity' in Jenkins, I. and Sloan, K. (eds) (1996), 40-64.

Jenkins, I. and Sloan, K. (eds) (1996), *Vases and Volcanoes: Sir William Hamilton and his Collection*, London: British Museum Press.

Jex-Blake, K. and Sellers, E. (1896), *The Elder Pliny's Chapters on the History of Art*, translated by K. Jex-Blake with commentary and historical introduction by Sellers, E., London and New York: Macmillan.

Jonas, H. (1963), *The Gnostic Religion*, Boston: Beacon.

Jones, A.H. M. (1940), *The Greek City: From Alexander to Justinian*, Oxford: Clarendon Press.

Jones, F.M. (1991), 'Realism in Petronius' in Hofman, H. (ed.) (1991), 105-120.

Jucker, H. (1950), *Von Verhältnis der Römer zur bildeden Kunst des Griechen*, Frankfurt am Main: V. Klostermann.

Juret, A. (1942), *Dictionnaire étymologique Grec et Latin*, Strassburg: Publications de la Faculté des lettres de l' Université.

Kalkmann, A. (1898), *Die Quellen der Kunstgeschichte des Plinius*, Berlin: Weidmannsche Buchhandlung.

Kavanagh, G. (ed.) (1991), *Museum Languages: Objects and Texts*, Leicester, London and New York: Leicester University Press.

Kennedy, D.F. (1993), *The Arts of Love: five studies in the discourse of Roman love elegy*, Cambridge: Cambridge University Press.

Kenney, E.J. and Clausen, W.V. (eds) (1982), *The Cambridge History of Classical Literature. II: Latin Literature*, Cambridge: Cambridge University Press.

Kent Hill, D. (1944), 'Hera, the sphinx' in *Hesperia*, 13, 353-60.

Kent, S. (ed.) (1990), *Domestic Architecture and the Use of Space: An interdisciplinary cross-cultural study*, Cambridge: Cambridge University Press.

Ker, W.C.A. (1919), 'Introduction' in Martial, Epigrams, Loeb CL, volume 1, London and Cambridge Mass.: W. Heinemann Ltd and Harvard University Press, vii-xviii.

Kerferd, G.B. (1972), 'The search for personal identity in Stoic thought' in *Bulletin of the John Rylands University Library of Manchester*, 55, 177-196.

Kidd, I.G. (1971), 'Stoic intermediates and the end of man' in Long, A. (ed.) (1971), 150-172.

King, A.D. (ed.) (1980), *Buildings and Society*, London: Routledge and Kegan Paul.

Kleiner, D.E.E. (1996), 'Imperial women as patrons of the arts in the early Empire' in Kleiner, D.E.E. and Matheson, S.B. (eds) (1996), 28-41.

Kleiner, D.E.E. and Matheson, S.B. (eds) (1996), *I Claudia: Women in Ancient Rome*, New Haven: Yale University Art Gallery/Austin: University of Texas Press.

Knell, S.J. (ed.) 1999, *Museums and the Future of Collecting*, Aldershot: Ashgate Publishing.

Knox, A.D. (1922), *Herodas: The Mimes and Fragments*, Cambridge: University Press.

Koch, G.F. (1967), *Die Kunstaustellung; Ihre Geschichte von den Anfängen bis zum Ausgang des 18. Jahrhunderts*, Berlin: Walter de Gruyter & Co.

Koller, H. (1954), *Die Mimesis in der Antike*, Bern: A. Francke.

Konstan, D. (1972), 'Epicurus on "up" and "down" (*Letters to Herodotus*, paragraph 60)' in *Phronesis*, 17, 269-278.

Kopytoff, I. (1986), 'The cultural biography of things: commoditization as process' in Appadurai, A., (ed.) (1986), 64-94.

Kresic, S. (1981), *Contemporary Literary Hermeneutics and Interpretation of Classical Texts*, Ottawa: University of Ottawa Press.

Kretschmer, P. (1920), 'Mythische Namen' in *Glotta*, 10, 51-57.

Kristeva, J. (1986), *The Kristeva Reader*, edited by T. Moi, Oxford: Blackwell.

Kroeber, A.L. (ed.) (1953), *Anthropology Today: An Encyclopaedic Inventory*, Chicago Illinois: University of Chicago Press.

Kroll, W. (1930), *Die Kosmologie des Plinius*, Abhandl. des Schlesischen Ges. für vaterländische Cultur, geisteswiss. Reihe. 3. Hefte. Breslau: Verlag von M. and H. Marcus.

Kurtz, D. and Boardman, J. (1971), *Greek Burial Customs*, London: Thames and Hudson.

Kyrieleis, H. (1993), 'The Heraion at Samos' in Marinatos, N. and Hägg, R. (eds) (1993), 125-153.

Lafon, X. (1981), 'À propos de "villae" republicaines: Quelques notes sur les programmes decoratifs et les commanditaires', in *L'Art Decoratif à Rome à la fin de la Republique et au debut du Principat*, Rome: École Française de Rome, Palais Farnèse, 151-172.

Lancaster, S. and Foddy, M. (1988), 'Self-extensions: a conceptualisation' in *Journal for the Theory of Social Behaviour*, 18 (1), 77-94.

Landwehr, C. (1985), *Die Antiken Gipsabgussen aus Baiae*, Berlin: Gebr. Mann Verlag.

Lane Fox, R.J. (1996), 'Theophrastus' *Characters* and the historian' in *PCPhS*, 42: 127-170.

Langdon, S. (1987), 'Gift exchange in Geometric sanctuaries' in Linders, T. and Nordquist, G. (eds) (1987), 107-113.

Laurens, P. (1980), '"Martial", ou l' épigramme grecque et latine de l' époque alexandrine à la fin de la Renaissance' in *L' Information Litteraire*, 32, 201-206.

Lausberg, M. (1982), *Das Einzeldistichon: Studien zum Antiken Epigramm*, Munich: W. Fink.

Laurence, R. and Wallace-Hadrill, A. (eds) (1997), *Domestic Space in Ancient Rome: Pompeii and Beyond*, Portsmouth, Journal of Roman Archaeology Supplement, 22: Society for the Promotion of Roman Studies.

Leach, E.W. (1982a), *Social Anthropology*, New York and Oxford: Oxford University Press.

Leach, E.W. (1982b), 'Patrons, painters, and patterns: the anonymity of Romano-Campanian painting and the transition from the second to the third style' in Gold, B. (ed.) (1982), 135-173.

Leach, E.W. (1988), *The Rhetoric of Space: Literary and Artistic Representations of Landscape in Republican and Augustan Rome*, Princeton: Princeton University Press.

Leary, T.J. (1996), *Martial Book XIV: The Apophoreta*, London: Duckworth.

Leen, A. (1991), 'Cicero and the rhetoric of art' in *AJPh*, 112, 229-245.

Lehmann, K. (1945), 'A Roman poet visits a museum' in *Hesperia*, XIV, 259-269.

Lehmann-Hartleben, K. (1941), 'The Imagines of Philostratus' in *Art Bulletin*, XXIII, 33ff.

Lévi-Strauss, C. (1969), *The Elementary Structures of Kinship*, London: Eyre and Spottiswoode (originally published in 1949).

Levick, B. (ed.) (1975), *The Ancient Historian and His Materials: Essays in Honour of C.E. Stevens on his seventieth birthday*, Farnborough: Gregg International.

Levidis, A. (1994), 'Prologos tou epimelete' (Prologue by the editor), in *Pliny the Elder, Peri tes Archaias Ellenekes Zografikes* (On the Ancient Greek Painting) – *35o Vivlio tes Fisikes Istorias* (35th Book of the 'Natural History'), translated by T. Roussos and A. Levidis, Athens: Agra (in Greek), 7-14.

Linders, T. (1972), *Studies in the Treasure Records of Artemis Brauronia found in Athens*, Stockholm: Swedish Institute of Athens, Lund: P. Aström, Sölveg. 2 (distr.).

Linders, T. (1975), *The Treasurers of the Other Gods in Athens and their Functions*, Beiträge zur Klassischen Philologie, Heft 62, Meisenheim am Glan: Hain.

Linders, T. and Nordquist, G. (eds) (1987), *Gifts to the Gods*, Proceedings of the Uppsala Symposium, 1985, Boreas 15, Uppsala: Academia Ubsaliensis; Stockholm: Almquist & Wiksell International.

Ling, R. (1991), *Roman Painting*, Cambridge: Cambridge University Press.

Lintott, A. (1986), 'How bad was Verres?' in *Omnibus*, 11, 1-4.

Lippold, G. (1923), *Kopien und Umbildungen griechischer Statuen*, Munich: Oskar Beck.

Lloyd, A.C. (1970), 'Activity and description in Aristotle and the Stoa' in *Proceedings of the British Academy*, 56, 227-240.

Lloyd, G.E.R. (1962), 'Right and left in Greek philosophy' in *JHS*, 82, 56-66.

Lobeck, C.A. (1843), *Pathologiae Sermonis Graeci*, (Prolegomena), Leipzig: Apud Weidmanns.

Loewenthal, A.I. and Harden, D.B. (1949), '*Vasa murrina*' in *JRS*, 39, 31-37.

Long, A.A. (ed.) (1971), *Problems in Stoicism*, London: Athlone Press.

Long, A.A. (1974), *Hellenistic Philosophy: Stoics, Epicureans, Sceptics*, London: Duckworth.

Long, A.A. (1983), 'Greek ethics after MacIntyre and the Stoic community of reason' in *Ancient Philosophy*, 3, 174-199.

Long, A.A. (1986), 'Pleasure and social utility - the virtues of being Epicurean' in Flashar, H. and Gigon, O. (eds) (1988), 283-316.

Long, A.A. (1991), 'Representation and the self in Stoicism', in Everson, S. (ed.) (1991), 102-120.

Long, A.A. (1993), 'Hellenistic ethics and philosophical power' in Green, P. (ed.) (1993), 138-167.

Long, A.A. and Sedley, D.N. (eds) (1987a), *The Hellenistic Philosophers*, volume 1, Cambridge: Cambridge University Press.

Long, A.A. and Sedley, D.N. (eds) (1987b), *The Hellenistic Philosophers*, volume 2: Greek and Latin texts with notes and bibliography, Cambridge: Cambridge University Press.

Lovatt, J.R. (1995), 'A People's Show means a People's Show' in *Museological Review*, 1 (2), 66-71.

Lovatt, J.R. (1997), 'The People's Show Festival in 1994: a survey' in Pearce, S.M. (ed.) (1997), 196-254.

Lovejoy, A.O. and Boas, G., (eds) (with suppplemetary essays by Albright, W.F. and Dumont, P.E.) (1997), *Primitivism and Related Ideas in Antiquity*, Baltimore and London: The Johns Hopkins University Press (first published in 1935).

Lowenthal, D. (1985), *The Past is a Foreign Country*, Cambridge: Cambridge University Press.

Lukes, S. (1973), *Individualism*, New York: Harper and Row.

Lumley, R. (ed.) (1988), *The Museum Time Machine: Putting Cultures on Display*, London: Routledge.

Maas, E. (1925), 'Thesauros', *RhM*, 74, 235-253.

MacDougal, E.B. (ed.) (1987), *Ancient Roman Villa Gardens*, Washington DC.: Dumbarton Oaks Research and Library Collection.

MacDougal, E.B. and Jashemscki, W.F. (eds) (1981), *Ancient Roman Gardens*, Dumbarton Oak Colloquium on the History of Landscape Architecture VII, Washington DC: Dumbarton Oaks Trustees for Harvard University.

MacGregor, A. (1983), *Tradescants' Rarities*, Oxford: Oxford University Press.

MacGregor, A. (ed.) (1994), *Sir Hans Sloane: Collector, Scientist, Antiquary, Founding Father of the British Museum*, London: British Museum Press and A. McAlpine.

MacIntyre, A. (1985), *After Virtue: A Study in Moral Theory*, London: Duckworth.

Mallwitz, A. (1972), *Olympia und seine Bauten*, Munich: Prestel-Verlag.

Manderscheid, H. (1981), *Die Sculpturenausstattung des kaiserzeitlichen Termenanlagen*, (*Monumenta Artis Romanae* 15), Berlin: Mann.

Marinatos, N. (1993), 'What were the Greek sanctuaries? A synthesis' in Marinatos, N. and Hägg, R. (eds) (1993), 228-233.

Marinatos, N. and Hägg, R. (eds) (1993), *Greek Sanctuaries: New Approaches*, London and New York: Routledge.

Marincola, J. (1997), *Authority and Tradition in Ancient Historiography*, Cambridge: Cambridge University Press.

Martin, L.H. (1987), *Hellenistic Religions: An Introduction*, New York and Oxford: Berg.

Martin, L.H. (1994), 'The anti-individualistic ideology of Hellenistic culture' in *Numen*, 41, 117-140.

Martin, L., Gutman, H. and Hutton, P. (eds) (1988), *Technologies of the Self: A Seminar with M. Foucault*, Amherst: The University of Massachussetts Press.

Martin, P.K. (1996), 'Tomorrow's history today? Post-modern collecting' in *History Today*, February, 5-8.

Martin, P.K. (1997), Contemporary popular collecting in Britain: The socio-cultural construction of identity at the end of second millenium AD, unpublished Ph.D. thesis submitted at the Department of Museum Studies, University of Leicester.

Martin, P.K. (1999a), 'Contemporary popular collecting' in Knell, S.J. (ed.) (1999), 73-76.

Martin, P.K. (1999b), *Popular Collecting and the Everyday Self: The Reinvention of Museums*, London: Leicester University Press.

Martindale, C. (1993), *Redeeming the Text: Latin poetry and the Hermeneutics of Reception*, Cambridge: Cambridge University Press.

Marvin, M. (1983), 'Freestanding sculptures from the Baths of Caracalla', *AJA*, 87, 378.

Marvin, M. (1989), 'Copying the Roman sculpture: the replica series' in *Retaining the Original: Multiple Originals, Copies and Reproductions*, Washington DC: National Gallery of Art, 20, 29-45.

Marx, K. (1867), *Capital, vol. I: A Critical Analysis of Capitalist Production*. Moscow: Progress Publishers.

Mason, P. (1994), 'From presentation to representation: Americana in Europe' in *Journal of the History of Collections* 6 (1), 1-20.

Mau, A. (1882), *Geschichte des decorativen Wandmalerei in Pompeji*, Berlin: G. Reimer.

Mau, A. (1899), *Pompeii: Its Life and Art*, London: Macmillan.

Mauss, M. (1970), *The Gift: Forms and Functions of Exchange in Archaic Societies*, translated by I. Cunnison, London: Cohen and West Ltd (originally published in 1925).

Mauss, M. (1979), *Sociology and Psychology: Essays*, translated by B. Brewster, London, Boston and Henley: Routledge and Kegan Paul.

May, J.M. (1988), *Trials of Character: The Eloquence of Ciceronian Ethos*, North Carolina Press: Chapel Hill and London.

McKay, A.G. (1977), *Houses, Villas, and Palaces of the Roman World*, London: Thames and Hudson.

Mendell, H. (1987), '*Topoi* on *topos*: the development of Aristotle's concept of place' in *Phronesis*, 32, 206-231.

Meyer, B.F. and Sanders, E.P. (eds) (1982), *Jewish and Christian Self-definition, vol.3: Self-definition in the Graeco-Roman World*, London: SCM Press Ltd.

Meyer, L. (1901), *Handbuch der Griechischen Etymologie*, vol. 3, Leipzig: S. Hirzel.

Michaelis, A. (1908), *A Century of Archaeological Discoveries*, London: J. Murray.

Michel, A. (1960), *Rhétorique et Philosophie chez Cicéron*, Paris: Presses Universitaires de France.

Michel, A. (1966), 'Cicéron et la phychologie de l'art' in *Maia*, 18, 3-19.

Michel, A. (1987), 'L' aestheticque de Pline l'Ancien' in *Helmantica*, 38, 55-67.

Middleton, D. and Edwards, D. (eds) (1990), *Collective Remembering*, London: Sage.

Miller, S.G. (1978), 'Excavations at Nemea-1977' in *Hesperia*, 47, 58-88.

Miller, S.G. (ed.) (1990), *Nemea: A Guide to the Site and Museum*, Berkeley: University of California Press.

Mitchell, L.G. (1997), *Greek Bearing Gifts: The Public Use of Private Relationships in the Greek World, 435-323 BC*, Cambridge: Cambridge University Press.

Mitchell, T.N. (1991), *Cicero the Senior Statesman*, New Haven: Yale University Press.

Mohler, S.L. (1927/8), 'Apophoreta' in *Classical Journal*, 23, 248-257.

Momigliano, A. (1950), 'Ancient history and antiquarianism', in *Journal of the Warburg and Courtauld Institutes*, XIII, 285-315.

Momigliano, A. (1969), 'Time in ancient historiography' in *Quatro contributo all storia degli studi classici e del mondo antico*, Roma: Edizioni di Storia e Letteratura, 1-41 (first published in *History and Theory*, Beiheft 6, 1966, 1-23).

Momigliano, A. (1977), 'Tradition and the classical historian', in Momigliano, A. (1977), *Essays in Ancient and Modern Historiography*, Oxford: Blackwell.

Momigliano, A. (1985), 'Marcel Mauss and the quest for the person in Greek biography and autobiography' in Carrithers, M., Collins, S., and Lukes, S. (eds) (1985), 83-92.

Momigliano, A. (1990a), 'The rise of antiquarian research' in Momigliano, A. (1990b), 54-79.

Momigliano, A. (1990b), *The Classical Foundations of Modern Historiography*, Berkeley: University of California Press.

Momigliano, A. (1993), *The Development of Greek Biography*, Cambridge Mass: Harvard University Press (originally published in 1971).

Mommsen, T. (1884), 'Eine Inschrift des älteren Plinius', *Hermes*, XIX, 644-648.

Moore, H. (1990), 'Paul Ricoeur: action, meaning and text' in Tilley, C. (ed.) (1990a), 85-120.

Moorhouse, A.C. (1940), 'A Roman view of art' in *Greece and Rome*, 10, 29-35.

Morford, M. (1986), 'Nero's patronage and participation in literature and the arts' in *ANRW*, II.32.3, 2003-2029.

Morgan, C. (1990), *Athletes and Oracles: The Transformation in Olympia and Delphi in the eighth century BC*, Cambridge: Cambridge University Press.

Morris, B. (1991), *Western Conceptions of the Individual*, Oxford and New York: Berg.

Morris, B. (1994), *Anthropology of the Self: the Individual in Cultural Perspective*, London: Pluto Press.

Morris, I. (1986), 'Gift and commodity in Archaic Greece' in *Man* (n.s.), 21(1), 1-17.

Morris, I. (1992), *Death-Ritual and Social Structure in Classical Antiquity*, Cambridge: Cambridge University Press.

Moulin, R. (1984), *The French Art Market: A Sociological Analysis*, New Brunswick, New Jersey: Rutgers University Press.

Moxon, I.S., Smart, J.D. and Woodman, A.J. (eds) (1986), *Past Perspectives: Studies in Greek and Roman Historical Writing*, Cambridge: Cambridge University Press.

Muensterberger, W. (1994), *Collecting: An Unruly Pasion. Psychological Perspectives*, New Jersey: Princeton University Press.

Müller, K. and Ehlers, W. (eds) (1965), *Petronius: Satyrica. Schelmengeschichten*, Munich: E. Heimeran.

Müller, K. and Ehlers, W. (eds) (1995), *Petronius: Satyrica. Schelmenszenen*, 4 Auflage, Munich: E. Heimeran.

Münzer, F. (1897), *Beiträge zur Quellenkritik der Naturgeschichte des Plinius*, Berlin: Weidemannsche Buchhandlung.

Murray, D. (1904), *The Museums: their History and their Use*, Glasgow: James MacLehose and Sons.

Murray, O. (1986), 'Life and society in ancient Greece' in Boardman, J., Griffin, J., Murray, O. (eds) (1986), 204-233.

Murray, O. (1990), 'Cities of reason' in Murray, O. and Price, S. (eds) (1990), 1-29.

Murray, O. and Price, S. (eds) (1990), *The Greek City: From Homer to Alexander*, Oxford: Clarendon Press.

Museums Association (1994/5), *Code of Practice for Museum Authorities*, in Museums Yearbook 1994/5 (edited by S. Barbour), Rhinegold Publishing Ltd, London, 445ff.

Nagy, J.F. (1981), 'The deceptive gift in Greek mythology' in *Arethusa*, 14 (2), 191-204.

Neudecker, R. (1988), *Die Skulpturen-ausstatung römischer Villen in Italien*, Mainz am Rhein: Verlag Philipp von Zabern.

Neugebauer, K.A. (1934), 'Herodes Atticus, ein antiker Kunstmäzen' in *Die Antike*, 10, 92-121.

Nevett, L. (1997), 'Perceptions of space in Roman Italy' in Rawson, B. and Weaver, P. (eds) (1997), 281-298.

Norden, E. (1898-1918), *Antike Kunstprosa*, I-II, Leipzig: B. G. Teubner.

Oberhummer, E. (1933), 'Μουσειον' in *RE*, XVI.1, 797-821.

Olmstead, A.D. (1987), *Stamp Collectors and Stamp Collecting*, Paper presented at the Popular Culture Association Annual Meeting, Antiques and Collecting Section, Montreal.

Olmstead, A.D. (1988), 'Morally controversial leisure: the social world of gun collectors' in *Symbolic Interaction*, 11, 277-287.

Olsen, B. (1990), 'Roland Barthes: from sign to text' in Tilley, C. (ed.) (1990a), 163-205.

Østby, E. (1993), 'Twenty-five years of research on Greek sanctuaries: a bibliography' in Marinatos, N. and Hägg, R. (eds) (1993), 192- 227.

Owen, G.E.L. (1979), 'Aristotle on time' in Barnes, J., Schofield, M., Sorabji, R. (eds) (1979), 140-158.

Palm, J. (1965), 'Bemerkungen zur Ekphrase in der griechischen Literatur' in *Kungliga Humanistiska vetenskapssamfundet*, 1, 108-211.

Panayotakis, C. (1995), *Theatrum Arbitri: Theatrical Elements in the Satyrica of Petronius*, Leiden: E. J. Brill.

Pantermalis, D. (1971), 'Zum Programm der Statuenausstatung in der Villa dei Papyri' in *Mitteilungen des Deutchen archäologischen Instituts athenische Abteilung* 86, 173-209.

Papaioannou, A.A. (1997), 'Archaiologia: e istoria tou onomatos' (Archaeology: the history of the name), in *Platon: Deltion tes Etaireias Ellinon Philologon* (Plato: Bulletin of the Society of Greek Philologists), 49, 142-165 (in Greek).

Pape, M. (1975), *Griechische Kunstwerke aus Kriegsbeute und ihre öffentliche Aufstellung in Rom*, Hamburg: privately published.

Pappalardo, U. (1990), 'L' eruzione pliniana del Vesuvio nel 79 d.c.: Ercolano', in Albore-Livadie, C. and Widemann, F. (eds) (1990), 205ff.

Parke, H.W. (1984), 'Croesus and Delphi' in *GRBS*, 25, 209-232.

Parker Pearson, M. and Richards, C. (eds) (1994), *Architecture and Order: Approaches to Social Space*, London and New York: Routledge.

Parsons, P.J. (1974), *P. Oxy.* 3010, 34-41.

Pearce, S.M. (1992), *Museums, Objects and Collections: A Cultural Study*, Leicester and London: Leicester University Press.

Pearce, S.M. (1993), 'Towards modernist collecting: Some European practices of the long term' in *Nordisk Museologi*, 2, 87-98.

Pearce, S.M. (1995), *On Collecting: An Investigation into Collecting in the European Tradition*, London and New York: Routledge.

Pearce, S.M. (1998), *Collecting in Contemporary Practice*, London: Sage Publications.

Pearce, S.M. (ed.) (1989), *Museum Studies in Material Culture*, Leicester and London: Leicester University Press.

Pearce, S.M. (ed.) (1995), *New Research in Museum Studies, 6: Art in Museums*, London: Athlone Press.

Pearce, S.M. (ed.) (1997), *Experiencing Material Culture in the Western World*, London and Washington: Leicester University Press.

Pellegrini, A. (1867), 'Orti di Asinio Pollione' in *Bulletino dell' Instituto di Correspondenza Archaeologia per l'anno 1867*, 109-119.

Pelling, C. (ed.) (1990), *Characterization and Individuality in Greek Literature*, Oxford: Clarendon Press.

Pensabene, P. (1983), 'Osservazioni sulla diffusione dei Mamri e sul lore Prezzo', in *Dialogui di archeologia*, 1, 55-63.

Perret-Clermont, A.-N. et Perret, J.-F. (1982), 'Les collectionneurs en herbe' in Hainard, J. and Kaehr, R. (eds) (1982), 169-179.

Peterson, T. (1920), *Cicero: A Biography*, Berkeley: University of California Press.

Pfister, F. (1909-12), *Der Reliquienkult im Altertum*, 2 vols, Gieben: A. Topelmann.

Picard, C. (1946), 'La pinacothèque de Colotès á Delos' in *Revue Arhaeologique*, ser. 6, 26, 99-101.

Platner, S.B. and Ashby, T. (1929), *A Topographical Dictionary of Ancient Rome*, London: Oxford University Press and H. Milford .

Pocock, J.G.A. (1962), 'The origins of study of the past: a comparative approach' in *Comparative Studies in Society and History*, 4, 209-246.

Polignac, F. de (1995), *Cults, Territory, and the Origins of the Greek City-State*, translated by J. Lloyd, Chicago: University of Chicago Press (first published in French with the title *La naissance de la cité grecque*, Paris: Éditions La Découverte, 1984).

Pollitt, J.J. (1974), *The Ancient View of Greek Art: Criticism, History, and Terminology*, New Haven and London: Yale University Press.

Pollitt, J.J. (1978), 'The impact of Greek art on Rome' in *TAPA*, 108, 155-174.

Pollitt, J.J. (1983), *The Art of Rome, c. 753 BC.-337 AD*, Cambridge: Cambridge University Press.

Pollitt, J.J. (1986), *Art in the Hellenistic Age*, Cambridge: Cambridge University Press.

Pomian, K. (1990), *Collectors and Curiosities: Paris and Venice, 1500-1800*, translated by E. Wiles-Portier, London: Polity Press (originally published in French, 1987).

Porter, G. (1991), 'Partial truths' in Kavanagh, G. (ed.) (1991), 101-118.

Porter, G. (1994), Studies in gender and representation in British history museums, unpublished Ph.D. thesis, submitted at the Department of Museum Studies, University of Leicester.

Poulot, D. (1985), 'L'invention de la bon volonté culturelle: L'image du musée au XIXe siecle' in *Le Mouvement Social*, no. 131 (April-June), 35-64.

Poulot, D. (1987), 'Musée et sociètè dans l'Europe moderne', *MEFR-Moyen Age/Temps Modernes*, 98, 991-1096.

Preisshofen, F. (1978), 'Kunsttheorie und Kunstbetrachtung' in *Le Classicisme à Rome aux Iers siécles avant et après J.-C.*, (Entretiens Sur l'Antiquité Classique, 25), Vandoeuvres: Fondation Hardt, 263-282.

Prellwitz, W. (1892), *Etymologische Wörterbuch der griechischen Sprache*, Göttingen: Vandenhoeck und Ruprecht.

Rabinowitz, P. (1986), 'Shifting sands, shifting standards: reading, interpretation, and literary judgement' in *Arethusa*, 9 (2), 115-134.

Radley, A. (1990), 'Artefacts, memory and a sense of the past' in Middleton, D. and Edwards, D. (eds) (1990), 46-59.

Raith, O. (1963), *Petronius, ein Epikureer*, Nuremberg: H. Carl.

Rapoport, A. (1980), 'Vernacular architecture and the cultural determinants of form' in King, A.D. (ed.) (1980), 283-305.

Rapoport, A. (1990), 'Systems of activities and systems of settings' in Kent, S. (ed.) (1990), 9-20.

Rawson, B. and Weaver, P. (eds) (1997), *The Roman Family in Italy*, Oxford: Clarendon Press.

Rawson, E. (1985), *Intellectual Life in the Late Roman Republic*, London: Duckworth.

Rawson, E. (1994), *Cicero: A Portrait*, Bristol: Bristol Classics Paperbacks.

Reardon, B.P. (ed.) (1971), *Erotica Antiqua*, Acta of the International Conference on the Ancient Novel held under the auspices of the Society for the Promotion of Hellenic Studies at the University College of North Wales, 12-17 July, 1976, Bangor [publisher uncertain].

Reardon, B.P. (ed.) (1989), *Collected Ancient Greek Novels*, Berkeley: University of California Press.

Reinach, M.S. (1889), 'Le musée de l' empereur Auguste' in *Revue d' Anthropologie*, IV, 28-56.

Reynolds, J. (1986), 'The Elder Pliny and his times' in French, R. and Greenaway, F. (eds) (1986), 1-10.

Rheims, M. (1959), *Art on the Market: Thirty-Five Centuries of Collecting and Collectors from Midas to Paul Getty*, translated by D. Pryce-Jones, London: Weidenfeld and Nicolson.

Richardson, L. jr. (1992), *A New Topographical Dictionary of Ancient Rome*, Baltimore and London: The Johns Hopkins University Press.

Richter, G.M.A., revised by J.D. Breckenridge (1982), 'The relation of Early Imperial Rome to Greek art' in *ANRW*, II.12.1, 3-23.

Ricoeur, P. (1978), *The Rule of Metaphor: Multi-disciplinary studies of the creation of meaning*, translated by R. Czerny, London: Routledge and Kegan Paul.

Ricoeur, P. (1981), *Hermeneutics and the Human Sciences: Essays on language, action and interpretation*, edited, translated and introduced by J.B. Thompson, Cambridge: Cambridge University Press.

Ricoeur, P. (1984), *The Reality of the Historical Past*, The Aquinas Lecture, Milwaukee: Marquette University Press.

Ridgway, B.S. (1970), *The Severe Style in Greek Sculpture*, Princeton: Princeton University Press.

Ridgway, B.S. (1971), 'The setting of Greek sculpture' in *Hesperia*, XL, 336-356.

Ridgway, B.S. (1984), *Roman Copies of Greek Sculpture: The Problem of the Originals*, Ann Arbor: University of Michigan Press.

Ridgway, B.S. (1989), 'Defining the issue: the Greek period' in *Retaining the Original: Multiple Originals, Copies and Reproductions*, Studies in the History of Art, Vol. 20, National Gallery of Art of Washington DC.

Ridgway, B.S. (1995), 'The wreck of Madhia, Tunisia, and the art market in early first century BC' in *JRA*, 8, 340-347.

Rigby, D., and Rigby, E. (1944), *Lock, Stock and Barrel: The Story of Collecting*, Philadelphia, PA: J.B. Lippincott.

Riggins, S.H. (ed.) (1994), *The Socialness of Things: Essays on the Socio-Semiotics of Objects*, Berlin and New York: Mouton de Gruyter.

Riggsby, A. (1997), '"Public" and "private" in Roman culture: the case of the cubiculum' in *JRA*, 10, 36-56.

Rist, J.M. (1969), *Stoic Philosophy*, London: Cambridge University Press.

Rist, J.M. (1982), *Human Value: A Study in Ancient Philosophical Ethics*, Leiden: E.J. Brill.

Robertson, M. (1975), *History of Greek Art*, Cambridge: Cambridge University Press.

Rohde, E. (1920), *Pscyhe: The Cult of Souls and Belief in Immortality among the Ancient Greeks*, translated by W.B. Hills, New York: Harcourt, Brace, Jovanovich.

Rolley, C. (1977), *Les trépieds à cuve clouée*, FdD V.3, Paris: Diffusion Boccard.

Römer, F. (1978), 'Plinius der Ältere: III Bericht' in *Anzeiger für des Altertumwissenschaft*, 31 (3-4), 129-205.

Rose, K.F.C. (1966), 'The Petronian inquisition: an auto-da-fé', *Arion*, 5, 275-301.

Rose, K.F.C. (1971), *The Date and Author of the Satyricon*, Mnemosyne Supplement no. 16, Leiden: Brill.

Rosenblatt, P.C., Walsh, R.P. and Jackson, A.J. (1976), *Grief and Mourning in Cross-cultural Perspective*, New York: HRAF Press.

Rostovtzeff, M.I. (1941), *The Social and Economic History of the Hellenistic World*, 2 vols, Oxford: Clarendon Press.

Rouveret, A. (1981), 'Commentaire' in *Pline l'Ancien, Histoire Naturelle*, Livre XXXVI, introduction, translation and commentary by J. André, R. Bloch and A. Rouveret, 1981, Paris: Budé, Belles Lettres, 123ff.

Rouveret, A. (1982), 'Peinture et "art de la mémoire"; le paysage et l'allégorie dans les tableaux grecs et romains' in *CRAI*, 572-588.

Rouveret, A. (1987), '"Toute la mémoire du monde": La notion de collection dans la *NH* de Pline' in *Helmantica*, 38, 115-133.

Rouveret, A. (1989), *Histoire et imaginaire de la peinture ancienne (Ve siècle av. J-C. - 1er siècle ap. J-C.)*, Rome: École Française de Rome.

Roux, G. (1954), 'Le val des Muses et les Musées chez les auteurs anciens' in *BCH*, 78, 22-48.

Rudmin, F.W. (ed.) (1991), *To Have Possessions: a Handbook on Ownership and Property*, Special issue of the *Journal of Social Behaviour and Personality*, 6 (6).

Ruggieri Tricoli, M.C. - Vacirca, M.D. (1998), *L'idea du Museo: Archetipi della comunicazione museale nel mondo antico*, Italia: Edizioni Lybra.

Runciman, W.G. (1990), 'Doomed to extinction: the *polis* as an evolutionary dead-end' in Murray, O. and Price, S. (eds) (1990), 347-368.

Rups, M. (1986), Thesauros: A study of the Treasury Building as found in Greek sanctuaries, Ph.D. thesis, The Johns Hopkins University, Ann Arbor, MI: University Microfilms International.

Sabine, G. (1973), *A History of Political Thought*, Hinsdale Illinois: Dryden Press.

Sahlins, M. (1972), *Stone Age Economics*, Chicago: Aldine.

Saisselin, R.G. (1984), *The Bourgeois and the Bibelot*, New Brunswick, New Jersey: Rutgers University Press.

Saller, R.P. (1983), 'Martial on patronage and literature' in *Classical Quarterly*, 33 (1), 246-257.

Sallmann, K. (1975), 'Plinius der Ältere 1938-1970' in *Lustrum* 18, 5-299 and 345-352.

Sallmann, K. (1987), 'La responsabilité de l'homme à façe de la nature' in *Pline l' Ancien. Temoin de son Temps*, Salamanca et Nantes: Universidad Pontificia, 251-266.

Salmon, P. (1958), *De la Collection au Musée*, Bruxelles: Office de Publicité.

Sanders, D. (1990), 'Behavioral conventions and archaeology: methods for the analysis of ancient architecture' in Kent, S. (ed.) (1990), 43-72.

Sandys, J.E. (1921), *A History of Classical Scholarship*, Cambridge: Cambridge University Press.

Sauron, G. (1980), 'Templa serena: À propos de la "villa des Papyri" d'Herculaneum: contribution à l'étude des comportments aristocratiques romain à la fin de la Republique' in *MEFR*, 92.1, 277-301.

Schachter, A. and Bingen, J. (eds) (1992), *Le Sanctuaire Grec*, (Entretiens sur l'Antiquité Classique), Vandoeuvres: Fondation Hardt.

Scheid-Tissinier, É. (1994), *Les usages du don chez Homere: Vocabulaire et pratiques*, Nancy: Presses Universitaires de Nancy.

Schlosser, J. (1908), *Kunst und Wunderkammern der Spätrenaissance*, Leipzig: Verlag von Klinkhardt & Biermann.

Schnapp, A. (1996), *The Discovery of the Past: The Origins of Archaeology*, London: British Museum Press (originally published in 1993, as *La Conquête du Passé*, Paris: Carré).

Schofield, M. and Striker, G. (eds) (1986), *The Norms of Nature: Studies in Hellenistic Ethics*, Cambridge and Paris: Cambridge University Press and Éditions de la Maison des Sciences de l' Homme.

Schofield, M. (1991), *The Stoic Idea of the City*, Cambridge: Cambridge University Press.

Schofield, M., Burnyeat, M. and Barnes, J. (eds) (1991), *Doubt and Dogmatism: Studies in Hellenistic Epistemology*, Oxford: Clarendon Press.

Schorske, C.E. (1985), *Fin-de-siècle Vienna: Politics and Culture*, Cambridge: Cambridge University Press.

Schulz, E. (1990), 'Notes on the history of collecting and museums' in *Journal of the History of Collections*, 2 (2), 205-218.

Schweitzer, B. (1932), *Xenocrates von Athen*, Halle: M. Niemeyer.

Schweitzer, B. (1948), *Die Bildniskunst der römischen Republik*, Leipzig: Koehler und Amelang.

Schweitzer, B. (1971), *Die geometrische Kunst Griechenlands*, Köln: Du Mont Schauberg.

Scodel, R. (1996), 'Δομων αγαλμα: virgin sacrifice and aesthetic object' in *TAPA*, 126, 111-128.

Seaford, R. (1995), *Reciprocity and Ritual: Homer and Tragedy in the Developing City-State*, Oxford: Oxford University Press.

Sedley, D.N. (1991), 'The protagonists' in Schofield, M., Burnyeat, M., Barnes, J., (eds) (1991), 1-19.

Seltzer, R.M. (ed.) (1989), *Religions in Antiquity. Selections from the Encyclopaedia of Religion*, New York: Macmillan.

Serbat, G. (1986), 'Pline l'Ancien. État présent des études sur sa vie, son oeuvre et son influence' in *ANRW*, II.32.4, 2069-2200.

Shackleton Bailey, D.R. (ed.) (1965), *Cicero's Letters to Atticus*, vol. 1, Cambridge: Cambridge University Press.

Shackleton Bailey, D.R. (ed.) (1978), *Cicero's Letters to his Friends*, Harmondsworth: Penguin.

Shackleton Bailey, D.R. (1971), *Cicero*, London: Duckworth.

Shanks, M. and Tilley, C. (1987a), *Re-constructing Archaeology*, Cambridge: Cambridge University Press.

Shanks, M. and Tilley, C. (1987b), *Social Theory and Archaeology*, Oxford: Polity Press.

Shelton, A.A. (1994), 'Cabinets of transgression: Renaissance collections and the incorporation of the New World' in Elsner, J. and Cardinal, R. (eds) (1994), 177-203.

Sherman, D.J. (1989), *Worthy Monuments: Art Museums and the Politics of Culture in Nineteenth-Century France*, Cambridge Mass.: Harvard University Press.

Sherman, D.J. and Rogoff, I. (eds) (1994), *Museums Culture: Histories, Discourses, Spectacles*, London: Routledge.

Showerman, G. (1904), 'Cicero's appreciation of Greek art', *AJPh*, 306-314.

Slater, N.W. (1987), '"Against interpretation": Petronius and art criticism' in *Ramus* 16, 165-176.

Slater, N.W. (1990), *Reading Petronius*, Baltimore and London: The Johns Hopkins University Press.

Small, J.P. (1997), *Wax Tablets of the Mind: Cognitive Studies in Memory and Literacy in Classical Antiquity*, London and New York: Routledge.

Smith, M.S. (ed.) (1975), *Petronius. Cena Trimalchionis*, Oxford: Clarendon Press.

Smith, M.S. (1985), 'A bibliography of Petronius (1945-1982)', in *ANRW*, II.32.3, 1624- 1665.

Snell, B. (1953), *The Discovery of Mind*, translated by T.G. Rosenmeyer, Cambridge Mass.: Harvard University Press.

Snodgrass, A. (1974), 'An ahistorical Homeric society?' in *JHS*, 94, 114-125.

Snodgrass, A. (1980), *Archaic Greece: The Age of Experiment*, London: Dent and Sons Ltd.

Sontag, S. (1982), *A Barthes Reader*, London: Jonathan Cape.

Sorabji, R. (1972), *Aristotle on Memory*, London: Duckworth.

Sorabji, R. (1983), *Time, Creation and the Continuum: Theories in Antiquity and the Early Middle Ages*, London: Duckworth.

Sorabji, R. (1986), 'Closed space and closed time' in *Oxford Studies in Ancient Philosophy*, IV, 215-231.

Sorabji, R. (1988), *Matter, Space and Motion: Theories in Antiquity and Their Sequel*, London: Duckworth.

Sourvinou-Inwood, C. (1990), 'What is *polis* religion?' in Murray, O. and Price, S. (ed.) (1990), 295-322.

Sourvinou-Inwood, C. (1995), *'Reading' Greek Death: To the End of the Classical Period*, Oxford: Clarendon Press.

Spriggs, M. (ed.) (1984), *Marxist Perspectives in Archaeology*, Cambridge: Cambridge University Press.

Stambaugh, E. (1988), *The Ancient Roman City*, Baltimore Md.: The Johns Hopkins University Press.

Starobinski, J. (1966), 'The idea of nostalgia' in *Diogenes*, 54 (summer), 81-103.

Stewart, A.F. (1977), 'To entertain an emperor: Sperlonga, Laokoon and Tiberius at the dinner-table' in *JRS*, 67, 76-90.

Stewart, A. (1979), *Attica: Studies in Athenian Sculpture of the Hellenistic Age*, Supplementary Paper No 14, London: Published by the Society for the Promotion of Hellenic Studies.

Stewart, S. (1993), *On Longing: Narratives of the Miniature, the Gigantic, the Souvenir, the Collection*, Durham and London: Duke University Press (originally published in 1984, London and Baltimore: The Johns Hopkins University Press).

Stocking, G. (ed.) (1986), *Objects and Others: Essays on Museums and Material Culture*, History of Anthropology Vol. III, University of Wisconsin Press.

Storr, A. (1983), 'The psychology of collecting' in *The Connoisseur*, June, 35-38.

Strong, D. (1966), *Greek and Roman Gold and Silver Plate*, London: Methuen.

Strong, D.E. (1975), 'Roman museums' in Strong, D. E., (ed.), *Archaeological Theory and Practice*, N.Y.: Seminar Press.

Strong, D.E. (1976), *Roman Art*, London: Pelican.

Suleiman, S.R. and Crosman, I. (1980), *The Reader in the Text: Essays on Audience and Interpretation*, Princeton: Princeton University Press.

Sullivan, J.P. (1963a), 'Satire and realism in Petronius' in Sullivan, J. P. (ed.) (1963b), 73-92.

Sullivan, J.P. (1968), *The Satyricon of Petronius. A Literary Study*, London: Faber.

Sullivan, J.P. (1985a), 'Petronius' Satyricon and its Neronian context' in *ANRW*, II.32.3, 1666-1686.

Sullivan, J.P. (1985b), *Literature and Politics in the Age of Nero*, Ithaca, New York: Cornell University Press.

Sullivan, J.P. (1991), *Martial: the unexpected classic: A literary and historical study*, Cambridge: Cambridge University Press.

Sullivan, J.P. (ed.) (1963b), *Critical essays on Roman literature - Satire*, London: Routledge and Kegan Paul.

Svoboda, K. (1960), 'Idées aesthetiques de Cicéron' in *Acta Sessionis Ciceronianae*, Warschau, 109-120.

Syme, R. (1979), 'Pliny the procurator' in Badian, E. (ed.) (1979), 742-773.

Syme, R. (1987), 'Carrière et amis consulaires de Pline' in *Helmantica*, 38, 223-231.

Szelest, H. (1986), 'Martial-eigentlichen Schoepter und hervorragendsten Verterer des römischen Epigrams' in *ANRW*, II.32.4, 2563-2623.

Tanner, J.J. (1992), 'Art as expressive symbolism: civic portraits in classical Athens' in *Cambridge Archaeological Journal*, 2 (2), 167-190.

Tanner, J.J. (1995), The invention of art history: religion, society and artistic differentiation in ancient Greece, unpublished Ph.D. thesis, University of Cambridge.

Tarn, W.W. (and Griffith, G.T.) (1952), *Hellenistic Civilisation*, London: Edward Arnold and Co.

Tatum, J. (ed.) (1994), *The Search for the Ancient Novel*, Baltimore and London: The Johns Hopkins University Press.

Taub, L.C. (1993), *Ptolemy's Universe: The Natural Philosophical and Ethical Foundations of Ptolemy's Astronomy*, Chicago: Open Court.

Taylor, C. (1989), *Sources of the Self: The Making of Modern Identity*, Cambridge: Cambridge University Press.

Taylor, F.H. (1948), *The Taste of Angels: A History to Art Collecting from Ramses to Napoleon*, Boston: Little, Brown and Company.

Thackray, J. (1996), '"The modern Pliny": William Hamilton and Vesuvius' in Jenkins, I. and Sloan, K. (eds) (1996), 65-74.

Thébert, Y. (1987), 'Private life and domestic architecture in Roman Africa' in Veyne, P. (ed.) (1987), 313-410.

Thomas, J. (1990), 'Same, other, analogue' in Baker, F. and Thomas, J. (eds) (1990), 18-23.

Thomas, N. (1994), 'Licensed curiosity: Cook's pacific voyages' in Elsner, J. and Cardinal, R. (eds) (1994), 116-136.

Thomas, R. (1992), *Literacy and Orality in Ancient Greece*, Cambridge: Cambridge University Press.

Thomas, R. (1997), 'Ethnography, proof and argument in Herodotus' *Histories*' in *PCPhS*, 43, 128-148.

Thompson, J.B. (1981), 'Introduction' in Ricoeur, P. (1981), 1-26.

Thompson, J.M.A., Basset, D.A., Duggan, A.J., Lewis, G.D. and Fenton, A. (eds) (1992), *Manual of Curatorship*, London: Butterworth and Heinemann.

Tilley, C. (1990b), 'Claude Lévi-Strauss: structuralism and beyond' in Tilley, C. (ed.) (1990a), 3-84.

Tilley, C. (1991), *Material Culture and Text: The Art of Ambiguity*, London: Routledge.

Tilley, C. (ed.) (1990a), *Reading Material Culture: Structuralism, Hermeneutics and Post-structuralism*, Oxford: Basil Blackwell.

Tomlinson, R.A. (1976), *Greek Sanctuaries*, London: Paul Elek.

Toohey, P. (1997), 'Trimalchio's constipation: periodizing madness, eros, and time' in Golden, M. and Toohey, P. (eds) (1997), 50-65.

Tournaire, A. (1902), *Fouilles de Delphes*, Tome II, Relevés et Restaurations, Paris: Boccard.

Toynbee, J.M.C. (1978), *Roman Historical Portraits*, London: Thames and Hudson.

Tuan, Y.-F. (1977), *Space and Place: The Perspective of Experience*, London: Edward Arnold Ltd.

Uhlenbrock, J.P. (ed.) (1990), *The Coroplast's Art: Greek Terracotttas of the Hellenistic World*, New Rochelle, New York: Caratzas.

Valenti, S. (1936), 'Cicerone collezionista' in *Atene e Roma*, III (IV), 236-270.

van Baal, J. (1976), 'Offering, sacrifice and gift' in *Numen*, 23 (3), 161-178.

van Bremen, R. (1993), 'Women and wealth' in Cameron, A. and Kuhrt, A. (eds) (1993), 223-242.

van Buren, A.W. (1938), 'Pinacothecae- with especial reference to Pompeii' in *Memoirs of the American Academy at Rome*, 15, 70-81.

van Holst, N. (1967), *Creators, Collectors and Connoisseurs: The Anatomy of Artistic Taste from Antiquity to the Present Day*, London: Thames and Hudson.

van Straten, F.T. (1981), 'Gifts for the gods' in Versnel, H. S. (ed.) (1981), 65-107.

van Straten, F.T. (1990), 'Votives and votaries in Greek sanctuaries' in Schachter, A. and Bingen, J. (eds) (1990), 247-285.

van Wees, H. (1992), *Status Warriors: War, Violence and Society in Homer and History*, Amsterdam: J.C. Gieben.

Vasaly, A. (1993), *Representations: Images of the World in Ciceronian Oratory*, Berkeley: University of California Press.

Vergo, P. (ed.) (1989), *The New Museology*, London: Reaktion Books.

Vermeule, C. (1968), 'Graeco-Roman statues: Purpose and setting' (in two parts), in *The Burlington Magazine*, nos. 787-788, vol. CX, October-November, 545-558, 607-613.

Vermeule, C. (1967), 'Greek sculpture and Roman taste' in *Bulletin of the Museum of Five Arts, Boston*, LXV (342), 175-192.

Vermeule, C. (1977), *Greek Sculpture and Roman Taste: The Purpose and Setting of Greco-Roman Art in Italy and the Greek Imperial East*, Ann Arbor: University of Michigan Press.

Vernant, J.-P. (1983a), 'Hestia-Hermes: the religious expression of space and movement in ancient Greece' in Vernant, J.-P. (1983b), 127-175.

Vernant, J.-P. (1983b), *Myth and Thought Among the Greeks*, London: Routledge and Kegan Paul.

Vernant, J.-P. (1991a), 'A general theory of sacrifice and slaying of the victim in the Greek *Thusia*' in Zeitlin, F. (ed.) (1991), 290-302 (first published in *Le sacrifice dans l'Antiquité*, Vandoeuvres: Fondation Hardt (Entretiens sur l'antiquité classique, 27), 1981, 1-21, in French).

Vernant, J.-P. (1991b), 'The individual within the city-state' in Vernant, J.-P. (1991) (edited by F. Zeitlin), *Mortals and Immortals: Collected Essays*, Princeton: Princeton University Press.

Vernant, J.-P. and Vidal-Naquet, P. (1981), *Tragedy and Myth in Ancient Greece*, translated by J. Lloyd, Brighton: Harvester Press.

Versnel, H.S. (ed.) (1981), *Faith, Hope and Worship: Aspects of Religious Mentality in the Ancient World*, Leiden: E.J. Brill.

Vessberg, O. (1941), *Studien zur Kunstgeschichte der römischen Republik*, Lund: C.W.K. Gleerup.

Veyne, P. (1961), 'Vie de Trimalchion' in *Annales économies-sociétés-civilisations*, 16, 213-247.

Veyne, P. (1963), 'Cave canem' in MEFR, 75, 59-66.
Veyne, P. (1964), 'Le "je" dans le Satyricon', in REL, 42, 301-324.
Veyne, P. (ed.) (1987), A History of Private Life: I. From Pagan Rome to Byzantium, Cambridge Mass.: Poelknap Press of Harvard University Press.
Vickers, M. (1997), 'Hamilton, geology, stone vases and taste' in Journal of the History of Collection, 9 (2), 263-274.
Vidal-Naquet, P. (1986), 'Divine time and human time' in Black Hunter: forms of thought and forms of society in the Greek world, translated by A. Szegedy-Maszak, Baltimore and London: The Johns Hopkins University Press.
Ville, G. (1964), 'Les coupes de Trimalchion figurant des gladiateurs et une série de verres sigillés gaulois' in Hommages à J. Bayet, Brussels: Collection Latomus 70, 722-733.
von Kraft-Ebbing, R. (1892), Psychopathia Sexualis, Stuttgart: F. Enke.
von Reden, S. (1994), Exchange in Ancient Greece, London: Duckworth.
Vygotsky, L.S. (1978), Mind in Society, Cambridge Mass.: Harvard University Press.
Wace, A.J. (1969), 'The Greeks and Romans as archaeologists' in Heizer, R.F. (ed.) (1969), 203-218 (originally published in 1949).
Walbank, F.W. (1982), The Hellenistic World, Cambridge Mass.: Harvard University Press.
Wallace-Hadrill, A. (ed.) (1989), Patronage in Ancient Society, London: Routledge.
Wallace-Hadrill, A. (1987), 'Time for Augustus: Ovid, Augustus, and the Fasti' in Whitby, M., Hardie, P., Whitby, M. (eds) (1987), 221-230.
Wallace-Hadrill, A. (1990), 'Pliny the Elder and man's unnatural history' in Greece and Rome, 37, 80-96.
Wallace-Hadrill, A. (1994), Houses and Society in Pompeii and Herculaneum, Princeton, New Jersey: Princeton University Press.
Wallace-Hadrill, A. (1996), 'Engendering the Roman house' in Kleiner, D.E.E. and Matheson, S.B. (eds) (1996), 104-115.
Walsh, K. (1992), The Representation of the Past: Museums and Heritage in the Post-Modern World, London and N.Y.: Routledge.
Walsh, P.G. (1970), The Roman Novel. The Satyricon of Petronius and the "Metamorphoses" of Apuleius, Cambridge: Cambridge University Press (reprinted in 1995 by Bristol Classical Press).
Walsh, P.G. (1974), 'Was Petronius a moralist?' in Greece and Rome, 21, 181-190.
Walsh, P.G. (ed.) (1996), Petronius: The Satyricon, Oxford: Clarendon Press.
Walter, H. (1976), Das Heraion von Samos. Ursprung und Wandel eines griechiechen Heiligtums, Munich: R. Piper.
Walter-Karydi, E. (1994), Die Nobilitierung des Wohnhauses; Lebensform und Architektur im spätklassischen Griechenland, Xenia, Heft 35, Konstanz: Universitätsverlag Konstanz.
Warden, P.G. and Romano, D.G. (1994), 'The course of glory: Greek art in a Roman context at the villa of the Papyri at Herculaneum' in Art History, 17 (2), 228-254.
Wasserman, G.R. (1981), Roland Barthes, Boston: Twayne Publications.
Watson, G. (1971), 'The natural law and Stoicism' in Long, A. (ed.) (1971), 216-238.
Watson, G. (1988), Phantasia in Classical Thought, Galway: Galway University Press.
Watson, G. (1994), 'The concept of "phantasia" from the late Hellenistic period to early Neoplatonism', in ANRW, II.36.7, 4765-4810.
Wehrli, F. (1968), Demetrios von Phaleron, Basel and Stuttgard: Schwabe.
Weinberg, G.D., Grace, V.R., Edwards, G.R., Robinson, H.S., Throckmorton, P. and Ralph, E.K. (1965), 'The Antikythera shipwreck reconsidered' in TAPhS, (n.s.) 55, 3ff.
Weiner, A. (1992), Inalienable Possessions: The paradox of keeping-while-giving, Berkeley: University of California Press.
Wernicke, K. (1894), 'Olympische Beiträge, II. Zur Geschichte des Heraion' in JDAI, 9, 101-114.

Whitby, M., Hardie, P. and Whitby, M. (eds) (1987), *Homo Viator: Classical Essays for John Bramble*, Bristol: Bristol Classical Press.

White, H. (1978), *Tropics of Discourse: Essays in Cultural Criticism*, Baltimore: The Johns Hopkins University Press.

White, P. (1978), 'Amicitia and the profession of poetry in early Imperial Rome' in *JRS*, 68, 74-92.

Whitley, J. (1987), 'Art history, archaeology and idealism: the German tradition', in Hodder, I. (ed.) (1987), 9-15.

Whitley, M.T. (1929), 'Children's interest in collecting', in *Journal of Educational Psychology*, 20, 249-261.

Wilkes, K. (1988), *Real People: Personal Identity without Thought Experiments*, Oxford: Clarendon Press.

Wilkinson, H. (1997), 'Mr Cropper and Mrs Brown: good and bad collectors in the work of A.S. Byatt and other recent fiction' in Pearce, S.M. (ed.) (1997), 95-113.

Will, E. (1979), *Histoire politique du monde hellénistique*, Nancy: impr. Berger-Levrault.

Williams, B. (1981), *Moral Luck: Philosophical Papers 1973-1980*, Cambridge: Cambridge University Press.

Williams, B. (1993), *Shame and Necessity*, Berkeley: University of California Press.

Williams, G. (1968), *Tradition and Originality in Roman Poetry*, Oxford: Clarendon Press.

Wilton, A. and Bignamini, I. (1997), *Grand Tour: The Lure of Italy in the Eighteenth Century*, London: Tate Gallery Publishing.

Winnicott, W.D. (1953), 'Transitional objects and transitional phenomenon' in *International Journal of Psychoanalysis*, 34 (2), 89-97.

Wiseman, T.P. (1986), 'Monuments and the Roman annalists' in Moxon, I.S., Smart, J.D. and Woodman, A.J. (eds) (1986), 87-100.

Wiseman, T.P. (1994), *Historiography and Imagination: eight essays on Roman culture*, Exeter: University of Exeter Press.

Witty, P. (1931), 'Sex differences in collecting interests' in *Journal of Educational Psychology*, 22, 221-228.

Wojcik, M.R. (1986), *La villa dei Papiri ad Ercolano: contributo alla riconstruzione dell' ideologia della nobilitas tardorepubblicana*, Rome: L' Erma di Bretschneider.

Woodruff, P. (1982), *Plato: Hippias Major*, Oxford: Basil Blackwell.

Wright, M.R. (1995), *Cosmology in Antiquity*, London: Routledge.

Wyke, M. (1994), 'Woman in the mirror: the rhetoric of adornment in the Roman world' in Archer, L.J., Fischler, S. and Wyke, M. (eds) (1994), 134-151.

Yates, F.A. (1966), *The Art of Memory*, London: Routledge and Kegan Paul.

Zanker, P. (1974), *Klassizistiche Statuen*, Mainz: P. von Zabern.

Zanker, P. (1978), 'Zur Funktion und Bedeutung griechischer Skulptur in des Römerzeit' *Le Classicisme à Rome aux Iers siécles avant et après J.-C.* (Entretiens Sur l'Antiquité Classique, 25), Vandoeuvres: Fondation Hardt, 283-314.

Zanker, P. (1979a), 'Die Villa als Vorbild des späten pompejanischen Wohngeschmacks' in *JdI*, 94, 460-523.

Zanker, P. (1979b), 'Zur Rezeption des hellenistischen Individualporträts in Rom und die den italischen Städten' in *Hellenismus in Mittelitalien*, (Kolloquium in Göttingen vom 5. bis 9. juni 1974), Göttingen: Vandenhoeck & Ruprecht.

Zanker, P. (1987), *Augustus und die Macht der Bilder*, Munich: C.H. Beck.

Zeitlin, F.I. (1971), 'Petronius as paradox: anarchy and artistic integrity' in *TAPA*, 102, 631-684.

Zeitlin, F.I. (1994), 'Gardens of desire in Longus's *Daphnis and Chloe*: nature, art, and imitation' in Tatum, J. (ed.) (1994), 148-172.

Zeitlin, F.I. (ed.) (1991), *Mortals and Immortals: Collected Essays – J.-P. Vernant*, Princeton: Princeton University Press.

Ziehen, L. (1936), 'Θησαυρος' in *RE*, VI.A.1, 1-7.

Zimmer, G. (1989), 'Das Sacrarium des C. Heius: Kunstraub und Kunstgeschmack in der späten Republik' in *Gymnasium*, 1989 (96), 493-520.

Zimmer, G. (1994), 'Republikanisches Kunstverstädnis: Cicero gegen Verres' in Hellenkemper Sallies, G. (ed.) (1994), 867-874.

Index

(References to illustrated material are in **bold** type)